SAN DIEGO

Welcome to San Diego

San Diego is a vacationer's paradise, with year-round temperatures in the seventies and near-constant sunshine. One of America's most family-friendly cities, San Diego is home to LEGOLAND, the New Children's Museum, and the famous San Diego Zoo. Sunbathers and surfers are guaranteed to find their perfect beach, and foodies find delights in artisanal breweries, local bistros, and gourmet restaurants. From the Broadway excitement of La Jolla Playhouse to the European feel of Little Italy to the nouveau-chic of the Gaslamp Quarter, San Diego has something for everyone.

TOP REASONS TO GO

★ **Sun and Surf:** Legendary beaches and surfing in La Jolla, Coronado, and Point Loma.

★ **Golf:** A concentration of beautiful courses with sweeping ocean views and light breezes.

★ **Outdoor Sports:** A perfect climate for biking, hiking, sailing—anything—outdoors.

★ **Family Time:** Fun for all ages at LEGOLAND, Balboa Park, the San Diego Zoo, and more.

★ **Great Eats:** Brewpubs, a wide mix of ethnic cuisines, and modern cafés delight diners.

★ **Shopping:** From hip boutiques and fine Mexican crafts to the upscale Fashion Valley Mall.

4

Contents

Fodor's InFocus

Lions and Tigers and Bears:
The World-Famous San Diego Zoo.... 95

MAPS

Chapter 1

EXPERIENCE
SAN DIEGO

12 ULTIMATE EXPERIENCES

San Diego offers terrific experiences that should be on every traveler's list. Here are Fodor's top picks for a memorable trip.

1 Shop and Dine in Seaport Village

Situated along the water, Seaport Village is a 14-acre, open-air shopping and dining complex that's home to shops and eateries, special events, and winding walking paths. Behind Seaport Village, The Headquarters at Seaport is a former police headquarters that's been transformed into an additional shopping and dining plaza. *(Ch. 3)*

2 Bet on a Horse

The Del Mar Racetrack sees about 12 races a day, July through early September. Be prepared for loud cheering, boozy cocktails, and dapper attire. *(Ch. 10)*

3 Explore Old Town

San Diego's oldest and most storied neighborhood is also California's earliest settlement. Today, it's a hub for Mexican restaurants, souvenir shops, and cultural and historical attractions and celebrations. *(Ch. 5)*

4 Seals in La Jolla Cove

Seals and sea lions love the Children's Pool Beach, but keep your distance. For good views from Coast Avenue, walk along the sea cliffs toward the seawall. *(Ch. 7)*

5 Visit a farmers' market

Thanks to California's bounty of fresh produce, San Diego's farmers' markets boast a cornucopia of quality foodstuff. Head to Little Italy on Saturdays and Hillcrest on Sundays. *(Ch. 3, 5)*

6 Eat Baja-style fish tacos

Featured on countless menus across town, fish tacos—battered and fried white fish filets, cabbage, pico de gallo, crema, fresh lime, corn tortillas—are San Diego's unofficial, must-try meal. *(Ch. 6, 8)*

7 Hike Mount Woodson

Mount Woodson is best known for a picturesque 6.4-mile loop that goes past well-known Potato Chip Rock. It's not an easy hike, taking most people about three hours to complete. *(Ch. 10)*

8 Explore the Gaslamp Quarter

Covering more than 16 city blocks, this bustling neighborhood is great for shopping, dining, and nightlife. Guided walking tours of the historic district are available. *(Ch. 1)*

9 Book a kayak tour or surf lesson in La Jolla Shores

One of the best local beaches for water sports, La Jolla Shores has a host of rental and tour companies located just steps from the sand. There's surf or stand-up paddleboard lessons, as well as snorkel and kayak tours. *(Ch. 7)*

10 Take the ferry to Coronado

The 15-minute ferry ride between downtown San Diego and Coronado provides great views of Downtown and Naval Air Station North Island. *(Ch. 9)*

11 Visit the tasting room of a local craft brewery

With more than 150 craft breweries spread throughout San Diego County, it's safe to say you'll have an easy time finding quality beer. *(Ch. 3, 5, 8, 10)*

12 Spend a day exploring Balboa Park

This 1,200-acre urban park houses 17 museums, performing arts venues, gardens, sculptures, and other attractions like the San Diego Zoo. *(Ch. 4)*

WHAT'S WHERE

1 Downtown. Streets are lined with nightclubs, boutiques, and restaurants, from the glam Gaslamp Quarter to the edgier East Village (home to PETCO Park). Seaport Village, the Embarcadero, and Little Italy are nearby.

2 Balboa Park, Bankers Hill, and San Diego Zoo. This 1,200-acre park has museums, performing arts venues, stunning Spanish Revival architecture, and the San Diego Zoo. Bankers Hill, on the park's west side, is an affluent neighborhood home to numerous eateries.

3 Old Town and Uptown. Old Town's pedestrian-friendly state park has historic buildings, galleries, and Mexican eateries. Uptown's a cluster of trendy neighborhoods north of Balboa Park. Hillcrest is the heart of the city's LGBT community, while hip North Park has boutiques, eateries, and bars. South Park has charming shops and cafés. Historic Mission Hills is between Old Town and Hillcrest, and northeast of it is Mission Valley.

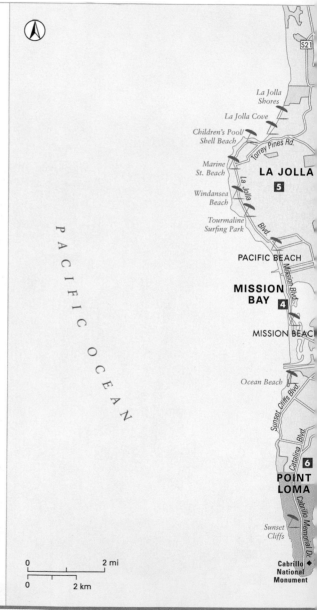

0 2 mi

0 2 km

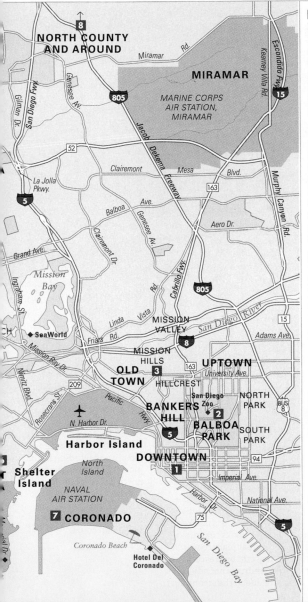

4 Mission Bay and the Beaches. Home to SeaWorld and a 4,600-acre aquatic park perfect for water activities. Mission Beach and Pacific Beach—full of surf shops, tattoo parlors, and beach bars—are nearby.

5 La Jolla. Picturesque cliffs and beaches, the famous seals, and a bevy of hotels, restaurants, galleries, and shops. Kearney Mesa's home to San Diego's Asian food mecca, Convoy District; nearby Clairemont also has good Asian food.

6 Point Loma Peninsula. The peninsula has grand houses, seafood eateries, Liberty Station, and Cabrillo National Monument. Harbor Island and Shelter Island are between the peninsula and Coronado, and farther north is Ocean Beach's Sunset Cliffs.

7 Coronado. An island-like peninsula across from the San Diego waterfront, the upscale area has the fabled Hotel Del Coronado, a naval base, and lots of shopping, dining, and sand.

8 North County and Around. Beach towns like Del Mar, Encinitas, Carlsbad; family attractions like LEGOLAND and the San Diego Zoo Safari Park; wineries in Temecula; and the Anza-Borrego Desert.

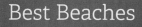

Best Beaches

CORONADO
Often praised for its sparkling sand, the island is home to Hotel del Coronado, a 130-year-old luxury hotel perfect for post-beach snacks; Del Beach, which is open to the public; and Dog Beach where pooches can run free sans leash.

TORREY PINES STATE BEACH
Situated at the base of a 1,500-acre natural reserve, La Jolla's Torrey Pines State Beach offers a long, narrow stretch of pristine beach framed by picturesque sea cliffs. Beachgoers can add a hike to their itinerary that starts or finishes on the sand, with plenty of lookout areas for great photo ops. Beyond the bluffs, a salt marsh provides seclusion from businesses and their associated street noise.

LA JOLLA SHORES
Pack up the whole family for a beach day in La Jolla Shores, which is known for its calm waves, two parks, and playground. Sea caves and underwater canyons that are part of La Jolla Underwater Park and Ecological Reserve—a marine protected area—attract kayakers and scuba divers.

DEL MAR CITY BEACH
In the upscale coastal neighborhood of Del Mar lies two beach parks that are popular for special events because of their stunning views of the Pacific. Seagrove Park is perched on the hill at the end of 15th Street, with benches for ocean gazing and winding paths along the bluffs. Farther north across the railroad tracks, Powerhouse Park offers easy beach access, a playground area, and a volleyball court.

MISSION BEACH
Located near SeaWorld San Diego, Mission Beach is home to a bustling boardwalk that's frequented by walkers, cyclists, and people-watchers. The bay is popular for water sports such as stand-up paddle boarding and Jet Skiing, but the beach is best known for Belmont Park, its oceanfront amusement park.

WINDANSEA BEACH
Seasoned surfers should head to La Jolla's Windansea Beach for powerful waves. Tucked away in a residential area, Windansea's entrance is marked by large rocks that make for a great place to watch or dry out, but recreational swimming is not advised here due to the strong surf.

La Jolla Shores

SWAMI'S STATE BEACH
West of the magnificent Self-Realization Fellowship Temple and Meditation Gardens in Encinitas, this beach draws surfers and yogis in with its Zen vibes, while others treat the steep staircase leading down to the beach as a workout, with a rewarding view of sea cliffs waiting at the bottom. At low tide, shells and other sea creatures are left behind for beachcombers to easily discover.

FLETCHER COVE BEACH PARK
Nestled in the heart of Solana Beach, Fletcher Cove Beach Park doubles as a recreational park and beach access area. Here you'll find a basketball court, playground, lawn area, and picnic tables. A paved ramp leads down to the crescent-shaped beach that's flanked by cliffs on both sides. For sweeping views of the ocean, position yourself at one of the lookouts outfitted with seating and/or binoculars—yup, binoculars are waiting for you.

BEACON'S BEACH
Follow the windy dirty path laden with switchbacks down to find Beacon's Beach in Encinitas, a well-known beach spot and favorite locals' hangout; on maps it may be labeled Leucadia State Beach. Since its entrance is hidden below sea cliffs on a one-way residential street, Beacon's Beach has an air of exclusivity. With plenty of space to spread out here, you won't have to infringe on sun-worshipping neighbors.

MOONLIGHT STATE BEACH
Fans of active beach days should head to this Encinitas beach. Volleyball courts, picnic tables, and playgrounds line the beach, with a concession stand, equipment rentals, and free Sunday concerts in high season.

What to Eat and Drink

SEAFOOD FRESH FROM THE OCEAN

You don't have to go far to find a bounty of fresh seafood in San Diego, most likely sourced from the waters off Southern California. Always check out the day's catch—usually served as a sandwich, salad, or plate—and what's been shucked on ice.

FISH TACOS

There's a great debate about who makes the best fish tacos in town. There are numerous options, but Rubio's Coastal Grill is credited with popularizing fish tacos in the U.S.; the original location is still in Pacific Beach. The original tacos have fried pollock, white sauce, salsa, cabbage, and a corn tortilla.

DISTILLERIES

San Diego is a craft beer town, but that hasn't stopped distilleries from cropping up. Cutwater Spirits has seven types of spirits and 14 ready-to-drink canned cocktails; Malahat Spirits specializes in small-batch, handcrafted rum, whiskey, and vodka; and You & Yours Distilling offers gin and vodka.

CRAFT BEER

Dubbed the "Capital of Craft," San Diego has more than 150 craft breweries, a movement that began with Karl Strauss Brewing Company in 1989. Since then, the San Diego Brewers Guild established an annual San Diego Beer Week every November, and a few neighborhoods have become craft brewery destinations in their own right including "Beeramar" (Miramar) and North Park's "Beer Boulevard" (30th Street).

MEXICAN FOOD

California burritos, carne asada fries, and fish tacos are common staples at the city's Mexican restaurants. If you can't make the trip to Tijuana, the most authentic San Diego alternative is Las Cuatro Milpas, a no-frills eatery that typically draws a line of people around the corner at lunchtime. For exceptional tacos of many varieties, head to Puesto, Galaxy Taco, or Lola 55.

ASIAN FOOD

The Convoy District in Kearny Mesa is San Diego's Asian food mecca. Here you'll find Chinese, Vietnamese, Thai, Japanese, Korean, and Filipino restaurants—all within a stone's throw of one another.

SUSHI

Sushi should be a no-brainer when visiting San Diego, especially for tourists from landlocked states who don't often get fresh fish.

VEGETARIAN FOOD

Californians are generally known to be health conscious, eating lots of fresh local produce (including adding avocado to everything) and exercising outdoors year-round. There are plentiful vegetarian and vegan options throughout the city.

SWEETS

Calories don't count on vacation, right? There are plenty of options to indulge in here including exquisite layered cakes, cookies, and classic French pastries. And we'd be remiss if we didn't mention the local chocolatiers. Artisan chocolate, bonbons and truffles, and flavored chocolate bars are yours for the tasting.

COFFEE

You'll be hard pressed to find a San Diego neighborhood that lacks a proper coffee shop these days, as many of the local roasters have recently expanded their operations and added new locations. Dark Horse Coffee Roasters, a handcrafted, small-batch roaster, has four San Diego locations. James Coffee Co. brews single-origin beans and custom blends at its three coffee shops. Bird Rock Coffee Roasters brews ethically sourced java at its five San Diego spots.

TIKI COCKTAILS

Tiki culture has obvious parallels to San Diego's tropical, laidback vacation vibe, so it's no surprise that the concept took root here with rum as the star spirit. Sure bets include The Grass Skirt, False Idol, and Fairweather Bar.

MARGARITAS

San Diego's mixologists have elevated the burgeoning cocktail scene, and margaritas can come skinny, spicy, or standard, with house-made sours and fresh-squeezed juices.

BEST BETS

Fodor's writers and editors have chosen our favorites to help you plan. Search individual chapters for more recommendations.

🍴 RESTAURANTS

BEST BUDGET ($-$$)
City Tacos, ch. 5
Piatti La Jolla, ch. 7
Soda & Swine, ch. 8

BEST MIDRANGE ($$-$$$)
Bankers Hill Bar + Restaurant, ch. 4
Herb & Wood, ch. 3
Trust, ch. 5
Urban Solace, ch. 5

BEST UPSCALE ($$$$)
Addison, ch. 10
A.R. Valentien, ch. 7
Born and Raised, ch. 3
George's at the Cove, ch. 7
Mille Fleurs, ch. 10

BEST BREAKFAST
Breakfast Republic, ch. 3
The Cottage, ch. 7
The Misson, ch. 3
Shorehouse Kitchen, ch. 7
Snooze, ch. 5

BEST ASIAN
Dumpling Inn, ch. 7
Phuong Trang, ch. 7
RakiRaki, ch. 7

BEST SUSHI
Azuki Sushi, ch. 4
j/wata Temaki Bar, ch. 7
Sushi Ota, ch. 6

BEST GASTROPUBS
Julian Beer Company, ch. 10
Stone Brewing Bistro, ch. 8

BEST ITALIAN
Buona Forchetta, ch. 5
Cucina Urbana, ch. 4
Romano's Restaurant, ch. 10
Trattoria Toscana, ch. 10
Vigilucci's Cucina Italiana, ch. 10

BEST MEXICAN
Las Cuatros Milpas, ch. 3
Galaxy Taco, ch. 7
Lola 55, ch. 3
Puesto, ch. 3
Salud!, ch. 3

BEST FISH TACOS
Pacific Beach Fish Shop, ch. 6
Rubio's Coastal Grill, ch. 6
South Beach Bar & Grille, ch. 8

BEST SEAFOOD
Blue Water Seafood Market, ch. 5
Eddie V's Prime Seafood, ch. 3
El Pescador Fish Market, ch. 7
The Fish Market, ch. 10
Fish 101, ch. 10
George's at the Cove, ch. 7
Point Loma Seafoods, ch. 8

BEST BRUNCH
Brockton Villa, ch. 3
Herringbone, ch. 7
The Little Lion, ch. 8
The Marine Room, ch. 7
Prep Kitchen Little Italy, ch. 3

BEST COCKTAILS
Campfire, ch. 10
Madison on Park, ch. 5
Whisknladle, ch. 7

BEST FOR DINING WITH KIDS
Draft South Mission, ch. 6
Liberty Public Market, ch. 8
URBN North Park, ch. 5
Waypoint Public, ch. 5

BEST OUTDOOR DINING
Casa de Reyes, ch. 5
The Crack Shack, ch. 3
Piatti La Jolla, ch. 7

BEST WATER VIEWS
Brockton Villa, ch. 7
Coasterra, ch. 8
Jake's Del Mar, ch. 10
JRDN, ch. 6
Tom Ham's Lighthouse, ch. 8
Waterbar, ch. 6

BEST WINE LISTS
AVANT, ch. 10
Bellamy's Restaurant, ch. 10
Mille Fleurs, ch. 10
3rd Corner Wine Shop and Bistro, ch. 8
Veladora, ch. 10

BEST DESSERTS
The Cravory, ch. 8
Eclipse Chocolate Bar + Bistro, ch. 5
Extraordinary Desserts, ch. 3, 5
Michele Coulon Dessertier, ch. 7
Le Parfait Paris, ch. 3

BEST VEGETARIAN
Cafe Gratitude, ch. 3
Kindred, ch. 5
Trilogy Sanctuary, ch. 7

🛏 HOTELS

BEST BUDGET *($-$$)*
Blue Sea Beach Hotel, *ch.* 6
Cosmopolitan Hotel Old Town, *ch.* 5
Crystal Pier Hotel and Cottages, *ch.* 6
Porto Vista Hotel, *ch.* 3

BEST MID-RANGE *($$-$$$)*
Hard Rock Hotel, *ch.* 3
1906 Lodge $$$, *ch.* 9
The Pearl Hotel, *ch.* 8
The Sofia Hotel, *ch.* 3

BEST UPSCALE *($$$$)*
Andaz San Diego, *ch.* 3
Grande Colonial, *ch.* 7
Hotel Del Coronado, *ch.* 9
Lodge at Torrey Pines, *ch.* 7
Rancho Valencia Resort & Spa, *ch.* 10
The U.S. Grant, *a Luxury Collection Hotel, ch.* 3

BEST BEACH
Beach Terrace Inn, *ch.* 10
Catamaran Resort and Spa, *ch.* 6

BEST POOL
Fairmont Grand Del Mar, *ch.* 10
Kimpton Solamar Hotel, *ch.* 3
Omni La Costa Resort & Spa, *ch.* 10
Park Hyatt Aviara Resort, *ch.* 10

BEST FOR ROMANCE
Carter Estate Winery and Resort, *ch.* 10
Orchard Hill Country Inn, *ch.* 10
Pelican Cove Inn, *ch.* 10
Ponte Vineyard Inn, *ch.* 10
La Valencia, *ch.* 7

BEST VIEWS
Coronado Island Marriott Resort, *ch.* 9

MOST TRENDY
Pendry San Diego, *ch.* 3

BEST FOR FAMILIES
Courtyard Marriott San Diego Airport Liberty Station, *ch.* 8
LEGOLAND Hotel, *ch.* 10
Loews Coronado Bay Resort, *ch.* 9
Ocean Palms Beach Resort, *ch.* 10
Paradise Point Resort and Spa, *ch.* 6

🍸 BARS

BEST BREWERIES
Bivouac Ciderworks, *ch.* 5
Stone Brewing World Gardens and Bistro, *ch.* 8

BEST MICROBREW SELECTION
Blind Lady Ale House, *ch.* 5
Hamilton's Tavern, *ch.* 5
Toronado, *ch.* 5

BEST ROOFTOP BARS
Altitude Sky Lounge, *ch.* 3
Cannonball, *ch.* 6
The Rooftop by STK, *ch.* 3
Top of the Park, *ch.* TK

BEST MARGARITAS
Baja Betty's, *ch.* 5
Blanco Tacos + Tequila, *ch.* 5
Cantina Mayahuel, *ch.* 5
Volcano Rabbit, *ch.* 3

BEST PIANO BARS
Red Tracton's, *ch.* 10
Westgate Hotel Plaza Bar, *ch.* 3

BEST WINE BARS
Vin de Syrah, *ch.* 3

BEST COCKTAILS
The Grant Grill, *ch.* 3
Madison on Park, *ch.* 5
Noble Experiment, *ch.* 3

BEST BARS
Fairweather, *ch.* 3
Seven Grand, *ch.* 5
Starlite, *ch.* 5
The Waterfront Bar & Grill, *ch.* 3

BEST FOR LIVE MUSIC
Belly Up, *ch.* 10
The Casbah, *ch.* 3
Humphreys Concerts by the Bay, *ch.* 8

BEST SPEAKEASIES
The Grass Skirt, *ch.* 6
Noble Experiment, *ch.* 3

BEST NOVELTY BARS
Bang Bang, *ch.* 3
False Idol, *ch.* 3

BEST LGBT-FRIENDLY BARS
Baja Betty's, *ch.* 5
Martinis Above Fourth, *ch.* 5
Rich's, *ch.* 5
Urban Mo's Bar and Grill, *ch.* 5

San Diego with Kids

BEACH FUN

A pail and shovel can keep kids entertained for hours at the beach—**Coronado Beach** is especially family-friendly. Be liberal with the sunscreen, even if it's cloudy.

If you're visiting in summer, check out Imperial Beach's **Sun and Sea Festival.** This sand castle competition in July even has a kids' contest.

Drop off the tweens and teens for a morning **surf lesson** and enjoy some guilt-free grown-up time. Or rent bikes for a casual family ride along the **Mission Bay boardwalk.** If that's not enough of an adventure, take your daring offspring on the **Giant Dipper,** an old wooden roller coaster at Mission Bay's **Belmont Park,** also home to a huge arcade and the Wave House.

TOP ATTRACTIONS

LEGOLAND California is a full day of thrills for kids 12 and under, while the **San Diego Zoo** and **San Diego Safari Park** satisfy all age groups and every kind of kid, from the curious (plenty of educational angles) to the boisterous (room to run around and lots of animals to imitate). They even have family sleepover nights in summer.

WINTER SIGHTINGS

If you're visiting in winter, try a **whale-watching** tour. Even if you don't see any migrating gray whales, the boat ride is fun. La Jolla's **Birch Aquarium** has enough glowing and tentacled creatures to send imaginations plummeting leagues under the sea.

MUSEUMS GEARED TO KIDS

An afternoon at the museum might elicit yawns until they spy all the neat stuff at Balboa Park's **San Diego Air and Space Museum,** which celebrates aviation and flight history with exhibitions that include actual planes. The **Fleet Science Center** inspires budding scientists with interactive exhibits and its IMAX dome theater. The **San Diego Model Railroad Museum** features miles and miles of model trains and track, including an incredibly detailed reproduction of the Tehachapi railroad circa 1952.

Downtown's **New Children's Museum** appeals to all age groups. With installations geared just for them and dry and wet art-making areas (less mess for you), kids can channel all that excess vacation energy into something productive. While they color and craft, you can admire the museum's ultra-contemporary, sustainable architecture.

TAKE ME OUT TO THE BALL GAME

Baseball buffs will have a blast at **PETCO Park,** where the San Diego Padres play all spring and summer. PETCO's Park at the Park, a grassy elevated area outside the stadium, offers stellar center-field views—plus all the action on a big screen—with a sandy play space if your kids get bored after a few innings.

TREATING YOUR TOTS

Pacific Beach's yummy **The Baked Bear** (✉ *4516 Mission Blvd.* ⊕ *www.thebakedbear.com*) offers customized ice-cream sandwiches that are sure to please. If toys trump sweet treats, check out the classics at **Geppetto's** (⊕ *www.geppettos-toys.com*), a family-run business with 10 locations throughout San Diego, including Old Town, La Jolla, and the Fashion Valley Mall.

Free Things to Do in San Diego

San Diego may levy an unofficial "sunshine tax," but it makes up for it with plenty of free stuff. Aside from the beaches, backcountry trails, and verdant city parks—all as free as the steadfast sun and endless blue skies—a little careful planning can land you cost-free (or very cheap) fun for the whole family.

FREE IN BALBOA PARK

Balboa Park hosts its one-hour **Twilight in the Park** concert series from June through August, Tuesday through Thursday at 6:30 pm. Sit under the stars and take in everything from Dixieland Jazz to Latin salsa. Also at the park, check out the **Spreckels International Organ Festival** concerts Monday at 7:30 pm, from June to September, as well as 2 pm Sunday matinee concerts throughout the year. Balboa Park's **Screen on the Green,** an outdoor movie screening, runs throughout August. The **Timken Museum of Art** in Balboa Park is free but a donation is suggested.

FREE CONCERTS

The **Del Mar Racetrack Summer Concert Series** features big-name local and national bands; it's technically free, though you still have to pay a few bucks for racetrack admission.

Also worth catching: Carlsbad's **TGIF Concerts in the Parks,** Friday at 6 pm; **Coronado Summer Concerts in the Park,** Sunday at 6 pm, May through September; the **Del Mar Twilight Concert Series,** Tuesday at 7 pm, June through August; and Encinitas' **Sunday Summer Concerts by the Sea,** 3 pm, July and August.

The annual **Adams Avenue Unplugged** festival in April and **Adams Avenue Street Fair** in September both hit pay dirt: blues, folk, country, jazz, indie, world, and more—all for free.

FREE (OR INEXPENSIVE) TASTINGS

Beer aficionados can take an $8, 45-minute tour of the 55,000-square-foot **Stone Brewing Company**—groups fill up fast, maybe because of the free tastings at the end. At **Alpine Beer Company,** it's not free, but it's cheap: up to four tasters are just $2 each. Wine lovers might pack a lunch and head for **Orfila Vineyards & Winery,** where picnic tables dot the pastoral landscape—the wine's not free, but the views are. Or spend an entire afternoon in **Temecula Wine Country.** Tastings typically aren't free, but you can find twofer coupons and other discounts at ⊕ *www.temeculawines.org.*

OCTOBER FREEBIES

October is Kids Free Month for tots under 11 at the **San Diego Zoo, SeaWorld, Balboa Park Museums,** and the **San Diego Safari Park.** Little ones can also snag meals on the house and more than 100 other perks throughout San Diego.

FREE MUSEUMS

The **MCASD** is always free for patrons under 25, and for everyone else the third Thursday of the month from 5 to 7 pm.

In February, you can pick up a free **Museum Month Pass** at San Diego libraries that offers half-off admission to 40 museums for the entire month.

Many of San Diego's museums offer a once-a-month free Tuesday, on a rotating schedule (see ⊕ *www.balboapark.org* for the schedule) to San Diego city and county residents and active military, and their families; special exhibitions often require separate admission.

What to Read and Watch

THE HOUSE OF BROKEN ANGELS BY LUIS ALBERTO URREA

Centered around three generations of a Mexican-American family, with a history in the California Territories since World War I, this is a full, happy novel about family love and heartbreak, teeming with big personalities and vivid characters.

THE GANGSTER WE ARE ALL LOOKING FOR BY LE THI DIEM THUY

The characters of Thuy's novel are Vietnamese refugees in the late '70s, adjusting to life in crowded bungalows and apartments of Normal Heights, Linda Vista, and East San Diego. The protagonist, a young girl, flees Vietnam with her father and is sponsored by a churchgoing family in San Diego after their long journey. The novel is based on the author's own childhood.

TIJUANA STRAITS BY KEM NUNN

Set in San Diego, San Ysidro, and the area around the Mexican border, the cast of characters is made up of washed-up surfers, gangsters, down-and-outs, and others at dire straits. The novel's suspenseful and entertaining storyline, full of chases, crimes, and mysterious circumstances across borders, is a glimpse at the gritty violence and adventures in the land between California and Mexico.

TOP GUN (1986)

This famous late '80s flick, starring a cocky Tom Cruise in pilot school, filmed most of its base scenes at the elite pilot school that it fictionalizes, the Naval Air Station Miramar in San Diego (it's since moved to Nevada). Other key scenes were filmed throughout San Diego county, in Oceanside, and at Kansas City Barbeque, a divey sports bar in San Diego's Embarcadero (the bar proudly displays memorabilia from the movie).

ANCHORMAN (2004)

In this raunchy comedy, Will Ferrell plays Ron Burgundy, a beloved San Diego news anchor who faces challenges to his job and sexist way of thinking when a female news anchor (Christina Applegate) comes on the scene. While the loud comedy boasts San Diego as its setting, much was filmed in L.A., with great pains taken to make everything look like San Diego.

TRAFFIC (2000)

This complex and moving film tackles the war on drugs through several different points of view and experiences of the people within it. San Diego scenes include the ritzy Ranch Bernardo Inn, La Jolla coast, the Hall of Justice courthouse in Downtown San Diego, Balboa Park and the botanical gardens, and the San Ysidro/Tijuana border crossing just south of San Diego.

FAST TIMES AT RIDGEMONT HIGH (1982)

This humorous coming-of-age film has become somewhat of a cult classic, but many people don't know it's based on the book and journalistic efforts of Cameron Crowe (the young Rolling Stone prodigy reporter). Cameron spent a year undercover in Clairemont High School in San Diego, and the book and movie tell the account of this wild, adolescent year and the characters he meets.

VERONICA MARS

A drama series starring Kristen Bell as a young crime-solver wrapped up in the (many) mysteries of her wealthy beachside town, seasons of Veronica Mars were filmed almost entirely in and around San Diego. A revival movie was also made about the cast of characters in 2014, and streaming network Hulu is doing an eight-episode limited series set to air in 2019.

Chapter 2

TRAVEL SMART SAN DIEGO

Updated by
Marlise Kast-Myers

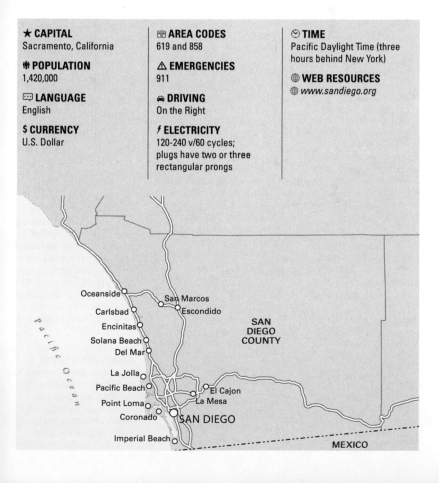

★ **CAPITAL**
Sacramento, California

👥 **POPULATION**
1,420,000

💬 **LANGUAGE**
English

$ **CURRENCY**
U.S. Dollar

📠 **AREA CODES**
619 and 858

⚠ **EMERGENCIES**
911

🚗 **DRIVING**
On the Right

⚡ **ELECTRICITY**
120-240 v/60 cycles;
plugs have two or three
rectangular prongs

⊘ **TIME**
Pacific Daylight Time (three
hours behind New York)

🌐 **WEB RESOURCES**
🌐 *www.sandiego.org*

Oceanside
San Marcos
Carlsbad
Escondido
Encinitas
Solana Beach
Del Mar

SAN
DIEGO
COUNTY

La Jolla
Pacific Beach
El Cajon
La Mesa
Point Loma
Coronado
SAN DIEGO

Imperial Beach

MEXICO

Pacific Ocean

San Diego: Know Before You Go

San Diego is a desirable destination for beachgoers, outdoor enthusiasts, and culture seekers—attracting more than 35 million visitors annually. Take the guess work out of packing and planning for your next trip to America's Finest City with these insider tips on what to expect, what to bring, and what to avoid.

BRING LAYERS

Known for having one of the most temperate climates in the country, San Diego's typical weather forecast is 70s and sunny. But tourists who have never visited the Southern California paradisiacal city are often surprised to find out how cool it gets at night. Many businesses and residences—particularly older buildings—do not have central heating or air conditioning, so it's advised to bring a light jacket or sweater for summer evenings, and heavier knits during winter. Coastal neighborhoods can turn particularly chilly from ocean breezes.

WEAR COMFY SHOES

San Diego's a walkable town, and based on the traffic and lack of parking, you should walk as much as possible. Balboa Park and the zoo are walkers' paradises, and all of Downtown is pedestrian-friendly.

IF YOU DECIDE TO GO TO MEXICO, BRING YOUR PASSPORT

San Diego's an international border city, located only 17 miles from Tijuana, making it easy to plan a trip to both cities in a single visit. But gone are the days when Americans could cross the border into Mexico and return by simply showing their driver's license. For the last decade, U.S. Customs and Border Protection has required Americans to show a valid passport to return home after a day of tacos and margaritas in Mexico. From San Diego, the easiest way to travel to the border is by taking the trolley ($5 round-trip) to San Ysidro on the blue line, and then walk across—retracing your steps on the way back. Check the CBP Border Wait Times mobile app for estimated wait times around the clock.

SAN DIEGO IS A NAVY TOWN

With more than 143,000 active-duty service members and another 241,000 veterans, San Diego has the largest military concentration in the world. While in town (especially Coronado), you will likely see service members walking in uniform, or catch them driving special military vehicles. The best opportunity to interact with them or visit an active military base is during Fleet Week San Diego, held each fall. Visitors can also take self-guided tours of decommissioned aircraft carrier USS Midway Museum, open to the public year-round. Naval Air Station North Island is the birthplace of naval aviation. Naval Base San Diego is home to the largest contingency of ships in the U.S. Pacific Fleet, and Naval Amphibious Base Coronado is headquarters to elite special forces commands including the U.S. Navy SEALs.

GOOD LUCK FINDING A HOTEL IF YOU'RE VISITING DURING COMIC-CON INTERNATIONAL

More than 130,000 people, including big-name celebrities, flock to San Diego Convention Center each July for Comic-Con International. You can expect area lodging to be at an all-time high during the convention (which lasts for about five days), with hotel rooms and Airbnb rentals booked several months in advance. People in cosplay take over the streets of downtown, with additional spectators there to people-watch—inevitably causing heavy traffic into and out of the Downtown area. Check the Comic-Con website for event dates to plan accordingly.

AVOID RUSH HOUR

San Diego does not have a good public transit system to effectively help the thousands of people who commute across the city every day, causing bad weekday traffic from about

7 to 10 am and 3 to 7 pm. The I-5 and I-805 that run north and south are arguably the worst, and the I-15 and I-8 can also get bad during peak drive times. But as the locals say, it's still never as bad as driving in Los Angeles.

COME PREPARED TO IMBIBE

Sure, you could drink mainstream beer like Budweiser in San Diego, but you'll be hard-pressed to find it on tap at local bars or restaurants. San Diego is proud of its booming craft beer industry, evidenced by the more than 150 craft breweries throughout the county that are loyally supported by locals. India Pale Ales are the most common brews, but you'll find other varieties being poured to please your palate, in addition to ciders, hard kombucha, and mead.

SAN DIEGO IS HOME TO MAJOR THEME PARKS

If you're bringing kids on a trip to San Diego, there won't be a shortage of places to entertain them. Take a day off from the beach to visit local amusement parks, including San Diego Zoo and Safari Park, SeaWorld, and LEGOLAND. Adjacent to San Diego Zoo, Balboa Park houses 17 museums, as well as restaurants, gardens, and other attractions. Expect larger crowds during the summer months, and shop for multi-park passes if you plan to park hop. ■TIP→ **Adult beverages are available for purchase at all area theme parks.**

"MAY GRAY, JUNE GLOOM"

This common phrase in San Diego essentially means you shouldn't expect to see the sun during those months. An offshore marine layer that forms overnight is typically burned off by mid-morning sun, but until then, it leaves a blanket of thick fog over much of the coastal area. During May and June, the marine layer often doesn't burn off at all, leaving the city with fall-like temps and cloud-covered beaches. For the warmest weather, visit San Diego during high season, between July and September.

PARKING CAN BE TRICKY

The electric scooter trend continues to be a divisive topic in San Diego, with some communities like Coronado banning them, while other areas encourage their use to get cars off the road and free up parking spots. There's an abundance of scooters sprinkled throughout Downtown, Balboa Park, and the beach communities, which are all accessed through a mobile app (depending on the brand) and cost $1 to activate. In San Diego, adults 18 years and older are no longer required to wear a helmet while riding, but it's still illegal to ride electric scooters on sidewalks. Dockless bikes are another rideshare option when headed to a crowded area or if you don't have a place to store your wheels.

TACO TUESDAYS ARE A WEEKLY TRADITION

If you like happy hour, then you'll love Taco Tuesdays in San Diego. Many local restaurants offer discounts on Tuesdays that may also include drink specials. And it's not just Mexican restaurants that join in the tradition—eateries of all types and every price point have tempting deals. Browse Instagram for drool-worthy #TacoTuesday posts to begin plotting out your next tortilla-filled meal.

STAY AWAY FROM THE SEALS

They might look cute and cuddly, but keep away from the seals and sea lions that congregate at La Jolla's Children's Pool Beach. Do not feed them, and go with the knowledge that these playful creatures often leave a strong odor of feces in their wake.

FLIP-FLOPS AND SHORTS ARE THE NORM

You won't find a more casual big city. Flip-flops are the favored footwear, shorts and beachy skirts comprise the summer uniform, and designer jeans qualify as dressing up. Dining out warrants a little research; some eateries barely toe the "no shirt, no shoes" rule, while others require more elegant attire.

SUNRISE, SUNSET

The beaches can't be beat, but battling the crazy summer crowds for a spot on the sand is far from relaxing. Take a stroll just after dawn, or find a secluded spot on the cliffs, for a more serene sunset.

Getting Here and Around

When traveling in the San Diego area, consider the big picture to avoid getting lost. Water lies to the west of the city. To the east and north, mountains separate the urban areas from the desert. If you keep going south, you'll end up in Mexico.

Walking (or riding the bus or trolley) is the way to go once you've reached a destination area. Balboa Park and the zoo are walkers' paradises, and all of Downtown, including the Gaslamp Quarter, Little Italy, Seaport Village, and Embarcadero, is pedestrian-friendly. In the heart of the city, numbered streets run west to east and lettered streets run north to south. The business district around the Civic Center, at 1st Avenue and C Street, is dedicated to local government and commerce.

✈ Air Travel

Flying time to San Diego is 5 hours from New York, 4 hours from Chicago, 3 hours from Dallas, and 45 minutes from Los Angeles.

AIRPORT

The major airport is San Diego International Airport (SAN), formerly called Lindbergh Field. Most airlines depart and arrive at Terminal 2. Southwest, Frontier, and Alaska Airlines are reserved for Terminal 1. Free, color-coded shuttles loop the airport and match the parking lot they serve. The long-term parking lot on Harbor Drive and Liberator Way is a shuttle ride to the terminals. Parking lots at Terminals 1 and 2 charge $32 per day and have covered parking and charging stations. The Cell Phone Lot for attended vehicles is convenient when picking up passengers. With only one runway serving two main terminals, San Diego's airport is too small to accommodate the heavy traffic of busy travel periods. Small problems including fog and rain can cause congested terminals and flight delays. Delays of 20–30 minutes in baggage claim aren't unusual.

Shopping and dining options include these popular spots: Einstein Bros. Bagel, Best Buy Express, Brighton Collectibles, Be Relax Spa, Phil's Barbecue, and Stone Brewing. In addition, if you have a flight delay, consider catching a 10-minute cab ride to the Gaslamp Quarter for last-minute shopping or a stroll around Downtown.

If you need travel assistance at the airport, Airport Ambassadors are stationed at the information centers in both terminals.

GROUND TRANSPORTATION

San Diego International Airport is 3 miles from Downtown. Shuttle vans, buses, and taxis run from the Transportation Plaza, reached via the skybridges from Terminals 1 and 2. The cheapest and sometimes most convenient shuttle is the Metropolitan Transit System's Flyer Route 992, red-and-white-stripe buses that serve the terminals at 10- to 15-minute intervals between 5 am and 11 pm. These buses have luggage racks and make a loop from the airport to Downtown along Broadway to 9th Avenue and back, stopping frequently within walking distance of many hotels; they also connect with the San Diego Trolley and Amtrak. The $2.25 fare includes transfer to local transit buses and the trolley, and you should have exact fare (in coins or bills) handy. Information about the Metropolitan Transit System's shuttles and buses, the San Diego Trolley, and Coaster commuter train can all be found on the joint transit website ⊕ *www.transit.511sd.com.*

If you're heading to North County, the MTS route 992 can drop you off across from the Santa Fe Depot, where you can take the Coaster commuter train as far north as Oceanside for $5.50.

Of the various airport shuttles, only SuperShuttle has tie-downs for wheelchairs.

Ground shuttle service is available between LAX and San Diego, but can be prohibitively expensive, with rates for the two-hour trip starting at $296, so a car rental may be a more economical option. All the shuttles listed at the end of this section offer the service.

Taxis departing from the airport are subject to regulated fares—($2.80 initial fee, $3 per mile). Taxi fare is about $20 plus tip to most Downtown hotels. The fare to Coronado runs about $30 plus tip. Limousine rates vary and are charged per hour, per mile, or both, with some minimums established.

✪ Boat Travel

Many hotels, marinas, and yacht clubs rent slips short-term. Call ahead, because available space is limited. The San Diego and Southwestern yacht clubs have reciprocal arrangements with other yacht clubs.

Flagship Cruises takes you between Downtown and Coronado in a nostalgic, old-school ferry every hour from 9 am to 9 pm. The ride lasts about 15 minutes and costs $5 each way; bicycles and Segways are free.

San Diego SEAL Tours, operated by Old Town Trolley, combine the best of land and sea, departing from Seaport Village daily. After exploring picturesque San Diego neighborhoods, the bus-boat hybrid

rolls right into the water for a cruise around the bay. The $42 tour is narrated with fun facts, too.

🚗 Car Travel

To fully explore sprawling San Diego—especially with kids in tow—consider renting a car. Nearly everything of interest can be found off I–5 or I–163, and the county's freeways are wide and easy to use. Traffic isn't a major issue if you avoid rush hour. Parking in urban areas is typically metered, Monday through Saturday, 8 to 6, unless otherwise marked. You may park for free outside those hours, and on Sunday and holidays. ■TIP→ Yellow commercial loading zones are fair game for parking after 6 pm. During special Downtown events, such as Padres games, you'll likely have to settle for one of the many paid parking structures—they cost around $20 close to the action. Parking at beaches is free for the most part, though tough to come by on sunny days unless you stake out a spot early.

A car is necessary for getting around greater San Diego on the sprawling freeway system and for visiting the North County beaches, mountains, and desert. Driving around San Diego County is pretty simple: most major attractions are within a few miles of the Pacific Ocean. Interstate 5, which stretches north–south from Oregon to the Mexican border, bisects San Diego. Interstate 8 provides access from Yuma, Arizona, and points east. Drivers coming from the Los Angeles area, Nevada, and the mountain regions beyond can reach San Diego on I–15. During rush hours there are jams on I–5 and on I–15 between I–805 and Escondido.

Getting Here and Around

There are a few border inspection stations along major highways in San Diego County, the largest just north of Oceanside on I–5 near San Clemente. Travel with your driver's license, and bring your passport if you're an international traveler.

Gas is widely available in San Diego County, except in rural areas. Outlets are generally open 24 hours and accept major credit cards that can be processed at the pump. Full service is not available, but you will usually find window-washing tools next to a pump; water and air are available somewhere on the property. All fuel in California is unleaded and sold at three price levels. Pricing is per gallon pumped and varies widely by season, location, and oil company provider. In San Diego gas tends to cost about 15% more than it does in many other California cities.

There are nearly 60 charging stations for electric vehicles in San Diego, located at Balboa Park, recreation centers, libraries, upscale hotels, and entertainment districts. A map of EV charging stations is available at ⊕ *www.sandiego.gov.*

PARKING

Meters in Downtown usually cost $1 to $2.50 an hour; enforcement is 10–8 every day but Sunday. ■ TIP→ **If you are headed to Horton Plaza, the mall validates for one hour with no purchase required.** Be extra careful around rush hour, when certain on-street parking areas become tow-away zones. Violations in congested areas can cost $45 or more. In the evening and during events in Downtown, parking spaces are hard to find. Most Downtown hotels offer valet parking service. The Convention Center has nearly 2,000 spaces that go for $15 to $35 for event parking. On game day at PETCO Park, expect to pay $10 to $35 for a parking space a short walk from the stadium. Other Downtown lots cost $10–$45 per day.

Balboa Park and Mission Bay have huge free parking lots, and it's rare not to find a space, though it may seem as if you've parked miles from your destination. Old Town has large lots surrounding the transit center, but parking spaces are still hard to find. Parking is more of a problem in La Jolla and Coronado, where you generally need to rely on hard-to-find metered street spots or expensive by-the-hour parking lots.

ROAD CONDITIONS

Highways are in good condition in the San Diego area. From 6 to 8:30 am and 3:30 to 6 pm, traffic is particularly heavy on I–5, I–8, I–805, and I–15. Before venturing into the mountains, check on road conditions; mountain driving can be dangerous. Check Caltrans or listen to radio traffic reports for information on the length of border waits from Mexico. For roadside assistance, dial 511 from a mobile phone.

RENTAL CARS

In California you must be 21 to rent a car, and rates may be higher if you're under 25. Some agencies will not rent to those under 25; check when you book. Children up to age eight or under 4'9" in height must be placed in safety or booster seats. For non–U.S. residents an international license is recommended but not required.

Rates fluctuate with seasons and demand, but generally begin at $39 a day and $250 a week for an economy car with air-conditioning, automatic transmission, and unlimited mileage. This doesn't include an 8.75% tax.

Ⓜ Public Transportation

Visit ⊕ *www.511sd.com*, which lists routes and timetables for the Metropolitan Transit System and North County Transit District. Local/urban bus fare is $2.25 one-way, or $5 for an unlimited day pass (exact change only; pay when you board). A one-way ride on the city's iconic red trolleys is $2.50; get your ticket at any trolley vending machine.

Under the umbrella of the Metropolitan Transit System, there are two major transit agencies in the area: San Diego Transit and North County Transit District (NCTD). You will need to buy a $2 compass card, available when you board for the first time, on which are loaded your destinations to use MTS. Day passes, available for 1 to 30 days and starting at $5, give unlimited rides on nonpremium regional buses and the San Diego Trolley. You can buy them from most trolley vending machines, at the Downtown Transit Store, and at Albertsons markets. A $12 Regional Plus Day Pass adds Coaster service and premium bus routes.

The bright-red trolleys of the San Diego Trolley light-rail system operate on three lines that serve Downtown San Diego, Mission Valley, Old Town, South Bay, the U.S. border, and East County. The trolleys operate seven days a week from about 5 am to midnight, depending on the station, at intervals of about 15 minutes. The trolley system connects with San Diego Transit bus routes—connections are posted at each trolley station. Bicycle lockers are available at most stations and bikes are allowed on buses and trolleys though space is limited. Trolleys can get crowded during morning and evening rush hours. Schedules are posted at each stop; on-time performance is excellent.

NCTD bus routes connect with Coaster commuter train routes between

Oceanside and the Santa Fe Depot in San Diego. They serve points from Del Mar north to San Clemente, inland to Fallbrook, Pauma Valley, Valley Center, Ramona, and Escondido, with transfer points within the city of San Diego. NCTD also offers special express-bus service to Qualcomm Stadium for select major sporting events. The Sprinter light rail provides service between Oceanside and Escondido, with buses connecting to popular North County attractions.

San Diego Transit bus fares range from $2.25 to $5; North County Transit District bus fares are $4. You must have exact change in coins and/or bills. Pay upon boarding. Transfers are not included; the $5 day pass is the best option for most bus travel and can be purchased onboard.

San Diego Trolley tickets cost $2.50 and are good for two hours, but for one-way travel only. Round-trip tickets are double the one-way fare.

Tickets are dispensed from self-service machines at each stop; exact fare in coins is recommended, although some machines accept bills in $1, $5, $10, and $20 denominations and credit cards. Ticket vending machines will return up to $10 in change. For trips on multiple buses and trolleys, buy a day pass good for unlimited use all day.

FRED (FREE RIDE EVERYWHERE DOWNTOWN)

These open-air electric vehicles offer free rides throughout the Downtown area. Riders can make a pickup request through the FRED app, or simply flag one down. ⊕ *www.thefreeride.com*

Getting Here and Around

🚗 Ride-Sharing

App-driven ride-sharing services such as Uber and Lyft are popular in San Diego. Drivers are readily available from most in-town destinations and also service the airport.

🚕 Taxi Travel

Cabs are a fine choice for trips to and from the airport and short jaunts around town. The approximate rates are: $2.80 for the first 1/10 mile, $3 each additional mile, and $24 per hour of waiting time. You can find taxi stands at the airport, hotels, major attractions, and shopping centers. Downtown, your best bet is to flag one down.

If you are heading to the airport from a hotel, ask about the flat rate, which varies according to destination; otherwise you'll be charged by the mile (which works out to $20 or so from any Downtown location). Taxi stands are at shopping centers and hotels; otherwise you must call and reserve a cab.

PEDICABS

These pedal-powered tricycles with a rear passenger area are a great way to get around Downtown. Just be sure to agree on a price before you start moving, or you could get taken for the wrong kind of ride.

🚆 Train Travel

Amtrak serves Downtown San Diego's Santa Fe Depot with daily trains to and from Los Angeles, Santa Barbara, and San Luis Obispo. Connecting service to Oakland, Seattle, Chicago, Texas, Florida, and points beyond is available in Los Angeles. Amtrak trains stop in San Diego North County at Solana Beach and Oceanside. You can obtain Amtrak timetables at any Amtrak station, or by visiting the Amtrak website.

Coaster commuter trains, which run daily between Oceanside and San Diego, stop at the same stations as Amtrak as well as others. The frequency is about every half hour during the weekday rush hour, with four trains on Saturday (with additional Friday and Saturday night service in spring and summer). One-way fares are $4 to $5.50, depending on the distance traveled. The Oceanside, Carlsbad, and Solana Beach stations have beach access. The Sprinter runs between Oceanside and Escondido, with many stops along the way.

Metrolink operates high-speed rail service ($17) between the Oceanside Transit Center and Union Station in Los Angeles.

Train vending machines accept all major credit cards. Reservations, which you can make online, are suggested for trains running on weekends between San Diego and Santa Barbara. Make your reservations early to get the best fares. For security reasons, Amtrak requires ticket holders to provide photo ID.

Essentials

⑪ Dining

What It Costs

$	$$	$$$	$$$$
RESTAURANTS			
under $18	$18–$27	$28–$35	over $35

San Diego is an up-and-coming culinary destination, thanks to its stunning Pacific Ocean setting, proximity to Mexico, diverse population, and the area's extraordinary farming community. Increasingly the city's veteran top chefs are being joined by a new generation of talented chefs and restaurateurs who are adding stylish restaurants with innovative food and drink programs to the dining scene at a record pace. Yes, visitors still are drawn to the San Diego Zoo and miles of beaches, but now they come for memorable dining experiences as well.

The city's culinary scene got a significant boost when San Diego emerged as one of the world's top craft beer destinations, with artisan breweries and gastropubs now in almost every neighborhood. San Diego also was on the cutting edge of the farm-to-table, Slow Food movement. Local sourcing is possible for everything from seafood to just-picked produce from a host of nationally recognized producers like Chino Farms and Carlsbad Aquafarm. The city's ethnically diverse neighborhoods with their modest eateries offering affordable authentic international cuisines add spice to the dining mix.

San Diego's distinct neighborhoods have their own dining personalities with friendly restaurants and bistros catering to every craving in this sun-blessed city. The trendy Gaslamp Quarter delights visitors looking for a broad range of innovative and international dining and nightlife, while bustling Little Italy offers a mix of affordable Italian fare and posh new eateries. Modern restaurants and cafés thrive in East Village, amid the luxury condos near PETCO Park.

The Uptown neighborhoods centered on Hillcrest—an urbane district with San Francisco flavor—are a mix of bars and independent restaurants, many of which specialize in ethnic cuisine. North Park, in particular, has a happening restaurant and craft beer scene, with just about every kind of cuisine you can think of, and laid-back prices to boot. And scenic La Jolla offers some of the best fine dining in the city with dramatic water views as an added bonus.

DINING HOURS
Unless otherwise noted, the restaurants listed in this guide are open daily for lunch and dinner. Lunch is typically served 11:30 am to 2:30 pm, and dinner service in most restaurants begins at 5:30 pm and ends at 10 pm, though a number of establishments serve until 11 pm or later on Friday and Saturday nights.

WHAT TO WEAR
In San Diego restaurants, generally a "come-as-you-are" attitude prevails. It's a casual city for men and women alike, but going-out dress is generally fashionable and fun, especially for celebratory or upscale dining. Very few dress-up places remain.

CHILDREN
Most San Diego restaurants welcome children and many have special kids' menus with food offerings targeted to younger palates and parents' pocketbooks. Some high-end and bar-oriented establishments may not be appropriate for children—if unsure, call the establishment for confirmation.

Essentials

PARKING

With the boom of new apartments and condominiums Downtown and in Little Italy, street parking near many restaurants can be frustrating, especially in the evenings and on weekends. Valet ($10–$15) parking in front of many major restaurants is easy and convenient. Some valet parking is subsidized by restaurants; call ahead for parking offers and suggestions. There are several parking garages and lots throughout Downtown with prices that fluctuate depending on events. Savvy locals use the limited free parking with validation at Downtown's Horton Plaza. For major Downtown events where parking is impossible, consider parking for free at the Old Town transit center and get a quick San Diego Trolley ride to stops in Little Italy, East Village, and the Gaslamp Quarter.

SMOKING

Smoking is banned in restaurants in California. The city of San Diego permits smoking on patios, but it's not allowed in the cities of Chula Vista, Del Mar, El Cajon, Encinitas, National City, and Solana Beach.

PRICES

Meals in San Diego popular dining spots can be pricey, especially in areas like La Jolla and the Gaslamp Quarter. Many other restaurants are very affordable or offer extra value with fixed-price menus, early-dining specials and early and late happy hours.

Prices in the reviews are the average cost of a main course at dinner or, if dinner is not served, at lunch.

🛏 Lodging

WHAT IT COSTS			
$	$$	$$$	$$$$
HOTELS			
under $161	$161–$230	$231–$300	over $300

In San Diego, you could plan a luxurious vacation at the beach, staying at a resort with panoramic ocean views, private balconies, and a full-service spa. Or you could stay Downtown, steps from the bustling Gaslamp Quarter, in a modern hotel featuring lively rooftop pools, complimentary wine receptions, and high-tech entertainment systems. But with some flexibility—maybe opting for a partial-view room a quick drive from the action—it's possible to experience San Diego at half the price.

Sharing the city's postcard-perfect sunny skies are neighborhoods and coastal communities that offer great diversity; San Diego is no longer the sleepy beach town it once was. In action-packed Downtown, luxury hotels cater to solo business travelers and young couples with trendy restaurants and cabana-encircled pools. Budget-friendly options can be found in smaller neighborhoods just outside the Gaslamp Quarter such as Little Italy and Uptown (Hillcrest, Mission Hills, and North Park).

You'll need a car if you stay outside Downtown, but the beach communities are rich with lodging options. Across the bridge, Coronado's hotels and resorts offer access to a stretch of glistening white sand that's often recognized as one of the best beaches in the country. La Jolla offers many romantic, upscale ocean-view hotels and some of the area's best restaurants and specialty shopping.

WHERE SHOULD I STAY?

	Neighborhood Vibe	Pros	Cons
Downtown	Downtown's hub is the Gaslamp Quarter, an action-packed area with many hotels, boutiques, restaurants, and clubs. Little Italy and Embarcadero areas are quieter.	Close to food and nightlife options for every age and taste. Quick walk or trolley ride to convention center. Won't need a car to get to many attractions.	Streets can be congested and noisy at night, particularly in the Gaslamp Quarter and East Village. Overnight parking is expensive.
Uptown and Old Town	Quieter area north of Downtown with more budget-friendly hotels. Old Town has a busy stretch of Mexican restaurants and historic sites.	Central location that's close to Balboa Park and major freeways. Good for business travelers. More inexpensive dining options.	Limited nightlife options. Feels more removed from San Diego's beachy vibe. Mission Valley area lacks character; it's filled with malls and car lots.
Mission Bay, Beaches, and SeaWorld	Relaxed and casual beachside area with many resorts, golf courses, and parks. Largest man-made aquatic park in the country.	Right on the water. Can splurge on Jet Skis and other water sports or stick to barbecues and public playgrounds. Close to SeaWorld.	Resorts are spaced far apart, and area is somewhat removed from central San Diego. Watch for high resort fees and other not-so-obvious charges.
La Jolla	The "jewel" of San Diego, an affluent coastal area with a small-town atmosphere. Has a range of luxury hotels and a few value choices.	Gorgeous views. Close to or right on the beach. Some of the best seafood restaurants and high-end shopping in the state. Safe area for walking.	Often congested, and parking can be nearly impossible in summer. Very expensive area. Has few hotels that cater to children.
Point Loma and Shelter Island	Areas by the bay have historic and resort hotels, beaches, and tourist-oriented restaurants. Point Loma is residential and home to many military families.	Great views of the city, bay, and beaches. Near the airport. Convenient for boaters. Hotels tend to be family-friendly, with large rooms and pools.	Isolated from the rest of the city; you'll spend significant time commuting to other parts of San Diego, such as La Jolla and Balboa Park.
Coronado	Coronado, home to the iconic Hotel del Coronado, is residential, home to many military families. It's the perfect place to bike, or relax on the beach.	Quiet, lovely neighborhood feel on an island with easy access to Downtown San Diego. Great beaches, restaurants, shopping, and nightlife.	This is an island, so you'll spend significant time commuting to other parts of San Diego, and parking can be tough.

Essentials

But it's easy to find a water view in any price range: surfers make themselves at home at the casual inns and budget stays of Pacific Beach and Mission Bay. If you're planning to fish, check out hotels located near the marinas in Shelter Island, Point Loma, or Coronado.

For families, Uptown, Mission Valley, and Old Town are close to SeaWorld and the San Diego Zoo, offering good-value accommodations with extras like sleeper sofas and video games. Mission Valley is ideal for business travelers; there are plenty of well-known chain hotels with conference space, modern business centers, and kitchenettes for extended stays.

When your work (or sightseeing) is done, join the trendsetters flocking to Downtown's Gaslamp Quarter for its eateries, lounges, and multilevel clubs that rival L.A.'s stylish scenes.

PARKING

Given the distances between attractions and limited public transportation routes, a car is almost a necessity for visitors to San Diego. That being said, a vehicle can significantly add to your expenses if you stay in the ritzier areas. Overnight parking in Coronado, La Jolla, and Downtown's Gaslamp Quarter can be as high as $50 per night; in Uptown and Mission Bay it usually runs $10 to $20.

RESERVATIONS

Book well in advance, especially if you plan to visit in summer, which is the busy season for most hotels. In spring and fall, conventions and sports events can fill every Downtown hotel room. When you make reservations, ask about specials. Several properties in the Hotel Circle area of Mission Valley offer reduced rates and even free tickets to the San Diego Zoo and other attractions. You can save on hotels and attractions by visiting the San Diego Tourism Authority website (⊕ www.sandiego.org) for special seasonal offers.

STAYING WITH KIDS

The area is full of hotels suited to a family's budget and/or recreational needs, and many allow kids under 18 to stay free with their parents. You'll find the most choices and diversity in and around Carlsbad near LEGOLAND, and Mission Bay, which is close to SeaWorld, beaches, parks, and Old Town.

SERVICES

Downtown hotels once catered primarily to business travelers, though the new boutique hotels are attracting hip leisure travelers to the area, while those at Mission Bay, in coastal locations such as Carlsbad and Encinitas, and at inland resort areas offer golf and other sports facilities, spa services, children's activities, and more. If you're traveling with pets, note that pet policies do change and some hotels require substantial cleaning fees of $50 to $100. At many San Diego hotels, even smoking outdoors is frowned on or prohibited.

PRICES

Note that even in the most expensive areas, you can find affordable rooms. High season is summer, and rates are lowest in fall. If an ocean view is important, request it when booking, but it will cost you.

Prices in the reviews are the lowest cost of a standard double room in high season. For expanded hotel reviews, facilities, and current deals, visit Fodors. com.

🧳 Shopping

San Diego's retail landscape has changed radically in recent years with the opening of several new shopping centers—some in historic buildings—that are focused more on locally owned boutiques than national retailers. Where once the Gaslamp was the place to go for urban apparel and unique home decor, many independently owned boutiques have decided to set up shop in the charming neighborhoods east of Balboa Park known as North Park and South Park. Although Downtown is still thriving, any shopping trip to San Diego should include venturing out to the city's diverse and vibrant neighborhoods.

Old Town is a must for pottery, ceramics, jewelry, and handcrafted baskets. Uptown is known for its mélange of funky bookstores, offbeat gift shops, and nostalgic collectibles and vintage stores. The beach towns offer the best swimwear and sandals. La Jolla's chic boutiques offer a more intimate shopping experience, along with some of the classiest clothes, jewelry, and shoes in the county. Point Loma's Liberty Station shopping area in the former Naval Training Center has art galleries, restaurants, and home stores. Trendsetters will have no trouble finding must-have handbags and designer apparel at the world-class Fashion Valley mall in Mission Valley, a haven for luxury brands such as Hermès, Gucci, and Jimmy Choo. The Carlsbad Outlets near LEGOLAND have nearly 100 designer outlet stores including Barneys New York, Coach, Kate Spade, Michael Kors, and Nike.

Enjoy near-perfect weather year-round as you explore shops along the scenic waterfront. The Headquarters at Seaport is an open-air shopping and dining center in the city's former Police Headquarters building. Here there are some big names, but mostly locally owned boutiques selling everything from gourmet cheese to coastal-inspired home accessories. Just next door, Seaport Village is still the place to go for trinkets and souvenirs. If you don't discover what you're looking for in the boutiques, head to Westfield Horton Plaza, the Downtown mall with more than 120 stores, public plaza, amphitheater, and fountains.

Most malls have free parking in a lot or garage, and parking is not usually a problem. Westfield Horton Plaza and some of the shops in the Gaslamp Quarter offer validated parking or valet parking.

OPENING HOURS

Shops near tourist attractions and the major shopping malls tend to open early and close late. Standard hours are typically 10 to 9 on weekdays and 10 to 10 on weekends. Smaller shops may close as early as 5 on weekdays and Sunday. It's best to call ahead to confirm hours if you have your heart set on visiting a particular shop.

OUTLET MALLS

Some hotels offer free shuttles to shopping centers, outlet malls, and nearby casinos. Check with the concierge for schedules.

🍸 Nightlife

The San Diego nightlife scene is much more diverse and innovative than it was just a decade ago. Back then, options were limited to the pricey singles-heavy dance clubs Downtown, the party-hearty atmosphere of Pacific Beach, and a handful of charmingly musty neighborhood dive bars popular with locals. Today, options in San Diego have expanded dramatically, boasting more than 150 craft

Essentials

breweries throughout the county, not to mention several stylish cocktail lounges.

The Gaslamp Quarter is still one of the most popular areas to go for a night on the town. Named for actual gaslights that once provided illumination along its once-seedy streets (it housed a number of gambling halls and brothels), the neighborhood bears only a trace of its debauched roots. Between the Gaslamp and nearby East Village, Downtown San Diego mostly comprises chic nightclubs, tourist-heavy pubs, and a handful of live music venues. Even most of the hotels Downtown have a street-level or rooftop bar—so plan on making it a late night if that's where you intend to bunk. On weekends, parking can be tricky; most lots run about $20, and though there is metered parking (free after 6 pm and all day Sunday), motorists don't give up those coveted spots so easily. Some restaurants and clubs offer valet, though that can get pricey.

Hillcrest is a popular area for LGBT nightlife and culture, whereas just a little bit east of Hillcrest, ever-expanding North Park features a diverse range of bars and lounges that cater to a twenty- and thirtysomething crowd, bolstering its reputation as the city's hipster capital. Nearby Normal Heights is a slightly less pretentious alternative, though whichever of these neighborhoods strikes your fancy, a cab from Downtown will run about the same price: $15.

Nightlife along the beaches is more of a mixed bag. Where the scene in Pacific Beach might feel like every week is spring break, La Jolla veers toward being more cost-prohibitive. And although Point Loma is often seen as a sleeper neighborhood in terms of nightlife, it's coming into its own with some select destinations.

If your drink involves caffeine and not alcohol, there's no shortage of coffee-houses in San Diego, and some of the better ones in Hillcrest and North Park stay open past midnight. Many of them also serve beer and wine, if the caffeine buzz isn't enough.

THE LOWDOWN

Step outside to smoke. Smoking is strictly outlawed indoors in public places in San Diego, and since 2014 that includes e-cigarettes or vaporizer pens.

What to wear. In the Gaslamp, East Village, and some of North Park's more upscale spots, dress code is strictly enforced: no flip-flops, ball caps, jerseys, or shorts at any of the city's swankier bars.

Last call for alcohol. The last chance for nightcaps is theoretically 2 am, but most bars stop serving around 1:30. Listen for the bartender's announcement.

WHAT'S GOING ON?

The city's daily paper, *The San Diego Union-Tribune* (⊕ *www.sandiegouniontribune.com*), has up-to-date entertainment listings, as well as the paper's more nightlife-heavy sister site *Pacific San Diego* (⊕ *www.pacificsandiego.com*), which provides event listings and editorial suggestions. San Diego has two alt-weeklies, of which *The Reader* (⊕ *www.sandiegoreader.com*) boasts more extensive online listings. *San Diego CityBeat* (⊕ *sdcitybeat.com*) is more selective with its recommendations, highlighting the edgier and more innovative cultural events.

San Diego magazine (⊕ *www.sandiego-magazine.com*) is a mainstream read for all walks of life; *Modern Luxury* (⊕ *sandiego.modernluxury.com*) is younger, more upscale, and au courant.

🎭 Performing Arts

A diverse and sophisticated arts scene probably isn't the first thing that visitors—or even locals—associate with San Diego. It's a destination for those who seek out its perennial sunshine, gorgeous beaches, and beautiful scenery. Even those within the arts scene readily admit their fiercest competition is the beach! But just a little to the right of the Pacific Ocean, there are some amazing and diverse artistic offerings to prove that San Diego can hold its own.

The theater scene in San Diego may not have the commercial appeal that Broadway does, but it more than makes up for it with talent. In fact, a long list of Broadway-bound productions started right here, including *Jersey Boys,* The Who's *Tommy, Dirty Rotten Scoundrels,* and *Memphis.*

Balboa Park's Old Globe Theatre is modeled after the Shakespearian Globe Theatre in England, and hosts both an annual Shakespeare Festival as well as contemporary plays. A little bit north is La Jolla Playhouse, which was founded by Gregory Peck in 1947, and has hosted dozens of world-premiere productions, in addition to star actors like Laura Linney and Neil Patrick Harris. The playhouse has also launched the Without Walls initiative, which places theater in a new context by removing the theater entirely.

Music also has a major presence in San Diego, courtesy of the world-class San Diego Opera, which performs major works by Puccini and Mozart, and the San Diego Symphony, which caters to a diverse audience thanks to both its classical concerts and its more accessible Summer Pops series.

Whether you fancy *rond de jambes* or something a bit more modern, San Diego's scene is *en pointe* for dance fans.

There's always something new and exciting happening with visual arts in San Diego. No longer limited to a collector's market, younger urban artists are making inroads with warehouse gallery spaces in Barrio Logan, while galleries in La Jolla and Little Italy showcase bold works of contemporary art on their walls. The annual San Diego Art Prize highlights rising figures in the visual arts realm, and in the field of architecture, Orchids and Onions honors the best and worst in structural design—and with a sense of humor at that.

TICKETS
Plan ahead and buy tickets early—ideally around the same time that you book your hotel. Not that you can't find an outlet that sells day-of-show tickets, but you'll run the risk of paying a grossly inflated price, and might not end up with good seats.

GALLERY AND MUSEUM NIGHTS
The art gallery and museum experience in San Diego isn't limited to the daytime—at night, a number of different museums and venues host after-business-hours events that attract a younger, cosmopolitan crowd.

🏃 Activities

With average daily temperatures of 70.5°F, San Diego is built for outdoor activities year-round. As you'd expect, the ocean is one of San Diego's most popular natural attractions. Surfers, swimmers, kayakers, divers, snorkelers, and paddle-boarders have 70 miles of shorefront to explore. What might surprise you is there

Essentials

is also great hiking, horseback riding, rock climbing, biking, and more.

The possibilities for outdoor activity really are endless and evidence of San Diego's outdoorsy spirit is apparent everywhere; you'll likely see runners swarming the waterfront and Balboa Park, groups of surfers bobbing in the water at dawn, hang gliders swooping off sandstone cliffs, and white sails gliding gracefully along the shore. Outdoor enthusiasts are as much a part of San Diego's landscape as the sea, sand, and hills, and if you want to get in on the action, it's easy. Companies offering kayak and snorkeling tours and rentals are prevalent, especially in the beach communities of La Jolla, Mission Beach, and on Coronado. If you want to learn to surf, sign up for a lesson at one of the many surf schools in La Jolla or rent a board in Mission Beach and go out on your own. If sightseeing is more your style you can head out on a fishing or whale-watching excursion aboard a charter boat or take a sunset stroll on a wide, sandy beach. At the end of the day at any beach in the county, you'll surely see a local ritual: everyone stops what they're doing to watch the sun's orange orb slip silently into the blue-gray Pacific.

[+] Safety

San Diego is generally a safe place for travelers who observe all normal precautions. Downtown can get a little rowdy at night, especially toward 2 am, when bars boot drunken patrons out on the sidewalks. The city also has a large homeless population, who often camp out on side streets not far from East Village. Most are harmless, aside from the occasional panhandling, but it's safest to stick to well-lighted, busy areas. Certain pockets of Balboa Park are frequented by drug dealers and prostitutes after hours; if you're attending a nighttime theater performance or art event, park nearby or use the valet.

Item	Average Cost
Cup of Coffee	$4
Glass of Wine	$11
Sandwich	$14
One-Mile Taxi Ride	$3
Museum Admission	$19

At the beach, check with lifeguards about any unsafe conditions such as dangerous riptides or water pollution. The San Diego Tourism Authority offers a print and Web version of Visitor Safety Tips, providing sensible precautions for many situations.

For police, fire, or ambulance, dial 911 (0 in rural areas).

$ Money

With the mild climate and proximity to the ocean and mountains, San Diego is popular with tourists and conventioneers and, accordingly, is a relatively expensive place to visit. Three-star rooms average between $200 and $280 per night in high season, but there is also a good variety of modest accommodations available. Meal prices compare to those in other large cities, and you can usually find excellent values by dining in smaller, family-run establishments. Admission to local attractions can cost anywhere from $10 to $90. Thankfully, relaxing on one of the public beaches or meandering through the parks and neighborhoods is free—and fun. ■ **TIP→ To save money on restaurants, spas, and boutiques, scour the** coupon section at www.sdreader.com or visit www.groupon.com.

Prices here are given for adults. Substantially reduced fees are almost always available for children, students, and senior citizens. Most museums in Balboa Park offer free admission to residents on Tuesdays.

💲 Tipping

Most people know that it's customary to tip waitstaff 15% to 20%, with 20% being the norm at high-end restaurants. But, what about bellhops, tour guides, and everyone in between? Here are a few helpful tips for tipping all the service people you might meet on your travels.
■ TIP→ **Many restaurants are starting to include an 18% service charge to bills for parties of six or more; sometimes it's stated on the menu, sometimes it's not.** If you're traveling with a large party, always check the bill before leaving a tip.

🛍 Packing

Plan on warm weather at any time of the year. Cottons, walking shorts, jeans, and T-shirts are the norm. Pack bathing suits and shorts regardless of the season. Few restaurants require a jacket and tie for men. Women may want to also bring something a little dressier than their sightseeing garb.

Evenings are cool, even in summer, so be sure to bring a sweater or a light jacket. Rainfall in San Diego isn't usually heavy; you won't need a raincoat except in winter, and even then, an umbrella may suffice.

Be sure you have comfortable walking shoes. Even if you don't walk much at

Tipping Guidelines for San Diego

Bartender	$1 to $5 per round of drinks, depending on the number of drinks
Bellhop	$1 to $5 per bag, depending on the level of the hotel
Hotel Concierge	$5 or more, if he or she performs a service for you
Hotel Doorman	$1 to $2 if he helps you get a cab
Hotel Maid	$1 to $3 a day (either daily or at the end of your stay, in cash)
Hotel Room-Service Walter	$1 to $2 per delivery, even if a service charge has been added
Porter at Airport or Train Station	$2 per bag
Skycap at Airport	$1 to $3 per bag checked
Taxi Driver	15% to 20%, but round up the fare to the next dollar amount
Tour Guide	10% of the cost of the tour
Valet Parking Attendant	$2 to $5, but only when you get your car

home, you will probably find yourself covering miles while sightseeing on your vacation. Also bring a pair of sandals or water shoes for the beach.

Sunglasses and sunscreen are a must in San Diego. Binoculars can also come in handy, especially if you're in town during whale-watching season, from December through mid-April, or planning to stargaze in the desert in the summer. If you plan

Essentials

on surfing, consider packing or renting a wet suit or rash guard depending on the season. In winter, water temperatures drop into the 50s and average around 72 degrees in the summer.

○ Restrooms

Major attractions and parks have public restrooms. In the Downtown San Diego area, you can usually use the restrooms at major hotels and fast-food restaurants.

○ Visitor Information

For general information and brochures before you go, contact the San Diego Tourism Authority, which publishes the helpful *San Diego Visitors Planning Guide.* When you arrive, stop by one of the local visitor centers for general information.

ONLINE RESOURCES

For a dining and entertainment guide to San Diego's most popular nightlife district, check out Gaslamp.org. For insider tips from a local perspective, try Local Wally's San Diego Tourist Guide. For information on the birthplace of California, search the Old Town San Diego organization's site. Browse the website of San Diego's premier upscale lifestyle magazine, *Ranch and Coast. San Diego Magazine* also has a useful site. Search the site of ArtsTix for half-price show tickets. For a comprehensive listing of concerts, performances, and art exhibits, check out the local alternative paper *San Diego Reader.* For edgier arts and culture listings, pick up the *San Diego Citybeat* alt-weekly.

Contacts

✈ Air Travel

AIRPORT SHUTTLES
Advanced Shuttle.
✉ 4350 Palm Ave., La Mesa ☎ 800/719–3499, 619/466–6885 ⊕ www. advancedshuttle.com.
San Diego Transit.
☎ 619/233–3004 ⊕ www.511sd.com. **SuperShuttle.** ✉ 123 Caminio de la Riena ☎ 800/258–3826 ⊕ www.supershuttle.com.

AIRPORTS San Diego International Airport. ✉ 3225 N. Harbor Dr., off I–5 ☎ 619/400–2400 ⊕ www. san.org.

⛴ Boat

MARINAS Best Western Island Palms Hotel & Marina. ✉ 2051 Shelter Island Dr. ☎ 619/222–0561 ⊕ www.islandpalms. com. **The Dana on Mission Bay.** ✉ 1710 W. Mission Bay Dr. ☎ 619/225–2141 ⊕ www.thedana.com.
Kona Kai Resort & Spa. ✉ 1551 Shelter Island Dr. ☎ 619/224–7547 ⊕ www. resortkonakai.com. **San Diego Marriott Marquis & Marina.** ✉ 333 W. Harbor Dr. ☎ 619/230–8955 ⊕ www.marriott.com. **San Diego Yacht Club.** ✉ 1011 Anchorage La. ☎ 619/221–8400 ⊕ www.sdyc.org.
Southwestern Yacht Club. ✉ 2702 Qualtrough St. ☎ 619/222–0438 ⊕ www. southwesternyc.org.

🚌 Bus and Trolley

North County Transit District. ☎ 760/966–6500 ⊕ www. gonctd.com . **San Diego Transit.** ☎ 619/233–3004 ⊕ www.511sd.com . **Transit Store.** ✉ 102 Broadway ☎ 619/234–1060 ⊕ www. sdmts.com.

🚗 Taxi

Orange Cab. ☎ 619/223–5555 ⊕ www.orange-cabsandiego.net. **Silver Cabs.** ☎ 619/280–5555 ⊕ www.sandiegosilver-cab.com. **Yellow Cab.** ☎ 619/444–4444 ⊕ www. driveu.com.

🚆 Train

Coaster. ☎ 760/966–6500 ⊕ www.gonctd.com/ coaster. **Metrolink.** ☎ 800/371–5465 ⊕ www. metrolinktrains.com.

👁 General Interest

ArtsTix. ⊕ www.sdartstix. com. **Local Wally's San Diego.** ⊕ www.localwal-ly.com. **Ranch & Coast** ⊕ www.ranchandcoast. com. **San Diego City-Beat** ⊕ www.sdcitybeat. com. **San Diego Magazine.** ⊕ www.sandiegomag-azine.com. **San Diego Reader.** ⊕ www.sandie-goreader.com.

The San Diego Union-Tribune. ⊕ www.sand-iegouniontribune.com.

📍 Visitor Info

Borrego Springs Chamber of Commerce . ☎ 760/767–5555 ⊕ www.borre-gospringschamber.com **California Welcome Center Oceanside.** ☎ 760/721–1101, 800/350–7873 ⊕ www.visitoceanside. org **Carlsbad Visitors Center.** ☎ 800/227–5722 ⊕ www. visitcarlsbad.com **Coronado Visitor Center.** ✉ 1100 Orange Ave., Coronado ☎ 619/435–7242 ⊕ www. coronadovisitorcenter.com **The Gaslamp Quarter Association.** ⊕ www.gaslamp. org . **Encinitas Chamber of Commerce.** ✉ 535 Encinitas Blvd., Suite 116, Encinitas ☎ 760/753–6041 ⊕ www.encinitaschamber. com **Julian Chamber of Commerce.** ☎ 760/765–1857 ⊕ www.visitjulian. com. **Old Town San Diego.** ⊕ www.oldtownsandiego. org.

Great Itineraries

One Day in San Diego

If you've only got 24 hours to spare, start at **Balboa Park**, the cultural heart of San Diego. Stick to El Prado, the main promenade, where you'll pass by peaceful gardens and soaring Spanish colonial revival architecture. Unless you're a serious museum junkie, pick whichever piques your interest—choices range from photography to folk art.

If you're with the family, don't even think of skipping the **San Diego Zoo**. You'll want to spend the better part of your day there, but make an early start of it so you can head for one of San Diego's **beaches** afterward while there's still daylight. Kick back under the late afternoon sun and linger for sunset. Or wander around **Seaport Village** and the **Embarcadero** before grabbing a bite to eat in the **Gaslamp Quarter.**

Alternate plan: Start at **SeaWorld** and end with an ocean-view dinner in **La Jolla.**

Four Days in San Diego

DAY 1
The one-day itinerary *above* also works for the first day of an extended visit. If you're staying in North County, though, you may want to bypass the zoo and head for the **San Diego Zoo Safari Park.** Here, you'll see herds of African and Asian animals acting as they would in the wild. Not included in the general admission, but worth it, are the park's "special experiences"—guided photo caravans, behind-the-scenes tours, and the Flightline, a zip line soaring above the animal enclosures.

Another North County option for families with little ones: **LEGOLAND** in Carlsbad. **Note:** The San Diego Zoo, the San Diego Safari Park, and LEGOLAND are all-day, wipe-the-kids-out adventures.

DAY 2
You might want to ease into your second day with a leisurely breakfast, followed by a 90-minute tour aboard the **San Diego SEAL Tours,** which departs from Seaport Village and Embarcadero daily. The bus-boat hybrid explores picturesque San Diego neighborhoods before rolling right into the water for a cruise around the bay, all with fun-facts narration.

Back on land, you can devote an hour or so to **Seaport Village,** a 14-acre waterfront shopping and dining complex. Meant to look like a 19th-century harbor, Seaport features 4 miles of cobblestone pathways bordered by lush landscaping and water features.

From there, stroll north to the **Embarcadero,** where you'll marvel at the **Maritime Museum's** historic vessels, including the *Star of India* (the world's oldest active sailing ship).

Explore San Diego's military might at the **USS** Midway **Museum;** the permanently docked aircraft carrier has more than 60 exhibits and 29 restored aircraft.

Spend the rest of your afternoon and evening in **Coronado,** a quick jaunt by ferry or bridge, or walk a few blocks north to the **Gaslamp Quarter,** where the shopping and dining will keep you busy for hours.

DAY 3
Set out early enough, and you might snag a parking spot near **La Jolla Cove,** where you can watch sea lions lounging on the beach at the **Children's Pool.** Then head up one block to Prospect Street, where you'll find the vaunted **La Valencia** hotel (called the "Pink Lady" for its blush-hue exterior) and dozens of posh boutiques and galleries.

If you're with kids, head for **La Jolla Shores,** a good beach for swimming and making sand castles, followed by a visit to the **Birch Aquarium** and a bite to eat at the popular **El Pescador Fish Market** ().

Once you've refueled, head for **Torrey Pines State Natural Reserve,** where you can hike down the cliffs to the state beach with breathtaking views in every direction. (If you're with small children, the trek might prove too challenging.)

For dinner, swing north to **Del Mar;** during racing season, the evening scene is happening.

DAY 4
Start the day with a morning visit to **Cabrillo National Monument,** a national park with a number of activities. Learn about 16th-century explorer Juan Rodríguez Cabrillo, take a gentle 2-mile hike on the beautiful Bayside Trail, look around the Old Point Loma Lighthouse, and peer at tide pools. ■ TIP➔ **Find out when low tide is before planning your itinerary.**

After Cabrillo, head to **Old Town,** where San Diego's early history comes to carefully reconstructed life. Old Town's Mexican restaurants aren't the city's best, but they're definitely bustling and kid-friendly, and frosty margaritas make an added incentive for grown-ups.

After that, spend a few hours exploring whatever cluster of neighborhoods appeals to you most. If you like casual coastal neighborhoods with a youthful vibe, head to **Pacific, Mission,** or **Ocean Beach,** or venture up to **North County** for an afternoon in **Encinitas,** which epitomizes the old California surf town.

If edgy and artsy are more your thing, check out the hip and ever-changing neighborhoods in **Uptown,** where you'll find super-cool shops, bars, and eateries.

Tips

■ It's easy to add a theater performance or a concert to any of these days. Some of the city's top venues are in Balboa Park, Downtown, and La Jolla.

■ If you plan to tour many of Balboa Park's museums, buy the **Balboa Park Explorer Pass,** which gets you into 16 attractions for $59, or the **Balboa Park Explorer Combo Pass,** which also gets you into the zoo ($103). Both passes are valid for seven consecutive days. Buy them online or at the **Balboa Park Visitor Center** (619/239–0512 ⊕ www.balboapark.org).

■ The **Trolley** and the **Coaster** are great ways to access foot-friendly neighborhoods up and down the coast. You can head almost anywhere from the **Santa Fe Depot** in Downtown (the cutting-edge Museum of Contemporary Art is next door).

Alternatives

You can easily fill four days or more with every imaginable outdoor activity, from swimming and surfing to hiking and stand-up paddleboarding. San Diego is an athletics-enthusiast's heaven—unless you're a skier.

In **winter,** include more indoor activities—the museums are fantastic—as well as a whale-watching trip.

In **summer,** check local listings for outdoor concerts, theater, and movie screenings.

A Walk Through San Diego's Past

Downtown San Diego is a living tribute to history and revitalization. The Gaslamp Quarter followed up a long stint of seediness, emerging as a glamorous place to live and play. Little Italy, once a bustling fishing village, also got a facelift.

WHERE IT ALL STARTED

Begin at the corner of 4th and Island. This is the location of the 150-year-old **Davis-Horton House,** a saltbox structure shipped around Cape Horn and assembled in the Gaslamp Quarter. Among its famous former residents: Alonzo Horton, the city's founder. Take a tour, keeping a lookout for the house's current resident: a lady ghost.

From there walk a block east to 5th Avenue and head north. Along the way, you'll see some of the 16½-block historic district's best-known Victorian-era commercial beauties, including the Italianate **Marston Building** (at F Street), the **Keating Building,** the **Spencer-Ogden Building,** and the **Old City Hall.** Architecture buffs should pick up a copy of *San Diego's Gaslamp Quarter,* a self-guided tour published by the Historical Society.

At E Street, head back over to 4th Avenue and you'll behold the **Balboa Theatre,** a striking Spanish Renaissance–style building that was constructed in 1923 and restored in 2007. Right next to it is **Westfield Horton Plaza** mall, which opened its doors in 1985. This multilevel mall played a huge role in downtown's revitalization, as entrepreneurs and preservationists realized the value of the Gaslamp Quarter. Pop across Broadway to check out the stately **U.S. Grant Hotel,** built in 1910 by the son of President Ulysses S. Grant.

A Walk Through San Diego's Past

HIGHLIGHTS:
Restored gas lamps that give the Gaslamp its name; the contrast of old and new architecture; Little Italy's sidewalk cafés.

WHERE TO START:
The Davis-Horton House, at the corner of 4th and Island avenues, is a short walk from most Downtown hotels. If you drive, park in a paid lot or at nearby Horton Plaza, which offers three free hours with validation (stamp your ticket at one of the validation machines).

LENGTH:
About 3 miles and three to four hours round-trip with stops. Take the Orange Line trolley from Santa Fe Depot back if you're tired.

WHERE TO STOP:
From Little Italy follow the same path back or head down Laurel St. to Harbor Dr. and wander along the waterfront until you hit Broadway.

BEST TIME TO GO:
Morning or early afternoon.

WORST TIME TO GO:
During rush hour.

WHERE TO REFUEL:
If your stomach is growling, head to Little Italy: mangia, mangia! Try Little Italy Food Hall ⊠ *550 W. Date St.* or Ironside Fish and Oyster ⊠ *1654 India St.*

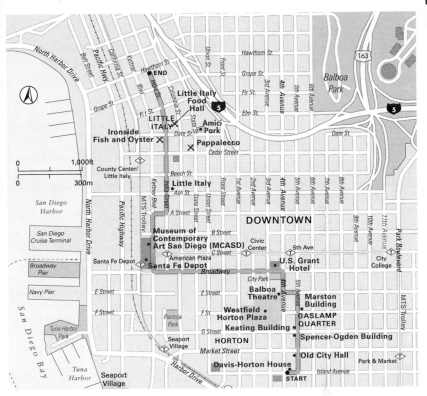

ART STOP

Follow Broadway west to Kettner Boulevard, where the **Museum of Contemporary Art San Diego (MCASD)** makes a bold statement with its steel-and-glass lines. It's definitely worth a wander, situated in the renovated baggage depot of the 1915 **Santa Fe Depot** (the station itself is also a stunner).

FROM FISHERMEN TO FASHIONISTAS

From there, head north on Kettner to A Street, make a quick right, and then take a left on India Street. This is the heart of **Little Italy,** which, at the turn of the 20th century, was a bustling Italian fishing village. The area fell into disarray

in the early 1970s due to a decline in the tuna industry and the construction of I-5, which destroyed 35% of the area. In 1996, a group of forward-thinking architects—commissioned by the city—developed new residential, retail, and public areas that coexist beautifully with the neighborhood's historic charms. Now, it's a vibrant urban center with hip eateries, bars, and shops. There are remnants of retro Little Italy, from authentic cafés (check out **Pappalecco,** a popular gelateria) to boccie ball matches played by old-timers at **Amici Park.**

On the Calender

JANUARY

Farmers Insurance Open. This is the Holy Grail for golf fans; the celeb-heavy tourney has been held at the scenic Torrey Pines Golf Course for decades. ⊕ *www.farmersinsuranceopen.com*

San Diego Brew Festival. More than 60 breweries are joined with a bevy of food trucks for a day of fun in the sun. ⊕ *www.sandiegobeerfest.com*

FEBRUARY

Gaslamp Quarter Mardi Gras. This block party invites revelers to let the good times roll. ⊕ *www.sdmardigras.com*

Museum Month. Half-price admission (with free pass) to more than 40 museums throughout the city. ⊕ *www.sandiego.org*

Winter Brew Fest. San Diego residents love their beer, and this event features more than 30 brews and live music in Balboa Park. ⊕ *www.sandiegobrewfest.com*

MARCH

Carlsbad Flower Fields. More than 60 acreas of giant ranunculus flowers bloom Mid-March through early May. ⊕ *www.theflowerfields.com*

Cherry Blossom Festival. The Japanese Friendship Garden at Balboa Park celebrates spring in bloom with cherry trees, cultural performances, Japanese street food, and beer and tea tastings. ⊕ *www.niwa.org*

APRIL

Adams Avenue Unplugged. The free event features 80 live musical performances staged inside 24 restaurants, bars, coffeehouses, and galleries on Adams Avenue. ⊕ *www.adamsavenuebusiness.com*

Humphreys Concerts by the Bay. Outdoor concerts—from rock and jazz to comedy and folk and everythng inbetween—run through October on Shelter Island. ⊕ *www.humphreysconcerts.com*

Mission Federal ArtWalk. Little Italy's annual event showcases local art talent on tent-lined streets. ⊕ *artwalksandiego.org*

MAY

Cinco de Mayo. Old Town is home to one of the country's biggest Cinco de Mayo celebrations with live music, lucha libra matches, lots of food, and much more. ⊕ *www.cincodemayooldtown.com*

Gator By The Bay. New Orleans comes to San Diego with blues, jazz, Louisiana food, and crawfish. ⊕ *www.gatorbythebay.com*

Temecula Valley Balloon and Wine Festival. Usually the last weeked of the month, the annual event has concerts with headliner entertainment, wine tasting and food pairings, and an evening Balloon Glow. ⊕ *www.tvbwf.com*

JUNE

San Diego County Fair. Over one million visitors come for a month of fun attractions including rides, concerts, and greasy fair favorites. ⊕ *sdfair.com*

San Diego Festival of the Arts. More than 190 award-winning artists display watercolors, sculpture, fine jewelry, photography, and more. ⊕ *www.sdfestivalofthearts.org*

JULY

Del Mar Races. Place your bets on your favorite horse at the Del Mar Racetrack from mid-July to Labor Day. ⊕ *www.dmtc.com*

San Diego Comic-Con. At this four-day comic book convention, thousands of fans unite for all things comics, sci-fi, fantasy, and anime. ⊕ *www.comic-con.org*

San Diego Pride. The city's vibrant LGBT Pride Festival celebrates diversity with four stages of live entertainment, cultural presentations, and vendor booths. ⊕ *sd-pride.org*

Summer Shakespeare Festival. The Old Globe's summer theater festival is the best way to enjoy Shakespeare under the stars. ⊕ *www.theoldglobe.org*

AUGUST

Bon Odori Festival. Family-friendly activities, Japanese festival foods, a tea and dessert garden, and cultural performances occur during this two-day event in the Japanese Friendship Garden. ⊕ *www.niwa.org/bonsd*

Chula Vista Lemon Festival. Celebrate Chula Vista's heritage as the "Lemon Capital of the World" with live entertainment, a kids' fun zone, and lots of lemons. ⊕ *thirdavenuevillage.com*

SAND-iego. Over Labor Day weekend, master sand sculptors create dimensional art, to be enjoyed along with tribute bands, food trucks, and rides for kids. ⊕ *www.ussandsculpting.com*

SEPTEMBER

KAABOO. A three-day "mix-perience" in Del Mar featuring top music acts, comedians, DJs, artists, and celebrity chefs. ⊕ *www.kaaboodelmar.com*

MCAS Miramar Air Show. The annual marine air show often features the Blue Angels. ⊕ *www.miramarairshow.com*

OCTOBER

Day of the Dead Festival. This free North Park festival incorporates Mexican-themed artisanal crafter purveyors, popular food trucks, and a select choice of beer, mezcal, and tequila vendors. ⊕ *www.dayofthedeadfestivalnorthpark.com*

Fleet Week San Diego. Men and women of the military are honored and celebrated with parades, entertainment, and daily events. ⊕ *fleetweeksandiego.org*

HalGLOWeen. The three-day event includes Halloween-themed music and dance parties, glowing "Boolahoops," special treats, and more. ⊕ *zoo.sandiegozoo.org*

Kids Free San Diego. Discounts, free meals, and free admission to attractions for kids throughout October. ⊕ *www.sandiego.org/promotions/kids-free*

NOVEMBER

Guild Fest. Hosted by the San Diego Brewers Guild, more than 60 independent breweries descend upon the Embarcadero. ⊕ *www.sdbeer.com*

San Diego Bay Wine & Food Festival. The West Coast's largest wine and culinary classic features wine-tasting seminars, cooking classes, and celebrity chef dinners. ⊕ *www.sandiegowineclassic.com*

DECEMBER

Balboa Park December Nights. Drawing 350,000 visitors the first Friday and Saturday of December, this event offers festive carolers, food, music, and dance. ⊕ *www.sandiego.gov/december-nights*

San Diego Bay Parade of Lights. Boats decked out for the holidays light up the harbor. ⊕ *www.sdparadeoflights.org*

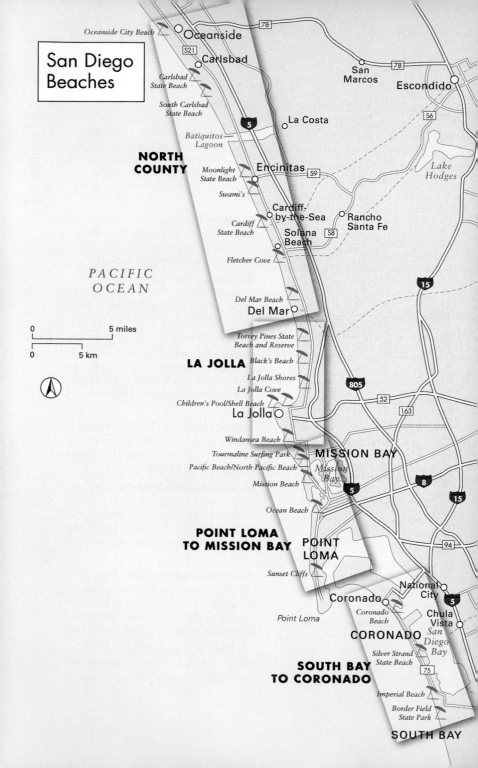

Chapter 3

DOWNTOWN

👁 **Sights** 🍴 **Restaurants** 🛏 **Hotels** 🛍 **Shopping** 🍸 **Nightlife**

★★★★★ ★★★★★ ★★★★★ ★★★★☆ ★★★★☆

NEIGHBORHOOD SNAPSHOT

GREAT EXPERIENCES DOWNTOWN

■ **Waterfront delights:** Stroll along the Embarcadero, explore Seaport Village, or enjoy a harbor cruise.

■ **Contemporary art for all ages:** From the stunning galleries of the Museum of Contemporary Art to the clever incorporation of art and play at the New Children's Museum, Downtown is the place for art.

■ **Maritime history:** Climb aboard and explore a wide array of vessels from sailing ships to submarines.

■ **Delicious dining:** The hip and high-style restaurants of Little Italy, the Gaslamp Quarter, and the East Village make Downtown San Diego a diner's delight.

■ **Happening Gaslamp:** It's hard to believe this hip neighborhood filled with street art, galleries, restaurants, and buzzing nightlife was once slated for the wrecking ball.

GETTING HERE

It's an easy drive into Downtown, especially from the nearby airport. There are reasonably priced parking lots (about $10 per day) along Harbor Drive, Pacific Highway, and lower Broadway and Market Street. Most restaurants offer valet parking at night, but beware of fees of $15 and up.

If you tire of exploring Downtown on foot, hop aboard a pedicab, hail the Free Ride Everywhere Downtown (FRED) shuttle, or rent a GoCar (three-wheel cars equipped with a GPS-guided audio tour).

PLANNING YOUR TIME

Most Downtown attractions are open daily, but the Museum of Contemporary Art is closed Wednesday and the New Children's Museum is closed on Tuesday during the school year. For guided tours of the Gaslamp Quarter Historic District, visit on Saturday. A boat trip on the harbor, or at least a hop over to Coronado on the ferry, is a must at any time of year. From December through March, when gray whales migrate between the Pacific Northwest and southern Baja, consider booking a whale-watching excursion from the Broadway Pier.

QUICK BITES

■ **Carnitas' Snack Shack - Embarcadero.** Indulge in some carnitas tacos, a BLT, or the "Triple Threat" pork sandwich at the Embarcadero outpost of this popular swine-heavy dining spot. **Known for:** the "Triple Threat" pork sandwich; amazing tacos. ⊠ 1004 *N. Harbor Dr., Embarcadero* ☎ 619/616–7675 ⊕ *www.carnitassnackshack.com.*

■ **Pappalecco.** Kids and adults alike will swoon over the addictive gelato at Pappalecco, while those seeking something savory can choose from a selection of panini and other snacks. ⊠ *1602 State St., Little Italy* ☎ 619/238–4590 ⊕ *www.pappalecco.com* ▭ *No credit cards.*

VISITOR INFORMATION

■ **San Diego Visitor Information Center.** This colorful and inviting visitor center is a great resource for information and discounts on hotels, restaurants, and local attractions. ⊠ *996 N. Harbor Dr., Embarcadero* ☎ 619/236–1242 ⊕ *www.sandiego.org.*

Nearly written off in the 1970s, today Downtown San Diego is a testament to conservation and urban renewal. Once derelict Victorian storefronts now house the hottest restaurants, and the Star of India, the world's oldest active sailing ship, almost lost to scrap, floats regally along the Embarcadero. Like many modern U.S. cities, Downtown San Diego's story is as much about its rebirth as its history. Although many consider Downtown to be the 16½-block Gaslamp Quarter, it actually comprises eight neighborhoods, including East Village, Little Italy, and Embarcadero.

Gaslamp Quarter

Considered the liveliest of the Downtown neighborhoods, the Gaslamp Quarter's 4th and 5th avenues are peppered with trendy nightclubs, swanky lounge bars, chic restaurants, and boisterous sports pubs. The Gaslamp has the largest collection of commercial Victorian-style buildings in the country. Despite this, when the move for Downtown redevelopment gained momentum in the 1970s, there was talk of bulldozing them and starting from scratch. In response, concerned history buffs, developers, architects, and artists formed the Gaslamp Quarter Council to clean up and preserve the quarter.

The majority of the quarter's landmark buildings are on 4th and 5th avenues, between Island Avenue and Broadway. If you don't have much time, stroll down 5th Avenue, where highlights include **Louis Bank of Commerce** (No. 835), **Old City Hall** (No. 664), **Nesmith-Greeley** (No. 825), and **Yuma** (No. 631) buildings. The Romanesque Revival **Keating Hotel** at 432 F Street was designed by the same firm that created the famous Hotel Del Coronado, the Victorian grande dame that presides over Coronado's beach. At the corner of 4th Avenue and F Street, peer into the **Hard Rock Cafe,** which occupies a

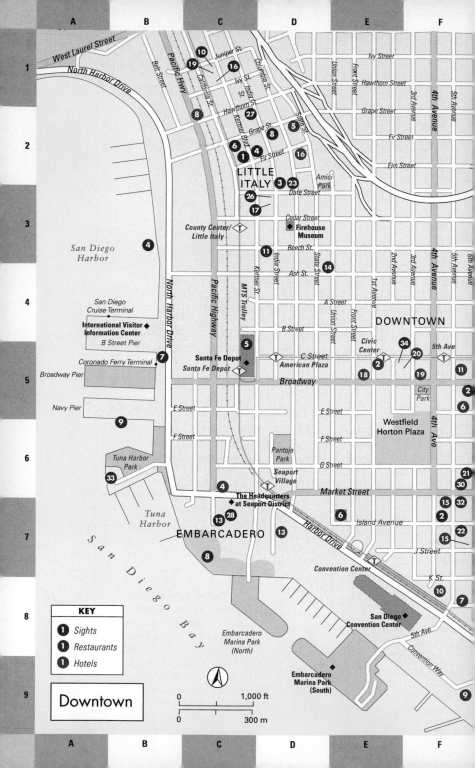

3

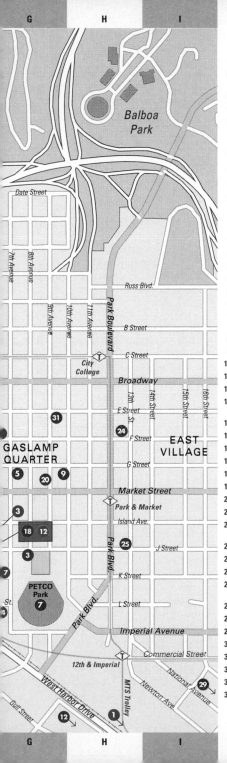

Sights ▼

1 Chicano Park............ **H9**
2 Gaslamp Museum at the Davis-Horton House..... **F7**
3 Little Italy Mercato ... **D3**
4 Maritime Museum...... **B3**
5 Museum of Contemporary Art San Diego (MCASD)..... **C5**
6 The New Children's Museum (NCM).......... **E7**
7 Petco Park.............. **G8**
8 Seaport Village........... **C7**
9 USS *Midway* Museum **B6**

Restaurants ▼

1 Bencotto................. **C2**
2 Biga **F5**
3 The Blind Burro **G7**
4 Born and Raised **C2**
5 Breakfast Republic **G6**
6 Café Gratitude........... **C2**
7 Carnitas' Snack Shack - Embarcadero............ **B5**
8 Cloak and Petal **D2**
9 Cowboy Star.............. **G6**
10 The Crack Shack......... **C1**
11 Craft & Commerce...... **D3**
12 Las Cuatro Milpas **G9**
13 Eddie V's Prime Seafood **C7**
14 Extraordinary Desserts **D4**
15 Havana 1920.............. **F7**
16 Herb & Wood.............. **C1**
17 Ironside Fish & Oyster . **D3**
18 Jsix **G7**
19 Juniper and Ivy **C1**
20 The Kebab Shop **G6**
21 Le Parfait Paris........... **F6**
22 Lionfish Modern Coastal Cuisine **F7**
23 Little Italy Food Hall..... **D3**
24 Lola 55.................... **H6**
25 The Mission **H7**
26 Prep Kitchen Little Italy **C3**
27 Puerto La Boca **C2**
28 Puesto.................... **C7**
29 ¡Salud! Barrio Logan..... **I9**
30 Searsucker............... **F6**
31 Tajima **G5**
32 Taka **F7**
33 Top of the Market....... **B6**
34 The Westgate Room..... **E5**

Hotels ▼

1 Andaz San Diego **G6**
2 The Bristol................ **E5**
3 Courtyard Marriott Gaslamp Quarter........ **G7**
4 Embassy Suites by Hilton San Diego Bay Downtown................ **C6**
5 Found Hotel.............. **D2**
6 Gaslamp Plaza Suites ... **F5**
7 Hard Rock Hotel **F8**
8 Hilton Garden Inn/ Homewood Suites....... **C2**
9 Hilton San Diego Bayfront................. **F9**
10 Hilton San Diego Gaslamp Quarter......... **F8**
11 Kimpton Hotel Palomar San Diego................. **F5**
12 Kimpton Hotel Solamar.................... **G7**
13 Manchester Grand Hyatt San Diego............... **D7**
14 Omni San Diego Hotel.. **G8**
15 Pendry San Diego **F7**
16 Porto Vista Hotel........ **D2**
17 San Diego Marriott Gaslamp Quarter........ **G7**
18 The Sofia Hotel........... **E5**
19 The U.S. Grant, a Luxury Collection Hotel, San Diego................. **F5**
20 The Westgate Hotel **E5**

restored turn-of-the-20th-century tavern with a 12-foot mahogany bar and a spectacular stained-glass domed ceiling.

The Gaslamp is a lively place—during baseball season, the streets flood with Padres fans, and festivals, such as Mardi Gras in February, ShamROCK on St. Patrick's Day, and Monster Bash in October, keep the party atmosphere going throughout the year.

Sights

Gaslamp Museum at the Davis-Horton House

HISTORIC SITE | The oldest wooden house in San Diego houses the Gaslamp Quarter Historical Foundation, the district's curator. Before developer Alonzo Horton came to town, Davis, a prominent San Franciscan, had made an unsuccessful attempt to develop the waterfront area. In 1850 he had this prefab saltbox-style house, built in Maine, shipped around Cape Horn, and assembled in San Diego (it originally stood at State and Market streets). Ninety-minute walking tours ($20) of the historic district leave from the house on Thursday at 1 pm (summer only) and Saturday at 11 am (year-round). If you can't time your visit with the tour, a self-guided tour map ($2) is available. ✉ *410 Island Ave., at 4th Ave., Gaslamp Quarter* ☎ *619/233–4692* 🌐 *www.gaslampfoundation.org* 🎟 *$5 self-guided, $10 with audio tour* 🕒 *Closed Mon.*

Restaurants

The historic heart of Downtown spread across 4th, 5th, and 6th avenues, the Gaslamp Quarter satisfies foodies, conventioneers, and night-clubbers with a wide choice of eateries and nightlife. Many are pricey, upscale chains and tourist-driven concepts, while others are stylish restaurants or casual gastropubs with local roots, featuring everything from sushi to authentic Mexican and aged steaks.

Trolley Dances

During the fall in San Diego, the commuter experience comes alive with dance performances at select trolley stops. A partnership between the Jean Isaacs Dance Theater and the city's Metropolitan Transit System, Trolley Dances (🌐 *www.sandiegodancetheater.org/trolleydances.html*) dancers give site-specific performances inspired by their environments, from historic Barrio Logan to the modern Downtown library. Get on the trolley for a tour ($40) to see the performances at each site.

Biga

$ | **ITALIAN** | An Italian food hall, bar, and café, this newly opened downtown eatery is an epicurean upgrade to lunchtime sandwich and pizza fare. The house-baked bread is some of the best in the city, and their pizza crust is the perfect balance of crisp and chewy. **Known for:** Calabrian BLT sandwich; warm octopus salad; Giulia pizza with prosciutto and fig. [$] *Average main: $15* ✉ *950 6th Ave., Suite C, Gaslamp Quarter* ☎ *619/794–0444* 🌐 *www.bigasandiego.com* 🕒 *Closed Mon.*

Breakfast Republic

$ | **AMERICAN** | Just because it's the most important meal of the day doesn't mean it can't also be flashy or innovative. Breakfast Republic adds some hipster flair to typical brunch fare with a menu that combines hearty southern staples (grits, jambalaya), Mexican food (chilaquiles, breakfast burritos) and over-the-top treats such as Oreo pancakes and s'mores French toast. **Known for:** rich, gooey pancakes and French toast; kombucha flights; kitschy decor. [$] *Average main: $12* ✉ *707 G St., Gaslamp Quarter* ☎ *619/501–8280* 🌐 *www.breakfastrepublic.com* 🕒 *No dinner.*

Havana 1920

$$ | **CUBAN** | A short walk up a flight of stairs transports diners into old Havana as Hemingway once knew it. True to its name, this still-young restaurant specializes in classic Cuban fare, such as empanadas, croquettes, and, of course, the Cubano sandwich. **Known for:** Cubano sandwich with fresh Cuban bread; strong yet refreshing daiquiris and mojitos; Latin jazz performers and salsa dancing. [$] *Average main: $20* ✉ *548 Fifth Ave., Gaslamp Quarter* ☎ *619/369–1920* 🌐 *www.havana1920.com.*

Jsix

$$$ | **AMERICAN** | Distressed brick walls, rustic wood tables, and vintage waterfront photos suits the restaurant's commitment to modern all-natural coastal cuisine with a Filipino twist. Locals, as well as guests at the adjacent boutique Hotel Solamar, savor menu items like shareable starters (lemon-tinged hummus or warm beet salad) and entrées that include Filpino standards like *pancit* noodles with vegetables; there are options like seared sea scallops or the J6 burger made with a top-secret grind as well. **Known for:** modern spin on Filipino food; open-air rooftop with skyline views; refreshing cocktails featuring ingredients like chamomile-infused gin and apricot liqueur. [$] *Average main: $30* ✉ *616 J St., Gaslamp Quarter* ☎ *619/531–8744* 🌐 *www.jsixrestaurant.com* ⏲ *No lunch.*

Lionfish Modern Coastal Cuisine

$$$ | **SEAFOOD** | One of several options inside the recently opened Pendry Hotel, Lionfish is a showcase for chef Jojo Ruiz's seafood-centric cuisine inside of a spacious, two-story room. The atmosphere is hip, yet aesthetically pleasing, though the menu itself is what's worth returning for, from the butter-poached king-crab leg to the wild mushroom and potato gnocchi. **Known for:** fresh seafood, including oysters and crab; nigiri (special sushi rice treated with vinegar) flights; elegant yet unconventional craft cocktails. [$] *Average main: $35* ✉ *435 Fifth Ave., Gaslamp Quarter* ☎ *619/738–7200 Pendry Hotel* 🌐 *www.lionfishsd.com.*

Le Parfait Paris

$ | **BAKERY** | Two French transplants have brought sleek Parisian style to Downtown San Diego and rows of eclairs, tarts, croissants, colorful macarons, and the aroma of espresso greet patrons as they enter a minimalist space. For something more substantial, look to their menu of crepes, panini, salads, and quiches; caffeinated drinks range from teas and coffee to a sweet lavender honey latte. **Known for:** open until midnight on Friday and Saturday, offering a more low-key postdinner alternative in the neighborhood; extensive macaron selection; pillow-soft pastries and chocolate-filled breads. [$] *Average main: $10* ✉ *555 G St., Gaslamp* ☎ *619/245–4457* 🌐 *leparfaitparis.com.*

Searsucker

$$$ | **AMERICAN** | Since opened by celebrity chef Brian Malarkey a few years ago, this high-energy flagship restaurant has become the Gaslamp's best for food and energetic atmosphere. Foodies from near and far savor the upscale down-home fare like small plates of biscuits with spicy honey, duck fat fries, and shrimp and grits. **Known for:** detailed, home-inspired decor; crispy duck fat fries; late-night menu on Friday and Saturday 11 pm–1 am. [$] *Average main: $30* ✉ *611 5th Ave., Gaslamp Quarter* ☎ *619/233–7327* 🌐 *www.searsucker.com.*

Taka

$$ | **JAPANESE** | Pristine fish imported from around the world and presented creatively attracts crowds nightly to this intimate Gaslamp restaurant. Table service is available inside and outside where an *omakase* (tasting menu) or eight-piece rolls can be shared and savored; take a seat at the bar to watch one of the sushi chefs preparing appetizers. **Known for:** uni sushi topped with wasabi; omakase

tasting menu; upscale sake offerings. [$] *Average main: $18* ✉ *555 5th Ave., Gaslamp Quarter* ☎ *619/338–0555* 🌐 *www.takasushi.com* ⏲ *No lunch.*

The Westgate Room

$$$ | FRENCH | Normandy-born chef Fabrice Hardel oversees the preparation of three meals a day at the Westgate Hotel, writing seasonal menus that mix French and Asian flavors. At dinner you're likely to find specials like grilled salmon with spring onions and shiitake mushrooms, as well as classics like Dover sole meunière and steak frites. **Known for:** opulent Sunday brunch buffet is one of the best in town; regal, formal setting; French-inspired cuisine with California flavors. [$] *Average main: $29* ✉ *Westgate Hotel, 1055 2nd Ave., Gaslamp Quarter* ☎ *800/522–1564* 🌐 *www.westgatehotel.com.*

Hotels

Smack in the middle of Downtown is the Gaslamp Quarter where you'll find nightlife options for every night of the week, ranging from gastropubs to clubs with celebrity DJs. For years, lodging options in this neighborhood were lacking in character, but the hotels themselves are becoming destinations in their own right, from the luxurious accommodations of the historic U.S. Grant to the EDM party scene at the Hard Rock or the stylish and trendy appeal of The Pendry, which opened in 2017. And though there are still a handful of budget hotels in the area, the Gaslamp is quickly becoming a go-to spot for glamorous accommodations.

★ Andaz San Diego

$$$$ | HOTEL | The lobby of the luxury, Hyatt-managed Andaz—with its dark, sexy vibe, tall columns wrapped in braided leather, buckets of chilled wine awaiting guests, and welcoming service—pretty much sums up the experience here: high-style stay without the attitude. **Pros:** luxurious rooms; romantic vibe; friendly service. **Cons:** noisy on weekends; not a good choice for families; small pool. [$] *Rooms from: $319* ✉ *600 F St., Gaslamp Quarter* ☎ *619/849–1234* 🌐 *www.sandiego.andaz.hyatt.com* 🛏 *159 rooms* 🍴 *No meals.*

The Bristol

$$$ | HOTEL | Mod pop art inspired by artists such as Andy Warhol and Ed Ruscha sets the tone at this casual boutique hotel. **Pros:** modern rooms; centrally located; good value. **Cons:** no restaurant; somewhat seedy area; street noise. [$] *Rooms from: $234* ✉ *1055 1st Ave., Gaslamp Quarter* ☎ *619/232–6141* 🌐 *www.thebristolsandiego.com* 🛏 *114 rooms* 🍴 *No meals.*

Courtyard Marriott Gaslamp Quarter

$$ | HOTEL | FAMILY | This is not your typical Courtyard by Marriott as the building has a historic past—it was the home of San Diego Trust and Savings Bank in 1928. **Pros:** great rooftop bar The Nolen; can accommodate families; 24-hour market. **Cons:** a little far from convention center and Petco Park; expensive valet parking; rooms are a bit small. [$] *Rooms from: $229* ✉ *530 Broadway, Gaslamp Quarter* ☎ *619/446–3000* 🌐 *www.sandiegocy.com* 🛏 *245 rooms* 🍴 *No meals.*

Gaslamp Plaza Suites

$$ | HOTEL | One of San Diego's first "skyscrapers," this 11-story structure has a central location and a vintage feel. **Pros:** historic building; good location a block from Horton Plaza; well priced. **Cons:** books up early; small, dated rooms; no room service. [$] *Rooms from: $200* ✉ *520 E St., Gaslamp Quarter* ☎ *619/232–9500* 🌐 *www.gaslampplaza.com* 🛏 *60 rooms* 🍴 *Free breakfast.*

★ Hard Rock Hotel

$$$ | HOTEL | Self-billed as a hip playground for rock stars and people who want to party like them, the Hard Rock is near Petco Park overlooking glimmering San Diego Bay. The interior oozes laid-back sophistication, and guest rooms include branded Sleep Like a Rock beds and the option of renting a guitar. **Pros:** central location; energetic scene; luxurious rooms. **Cons:** pricey drinks; some attitude; party scene tends to be loud. *[$] Rooms from: $249 ✉ 207 5th Ave., Gaslamp Quarter ☎ 619/702–3000, 866/751–7625 🌐 www.hardrockhotelsd.com 🛏 420 rooms 🍴 No meals.*

Hilton San Diego Bayfront
$$ | **HOTEL** | **FAMILY** | This contemporary 30-story hotel overlooking San Diego Bay strives for a boutique feel. **Pros:** close to the convention center and Petco Park; allergy-friendly rooms available; excellent views. **Cons:** expensive valet parking; not as family-friendly as other area hotels; no fridge or minibar in the rooms. *[$] Rooms from: $214 ✉ 1 Park Blvd., Gaslamp Quarter ☎ 619/564–3333 🌐 hilton-bayfront.thehotelsinsandiego.com 🛏 1190 rooms 🍴 No meals.*

Hilton San Diego Gaslamp Quarter
$$$ | **HOTEL** | The moment you experience the cozy lounge spaces and wood accents of the Hilton's modern and sophisticated lobby, you realize this isn't your run-of-the-mill chain hotel—room perks include pillow-top mattresses, down comforters, and spacious work desks. **Pros:** nice decor; upscale lofts; near restaurants and shops. **Cons:** noisy area; pricey parking; Wi-Fi is free for Hilton's Honors loyalty program members. *[$] Rooms from: $289 ✉ 401 K St., Gaslamp Quarter ☎ 619/231–4040, 800/445–8667 🌐 www3.hilton.com 🛏 273 rooms 🍴 No meals.*

Kimpton Hotel Palomar San Diego
$$$ | **HOTEL** | A few blocks from the heart of the Gaslamp Quarter, this swanky Kimpton hotel features luxurious guest rooms and a popular rooftop lounge. **Pros:** modern rooms; centrally located; complimentary evening wine hour. **Cons:** expensive parking; noisy part of town; most rooms' views leave something to be desired. *[$] Rooms from: $239 ✉ 1047 5th Ave., Gaslamp Quarter ☎ 619/515–3000 🌐 www.hotelpalomar-sandiego.com 🛏 211 rooms 🍴 No meals.*

★ Kimpton Hotel Solamar
$$$ | **HOTEL** | **FAMILY** | Best known for Upper East Bar, its poolside rooftop bar, and stylish lobby decor, Solamar's guest rooms reflect this urban escape's mixture of luxury and fun, with prints galore and subtle nods to San Diego's happy beach culture. **Pros:** great restaurant; attentive service; upscale rooms. **Cons:** busy valet parking; daily facility fee; no coffeemaker or teakettle in rooms. *[$] Rooms from: $279 ✉ 435 6th Ave., Gaslamp Quarter ☎ 619/819–9500, 877/230–0300 🌐 www.hotelsolamar.com 🛏 235 rooms 🍴 No meals.*

Omni San Diego Hotel
$$$ | **HOTEL** | Business travelers who also want to catch a baseball game flock to this modern masterpiece that occupies the first 21 floors of a 32-story highrise overlooking Petco Park. **Pros:** great views; good location; modern setting. **Cons:** busy; crowded during baseball season; pricey valet parking. *[$] Rooms from: $278 ✉ 675 L St., Gaslamp Quarter ☎ 619/231–6664, 800/843–6664 🌐 www.omnihotels.com 🛏 511 rooms 🍴 No meals.*

★ Pendry San Diego
$$$$ | **HOTEL** | Opened in early 2017, the Pendry San Diego is the Gaslamp's newest stunner. **Pros:** well-situated in Gaslamp Quarter; excellent dining options; complimentary coffee in the mornings. **Cons:** pricey room rates; meals are expensive; not very family-friendly. *[$] Rooms from: $480 ✉ 550 J St., Gaslamp Quarter ☎ 619/738–7000 🌐 www.pendryhotels.com 🛏 317 rooms 🍴 No meals.*

San Diego Marriott Gaslamp Quarter
$$$ | **HOTEL** | The 22-story Marriott sits amid the Gaslamp's restaurants and boutiques, near a trolley station, the convention center, and Petco Park. **Pros:** good views; modern decor; central location.

Cons: rooftop bar can get rowdy; no pool; small rooms. [$] *Rooms from: $269* ✉ *660 K St., Gaslamp Quarter* ☎ *619/696–0234* 🌐 *www.sandiegogaslamphotel.com* 🛏 *306 rooms* 🍴 *No meals.*

★ The Sofia Hotel

$$$ | HOTEL | This stylish and centrally located boutique hotel may have small rooms, but it more than compensates with pampering extras like motion-sensor temperature controls, a Zen-like 24-hour yoga studio, an updated lobby, and a brand-new spa suite. **Pros:** upscale amenities; historic building; near shops and restaurants. **Cons:** busy area; small rooms; spotty Wi-Fi. [$] *Rooms from: $259* ✉ *150 W. Broadway, Gaslamp Quarter* ☎ *619/234–9200, 800/826–0009* 🌐 *www.thesofiahotel.com* 🛏 *211 rooms* 🍴 *No meals.*

★ The U.S. Grant, a Luxury Collection Hotel

$$$$ | HOTEL | The U.S. Grant may be more than a hundred years old (it first opened in 1910) but thanks to a top-to-bottom renovation in 2017, this grand old dame is now one of the most glamorous hotels in Southern California. **Pros:** sophisticated rooms; great location; near shopping and restaurants. **Cons:** street noise can be heard from the guest rooms; no in-room minibars or coffeemakers; surrounded by many major construction projects downtown. [$] *Rooms from: $304* ✉ *326 Broadway, Gaslamp Quarter* ☎ *619/232–3121, 800/325–3589* 🌐 *www.marriott.com* 🛏 *270 rooms* 🍴 *No meals.*

The Westgate Hotel

$$$ | HOTEL | A modern high-rise near Horton Plaza hides San Diego's most opulent old world–style hotel—the lobby is outfitted with bronze sculptures and Baccarat chandeliers—where staff greet guests with old-fashioned charm and politeness; other Downtown hotels have flashier amenities but you won't find one with greater class. **Pros:** affordable luxury; serene rooftop pool deck; San Diego Trolley stops right outside the door. **Cons:** dated guest rooms; mandatory facility fee; next to courthouse. [$] *Rooms from: $299* ✉ *1055 2nd Ave., Gaslamp Quarter* ☎ *619/238–1818, 800/522–1564* 🌐 *www.westgatehotel.com* 🛏 *223 rooms* 🍴 *No meals.*

🍸 Nightlife

The Gaslamp Quarter is still one of the most popular areas to go for a night on the town. Named for actual gaslights that once provided illumination along its once-seedy streets (it housed a number of gambling halls and brothels), the neighborhood bears only a trace of its debauched roots. Partygoers line up behind velvet ropes to dance inside Downtown's most exclusive clubs.

BARS

Altitude Sky Lounge

PIANO BARS/LOUNGES | Location is everything at this sophisticated lounge on the roof of the 22-floor San Diego Marriott Gaslamp Quarter. The views of the Downtown skyline and Petco Park will give you a natural high. ✉ *San Diego Marriott Gaslamp Quarter, 660 K St., Gaslamp Quarter* ☎ *619/696–0234* 🌐 *www.sandiegogaslamphotel.com.*

barleymash

BARS/PUBS | This gigantic space can resemble either a raucous club or a sports bar, depending on what night you're there. But the drinks are strong and reasonably priced, and the reclaimed wood decor makes for an intimate atmosphere, even when the DJs are spinning mostly Top 40. ✉ *600 5th Ave., Gaslamp Quarter* ☎ *619/255–7373* 🌐 *www.barleymash.com.*

Coin Op

BARS/PUBS | Step back into the '80s with this kitschy yet vibrant hybrid of bar and video arcade. The room is stocked with vintage arcade cabinet games like Galaga and Pac-Man, as well as Skee-Ball and other childhood favorites. Yet unlike those trips to the arcade, Coin Op features a rotating menu of craft cocktail creations, including punch bowls, to make those pinball tournaments even more spirited. ■ TIP→ **Come on the first Sunday of the month for free games all day long.** ✉ *789 Sixth Ave., Gaslamp Quarter* ☎ *619/546– 6441* ⊕ *www.coinopgaslamp.com.*

★ The Grant Grill

BARS/PUBS | Though the Grant Grill—located on the ground floor of the historic U.S. Grant Hotel—is a full-service restaurant, it's built up a reputation in recent years for stepping up San Diego's craft cocktail game. The cocktail menu is updated seasonally with fresh ingredients and themes (one recently featured a mini "Voodoo" doll frozen inside of a large ice cube), all of which are both innovative and palate pleasant. The atmosphere is comfortable and elegant, even on its busiest nights. ✉ *U.S. Grant Hotel, 326 Broadway, Gaslamp Quarter* ☎ *619/744– 2077* ⊕ *www.grantgrill.com.*

Hard Rock Hotel

DANCE CLUBS | A-list wannabes (and a few real celebs) gather in two bars, the loungey 207 off the lobby and the rooftop Float. The latter's Intervention and Wintervention daytime parties feature some of the world's biggest DJ names, or if you prefer a rock show, head to Maryjane's Underground at 207. Maybe you can't be a rock star, but you might as well party like one. Just be prepared to spend like one, too. ✉ *207 5th Ave., Gaslamp Quarter* ☎ *619/702–3000* ⊕ *hardrockhotelsd. com.*

The Nolen

BARS/PUBS | Panoramic views, warm and welcoming firepits, and beer-forward "hop-tails" (cocktails that have beer in them) are the attraction at this rooftop destination, situated atop the Courtyard by Marriott San Diego Gaslamp/Convention Center. ✉ *453 6th Ave., Downtown* ☎ *619/796–6536* ⊕ *www.thenolenrooftop.com.*

Prohibition

PIANO BARS/LOUNGES | This underground jazz lounge lives up to its name with a slinky speakeasy style. Red lighting, dark wood, and leather tufted couches provide a cozy 1920s–'30s-inspired backdrop to the live jazz on weekends. ✉ *548 5th Ave., Gaslamp Quarter* ☎ *619/501–1919* ⊕ *prohibitionsd.com.*

★ The Rooftop by STK

DANCE CLUBS | At this rooftop bar and lounge atop the Andaz hotel, a fashionable crowd sips cocktails poolside while gazing at gorgeous views of the city. Thursday through Saturday, the scene heats up with a DJ spinning dance music, while velvet ropes and VIP bottle service please the A-listers (like Prince Harry) in the crowd. ✉ *Andaz San Diego, 600 F St., Gaslamp Quarter* ☎ *619/814–2060* ⊕ *www.hyatt.com/en-US/hotel/california/ andaz-san-diego/sanas/dining.*

Upper East

PIANO BARS/LOUNGES | The trendy poolside bar on the fourth floor of the swank Hotel Solamar is a sexy spot to people-watch while sipping sangria or chili-mango margaritas and noshing on snacks from the "Slow Food" menu. On cool evenings, reserve a cabana or warm up next to one of the roaring firepits. ✉ *Hotel Solamar, 435 Sixth Ave., Gaslamp Quarter* ☎ *619/531–8744* ⊕ *www.hotelsolamar. com.*

Volcano Rabbit

BARS/PUBS | Featuring Downtown's largest selection of tequila, Volcano Rabbit has weekend DJs, a late-night menu, and the award-winning passionfruit margaritas that are made with a punchy puree and liqueur that brings out the fruit's sweet-tart flavor. ✉ *527 5th Ave., Gaslamp Quarter* ☎ *619/232–8226* ⊕ *volcanorabbitsd.com.*

COMEDY AND CABARET
American Comedy Co.

COMEDY CLUBS | At this underground space modeled after the legendary comedy clubs in New York, there's not a bad seat in the house—which is especially great since the venue pulls in some of the hugest names in stand-up comedy. ✉ *818 6th Ave., Gaslamp Quarter* ☎ *619/795–3858* ⊕ *www.americancomedyco.com.*

DANCE CLUBS
Bang Bang
DANCE CLUBS | Part sushi bar and part discotheque, Bang Bang offers both a good culinary game as well as a lineup of superstar DJs providing beats and breaks. It's become famous for its bathroom decor, adorned with images of actor and heartthrob Ryan Gosling. ✉ *526 Market St., Gaslamp Quarter* ☎ *619/677–2264* ⊕ *www.bangbangsd.com.*

Fluxx
DANCE CLUBS | Arguably the hottest club in the Gaslamp, this Vegas-style, multitheme space is packed to the gills on weekends with pretty people dancing to house and electro music and dropping major cash at the bar. ■ TIP→ **Get here early for a lower cover and to avoid the epic lines that snake around the block.** ✉ *500 4th Ave., Gaslamp Quarter* ☎ *619/232–8100* ⊕ *www.fluxxsd.com.*

Omnia
DANCE CLUBS | If the bright and flashy spectacle of Omnia feels a little bit more like Las Vegas than San Diego, it might be helpful to know that it actually has a Vegas counterpart. Top international EDM artists make stops here when they come to town, making it a necessary destination for BPM-seeking nightcrawlers. ✉ *454 6th Ave., Downtown* ☎ *619/544–9500.*

Oxford Social Club
DANCE CLUBS | A luxurious new downtown nightclub beneath the Pendry Hotel, Oxford Social Club has become one of San Diego's trendiest new clubs, with a predictably ample-sized line outside on weekends. But once inside, the place is spacious and comfortable, with plush bench seating and strong cocktails, plus table reservations and bottle service for the high rollers. ✉ *Pendry Hotel, 435 Fifth Ave., Gaslamp Quarter* ☎ *619/738–7040* ⊕ *www.theoxfordsd.com.*

Sevilla
DANCE CLUBS | For more than two decades, Cafe Sevilla and the Sevilla nightclub have brought a Latin flavor to the Gaslamp Quarter through a mix of contemporary and traditional Spanish and Latin American music. Get fueled up at the tapas bar before venturing downstairs for dancing. Salsa lessons during the week provide an especially memorable experience. ✉ *353 5th Ave., Gaslamp Quarter* ☎ *619/245–1138* ⊕ *www.sandiego.sevillanightclub.com.*

PIANO BARS
★ Westgate Hotel Plaza Bar
PIANO BARS/LOUNGES | The old-money surroundings, including leather-upholstered seats, marble tabletops, and a grand piano, supply one of the most elegant and romantic settings for a drink in San Diego. ✉ *1055 2nd Ave., Gaslamp Quarter* ☎ *619/238–1818* ⊕ *www.westgatehotel.com.*

ROCK, POP, HIP-HOP, FOLK, AND BLUES CLUBS
House of Blues
MUSIC CLUBS | The local branch of the renowned music chain is decorated floor to ceiling with colorful folk art and features three different areas to hear music. There's something going on here just about every night of the week, and the gospel brunch on select Sundays is one of the most praiseworthy events in town. Can we get a hallelujah? ✉ *1055 5th Ave., Gaslamp Quarter* ☎ *619/299–2583* ⊕ *www.houseofblues.com.*

WINE BARS
★ Vin de Syrah
WINE BARS—NIGHTLIFE | This "spirit and wine cellar" sends you down a rabbit hole (or at least down some stairs) to a whimsical spot straight out of Alice in

Wonderland. Behind a hidden door (look for a handle in the grass wall), you'll find visual delights (grapevines suspended from the ceiling, vintage jars with flittering "fireflies," cozy chairs nestled around a faux fireplace and pastoral vista) that rival the culinary ones—the wine list is approachable and the charcuterie boards are exquisitely curated. ■TIP→ **More than just a wine bar, the cocktails are also worth a try.** ⊠ *901 5th Ave., Gaslamp Quarter* ☏ *619/234–4166* ⊕ *www.syrahwineparlor.com.*

Performing Arts

DANCE

Whether you fancy *rond de jambes* or something a bit more modern, San Diego's scene is *en pointe* for dance fans.

California Ballet Company

DANCE | The company performs high-quality contemporary and classical works September–May at the **Civic Theatre.** The *Nutcracker* is staged annually around the holiday season. ⊠ *San Diego Civic Theatre, 1100 3rd Ave., Gaslamp* ☏ *858/560–5676* ⊕ *www.californiaballet.org.*

City Ballet

DANCE | The ballet holds performances at the **Spreckels Theatre** and a few other area venues from November through May. At Christmastime, they dance a mean *Nutcracker.* ⊠ *Spreckels Theatre, 121 Broadway #600, Gaslamp* ☏ *858/272–8663* ⊕ *www.cityballet.org.*

MUSIC

Balboa Theatre

MUSIC | This renovated theater offers a variety of performances including ballet, music, plays, and even stand-up comedy. In addition to architectural splendor, the space offers unsurpassed acoustics . ⊠ *868 4th Ave., Gaslamp Quarter* ☏ *800/854–2196* ⊕ *www.sandiegotheatres.org.*

★ Copley Symphony Hall

MUSIC | The great acoustics here are surpassed only by the incredible Spanish baroque interior. Not just the home of the San Diego Symphony Orchestra, the renovated 2,200-seat 1920s-era theater has also hosted major stars like Elvis Costello, Leonard Cohen, and Sting. ⊠ *750 B St., Gaslamp* ☏ *619/235–0804* ⊕ *www.sandiegosymphony.org.*

San Diego Opera

MUSIC | Drawing international performers, the opera's season runs January–April. Past performances have included *Die Fledermaus, Faust, Idomeneo,* and *La Bohème,* plus solo concerts by such talents as Renée Fleming. ⊠ *Civic Theatre, 1100 3rd Ave., Gaslamp* ☏ *619/533–7000* ⊕ *www.sdopera.com.*

San Diego Symphony Orchestra

MUSIC | The orchestra's events include classical concerts and summer and winter pops, nearly all of them at Copley Symphony Hall. The outdoor Summer Pops series is held on the Embarcadero, on North Harbor Drive beyond the convention center. ⊠ *Box office, 750 B St., Gaslamp* ☏ *619/235–0804* ⊕ *www.sandiegosymphony.org.*

Spreckels Theatre

THEATER | A landmark theater erected in 1912, the Spreckels hosts comedy, dance, theater, and concerts. Good acoustics and old-time elegance make this a favorite local venue. ⊠ *121 Broadway, Suite 600, Gaslamp* ☏ *619/235–9500* ⊕ *www.spreckels.net.*

THEATER

Horton Grand Theatre

THEATER | After being home to the long-running Triple Espresso, the Horton Grand Theatre hosts productions from the likes of San Diego Musical Theatre as well as Intrepid Theatre Company, whose shows include *Who's Afraid of Virginia Woolf?* and *Woody Guthrie's American Song.* ⊠ *Hahn Cosmopolitan*

Theatre, 444 4th Ave., Gaslamp Quarter
☎ *858/560–5740.*

San Diego Civic Theatre
THEATER | The home of the San Diego Opera, the Civic Theatre is the city's largest performing arts venue, with musicals, theatrical productions, and concerts held throughout the year. ☒ *1100 3rd Ave., Gaslamp* ☎ *619/570–1100* ⊕ *www.sandiegotheatres.org.*

Activities

BICYCLING
The Bike Revolution
BICYCLING | Choose from a wide array of rentals, from road bikes to cruisers, and embark on a ride along the Downtown waterfront, up the hill to Balboa Park, or hop on the ferry to Coronado Island for a leisurely ride around the idyllic island. ☒ *522 6th Ave., Gaslamp Quarter* ☎ *619/564–4843* ⊕ *www.thebikerevolution.com* ⌚ *From $20.*

👜 Shopping

The mix of retailers in the historic heart of San Diego changes frequently, but there are always boutiques in the Victorian buildings and renovated warehouses along 4th and 5th avenues. Also in the quarter are the usual mall stores and gift shops. Some stores close early, starting as early as 5 pm, and many are closed Sunday or Monday.

CLOTHING AND ACCESSORIES
Blends
SHOES/LUGGAGE/LEATHER GOODS | Minimalist decor provides a perfect backdrop for the wild colors and patterns featured on original sneakers from Adidas, Nike, Vans, and other in-demand brands. Prices are steep, but many of the urban styles are unique. ☒ *719 8th Ave., Gaslamp Quarter* ☎ *619/233–6126* ⊕ *blendsus.com.*

Goorin Bros. Hats
JEWELRY/ACCESSORIES | Established in Pittsburgh in 1895, this company has helped make hats hip again with its stylish takes on fedoras, bowlers, and Panama hats. The San Diego location occupies the first floor of the historic Yuma building, a former brothel in the red light district. ☒ *631 5th Ave., Gaslamp Quarter* ☎ *619/450–6303* ⊕ *www.goorin.com.*

FOOD AND WINE
Wine Bank
WINE/SPIRITS | This overwhelmingly stocked emporium with a large selection of wines also features a long list of other beverages, from rums and tequilas to mezcals and local craft beers. ☒ *363 Fifth Ave., #100, Gaslamp Quarter* ☎ *619/234–7487* ⊕ *www.sdwinebank.com.*

MUSIC STORES
FeeLit Records
MUSIC STORES | This all-vinyl record shop features a wide selection from curated new releases to budget used records, that cross a wide spectrum of genres: rock, pop, dance, punk, metal, R&B, and hip-hop. ☒ *909 E St., Gaslamp Quarter* ☎ *707/733–3548* ⊕ *www.feelitrecords.com.*

SPECIALITY SHOPS
Magic Shop San Diego
SPECIALTY STORES | Like something out of a bygone era, this shop stocks an impressive amount of magic supplies, games, books, magazines, and other items for the beginner or professional prestidigitator. ☒ *827 4th Ave., Gaslamp Quarter* ☎ *619/738–8350* ⊕ *www.magicshopsandiego.com.*

Embarcadero

The **Embarcadero** cuts a scenic swath along the harborfront and connects today's Downtown San Diego to its maritime routes. The bustle of Embarcadero comes less these days from the activities of fishing folk than from the throngs of tourists, but this waterfront walkway, stretching from the Convention Center to the Maritime Museum, remains the nautical soul of the city. There are several seafood restaurants here, as well as sea vessels of every variety—cruise ships, ferries, tour boats, and Navy destroyers.

On the north end of the Embarcadero at Ash Street you'll find the **Maritime Museum.** South of it, the **B Street Pier** is used by ships from major cruise lines while tickets for harbor tours and whale-watching trips are sold at the foot of **Broadway Pier.** The terminal for the Coronado Ferry lies in between. Docked at the **Navy Pier** is the decommissioned **USS** Midway. At the foot of G Street, **Tuna Harbor** was once the hub of one of San Diego's earliest and most successful industries, commercial tuna fishing. The pleasant Tuna Harbor Park offers a great view of boating on the bay and across to any aircraft carriers docked at the North Island naval base. A few blocks south, **Embarcadero Marina Park North** is an 8-acre extension into the harbor from the center of **Seaport Village.** It's usually full of kite fliers, in-line skaters, and picnickers. Seasonal celebrations, including San Diego's Parade of Lights, the Port of San Diego Big Balloon Parade and the Big Bay July 4 Celebration, are held here and at the similar **Embarcadero Marina Park South.** The **San Diego Convention Center,** on Harbor Drive between 1st and 6th avenues, is a waterfront landmark designed by Canadian architect Arthur Erickson. The backdrop of blue sky and sea complements the building's nautical lines. The center often holds trade shows that are open to the public, and tours of the building are available.

A huge revitalization project is underway along the northern Embarcadero. The overhaul seeks to transform the area with large mixed-use development projects, inviting parks, walkways, and public art installations. The redevelopment will eventually head south along the waterfront, with plans underway for a major overhaul of the entire Central Embarcadero and Seaport Village.

◉ Sights

★ Maritime Museum
MARINA | FAMILY | From sailing ships to submarines, the Maritime Museum is a must for anyone with an interest in nautical history. This collection of restored and replica ships affords a fascinating glimpse of San Diego during its heyday as a commercial seaport. The jewel of the collection, the *Star of India,* was built in 1863 and made 21 trips around the world in the late 1800s. Saved from the scrap yard and painstakingly restored, the windjammer is the oldest active iron sailing ship in the world. The newly constructed *San Salvador* is a detailed historic replica of the original ship first sailed into San Diego Bay by explorer Juan Rodriguez Cabrillo back in 1542. And, the popular HMS *Surprise* is a replica of an 18th-century British Royal Navy frigate. The museum's headquarters are on the *Berkeley,* an 1898 steam-driven ferryboat, which served the Southern Pacific Railroad in San Francisco until 1958.

Numerous cruises of San Diego Bay are offered, including a daily 45-minute narrated tour aboard a 1914 pilot boat and 3-hour weekend sails aboard the topsail schooner the *Californian,* the state's official tall ship, and 75-minute tours aboard a historic swift boat, which highlights the city's military connection. Partnering with the museum, the renowned yacht *America* also offers sails on the bay, and whale-watching excursions are available in winter. ⊠ *1492 N. Harbor Dr., Embarcadero* ☎ *619/234–9153* ⊕ *www.sdmaritime.org* ⊉ *$18.*

★ Museum of Contemporary Art San Diego (MCASD)
MUSEUM | At the Downtown branch of the city's contemporary art museum, explore the works of international and regional artists in a modern, urban space. The

Built in 1863, the Maritime Museum's *Star of India* is often considered to be a symbol of San Diego.

Jacobs Building—formerly the baggage building at the historic Santa Fe Depot—features large gallery spaces, high ceilings, and natural lighting, giving artists the flexibility to create large-scale installations. MCASD's collection includes many Pop Art, minimalist, and conceptual works from the 1950s to the present. The museum showcases both established and emerging artists in temporary exhibitions, and has permanent, site-specific commissions by Jenny Holzer and Richard Serra. ⊠ *1100 and 1001 Kettner Blvd., Downtown* ☎ *858/454–3541* ⊕ *www.mcasd.org* ⊠ *$10; free 3rd Thurs. of the month 5–7* ☉ *Closed Wed.*

★ The New Children's Museum (NCM)

MUSEUM | FAMILY | The NCM blends contemporary art with unstructured play to create an environment that appeals to children as well as adults. The 50,000-square-foot structure was constructed from recycled building materials, operates on solar energy, and is convection-cooled by an elevator shaft. It also features a nutritious and eco-conscious café. Interactive exhibits include designated areas for toddlers and teens, as well as plenty of activities for the entire family. Several art workshops are offered each day, as well as hands-on studios where visitors are encouraged to create their own art. The studio projects change frequently and the entire museum changes exhibits every 18 to 24 months, so there is always something new to explore. The adjoining 1-acre park and playground is across from the convention center trolley stop. ⊠ *200 W. Island Ave., Embarcadero* ☎ *619/233–8792* ⊕ *www.thinkplaycreate.org* ⊠ *$14* ☉ *Closed Tues.*

Seaport Village

PEDESTRIAN MALL | FAMILY | You'll find some of the best views of the harbor at Seaport Village, three bustling shopping plazas designed to reflect the New England clapboard, and Spanish Mission architectural styles of early California. On a prime stretch of waterfront the dining, shopping, and entertainment complex connects the harbor with hotel towers and the convention center. Specialty

Ferry to Coronado

Coronado Ferry. Fifteen-minute ferries connect two locations along the Downtown San Diego waterfront with the Coronado Ferry Landing. Boats depart on the hour from the Broadway Pier on the Embarcadero and on the half hour from Coronado Ferry Landing to the Embarcadero during operating hours. Between the San Diego Convention Center and the Coronado Ferry Landing, service departs every 30 minutes during operating hours. Buy tickets at the Broadway Pier, 5th Avenue Landing, or Coronado Ferry Landing. To reach the heart of downtown Coronado from the Ferry Landing, you can rent a bike at the landing (or bring one with you), or catch the 904 shuttle bus that runs along Orange Avenue. Ferry service is operated by Flagship Cruises. ⊠ *Broadway Pier on the Embarcadero, 990 N. Harbor Dr., San Diego* ☎ *619/234–4111, 800/442–7847* ⊕ *www.flagshipsd.com* ⊠ *Ferry $4.75 one way.*

shops offer everything from a kite store and swing emporium to a shop devoted to hot sauces. You can dine at snack bars and restaurants, many with harbor views.

Live music can be heard daily from noon to 4 at the main food court. Additional free concerts take place every Sunday from 1 to 4 at the East Plaza Gazebo. The **Seaport Village Carousel** (rides $3) has 54 animals, hand-carved and hand-painted by Charles Looff in 1895. Across the street, the **Headquarters at Seaport Village** converted the historic police headquarters into several trendsetting shops and restaurants. ⊠ *849 W. Harbor Dr., Downtown* ☎ *619/235–4014 office and events hotline* ⊕ *www.seaportvillage.com.*

★ **USS *Midway* Museum**

MILITARY SITE | FAMILY | After 47 years of worldwide service, the retired USS *Midway* began a new tour of duty on the south side of the Navy pier in 2004. Launched in 1945, the 1,001-foot-long ship was the largest in the world for the first 10 years of its existence. The most visible landmark on the north Embarcadero, it now serves as a floating interactive museum—an appropriate addition to the town that is home to one-third of the

Pacific fleet and the birthplace of naval aviation. A free audio tour guides you through the massive ship while offering insight from former sailors. As you clamber through passageways and up and down ladder wells, you'll get a feel for how the *Midway*'s 4,500 crew members lived and worked on this "city at sea."

Though the entire tour is impressive, you'll really be wowed when you step out onto the 4-acre flight deck—not only the best place to get an idea of the ship's scale, but also one of the most interesting vantage points for bay and city skyline views. An F-14 Tomcat jet fighter is just one of many vintage aircraft on display. Free guided tours of the bridge and primary flight control, known as "the Island," depart every 10 minutes from the flight deck. Many of the docents stationed throughout the ship served in the Navy, some even on the *Midway*, and they are eager to answer questions or share stories. The museum also offers multiple flight simulators for an additional fee, climb-aboard cockpits, and interactive exhibits focusing on naval aviation. There is a gift shop and a café with pleasant outdoor seating. This is a wildly popular stop, with most visits lasting several hours. ⚠ **Despite efforts to provide accessibility throughout the ship, some areas can only be reached via fairly steep steps; a video tour of these areas is available on the hangar deck.** ✉ *910 N. Harbor Dr., Embarcadero* ☎ *619/544–9600* 🌐 *www.midway.org* 🎟 *$21.*

🍴 Restaurants

This walkable Downtown bayfront strip between the iconic County Administration building and the convention center offers visitors access to historic maritime destinations and dining options served up with spectacular views.

Carnitas' Snack Shack - Embarcadero
$ | **AMERICAN** | Indulge in some carnitas tacos, a BLT, or the "Triple Threat" pork sandwich at the Embarcadero outpost of this popular swine-heavy dining spot. **Known for:** the "Triple Threat" pork sandwich; amazing tacos. [$] *Average main: $9* ✉ *1004 N. Harbor Dr., Embarcadero* ☎ *619/616–7675* 🌐 *www.carnitassnackshack.com.*

★ Eddie V's Prime Seafood
$$$ | **SEAFOOD** | Don't be put off by the name, or that it is part of a small chain. This fine-dining restaurant at the Headquarters at Seaport in Downtown has won a devoted following for classic seafood, casual but sophisticated settings, and nightly live jazz. **Known for:** wallet-friendly happy hour deals; indulgent truffled mac and cheese. [$] *Average main: $34* ✉ *789 W. Harbor Dr., Embarcadero* ☎ *619/615–0281* 🌐 *www.eddiev.com* 🕒 *No lunch.*

★ Puesto
$ | **MEXICAN** | Bold graffiti graphics, chandeliers with tangled telephone wires, and beat-heavy music energize this Downtown eatery that celebrates Mexican street food with a modern twist. Settle into one of the interior rooms or the sunny patio under orange umbrellas to sip margaritas and other specialty cocktails, Baja wines, or fruity aguas frescas made daily. **Known for:** taco trio plates; unique Parmesan guacamole; fruit-infused margaritas made in-house. [$] *Average main: $16* ✉ *789 W. Harbor Dr., Downtown* ☎ *619/233–8880* 🌐 *www.eatpuesto.com.*

Top of the Market
$$$ | **SEAFOOD** | With its bay views from Point Loma to the Coronado Bridge, this upscale seafood house is just right for a memorable evening. The romantic teak-paneled dining room and a deck that sits over the water are popular spots for visitor splurges and locals celebrating special occasions. **Known for:** romantic atmosphere; smoked fish appetizers. [$] *Average main: $35* ✉ *750 N. Harbor Dr., Embarcadero* ☎ *619/234–4687* 🌐 *www.sdtopofthemarket.com.*

🛏 Hotels

Embassy Suites by Hilton San Diego Bay Downtown
$$$ | **HOTEL** | **FAMILY** | The front door of each spacious, contemporary suite here opens out onto a 12-story atrium. **Pros:** harbor-facing rooms have spectacular views; spacious accommodations; good location. **Cons:** busy area; ho-hum decor; limited dining options. [$] *Rooms from: $269* ✉ *601 Pacific Hwy., Embarcadero* ☎ *619/239–2400, 800/362–2779* 🌐 *www.sandiegobay.embassysuites.com* 🛏 *341 suites* 🍽 *Free breakfast.*

Manchester Grand Hyatt San Diego
$$$ | **HOTEL** | **FAMILY** | Primarily a draw for business travelers, this hotel between Seaport Village and the convention center also works well for leisure and family travelers. **Pros:** great views; conference facilities; good location; spacious rooms. **Cons:** lots of convention-goers; some trolley noise; not as stylish as many other downtown hotels. [$] *Rooms from: $259* ✉ *1 Market Pl., Embarcadero* ☎ *619/232–1234, 800/233–1234* 🌐 *www.manchester.grand.hyatt.com* 🛏 *1628 rooms* 🍽 *No meals.*

♉ Nightlife

Scenic drinking spots and higher bar tabs overlook tall ships and naval history.

BARS

The Lion's Share

PIANO BARS/LOUNGES | Hemingway would have loved this exquisitely designed brick-and-wood bar that serves up equally exquisite craft cocktails that, while pricey, are definitely made for sipping. The place attracts a sophisticated crowd and is highly recommended for those looking to impress a special someone. ⊠ *629 Kettner Blvd., Embarcadero* ☎ *619/564–6924* ⊕ *lionssharesd.com.*

Top of the Hyatt

PIANO BARS/LOUNGES | This lounge at the Manchester Grand Hyatt crowns the tallest waterfront building in California, affording great views of San Diego Bay, including Coronado to the west, Mexico to the south, and Point Loma and La Jolla to the north. It's pricey and pretentious (don't you dare wear flip-flops), but this champagne-centric bar is great for catching a sunset or celebrating an anniversary. ⊠ *1 Market Pl., Embarcadero* ☎ *619/232–1234* ⊕ *topofthehyatt.com.*

🏃 Activities

BICYCLING

Wheel Fun Rentals

BICYCLING | Surreys, cruisers, mountain bikes, and tandems, among other two-, three-, and four-wheeled contraptions, are available at the Downtown Holiday Inn and a number of other locations around San Diego; call or visit the website for details. ⊠ *1355 N. Harbor Dr., Embarcadero* ☎ *619/342–7244* ⊕ *www.wheelfunrentals.com* ⊠ *From $32.*

SAILING AND BOATING

Flagship Cruises & Events

BOATING | Get on board here for harbor tours, two-hour dinner and brunch cruises, and a ferry to Coronado. ⊠ *990 N. Harbor Dr., Embarcadero* ☎ *619/234–4111, 800/442–7847 reservations* ⊕ *www.flagshipsd.com* ⊠ *From $27.*

Hornblower Cruises and Events

BOATING | This outfit operates harbor cruises, sunset cocktail and dining cruises, whale-watching excursions, and yacht charters. ⊠ *970 N. Harbor Dr., Embarcadero* ☎ *619/686–8700, 619/686–8715 ticket booth* ⊕ *www.hornblower.com* ⊠ *From $27.*

WHALE-WATCHING CRUISES

Whale-watching season peaks in January and February, when thousands of gray whales migrate south to the warm weather, where they give birth to their calves. If you want a closer look, charter boats and cruises host whale-watching excursions.

Flagship Cruises & Events

WHALE-WATCHING | Join one of the twice-daily whale-watching trips during the season from December through April. Tours are led by naturalists from Birch Aquarium at Scripps. ⊠ *990 N. Harbor Dr., Embarcadero* ☎ *619/234–4111, 800/442–7847 reservations* ⊕ *www.flagshipsd.com* ⊠ *From $43.*

Hornblower Cruises and Events

WHALE-WATCHING | Yachts take passengers to catch a glimpse of gray whales and perhaps an occasional school of dolphins. Live narration is provided by experts from the San Diego Natural History Museum. ⊠ *970 N. Harbor Dr., Embarcadero* ☎ *619/686–8700, 619/686–8715 ticket booth* ⊕ *www.hornblower.com* ⊠ *From $48.*

🛍 Shopping

The new Headquarters at Seaport shopping district is breathing new life into the somewhat touristy San Diego waterfront. Spanning 14 acres and offering more than 50 shops and 17 restaurants, Seaport Village remains popular for souvenirs and entertainment.

SHOPPING CENTERS

★ The Headquarters at Seaport

OUTDOOR/FLEA/GREEN MARKETS | This new upscale shopping and dining center is in the city's former police headquarters, a beautiful and historic Mission-style building featuring an open courtyard with fountains. Restaurants and shops, many locally owned, occupy former jail facilities and offices. Pop into **Urban Beach House** for coastal-inspired fashion from popular surf brands for men and women, including accessories and home decor. Swing by **Madison San Diego** for a great selection of leather goods and accessories, from apparel and handbags to belts and travel accessories. **Dallmann Fine Chocolates** sells truffles in flavors like bananas Foster and coconut curry. **Venissimo Cheese** dishes up the best cheese from around the world, from goat milk chevre filled with Italian truffle salt to French triple crème brie topped with tangy cranberries. **Geppetto's** has been a San Diego staple for more than 40 years, offering classic toys and games that inspire creativity for the entire family. ⊠ *789 W. Harbor Dr., Downtown* ☎ *619/235–4013* ⊕ *theheadquarters.com.*

Seaport Village

SHOPPING CENTERS/MALLS | If you're looking for trinkets and souvenirs, this is the place. This complex of kitschy shops and waterfront restaurants has upped its hip factor with boutiques like **San Pasqual** wine bar; bamboo clothing–maker **Cariloha**; and **Frost Me Gourmet Cupcakes,** the bakery known for its win on Cupcake Wars Season 9. While there, keep an eye out for **Urban Girl Accessories** to find an eclectic mix of clothing and gifts from name brands and local artisans, and stop by **Village Hat Shop** to browse their collection of 50,000 fedoras, bowlers, cowboy, and custom embroidered hats. In addition to shopping, the village has views of the bay, fresh breezes, and great strolling paths. A hand-carved historic carousel and frequent public entertainment are among the attractions. Seaport Village is within walking distance of hotels, the San Diego Convention Center, and the San Diego Trolley. ⊠ *849 W. Harbor Dr., at Pacific Hwy., Downtown* ☎ *619/235–4014* ⊕ *www.seaportvillage.com/shopping.*

East Village

The most ambitious of the Downtown projects is **East Village,** not far from the Gaslamp Quarter, and encompassing 130 blocks between the railroad tracks up to J Street, and from 6th Avenue east to around 10th Street. Sparking the rebirth of this former warehouse district was the 2004 construction of the San Diego Padres' stunning 42,000-seat baseball stadium, **Petco Park,** where games are rarely rained out.

The **Urban Art Trail** has added pizzazz to drab city thoroughfares by transforming such things as trash cans and traffic controller boxes into works of art. As the city's largest Downtown neighborhood, East Village is continually broadening its boundaries with its urban design of redbrick cafés, spacious galleries, rooftop bars, sleek hotels, and warehouse restaurants.

◉ Sights

Petco Park

SPORTS VENUE | FAMILY | Petco Park is home to the city's major league baseball team, the San Diego Padres. The ballpark is strategically designed to give fans a view of San Diego Bay, the skyline, and Balboa Park. Reflecting San Diego's beauty, the stadium is clad in sandstone from India to evoke the area's cliffs and beaches; the 42,000 seats are dark blue, reminiscent of the ocean, and the exposed steel is painted white to reflect the sails of harbor boats on the bay. The family-friendly lawnlike berm, "Park at the Park," is a popular and affordable place for fans to view the game. The ballpark underwent a huge effort to improve

Home of the San Diego Padres, Petco Park offers behind-the-scenes tours.

dining in the park, and local food vendors and craft breweries now dominate the dining options. Behind-the-scenes guided tours of Petco, including the press box and the dugout, are offered throughout the year. ✉ *100 Park Blvd., East Village* ☎ *619/795–5011 tour hotline* 🌐 *sandiego.padres.mlb.com* 🎟 *$20 tour.*

🍴 Restaurants

Revived with the opening of the San Diego Padres stadium, Petco Park, this trendy high-rise residential area is an eclectic mix of hip gastropubs, wine bars, and cafés serving everything from French bistro fare to Baja-Mexican, burgers, and artisan-baked bread.

The Blind Burro

$$ | **MODERN MEXICAN** | **FAMILY** | East Village families, baseball fans heading to or from Petco Park, and happy-hour bound singles flock to this airy restaurant with Baja-inspired food and drink. Traditional margaritas get a fresh kick from fruit juices or jalapeño peppers; other libations include sangria and Mexican beers, all perfect pairings for house-made guacamole, ceviche, or salsas with chips. **Known for:** house margarita with fruit infusions; surf-and-turf Baja-style tacos; gluten-free menu. [$] *Average main: $18* ✉ *639 J St., East Village* ☎ *619/795–7880* 🌐 *www.theblindburro.com.*

Cowboy Star

$$$$ | **STEAKHOUSE** | Special-occasion diners, conventioneers on expense accounts, and meat-loving locals haunt this surprisingly intimate dining room for great beef expertly prepared. The wood-and-brick interior has leather accents, Western landscapes, and vintage Old West photos, and servers wear white shirts and stylish denim aprons, all creating a relaxed urban-cowboy ambience. **Known for:** on-site butcher shop selling premium steaks, sausages, and charcuterie; 35-day dry-aged beef. [$] *Average main: $53* ✉ *640 10th Ave., East Village* ☎ *619/450–5880* 🌐 *www.cowboystarsd.com* 🕒 *No lunch Sat.–Mon.*

The Kebab Shop

$ | **MEDITERRANEAN** | At its five San Diego locations—East Village, Little Italy, Mira Mesa, Mission Valley, and Rancho Bernardo—this fast-food Mediterranean eatery offers a mix of slowly cooked rotisserie meats, grilled to-order seafood, and crispy falafel served on plates of saffron rice or wrapped in grilled flatbread. Fresh tabbouleh, 10 Mediterranean salads, and baklava desserts round out the meals. **Known for:** rotisserie meats including chicken, beef, and lamb; creamy garlic yogurt sauce. [$] *Average main: $8* ✉ *630 9th Ave., East Village* ☎ *619/525–0055* 🌐 *www.thekebabshop.com.*

Lola 55

$ | **MEXICAN** | This is the place for exceptional, elevated tacos that won't break the bank. Don't miss Happy Hour, Sunday–Friday from 2–6 pm, where margaritas and Modellos are $4. **Known for:** great cocktails; great tacos; gluten-free and vegan options. [$] *Average main: $5* ✉ *1290 F St., East Village* 🌐 *lola55.com.*

The Mission

$ | **AMERICAN** | Healthy, creative dishes and a friendly staff make this art-filled East Village café a local favorite for breakfast and lunch. Hungry San Diegans wait 30 minutes or more to enjoy fluffy scrambled eggs with chicken apple sausage or strawberry banana pancakes with a side of eggs and bacon. **Known for:** Mexican-influenced breakfast dishes like chilaquiles; French toast made with house-baked cinnamon bread; busy breakfast scene especially on weekends. [$] *Average main: $10* ✉ *1250 J St., East Village* ☎ *619/232–7662* 🌐 *www.themissionsd.com* ⏲ *No dinner.*

Tajima

$ | **JAPANESE** | With four other locations in the city—Hillcrest, North Park, and two outposts in Kearny Mesa—Tajima has become a favorite source for ramen-hungry San Diegans. Climb into a cozy booth and order a Japanese craft beer or sake before diving into one of the five types of ramen—all of which come in hefty portions with affordable price tags—including an excellent vegan version with spinach noodles. **Known for:** spicy sesame ramen with spicy ground pork and fried garlic; affordable and hefty portions; karaage fried chicken. [$] *Average main: $10* ✉ *901 E St., East Village* ☎ *619/431–5820* 🌐 *www.tajimasandiego.com.*

Western Metal Supply

Initially scheduled for demolition to make room for Petco Park, the historic Western Metal Supply Co. was instead incorporated into the ballpark and supports the left-field foul pole. Great care was taken to retain the historic nature of the building's exterior despite extensive interior renovations. Built in 1909, the four-story structure originally manufactured wagon wheels and war supplies, and today holds the Padres' Team Store, food and beverage outlets, and rooftop seating.

Nightlife

East Village, just outside of the Gaslamp, is a little more cutting edge. This up-and-coming urban hood has upscale style mashed with hip, underground dives. Most of its destinations are within close quarters to Petco Park, so on game night, the neighborhood is particularly lively. Not that it's quiet any other night; popular hangouts like East Village Tavern and Bowl, and Bar Basic are reliably crowded haunts, so show up early.

BARS

Bar Basic

BARS/PUBS | This spot is always bustling, in part because it's *the* place to be seen for Padres fans or anyone else attending events at Petco Park. True to its name,

Basic reliably dishes up simple pleasures: strong drinks and hot, coal-fired pizza. The garage-style doors roll up and keep the industrial-chic former warehouse ventilated during the balmy summer. ⊠ *410 10th Ave., East Village* ☎ *619/531–8869* ⊕ *www.barbasic.com.*

East Village Tavern & Bowl

BARS/PUBS | Twelve bowling lanes means no more hauls to the suburbs to channel one's inner Lebowski. Lane rental is pricey during prime times, but reasonable if you consider that some nearby clubs charge a Jackson just for admission, though reservations are definitely recommended. From the expansive bar area you can watch sports on 33 flat screens, and the satellite radio plays an assortment of alt- and classic rock. ⊠ *930 Market St., East Village* ☎ *619/677–2695* ⊕ *www.tavernbowl.com.*

★ Fairweather

BARS/PUBS | Hidden in plain sight next to Petco Park, Fairweather is an urban tiki oasis with a top-notch cocktail menu that boasts classics like daiquiris and their signature frozen piña colada alongside modern interpretations of old-school tiki drinks like corpse revivers and mai tais. ■TIP→ **Come by during Comic-Con in July to view the parade of costumed characters while sipping rum refreshment on the balcony.** ⊠ *793 J St., 2nd fl., East Village* ☎ *619/578–2392* ⊕ *www.fairweatherbar. com.*

★ Noble Experiment

PIANO BARS/LOUNGES | There are a handful of speakeasy-style bars in San Diego, though none deliver so far above and beyond the novelty quite like this cozy-yet-swank cocktail lounge hidden in the back of a burger restaurant. Seek out the hidden door (hint: look for the stack of kegs), tuck into a plush leather booth next to the wall of golden skulls, and sip on the best craft cocktails in the city. ■TIP→ **Reservations are almost always a must, so be sure to call ahead.** ⊠ *777 G St.,*

East Village ☎ *619/888–4713* ⊕ *nobleexperimentsd.com.*

Punch Bowl Social

BARS/PUBS | Punch Bowl Social—which also has locations in Atlanta, Austin, and Denver—is essentially three different concepts all wrapped up in one wildly entertaining time. It's a cocktail bar, boasting favorites including mules and daiquiris, along with modern twists and even spiked milkshakes. It's also a diner, with fare that ranges from breakfast nachos to fried-chicken sandwiches. And most importantly, it's a game room, complete with darts, pinball, and even a bowling alley. No matter what, though, get one of those milkshakes—they're dangerously good. ⊠ *1485 E St., East Village* ☎ *619/452–3352* ⊕ *www.punchbowlsocial.com.*

You & Yours

BARS/PUBS | A refreshing alternative to the sensory overload in some of the bars downtown, You & Yours is a local gin and vodka distillery that also serves up a number of excellent cocktails inside its tasting room. The atmosphere is modern, relaxed, and airy; the clientele low-key; and the gin itself is outstanding. ⊠ *1495 G St., East Village* ☎ *619/955–8755* ⊕ *www.youandyours.com.*

Little Italy

Home to many in San Diego's design community, Little Italy exudes a sense of urban cool. The main thoroughfare, India Street, is filled with lively cafés, chic shops, and many of the city's trendiest restaurants. Little Italy is one of San Diego's most walkable neighborhoods, and a great spot to wander. Art lovers can browse gallery showrooms, while shoppers adore the Fir Street cottages. The neighborhood bustles each Saturday during the wildly popular Mercato farmers' market, and at special events throughout the year such as Artwalk in spring and FESTA! each fall. The website Little Italy San Diego (🌐 *www.littleitalysd.com*) has detailed info about neighborhood shops and events.

The neighborhood is also authentic to its roots and marked by old-country charms: church bells ring on the half hour, and Italians gather daily to play boccie in Amici Park. After an afternoon of gelati and espresso, you may just forget that you're in Southern California.

👁 Sights

Little Italy Mercato

MARKET | Each Saturday tourists and residents alike flock to the Little Italy Mercato, one of the most popular farmers' markets in San Diego. Over 150 vendors line Date Street selling everything from paintings and pottery, to flowers and farm-fresh eggs. Come hungry, as several booths and food trucks serve prepared foods. Alternatively, the neighborhood's many cafés and restaurants are just steps away. The Mercato is a great opportunity to experience one of San Diego's most exciting urban neighborhoods. ✉ *Date and India Sts., Little Italy* 🌐 *www.littleitalysd.com/events/mercato.*

🍴 Restaurants

One of San Diego's oldest and liveliest neighborhoods steeped in the city's Italian and Portuguese fishing culture, Little Italy is known for its bustling nightlife and Italian fine and casual dining mixed with trendy new eateries, dessert destinations, sidewalk cafés, and a few late-night bars.

Bencotto

$$ | **ITALIAN** | The ultramodern Italian eatery with young Milanese owners gets cheers for its design and cuisine from hip Little Italy residents and visitors alike. Diners linger over drinks and house-made pasta at the friendly long bar and more intimate upstairs dining room. **Known for:** mix-and-match pasta entrées; gluten-free pasta options; traditional Italian tiramisu. [$] *Average main: $24* ✉ *750 W. Fir St., Little Italy* ☎ *619/450–4786* 🌐 *www.lovebencotto.com* ⏲ *No lunch Mon.*

★ Born and Raised

$$$$ | **STEAKHOUSE** | The name is cheeky if a little morbid; the title refers to the restaurant's speciality—steak. It's a twist on a classic steak house, with a menu full of aged, prime cuts of beef served with a number of sauces, or perhaps try the tableside-prepared steak Diane with flambéed jus. **Known for:** tableside Caesar salad; aged New York steak; cheeky, glamorous decor. [$] *Average main: $45* ✉ *1909 India St., Little Italy* ☎ *619/202–4577* 🌐 *www.bornandraisedsteak.com.*

Café Gratitude

$ | **VEGETARIAN** | Food is served with a side of spiritual enlightenment at this plant-based eatery where friendly, Zen-ed out servers help you navigate the lengthy menu after offering the thoughtful question of the day. All menu items—including the potent wellness shots that can detoxify livers and boost immunity—are

San Diego's Bounty 👁

Sunny San Diego is one of the premier agricultural areas in the country. Visit a farmers' market and have a taste: spring is the season for cherimoyas and strawberries, summer brings peaches and boysenberries, autumn is the time for apples and pears, and winter is abundant with tangerines and grapefruit. There's a different market every day of the week, including the popular Little Italy market. Check the list of farmers' markets around the county at 🌐 *www.sdfarmbureau.org.*

named after positive affirmations. **Known for:** bowl entrées with rice or quinoa; wellness tonic drinks; desserts that taste equally delicious without any dairy. $ *Average main: $16 ⊠ 1980 Kettner Blvd., Little Italy* ☎ *619/736–5077* ⊕ *www.cafegratitude.com.*

Cloak and Petal

$$ | JAPANESE FUSION | More than simply a sushi restaurant, Cloak and Petal offers up "Japanese tapas," with a menu of small bites that range from fresh sashimi to wagyu beef lettuce cups. Even more stunning is the visual appeal, including a giant cherry blossom tree behind the bar. **Known for:** tiki drinks with Far East ingredients; unconventional sushi rolls; decor that's a feast for the eyes. $ *Average main: $21 ⊠ 1953 India St., Little Italy* ☎ *619/501–5505* ⊕ *www.cloakandpetal.com.*

★ The Crack Shack

$ | AMERICAN | FAMILY | Next to his successful fine dining restaurant, Juniper and Ivy, celebrity chef Richard Blais has opened this more casual eatery complete with a walk-up counter, picnic-style tables, a boccie court, and a giant rooster—a nod to the egg- and chicken-themed menu. Ingredients are sourced from high-quality vendors and used for sandwiches, of which the fried chicken varieties shine, as well as salads and sides like fluffy minibiscuits with a miso-maple butter and a Mexican spin on poutine. **Known for:** Señor Croque fried chicken sandwich with smoked pork belly; biscuits with miso-maple butter; all-outdoor seating with boccie court. $ *Average main: $12 ⊠ 2266 Kettner Blvd., Little Italy* ☎ *619/795–3299* ⊕ *www.crackshack.com.*

Craft & Commerce

$ | MODERN HAWAIIAN | The redesigned Little Italy restaurant-bar oozes slightly surreal cool. Crammed book shelves line the walls, banquettes and mirrors are scrawled with sayings, and taxidermy appears in odd settings like a lion

preying on a hog above the bar. **Known for:** wood-fired cuisine including grilled oysters and fire-roasted eggplant dip; refreshing craft cocktails infused with cucumber, grapefruit, or apple. $ *Average main: $15 ⊠ 675 W. Beech St., Little Italy* ☎ *619/269–2202* ⊕ *www.craft-commerce.com.*

★ Extraordinary Desserts

$ | CAFÉ | For Paris-perfect cakes and tarts embellished California-style with fresh flowers, head to this sleek, serene branch of Karen Krasne's pastry shop and café. The space with soaring ceilings hosts breakfasts, lunches, and light dinners, accompanied by a wide selection of teas, coffee, organic wines, and craft beers. **Known for:** blueberry coffee cake for breakfast; chocolate dulce de leche cake; house-made dips including onion dip and Parmesan pesto. $ *Average main: $14 ⊠ 1430 Union St., Little Italy* ☎ *619/294–7001* ⊕ *www.extraordinarydesserts.com.*

★ Herb & Wood

$$ | AMERICAN | Design lovers will fall for celebrity chef Brian Malarkey's sprawling restaurant, a former art store that has been refashioned into four luxe spaces in one—an entryway lounge, outdoor lounge, fireplace-dotted patio, and the main dining room, which is flanked by beaded chandeliers, lush banquettes, and paintings in rich jewel tones. The menu is heavy on wood-roasted dishes, many of which are apt for sharing like the roasted baby carrots or hiramasa with crispy quinoa. **Known for:** roasted baby carrots with cashew sesame dukkah; pillow-soft oxtail gnocchi; the secret menu Parker House rolls topped with Maldon sea salt. $ *Average main: $20 ⊠ 2210 Kettner Blvd., Little Italy* ☎ *619/955–8495* ⊕ *www.herbandwood.com* ☽ *No lunch.*

Ironside Fish & Oyster

$$ | SEAFOOD | Hundreds of piranhas cover one wall of this soaring, nautically themed dining room dedicated to fresh seafood in all its guises. At the raw bar with its refrigerated metal top, a half dozen or more varieties of oysters are available for slurping, along with drinks from the booklet-size cocktail menu. **Known for:** $1 oysters during weekday happy hour; extensive cocktail menu; fresh whole fish with simple sides is a bargain at less than $25. [$] *Average main: $24* ✉ *1654 India St., Little Italy* ☎ *619/269–3033* 🌐 *www.ironsidefishandoyster.com.*

Juniper and Ivy
$$$ | **MODERN AMERICAN** | Celebrity chef Richard Blais's addition to San Diego's restaurant scene fills an open-beamed space with seating for 250 and an open stainless-steel dream kitchen where diners can watch the chef and team in action. Blais sources local farm-fresh ingredients for his "left coast cookery" with a molecular gastronomy twist. **Known for:** California-Baja-inspired carne crudo asada topped with quail eggs; off-menu "In & Haute" burger; very shareable Yodel chocolate dessert. [$] *Average main: $35* ✉ *2228 Kettner Blvd., Little Italy* ☎ *619/269–9036* 🌐 *www.juniperandivy.com* 🕒 *No lunch.*

Little Italy Food Hall
$ | **FUSION** | **FAMILY** | A recently opened, chic update on the food court, Food Hall brings together a half-dozen different innovative food counters to offer quick bites vastly more interesting than mall fare. Among its offerings are the seafood-centric Single Fin Kitchen and Wicked Maine Lobster, and an update on a local delicacy, Not Not Tacos. **Known for:** fusion tacos; bustling crowds of Mercato shoppers; beer/wine cart dispensing refreshments in the outdoor seating area. [$] *Average main: $10* ✉ *550 W. Date St., Suite B, Little Italy* ☎ *619/269–7187* 🌐 *www.littleitalyfoodhall.com.*

★ Prep Kitchen Little Italy
$$ | **MODERN AMERICAN** | Urbanites craving a hip casual setting and gourmet menu pack architectural salvage-styled Prep Kitchen Little Italy, tucked upstairs above a busy corner in this thriving neighborhood. With first-date cocktails, after-work brews, or birthday champagne, diners relish familiar choices like meatball sandwiches, chops, and pork belly with kimchi Brussels. **Known for:** weekend brunch featuring popular chilaquiles dish; bacon-wrapped dates; $6 tapas during the daily happy hour. [$] *Average main: $23* ✉ *1660 India St., Little Italy* ☎ *619/398–8383* 🌐 *www.prepkitchenlittleitaly.com.*

Puerto La Boca
$$ | **ARGENTINE** | Located on the fringe of Little Italy's bustling restaurant scene, this intimate Argentine steak house is named for a Buenos Aires waterfront neighborhood home to generations of Italian immigrants. The dimly lighted spot may not be as trendy as other dining spots here, but it's still a romantic and comfortable destination for visitors and neighborhood regulars. **Known for:** tasty happy hour munchies; extensive wine list includes some delicious Malbecs from Mendoza; Argentinean-style steaks, including the signature skirt steak. [$] *Average main: $27* ✉ *2060 India St., Little Italy* ☎ *619/234–4900* 🌐 *www.puertolaboca.com.*

Hotels

Found Hotel
$ | **B&B/INN** | You'll find more amenities at other Downtown hotels but it's hard to beat this property's value and charm. **Pros:** good location; historic property; welcoming staff. **Cons:** some shared baths; no parking; not great for couples or families. [$] *Rooms from: $139* ✉ *505 W. Grape St., Little Italy* ☎ *619/230–1600, 800/518–9930* 🌐 *sandiego.foundhotels.com* 🛏 *23 rooms* 🍴 *Free Breakfast.*

Hilton Garden Inn/Homewood Suites
$$$ | **HOTEL** | **FAMILY** | Two brands from Hilton Hotels now share a building in Little Italy two blocks from the bay, giving guests more space to spread out and be relatively within budget. **Pros:**

modern guest rooms; plenty of tech conveniences; quiet neighborhood at night. **Cons:** on a busy block; valet parking only; limited amenities. $ *Rooms from: $235* ✉ *2137 Pacific Hwy., Little Italy* ☏ *619/696–7000 Homewood Suites, 619/696–6300 Hilton Garden Inn* ⊕ *www.sandiegohiltonhotels.com* ⌨ *364 rooms* ⦿ *Free Breakfast.*

Porto Vista Hotel
$ | **HOTEL** | This former budget motel has transformed into a contemporary hotel-motel with modern furnishings, a stylish restaurant and lounge, a fitness center, and even a hair salon. **Pros:** great location in Little Italy; complimentary airport shuttle; scenic views from restaurant. **Cons:** can be noisy; rooms need updating; limited amenities. $ *Rooms from: $160* ✉ *1835 Columbia St., Little Italy* ☏ *619/544–0164* ⊕ *www.portovistasd.com* ⌨ *191 rooms* ⦿ *No meals.*

🍸 Nightlife

Amid its arty galleries and boutiques, Little Italy houses several popular open-air beer bars.

BARS
★ False Idol
BARS/PUBS | A walk-in refrigerator harbors the secret entrance to this tiki-themed speakeasy, which is attached to Craft & Commerce. Beneath fishing nets full of puffer-fish lights and elaborate tiki-head wall carvings, the knowledgeable staff serves up creative takes on tropical classics with the best selection of rums in town. ■ TIP→ **The bar fills up quickly, especially on weekends. Make a reservation online a week or more in advance.** ✉ *675 W. Beech St., Little Italy* ⊕ *falseidoltiki.com.*

The Waterfront Bar & Grill
BARS/PUBS | It isn't really *on* the waterfront, but San Diego's oldest bar was once the hangout of Italian fishermen. Most of the collars are now white, and patrons enjoy an excellent selection of beers, along with chili, burgers, fish-and-chips, and other great-tasting grub, including fish tacos. Get here early, as there's almost always a crowd. ✉ *2044 Kettner Blvd., Little Italy* ☏ *619/232–9656* ⊕ *www.waterfrontbarandgrill.com.*

BREWPUBS
★ Ballast Point Brewing Co.
BREWPUBS/BEER GARDENS | Until recently, you had to head to the Miramar/Scripps Ranch area for a tasting at Ballast Point, but now there's a local taproom in Little Italy. The Sculpin IPA is outstanding. ✉ *2215 India St., Little Italy* ☏ *619/255–7213* ⊕ *www.ballastpoint.com.*

Karl Strauss' Brewing Company
BARS/PUBS | San Diego's first microbrewery now has multiple locations, but the original one remains a staple. This locale draws an after-work crowd for pints of Red Trolley Ale and later fills with beer connoisseurs from all walks of life to try Karl's latest concoctions. The German-inspired pub food is above average. ✉ *1157 Columbia St., Little Italy* ☏ *619/234–2739* ⊕ *www.karlstrauss.com.*

MUSIC CLUB
★ The Casbah
MUSIC CLUBS | This small club near the airport, the unofficial headquarters of the city's indie music scene, has a national reputation for showcasing up-and-coming acts of all genres. Nirvana, Smashing Pumpkins, and the White Stripes all played here on the way to stardom. ✉ *2501 Kettner Blvd., Middletown* ☏ *619/232–4355* ⊕ *www.casbahmusic.com.*

NIGHT BAY CRUISES
Flagship Cruises and Events
ENTERTAINMENT CRUISE | Flagship Cruises welcomes guests aboard with a glass of champagne as a prelude to nightly dinner-dance and holiday cruises. ✉ *990 N. Harbor Dr., Little Italy* ☏ *619/234–4111* ⊕ *www.flagshipsd.com.*

Hornblower Cruises

ENTERTAINMENT CRUISE | Take a dinner-dance cruise aboard the *Lord Hornblower*—the trip comes with fabulous views of the San Diego skyline. ⊠ *970 N. Harbor Dr., Little Italy ⊕ hornblower.com.*

🛍 Shopping

With more than 33,500 square feet of retail, Little Italy is the place to find contemporary art, modern furniture, and home accessories. It's also an especially fun place to visit during holiday celebrations and special events like ArtWalk in April and Taste of Little Italy in June. The weekly Saturday farmers' market is one of the city's best, and brings people from all over the county to the neighborhood (⊕ *www.sdweeklymarkets.com*). Many shops have a strong European ambience, and shoppers will find enticing wares that include colorful ceramics, hand-blown glassware, modern home accents, and designer shoes. Kettner Boulevard and India Street north of Grape Street are considered the North Little Italy Art and Design District.

CLOTHING AND ACCESSORIES

Azzurra Capri

CLOTHING | Walking into this white shop with blue trim will transport you instantly to Italy's stylish and sophisticated Amalfi Coast. Inspired by the island of Capri, this upscale boutique stocks swimsuits, resort wear, cashmere scarves, and handmade Italian leather sandals adorned with things like Swarovski crystals and turquoise. ⊠ *1840 Colombia St., Little Italy ☎ 619/230–5116 ⊕ azzurracapri.com.*

Vocabulary Boutique

CLOTHING | A local favorite for its friendly vibe and stylish inventory, this cozy boutique often stars in regional fashion shoots. It's known for unique, affordable outfits for women, men, and kids, as well as accessories, home decor, paper, and gift items. ⊠ *414 W. Cedar St., Little Italy*

☎ *619/203–4066 ⊕ www.vocabularyboutique.com.*

FOOD AND WINE

Bottlecraft Beer Shop

SPECIALTY STORES | This boutique beer shop and tasting room stocks the best craft beer from San Diego and around the world, from double IPAs and pale ales to saisons and wheat beers. Owner Brian Jensen offers a wealth of knowledge on the local craft beer scene. Bottlecraft now has additional locations in North Park and Liberty Station. ⊠ *2252 India St., Little Italy ☎ 619/487–9493 ⊕ bottlecraftbeer.com.*

HOME ACCESSORIES AND GIFTS

Architectural Salvage of San Diego

ANTIQUES/COLLECTIBLES | If you have any interest in home design and renovation, this shop that specializes in reusing old materials should be top of your list. The warehouse space is filled with unusual building and decorative materials, as well as items that come from various time periods throughout the 1900s. Products range from stained-glass windows and light fixtures to cabinets and doors in styles ranging from Victorian to Craftsman. ⊠ *2401 Kettner Blvd., Little Italy ☎ 619/696–1313 ⊕ www.architecturalsalvagesd.com.*

Blick Art Materials

BOOKS/STATIONERY | Besides supplying local artists with their tools, Blick also carries art books, fine stationery and pens, ornate gift wrap, and beautiful leather-bound journals. ⊠ *1844 India St., Little Italy ☎ 619/687–0050 ⊕ www. dickblick.com.*

Love & Aesthetics

HOUSEHOLD ITEMS/FURNITURE | Located inside one of the cozy yet stylish Fir Street Cottages, this boutique offers a variety of home goods that defy conservative decor aesthetics. From trendy Jonathan Adler furnishings to psychedelic pillows, plates, lamps, and even bespoke cannabis accessories (it's legal in California), this is not your run-of-the-mill housewares emporium. ⊠ *621 W. Fir St., Little Italy* ☎ *619/546–6143* ⊕ *www. loveandaesthetics.com.*

Vitreum
CERAMICS/GLASSWARE | The Japanese artist Takao owns this gallery-like shop that sells beautifully handcrafted home-decor items—tableware, glass vases, tea sets, and decorative gifts. ⊠ *619 W. Fir St., Little Italy* ☎ *619/237–9810* ⊕ *www. vitreum-us.com.*

SHOPPING CENTERS
The James Coffee Space
SHOPPING CENTERS/MALLS | This spacious warehouse building bears James Coffee's logo on the front and the intoxicating scent of its pour-over brews inside, but the building houses considerably more than just the local coffee roaster. Its tenants include James At Home, which sells coffee home-brewing accessories and equipment; Specs Optometry; papergoods vendor Card Shop SD; stylish men's apparel in ZB Savoy; and natural bath products at Apothebeauty. ⊠ *2355 India St., Little Italy* ☎ *619/756–7770* ⊕ *www.jamescoffeeco.com.*

Barrio Logan

San Diego's Mexican-American community is centered in Barrio Logan, under the San Diego–Coronado Bay Bridge on the downtown side. Chicano Park, spread along National Avenue from Dewey to Crosby streets, is the barrio's recreational hub. It's worth taking a short detour to see the huge murals of Mexican history painted on the bridge supports at National Avenue and Dewey Street; they're among the best examples of folk art in the city. Art enthusiasts will also enjoy the burgeoning gallery scene in the Barrio Logan neighborhood, rapidly becoming a hub for artists in San Diego.

GETTING HERE AND AROUND
Barrio Logan is located right off Interstate 5, at the Cesar E. Chavez Parkway exit. Driving is the easiest way to get there, especially coming from Downtown—in fact, it's only a mile from Petco Park, and easily accessible via Imperial and Logan avenues. However, the Blue Line trolley also stops in Barrio Logan, and several bus lines also cross through the neighborhood, including the 9, 6, 20, 705, and 923.

When staying downtown, Barrio Logan is also just a 15-minute walk, but with its somewhat isolated location under a bridge, visitors should exercise caution visiting the Chicano Park murals after dark.

◉ Sights
★ Chicano Park
PUBLIC ART | **FAMILY** | The cultural center of the Barrio Logan neighborhood, Chicano Park—designated a National Historic Landmark in 2017—was born in 1970 from the activism of local residents who occupied the space after the state rescinded its promise to designate the land a park. Signed into law a year later, the park is now a protected area that brings together families and locals for both public and private events, a welcoming gathering space as well as an outdoor gallery featuring large murals documenting Mexican-American history and Chicano activism. Every year Chicano Park Day is held on April 21, filling the park with the sights and sounds of music, dancers, vintage cars, and food and clothing vendors. ⊠ *Logan Ave. and Cesar Chavez Pkwy., Barrio Logan* ⊕ *chicano-park.com; www.chicanoparksandiego.com.*

🍴 Restaurants
Las Cuatros Milpas
$ | **MEXICAN** | One of the oldest restaurants in San Diego, having opened in 1933, Las Cuatros Milpas feels like a

closely held secret in Barrio Logan. Open daily until 3 pm, it almost inevitably attracts a big lunchtime rush, though the wait is worth it for the homemade tortillas, beans with chorizo, and rolled tacos. **Known for:** homemade tortillas; checkered picnic tables; chorizo con huevos. $ *Average main: $5* ⊠ *1857 Logan Ave., Barrio Logan* ☎ *619/234–4460* ⊘ *Closed Sun.* ⊟ *No credit cards.*

★ ¡Salud!

$ | **MEXICAN** | The line that inevitably wraps around the building is indicative of the quality of the tacos and the large selection of local craft beers on tap. Indeed, these are some of the best tacos in all of San Diego, ranging from the classic carne asada and Baja fish tacos to fried-shell beef tacos and Califas, which features french fries inside the tortilla. Just remember—alcohol isn't allowed at the outdoor tables. **Known for:** Baja-style street tacos; Pruno de Piña (beer and fermented pineapple); churros and ice cream. $ *Average main: $3* ⊠ *2196 Logan Ave., Barrio Logan* ☎ *619/255–3856* ⊕ *www.saludsd.com.*

ⓨ Nightlife

Border X Brewing

BREWPUBS/BEER GARDENS | Barrio Logan's first local craft brewery, Border X has a tap list full of brews inspired by Mexican recipes such as the Jamaica-like Blood Saison (with Hibiscus) and Abuelita's Chocolate Stout, featuring cocoa and cinnamon flavors. The taproom is lively most weekends, with sounds of cumbia music soundtracking the revelry. Border X also serves tacos, which always pair well with a refreshing lager. ⊠ *2181 Logan Ave., Barrio Logan* ☎ *619/501–0503* ⊕ *www. borderxbrewing.com.*

🎭 Performing Arts

Bread & Salt

ART GALLERIES—ARTS | The spacious factory setting that houses Bread & Salt feels like a modern art warehouse, though its name nods to its long history as a former Wonder Bread factory. Still adorned with much of the industrial machinery and exposed brick, Bread & Salt now houses rotating exhibits from local and national artists, as well as group events such as motorcycle shows and live music showcases. It's also a partner with the La Jolla Athenaeum, and puts on jazz concerts throughout the year. ⊠ *1955 Julian Ave., Barrio Logan* ☎ *858/454–5872* ⊕ *www. breadandsaltsandiego.com.*

Chapter 4

BALBOA PARK, BANKERS HILL, AND SAN DIEGO ZOO

Updated by
Claire Deeks Van Der Lee

⦿ Sights	🍴 Restaurants	🏨 Hotels	🛍 Shopping	🍸 Nightlife
★★★★★	★★★☆☆	★☆☆☆☆	★★★☆☆	★☆☆☆☆

NEIGHBORHOOD SNAPSHOT

GREAT EXPERIENCES

■ **San Diego Zoo:** San Diego's best-loved attraction, the world-renowned zoo, is set amid spectacular scenery in the heart of Balboa Park.

■ **Museums galore:** Automobiles and spacecraft, international folk art and baroque masters, dinosaur fossils and mummified humans—there is something for everyone at Balboa Park's many museums.

■ **The great outdoors:** Escape down a hiking trail, try your hand at a new sport, or just soak in the sunshine from your own stretch of grass. You may even forget you are in the middle of the city.

■ **Gorgeous gardens:** From the lush tropical feel of the Botanical Building to the refined design of the Rose Garden, Balboa Park's intricate gardens and landscaping are sure to delight.

■ **Free cultural events:** The park is full of freebies, from weekly concerts at the organ pavilion to annual events like Earth Day and December Nights.

GETTING AROUND

Although Balboa Park is massive, many of its star attractions are located quite close to each other. That said, exploring the park can lead to a lot of walking, particularly if you throw in a trip to the zoo or take on one of the many hiking trails. The park's free tram service stops at several spots around the park, and can give tired feet a welcome rest at the end of a long day.

QUICK BITES

Quick snacking opportunities abound throughout the park, from cafés tucked in among the museums and grounds, to hot dog, tamale, or ice-cream carts along the walkways and plazas. Good bets include the sushi, noodles, and, of course, tea at the **Tea Pavilion** outside the Japanese Friendship Garden; the flatbreads, smoothies and ice cream at **Craveology** adjacent to the Fleet Science Center, or the **Cafe in the Park,** an espresso bar serving salads, panini, and baked goods inside the Casa de Balboa.

GETTING HERE

■ Located just north of Downtown, Balboa Park is easily reached from both Interstate 5 and Highway 163. The most spectacular approach is from 6th Avenue over the Cabrillo Bridge. There are also several entrances off Park Boulevard.

■ Balboa Park is served by public buses, particularly the No. 3, 7, and 120 lines. Taxis can often be found inside the park near the visitor center and lined up outside the zoo.

VISITOR INFORMATION

■ **House of Hospitality.** The visitor center located here is an excellent resource for planning your visit to the park. Check the website before you go or spend a few minutes at the center when you arrive. They also offer a free mobile app with information on sites, special events, and useful tips to help maximize your time. ✉ 1549 El Prado, Balboa Park ☎ 619/239–0512 ⊕ www.balboapark.org.

Overlooking Downtown and the Pacific Ocean, 1,200-acre Balboa Park is the cultural heart of San Diego. This is where you'll find most of the city's museums, art galleries, the Tony Award–winning Old Globe Theatre, and the world-famous San Diego Zoo. Often referred to as the "Smithsonian of the West" for its concentration of museums, Balboa Park is also a series of botanical gardens, performance spaces, and outdoor playrooms endeared to the hearts of residents and visitors alike.

Thanks to the "Mother of Balboa Park," Kate Sessions, who suggested hiring a landscape architect in 1889, wild and cultivated gardens are an integral part of the park, featuring 350 species of trees. What Balboa Park would have looked like had she left it alone can be seen at Florida Canyon (between the main park and Morley Field, along Park Boulevard)—an arid landscape of sagebrush, cactus, and a few small trees.

In addition, the captivating architecture of Balboa's buildings, fountains, and courtyards gives the park an enchanted feel. Historic buildings dating from San Diego's 1915 Panama–California International Exposition are strung along the park's main east–west thoroughfare, El Prado, which leads from 6th Avenue eastward over the Cabrillo Bridge (formerly the Laurel Street Bridge), the park's official gateway. If you're a cinema fan, many of the buildings may be familiar—Orson Welles used exteriors of several Balboa Park buildings to represent the Xanadu estate of Charles Foster Kane in his 1941 classic, *Citizen Kane*. Prominent among them was the California Building, whose 200-foot tower, housing a 100-bell carillon that tolls the hour, is El Prado's tallest structure. Missing from the black-and-white film, however, was the magnificent blue of its tiled dome shining in the sun.

The parkland across the Cabrillo Bridge, at the west end of El Prado, is set aside for picnics and athletics. Cyclists and skaters zip along Balboa Drive, which leads to the highest spot in the park, Marston Point, overlooking Downtown. At the green beside the bridge, ladies and gents in all-white outfits meet on summer afternoons for lawn-bowling tournaments.

East of Plaza de Panama, El Prado becomes a pedestrian mall a nd ends at a footbridge that crosses over Park Boulevard, the park's main north–south thoroughfare, to the perfectly tended Rose Garden, which has more than 2,000 rosebushes. In the adjacent Desert Garden, trails wind around cacti and succulents from around the world. Palm Canyon, north of the Spreckels Organ Pavilion, has more than 50 varieties of palms along a shady bridge. Pepper Grove, along Park Boulevard south of the museums, has lots of picnic tables as well as play equipment.

Bankers Hill is a small neighborhood west of Balboa Park, with gorgeous views ranging from Balboa Park's greenery in the east to the San Diego Bay in the west. It's home to some of San Diego's long-standing restaurant destinations.

Balboa Park Planner

Best Times to Visit

San Diego's ideal climate and sophis-ticated horticultural planning make visiting Balboa Park a year-round delight. However, summer brings longer opening hours, additional concerts at the Spre-ckels Organ Pavilion, and the beloved Shakespeare Festival at the Old Globe's outdoor stage.

Open Hours

Most of the park's museums and attrac-tions are open from 10 or 11 am until 4 or 5 pm, with the zoo opening earlier. Some offer extended hours during the summer. Many of the park's museums are closed on Monday. Balboa Park is beautiful by night, with the buildings along El Prado gorgeously illuminated. The Prado restau-rant and the Old Globe Theatre keep this

portion of the park from feeling deserted after dark.

Planning Your Time

It's impossible to cover all of Balboa Park's museums and attractions in one day, so choose your focus before you head out. If you plan on visiting the San Diego Zoo, expect to spend at least half the day there, leaving no more than a couple of hours to explore Balboa's other attractions afterward. *See the highlighted listing for more information about the San Diego Zoo.* Otherwise, check out these itineraries.

Two Hours: To help maximize your time, rent one of the audio headsets that guide you on a 60-minute tour of the park's history, architecture, and horticulture. Pick a garden of interest to explore or drop down into Palm Canyon. Spend the remainder of your time relaxing in front of the Botanical Building or around the Bea Evenson Fountain.

Half Day: Spend a little more time at the sights above, then select a museum to explore. Alternatively, take a stroll through the Japanese Friendship Garden. Afterward, you might have time for a quick ride on the carousel or a browse around the studios of the Spanish Village Art Center. Cap things off with lunch at Panama 66 in the Sculpture Garden.

Full Day: Consider purchasing a one-day discount pass from the visitor center if you want to tackle several museums. Depending on when you visit, enjoy a free concert at the Spreckels Organ Pavilion, a cultural dance at the House of Pacific Relations International Cottages, or join a guided walking tour. Active types can hit one of the more intensive hiking trails, while others can rest their feet at an IMAX or 3-D movie in the Fleet Center or Natural History Museum, respective-ly. In the evening, dine at the beautiful

Prado restaurant or catch a show at the Old Globe Theatre.

What's Free When

Many freebies can be found in Balboa Park, both on a weekly basis and at special times of the year. Free **Ranger Tours** depart from the visitor center Tuesday and Sunday at 11 am providing an overview of the history, architecture, and horticulture of the park. On Saturday at 10 am, volunteers offer a rotating selection of thematic **Offshoot Tours,** also free of charge and departing from the visitor center. If you prefer to explore on your own, head to the visitor center to pick up a free garden tour map.

The free concerts at the **Spreckels Organ Pavilion** take place Sunday afternoon at 2 pm year-round and on Monday evening in summer. Also at the Speckels Organ Pavilion, the **Twilight in the Park Summer Concert Series** offers various performances Tuesday, Wednesday, and Thursday from 6:30 to 7:30.

The **Timken Museum of Art, Museum of Photographic Arts,** and **San Diego History Center** offer free admission (a donation is suggested), or pay-what-you-wish admission pricing. Admission to the **House of Pacific Relations International Cottages** is also free, although they are only open on Sunday. You can explore the studios at the **Spanish Village Art Center** at no charge, although you just might be tempted to purchase a unique souvenir.

A fantastic deal for residents of San Diego County and active-duty military and their families is **Free Tuesdays in the Park,** a rotating schedule of free admission to most of Balboa Park's museums.

The **San Diego Zoo** is free for kids under 12 the whole month of October.

The **December Nights** festival on the first Friday and Saturday of that month includes free admission (and later hours)

to most of the Balboa Park museums. The outdoor events during the festival make it something not to miss.

Discount: Explorer Pass

The visitor center offers a selection of Balboa Park Explorer passes that are worth considering if you plan on visiting several museums. The Explorer ($59 adult, $32 children ages 3–12) offers one-time admission to 16 museums and attractions over the course of seven days. If you are also planning on visiting the zoo, the Zoo/Passport Combo might be a good choice ($101 adult, $66 child). A single-day pass includes entry to your choice of 5 out of the 16 options ($48 adult, $29 child).

Tips

Hop aboard the free trams that run every 10 to 20 minutes, 9 am to 6 pm daily, with extended summer hours.

Wear comfortable shoes—you'll end up walking more than you might expect. Bring a sweater or light jacket for the evening drop in temperature.

Don't be afraid to wander off the main drag. Discovering a hidden space of your own is one of the highlights of a trip to Balboa.

Balboa Park is a good bet for the odd rainy day—the museums are nice and dry, and many of the park's buildings are connected by covered walkways.

Make reservations for the Prado restaurant; it's popular with both visitors and locals alike.

If you aren't receiving a discount at one of the museums where San Diego residents get in for free on Tuesday, consider avoiding them on Tuesday, as they can become overcrowded.

Don't overlook the 6th Avenue side of the park, between the Marston House and the Cabrillo Bridge. There are several pathways and open fields that make for a quiet escape.

Parking

Parking within Balboa Park, including at the zoo, is free. From the Cabrillo Bridge, the first parking area you come to is off El Prado to the right. Don't despair if there are no spaces here; you'll see more lots as you continue along toward Pan American Plaza. Alternatively, you can park at Inspiration Point on the east side of the park, off Presidents Way. Free trams run from Inspiration Point to the visitor center and museums. Valet parking is available outside the House of Hospitality on weekends.

Balboa Park and the San Diego Zoo

BALBOA PARK WALK

Although Balboa Park as a whole is huge, many of its top attractions are located within reasonable walking distance. A straight shot across the **Cabrillo Bridge,** through the **Plaza de Panama,** and on to the **Bea Evenson Fountain** will take you past several of the park's architectural gems, including the **House of Hospitality.** Many of the park's museums are housed in the buildings lining the way. This route also encompasses the **Alcazar Garden** and **Botanical Building.** From the fountain, a quick jaunt across the pedestrian footbridge leads you into the **Desert Garden** and the **Inez Grant Parker Memorial Rose Garden.** Back at the fountain, your walking tour can continue by heading north toward the **San Diego Zoo.** This will take you past the **Spanish Village Art Center, Carousel,** and **Miniature Railroad.** Alternatively, double back to the Plaza de Panama and head south toward the **Spreckels**

Organ Pavilion. Continuing on from here, a loop will take you past **Palm Canyon,** the **International Cottages,** the **Marie Hitchcock Puppet Theater,** several more museums, and the **Japanese Friendship Garden.**

While the aforementioned routes provide a broad overview, there are several walking opportunities for those seeking more focused explorations of the park. Those wishing to experience the numerous gardens in depth will appreciate the excellent "Gardens of Balboa Park Self-Guided Walk," available free of charge at the visitor center. History and architecture buffs might consider buying a self-guided walking tour pamphlet from the visitor center, or taking the briefer audio tour. Opportunities for hiking abound, from a brief journey through **Palm Canyon** to more strenuous hikes through **Florida Canyon** or on the **Old Bridle Trail.** Stop in the visitor center for maps and guidance before setting out.

◉ Sights

Alcazar Garden

GARDEN | You may feel like royalty here as you rest on the benches by the exquisitely tiled fountains—the garden's highlight—and it's no wonder: the garden's landscaping was inspired by the gardens surrounding the Alcazar Castle in Seville,

Spain. The garden is open year-round, allowing for a seasonally shifting color palette. The flower beds, for example, are ever-changing horticultural exhibits featuring more than 7,000 annuals for a nearly perpetual bloom. ⊠ *1439 El Prado, Balboa Park* ⊕ *www.balboapark.org.*

★ Balboa Park Carousel

CAROUSEL | FAMILY | Suspended an arm's length away on this antique merry-go-round is the brass ring that could earn you an extra free ride (it's one of the few carousels in the world that continue this bonus tradition). Hand-carved in 1910, the carousel features colorful murals, big-band music, and bobbing animals including zebras, giraffes, and dragons; real horsehair was used for the tails. ⊠ *1889 Zoo Pl., behind zoo parking lot, Balboa Park* ☎ *619/239–0512* ⊕ *www.balboapark.org* ⊠ *$3* ⊘ *Closed weekdays Labor Day–mid-June.*

Balboa Park Miniature Railroad

TRANSPORTATION SITE (AIRPORT/BUS/FERRY/TRAIN) | FAMILY | Adjacent to the zoo parking lot and across from the carousel, a pint-size 48-passenger train runs a ½-mile loop through four tree-filled acres of the park. The engine of this rare 1948 model train is one of only 50 left in the world. ⊠ *2885 Zoo Pl., Balboa Park* ☎ *619/239–0512* ⊠ *$3* ⊘ *Closed weekdays Sept.–May, except during school holidays.*

Bea Evenson Fountain

FOUNTAIN | A favorite of barefoot children, this fountain shoots cool jets of water upwards of 50 feet. Built in 1972 between the Fleet Center and Natural History Museum, the fountain offers plenty of room to sit and watch the crowds go by. ⊠ *Balboa Park* ✛ *East end of El Prado* ⊕ *www.balboapark.org.*

★ Botanical Building

GARDEN | The graceful redwood-lath structure, built for the 1915 Panama–California International Exposition, now houses more than 2,000 types of tropical and subtropical plants plus changing seasonal flower displays. Ceiling-high tree ferns shade fragile orchids and feathery bamboo. There are benches beside miniature waterfalls for resting in the shade. The rectangular pond outside, filled with lotuses and water lilies that bloom in spring and fall, is popular with photographers. ⊠ *1549 El Prado, Balboa Park* ☎ *619/239–0512* ⊕ *www.balboapark.org* ⊠ *Free* ⊘ *Closed Thurs.*

Cabrillo Bridge

BRIDGE/TUNNEL | The official gateway into Balboa Park soars 120 feet above a canyon floor. Pedestrian-friendly, the 1,500-foot bridge provides inspiring views of the California Tower and El Prado beyond. ■TIP➔ **This is a great spot for photo-capturing a classic image of the park.** ⊠ *Balboa Park* ✛ *On El Prado, at 6th Ave. park entrance* ⊕ *www.balboapark.org.*

Fleet Science Center

MUSEUM | FAMILY | Interactive exhibits here are artfully educational and for all ages: older kids can get hands-on with inventive projects in Studio X, while the five-and-under set can be easily entertained with interactive play stations like the Ball Wall and Fire Truck in the center's Kid City. The IMAX Dome Theater, which screens exhilarating nature and science films, was the world's first, as was the Fleet's "NanoSeam" (seamless) dome ceiling that doubles as a planetarium. ⊠ *1875 El Prado, Balboa Park* ☎ *619/238–1233* ⊕ *www.rhfleet.org* ⊠ *The Fleet experience includes gallery exhibits and 1 IMAX film $21.95; additional cost for special exhibits or add-on 2nd IMAX film or planetarium show.*

House of Pacific Relations

ARTS VENUE | This is not really a house but a cluster of red tile–roof stucco cottages representing 34 foreign countries. The word "pacific" refers to the goal of maintaining peace. The cottages, decorated with crafts and pictures, are open weekend afternoons, when you can chat with transplanted natives and try out different ethnic foods. Folk-song

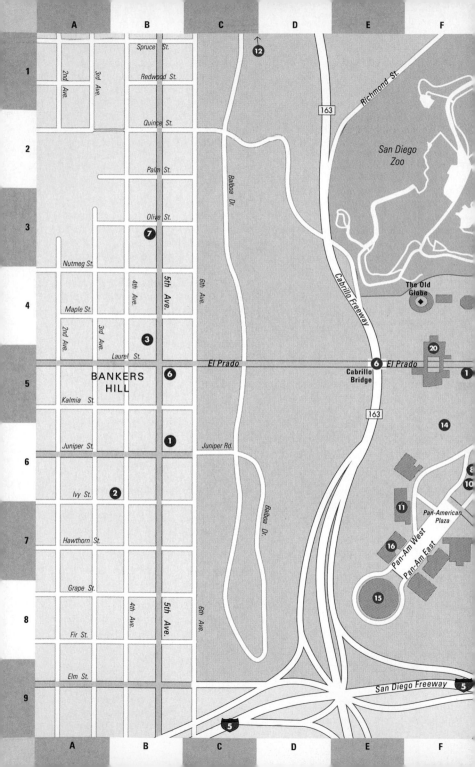

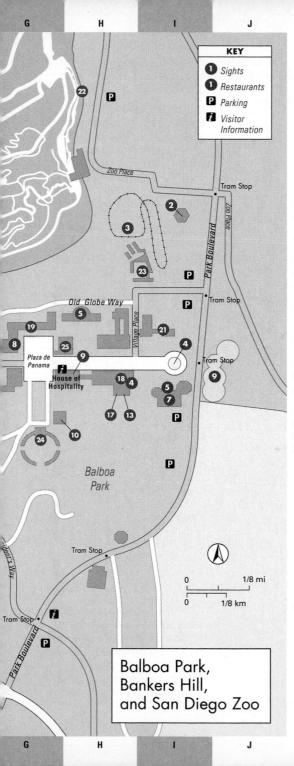

4

Balboa Park, Bankers Hill, and San Diego Zoo

BALBOA PARK AND THE SAN DIEGO ZOO

KEY

- **1** Sights
- **1** Restaurants
- **P** Parking
- **i** Visitor Information

and dance performances are presented on the outdoor stage around 2 pm most Sundays—check the schedule at the park visitor center. Across the road from the cottages, but not affiliated with them, is the Spanish colonial–style **United Nations Building.** Inside, the United Nations Association's International Gift Shop, open daily, has reasonably priced crafts, cards, and books. ⊠ *2191 Pan American Pl., Balboa Park* ☎ *619/234–0739* ⊕ *www. sdhpr.org* ✉ *Free, donations accepted* ⊗ *Closed weekdays.*

★ Inez Grant Parker Memorial Rose Garden and Desert Garden

GARDEN | These neighboring gardens sit just across the Park Boulevard pedestrian bridge and offer gorgeous views over Florida Canyon. The formal rose garden contains 1,600 roses representing nearly 130 varieties; peak bloom is usually in April and May. The adjacent Desert Garden provides a striking contrast, with 2.5 acres of succulents and desert plants seeming to blend into the landscape of the canyon below. ⊠ *2525 Park Blvd., Balboa Park* ⊕ *www.balboapark.org.*

Japanese Friendship Garden

GARDEN | A koi pond with a cascading waterfall, a cherry tree grove, and the serene Inamori tea pavilion are highlights of the park's authentic Japanese garden, designed to inspire contemplation and evoke tranquility. You can wander the various peaceful paths spread over 12 acres, and meditate in the traditional stone and Zen garden. ⊠ *2215 Pan American Rd., Balboa Park* ☎ *619/232–2721* ⊕ *www. niwa.org* ✉ *$12, special exhibits are an additional $4–$5.*

Marie Hitchcock Puppet Theater

ARTS VENUE | FAMILY | Performances incorporate marionettes, hand puppets, rod puppets, shadow puppets, and ventriloquism, while the stories range from traditional fairy tales to folk legends and contemporary puppet plays. Kids stare wide-eyed at the short, energy-filled productions. ⊠ *2130 Pan American Pl.,*

Balboa Park ☎ *619/544–9203* ⊕ *www. balboaparkpuppets.com* ✉ *$5* ⊗ *Closed Mon. and Tues.*

Marston House Museum & Gardens

GARDEN | George W. Marston (1850–1946), a San Diego pioneer and philanthropist who financed the architectural landscaping of Balboa Park—among his myriad other San Diego civic projects—lived in this 16-room home at the northwest edge of the park. Designed in 1905 by San Diego architects Irving Gill and William Hebbard, it's a classic example of the American Arts and Crafts style, which emphasizes simplicity and functionality of form. On the 5-acre grounds is a lovely English Romantic garden, as interpreted in California. The house may only be visited by guided tour. ■TIP→ **Call for information about specialty tours of the gardens, historic 7th Ave., and the Bankers Hill neighborhood.** ⊠ *3525 7th Ave., Balboa Park* ☎ *619/298–3142* ⊕ *www.marstonhouse.org* ✉ *$15* ⊗ *Closed Mon.–Thurs.* ☞ *Tours offered every ½ hour and last 40–45 min; last tour is 4 pm.*

Museum of Photographic Arts

MUSEUM | World-renowned photographers such as Ansel Adams, Imogen Cunningham, Henri Cartier-Bresson, and Edward Weston are represented in this museum's permanent collection, which includes everything from 19th-century daguerreotypes to contemporary photojournalism prints. In addition to selections from its own collection, the museum hosts excellent traveling exhibits. Photos rotate frequently, so call ahead if you're interested in something specific to find out if it is currently on display. ■TIP→ **MOPA is also known for its film screenings. Check the website for upcoming showings.** ⊠ *Casa de Balboa, 1649 El Prado, Balboa Park* ☎ *619/238–7559* ⊕ *www.mopa.org* ✉ *Pay what you wish pricing* ⊗ *Closed Mon.*

Balboa Park is home to gardens and the Spreckels Organ Pavilion, which hosts free concerts every Sunday at 2 pm.

Palm Canyon

CANYON | Enjoy an instant escape from the buildings and concrete of urban life in this Balboa Park oasis. Lush and tropical, with hundreds of palm trees, the 2-acre canyon has a shaded path perfect for those who love walking through nature. ✉ *1549 El Prado, south of House of Charm, Balboa Park.*

★ San Diego Air & Space Museum

MUSEUM | **FAMILY** | By day, the streamlined edifice looks like any other structure in the park; at night, outlined in blue neon, the round building appears—appropriately enough—to be a landed UFO. Every available inch of space in the rotunda is filled with exhibits about aviation and aerospace pioneers, including examples of enemy planes from the world wars. In all, there are more than 60 full-size aircraft on the floor and hanging from the rafters. In addition to exhibits from the dawn of flight to the jet age, the museum displays a growing number of space-age exhibits, including the actual *Apollo 9* command module. To test your own skills, you can ride in a two-seat Max Flight simulator or try out the Talon Racing simulator. Movies in the 3-D/4-D theater are included with admission. ✉ *2001 Pan American Pl., Balboa Park* ☎ *619/234–8291* ⊕ *www.sandiegoairandspace.org* ✉ *Museum $19.95 (more for special exhibitions); Flight Simulators $5–$8 extra; restoration tour $5 extra and subject to availability.*

San Diego Automotive Museum

MUSEUM | Even if you don't know a choke from a chassis, you're bound to admire the sleek designs of the autos in this impressive museum. On rotating display are gems from the museum's core collection of vintage motorcycles and cars—ranging from a pair of Steve McQueen's dirt bikes and an extremely rare Bizzarrini (only three were ever made), to a 1981 silver Delorean (remember the time machine in *Back to the Future*?)—as well as a series of visiting special exhibits. Be sure to see the *Fabulous Car of Louis Mattar,* which was ingeniously kitted out to set the cross-country endurance record in 1952 (6,320 miles nonstop from

Balboa's Best Bets

With so much on offer, Balboa Park truly has something for everyone. Here are some best bets based on area of interest.

Architecture Buffs
Bea Evenson Fountain
Cabrillo Bridge
House of Hospitality

Arts Aficionados
Museum of Photographic Arts
San Diego Museum of Art
Spanish Village Art Center
Spreckels Organ Pavilion
Timken Museum of Art

Cultural Explorers
House of Pacific Relations

History Junkies
San Diego History Center
San Diego Museum of Man

Kids of All Ages
Balboa ParkCarousel
Marie Hitchcock Puppet Theater
Balboa Park Miniature Railroad
San Diego Model Railroad Museum
San Diego Zoo

Nature Lovers
Alcazar Garden
Botanical Building
Inez Grant Parker Memorial Rose Garden
Japanese Friendship Garden
Palm Canyon

Science and Technology Geeks
Fleet Science Center
San Diego Air & Space Museum
San Diego Automotive Museum

San Diego to New York City and back, refueling from a moving gas truck); a video display shows highlights such as Mattar and his codrivers changing the tire while in motion and pouring a glass of water from the onboard tap. There's also an ongoing automobile restoration program and an extensive automotive research library. ⊠ *2080 Pan American Plaza, Balboa Park* ☎ *619/231–2886* ⊕ *www.sdautomuseum.org* ✉ *$10.*

San Diego History Center
MUSEUM | The San Diego Historical Society maintains its research library in the basement of the Casa de Balboa and organizes shows on the first floor. Permanent and rotating exhibits, which are often more lively than you might expect, survey local urban history after 1850, when California entered the Union. A 100-seat theater hosts public lectures, workshops, and educational programs, and a gift shop carries a good selection of books on local history as well as reproductions of old posters and other historical collectibles. ⊠ *Casa de Balboa, 1649 El Prado, Balboa Park* ☎ *619/232–6203* ⊕ *www.sandiegohistory.org* ✉ *Free (donations encouraged).*

San Diego Model Railroad Museum
MUSEUM | FAMILY | When the exhibits at this 27,000-square-foot museum are in operation, you can hear the sounds of chugging engines, screeching brakes, and shrill whistles. Local model railroad clubs built and maintain the four main displays, which represent California railroads in "miniature," with the track

laid on scale models of San Diego County terrain. Out back, the Centennial Railway Garden features replicas of the streetcars and scenes of Balboa Park during the 1915 Exposition. The Toy Train Gallery has an interactive Lionel exhibit and whimsical vignettes. ⊠ *Casa de Balboa, 1649 El Prado, Balboa Park* ☎ *619/696–0199* ⊕ *www.sdmrm.org* 🎟 *$11.50* 🕙 *Closed Mon.*

★ San Diego Museum of Art

MUSEUM | Known for its Spanish baroque and Renaissance paintings, including works by El Greco, Goya, Rubens, and van Ruisdael, San Diego's most comprehensive art museum also has strong holdings of South Asian art, Indian miniatures, and contemporary California paintings. The museum's exhibits tend to have broad appeal, and if traveling shows from other cities come to town, you can expect to see them here. Free docent tours are offered throughout the day. An outdoor Sculpture Court and Garden exhibits both traditional and modern pieces. Enjoy the view over a craft beer and some locally sourced food in the adjacent Panama 66 courtyard restaurant. ■**TIP**➜ **The museum hosts "Art After Hours" most Friday nights, with discounted admission 5–8 pm.** ⊠ *1450 El Prado, Balboa Park* ☎ *619/232–7931* ⊕ *www.sdmart.org* 🎟 *$15; $5 Fri. 5–8 pm; sculpture garden free* 🕙 *Closed Wed.*

★ San Diego Museum of Man

MUSEUM | **FAMILY** | If the facade of this building—the landmark California Building—looks familiar, it's because filmmaker Orson Welles used it and its dramatic tower as the principal features of the Xanadu estate in his 1941 classic, *Citizen Kane*. Closed for 80 years, the tower was recently reopened for public tours. An additional timed ticket and a climb up 125 steps is required, but the effort will be rewarded with spectacular 360-degree views of the coast, Downtown, and the inland mountains. Back

History Revealed 👁

While demurely posing as a butterfly garden today, the Zoro Garden has a racy history—tucked between the Casa de Balboa and the Fleet Center, this area showcased a nudist colony during the 1935–36 Exposition.

inside, exhibits at this highly respected anthropological museum focus on Southwestern, Mexican, and South American cultures. Carved monuments from the Mayan city of Quirigua in Guatemala, cast from the originals in 1914, are particularly impressive. Exhibits might include examples of intricate beadwork from across the Americas, the history of Egyptian mummies, or the lifestyles of the Kumeyaay peoples, Native Americans who live in the San Diego area. ⊠ *California Bldg., 1350 El Prado, Balboa Park* ☎ *619/239–2001* ⊕ *www.museumofman. org* 🎟 *$13; special exhibits extra; Tower tickets (including museum admission) $23* 🤙 *Tower tours are timed-entry and can be booked in advance through website or on arrival at museum.*

San Diego Natural History Museum

MUSEUM | **FAMILY** | There are 7½ million fossils, dinosaur models, and even live reptiles and other specimens under this roof. Favorite exhibits include the Foucault Pendulum, suspended on a 43-foot cable and designed to demonstrate the Earth's rotation, and *Ocean Oasis*, the world's first large-format film about Baja California and the Sea of Cortés. Permanent exhibits highlight citizen scientists and the regional environment, and traveling exhibits also make a stop here. Included in admission are 3-D films shown at the museum's giant-screen theater. ■TIP→ **Check the website for information about films, lectures, and free guided nature walks.** ✉ *1788 El Prado, Balboa Park* ☎ *619/232–3821* ⊕ *www.sdnhm.org* 💲 *$19.95; extra for special exhibits.*

★ San Diego Zoo

ZOO | **FAMILY** | Balboa Park's—and perhaps the city's—most famous attraction is its 100-acre zoo. Nearly 4,000 animals of some 800 diverse species roam in hospitable, expertly crafted habitats that replicate natural environments as closely as possible. The flora in the zoo, including many rare species, is even more dear than the fauna. Walkways wind over bridges and past waterfalls ringed with tropical ferns; elephants in a sandy plateau roam so close you're tempted to pet them.

Exploring the zoo fully requires the stamina of a healthy hiker, but open-air double-decker buses that run throughout the day let you zip through three-quarters of the exhibits on a guided 35- to 40-minute, 3-mile tour. There are also express buses, used for quick transportation, that make five stops around the grounds and include some narration. The Skyfari Aerial Tram, which soars 170 feet above the ground, gives a good overview of the zoo's layout and, on clear days, a panorama of the park, downtown San Diego, the bay, and the ocean, far beyond the San Diego–Coronado Bridge. ■TIP→ **Unless you come early, expect to wait for the regular bus, and especially for the top tier—the line can take more than 45 minutes; if you come at midday on a weekend or school holiday, you'll be doing the in-line shuffle for a while.**

Don't forget the San Diego Safari Park, the zoo's 1,800-acre extension to the north at Escondido. ✉ *2920 Zoo Dr., Balboa Park* ☎ *619/234–3153,* ⊕ *www.sandiegozoo.org* 💲 *$54 adult, $44 children ages 3–11 (includes Skyfari and bus tour).*

★ Spanish Village Art Center

MUSEUM | More than 200 local artists, including glassblowers, enamel workers, wood carvers, sculptors, painters, jewelers, and photographers work and give demonstrations of their craft on a rotating basis in these red tile–roof studio-galleries that were set up for the 1935–36 exposition in the style of an old Spanish village. The center is a great source for memorable gifts. ✉ *1770 Village Pl., Balboa Park* ☎ *619/233–9050* ⊕ *www.spanishvillageart.com* 💲 *Free.*

★ Spreckels Organ Pavilion

ARTS VENUE | The 2,400-bench-seat pavilion, dedicated in 1915 by sugar magnates John D. and Adolph B. Spreckels, holds the 4,518-pipe Spreckels Organ, the largest outdoor pipe organ in the world. You can hear this impressive instrument at one of the year-round, free, 2 pm Sunday concerts, regularly performed by the city's civic organist Raúl Prieto Ramírez and guest artists—a highlight of a visit to Balboa Park. On Monday evenings from late June to mid-August, internationally renowned organists play evening concerts. At Christmastime the park's Christmas tree and life-size Nativity display turn the pavilion into a seasonal wonderland. ✉ *2211 Pan American Rd., Balboa Park* ☎ *619/702–8138* ⊕ *spreckelsorgan.org.*

Timken Museum of Art

MUSEUM | Though somewhat out of place architecturally, this small and modern structure, made of travertine imported from Italy, is a jewel box. The museum houses works by major European and American artists as well as a superb collection of Russian icons. ✉ *1500 El Prado, Balboa Park* ☎ *619/239–5548* ⊕ *www.timkenmuseum.org* 💲 *Free, donations encouraged* ☉ *Closed Mon.*

Continued on page 102

Polar bear, San Diego Zoo

LIONS AND TIGERS AND BEARS:
The World-Famous San Diego Zoo

From diving polar bears and 6-ton elephants to swinging great apes, San Diego's most famous attraction has it all. Nearly 4,000 animals representing 800 species roam the 100-acre zoo in expertly crafted habitats that replicate the animals' natural environments. The pandas may have gone home (in 2019), but there are plenty of other cool creatures to see here, from teeny-tiny mantella frogs to two-story-tall giraffes. But it's not all just fun and games. Known for its exemplary conservation programs, the zoo educates visitors on how to go green and explains its efforts to protect endangered species.

SAN DIEGO ZOO TOP ATTRACTIONS

Underwater viewing area at the Hippo Trail

❶ Children's Zoo (Discovery Outpost). Goats and sheep beg to be petted, and there is a viewer-friendly nursery where you may see baby animals bottle-feed and sleep peacefully in large cribs.

❷ Monkey Trails and Forest Tales (Lost Forest). Follow an elevated trail at treetop level and trek through the forest floor observing African mandrill monkeys, Asia's clouded leopard, the rare pygmy hippopotamus, and Visayan warty pigs.

❸ Orangutan and Siamang Exhibit (Lost Forest). Orangutans and siamangs climb and swing in this lush, tropical environment lined with 110-foot-long and 12-foot-high viewing windows.

4 Scripps, Parker, and Owens Aviaries (Lost Forest). Wandering paths climb through the enclosed aviaries where brightly colored tropical birds swoop between branches inches from your face.

5 Tiger Trail (Lost Forest). The mist-shrouded trails of this simulated rainforest wind down a canyon. Tigers, Malayan tapirs, and Argus pheasants wander among the exotic trees and plants.

6 Hippo Trail (Lost Forest). Glimpse huge but surprisingly graceful hippos frolicking in the water through an underwater viewing window and buffalo cavorting with monkeys on dry land.

7 Gorilla Exhibit (Lost Forest). The gorillas live in one of the zoo's bioclimatic zone exhibits modeled on their native habitat with waterfalls, climbing areas, and an open meadow. The sounds of the tropical rain forest emerge from a 144-speaker sound system that plays CDs recorded in Africa.

8 Africa Rocks. This massive exhibit consists of six different rocky habitats designed to showcase the diversity of topography and species on the African continent. Penguins, meerkats, and a band of baboons are just a few of the animals that call this ambitious exhibit home.

Lories at Owen's Aviary

9 Sun Bear Forest (Asian Passage). Playful beasts claw apart the trees and shrubs that serve as a natural playground for climbing, jump¬ing, and general merrymaking.

10 Polar Bear Plunge (Polar Rim). Watch polar bears take a chilly dive from the underwater viewing room. There are also Siberian reindeer, white foxes, and other Arctic creatures here. Kids can learn about the Arctic and climate change through interactive exhibits.

11 Elephant Odyssey. Get a glimpse of the animals that roamed Southern California 12,000 years ago and meet their living counterparts. The 7.5-acre, multispecies habitat features elephants, California condors, jaguars, and more.

12 Koala Exhibit (Outback). The San Diego Zoo houses the largest number of koalas outside Australia. Walk through the exhibit for photo ops of these marsupials from Down-Under curled up on their perches or dining on eucalyptus branches.

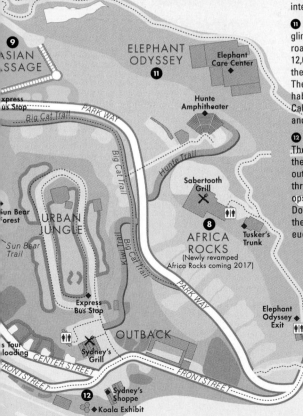

MUST-SEE ANIMALS

❶ GORILLA

This troop of primates engages visitors with their human-like expressions and behavior. The youngsters are sure to delight, especially when hitching a ride on mom's back. Up-close encounters might involve the gorillas using the glass partition as a backrest while peeling cabbage. By dusk the gorillas head inside to their sleeping quarters, so don't save this for your last stop.

❷ ELEPHANT

Asian and African elephants coexist at the San Diego Zoo. The larger African elephant is distinguished by its big flapping ears—shaped like the continent of Africa—which it uses to keep cool. An elephant's trunk has over 40,000 muscles in it—that's more than humans have in their whole body.

❸ ORANGUTAN

Bornean and Sumatran orangutans have been entertaining San Diego visitors since 1928. The exhibit has rope climbing structures, a man-made "termite mound" that's often filled with treats, rocky caves, and tall "sway poles" that allow the orangutans to swing like they would in trees. Don't be surprised if the orangutans come right up to the glass to observe the humans observing them!

❹ KOALA

While this collection of critters is one of the cutest in the zoo, don't expect a lot of activity from the koala habitat. These guys spend most of their day curled up asleep in the branches of the eucalyptus tree—they can sleep up to 20 hours a day. Although eucalyptus leaves are poisonous to most animals, bacteria in koalas' stomachs allow them to break down the toxins.

❺ POLAR BEAR

The trio of polar bears is one of the San Diego Zoo's star attractions, and their brand-new exhibit gets you up close and personal. Visitors sometimes worry about polar bears living in the warm San Diego climate, but there is no cause for concern. The San Diego-based bears eat a lean diet, thus reducing their layer of blubber and helping them keep cool.

Did You Know?

Red pandas aren't actually pandas, but more like skunks or raccoons in your backyard. With the giant pandas gone from the San Diego Zoo though, the red pandas are an adorable alternative.

PLANNING YOUR DAY AT THE ZOO

Left: Main entrance of the San Diego Zoo. Right: Sunbear

PLANNING YOUR TIME

Plan to devote at least a half-day to exploring the zoo, but with so much to see it is easy to stay a full day or more.

If you're on a tight schedule, opt for the guided **35 minute bus tour** that lets you zip through three-quarters of the exhibits. However, lines to board the busses can be long, and you won't get as close to the animals.

Another option is to take the **Skyfari Aerial Tram** to the far end of the park, choose a route, and meander back to the entrance. The Skyfari trip gives a

good overview of the zoo's layout and a spectacular view.

The **Elephant Odyssey**, while accessible from two sides of the park, is best entered from just below the Polar Rim. The extremely popular **Panda exhibit** can develop long lines, so get there early.

The zoo offers several entertaining **live shows** daily. Check the website or the back of the map handed out at the zoo entrance for the day's offerings and showtimes.

BEFORE YOU GO

■ To avoid ticket lines, purchase and print tickets online using the zoo's Web site.

■ To avoid excessive backtracking or a potential meltdown, plan your route along the zoo map before setting out. Try not to get too frustrated if you lose your way, as there are exciting exhibits around every turn and many paths intersect at several points.

■ The zoo offers a variety of program extras, including behind-the-scenes tours, backstage pass animal encounters, and sleepover events. Call in advance for pricing and reservations.

AT THE ZOO

■ Don't forget to explore at least some of the exhibits on foot—a favorite is the lush Tiger Trail.

■ If you visit on the weekend, find out when the Giraffe Experience is taking place. You can purchase leaf–eater biscuits to hand feed the giraffes!

■ Splurge a little at the gift shop: your purchases help support zoo programs.

■ The zoo rents strollers, wheelchairs, and lockers; it also has a first-aid office, a lost and found, and an ATM.

Fern Canyon, San Diego Zoo

GETTING HERE AND AROUND

The zoo is easy to get to, whether by bus or car.

Bus Travel: Take Bus No. 7 and exit at Park Boulevard and Zoo Place.

Car Travel: From Downtown, take Route 163 north through Balboa Park. Exit at Zoo/Museums (Richmond Street) and follow signs.

Several options help you get around the massive park: express buses loop through the zoo and the Skyfari Aerial Tram will take you from one end to the other. The zoo's topography is fairly hilly, but moving sidewalks lead up the slopes between some exhibits.

QUICK BITES

There is a wide variety of food available for purchase at the zoo from food carts to ethnic restaurants such as the Pan-Asian **Hua Mei Cafe**.

One of the best restaurants is **Albert's**, near the Gorilla exhibit, which features grilled fish, homemade pizza, and fresh pasta along with a full bar.

SERVICE INFORMATION

✉ 2920 Zoo Dr., Balboa Park
☎ 619/234–3153
🌐 www.sandiegozoo.org

SAN DIEGO ZOO SAFARI PARK

About 45 minutes north of the zoo in Escondido, the 1,800-acre San Diego Zoo Safari Park is an extensive wildlife sanctuary where animals roam free—and guests can get close in escorted caravans and on backcountry trails. This park and the zoo operate under the auspices of the San Diego Zoo's nonprofit organization; joint tickets are available.

🍴 Restaurants

The culinary heart of this museum-filled urban park is the Prado, a stylish sit-down restaurant with a sunny patio. Other dining is limited to museum and zoo food stands, cafés, and food carts.

Cafe in the Park

$ | DELI | Located in the Casa del Balboa building near the San Diego History Center, this café is a convenient stop for a quick breakfast or lunch, or a midday coffee break. The café offers a good selection of pastries, panini, soups, and salads, and a few indoor tables in case you find yourself there on the odd rainy day. **Known for:** convenient location along the park's main drag; all-day menu; specialty coffees. [$] *Average main: $8* ✉ *Casa del Balboa, 1549 El Prado, Balboa Park* ✥ *near the San Diego History Center* ☎ *619/331–1992* ⏲ *No dinner.*

Craveology

$ | AMERICAN | FAMILY | Enjoy views of the Bea Evenson Fountain from the patio of this quick lunch option outside the Fleet Science Center. The menu offers everything from flatbreads, sandwiches, and soups to smoothies, specialty coffees, and soft-serve ice cream. **Known for:** fountain views; smoothies and specialty coffees; color-changing ice cream spoons. [$] *Average main: $9* ✉ *1875 El Prado, Balboa Park* ✥ *outside the Fleet Science Center* ☎ *619/238–1233* 🌐 *www.rhfleet.org.*

Panama 66

$ | AMERICAN | Adding a dose of hip to Balboa Park, this gastropub, located adjacent to the San Diego Museum of Art's sculpture garden, offers a stylish pit-stop pre-theater or between museum-hopping. The menu features upscale pub fare with several vegan options as well as a weekend brunch. **Known for:** rotating cocktails pegged to museum exhibits; live music most nights; local San Diego and Tijuana brews. [$] *Average main: $12* ✉ *1450 El Prado, Balboa Park* ☎ *619/696–1966* 🌐 *www.panama66.com* ⏲ *No dinner Mon. and Tues. Labor Day–Memorial Day.*

The Prado at Balboa Park

$$$ | ECLECTIC | This lovely restaurant in the historic House of Hospitality makes contemporary fare, friendly service, and patio dining available to legions of museum- and theatergoers who come to Balboa Park. The bar is a fashionable destination for creative drinks and light nibbles, while the dining room's specialties range from fish tacos and paella to unusual surf-and-turf combos. **Known for:** post-theater happy hour; Latin-inspired cocktails heavy on rum and citrus juices; striking Spanish-Moorish architectural details. [$] *Average main: $29* ✉ *1549 El Prado, Balboa Park* ☎ *619/557–9441* 🌐 *www.pradobalboa.com* ⏲ *No dinner Mon.*

Tea Pavilion

$ | JAPANESE | Grab some noodles, sushi, or Japanese tea and treats at this pavilion located in the center of the park. The large outdoor patio is a great place to rest and recharge before seeking tranquility in the adjacent Japanese Friendship Garden. **Known for:** spacious patio; extensive tea selection; Japanese snacks and sweets. [$] *Average main: 9* ✉ *2215 Pan American Way, Balboa Park* ☎ *619/231–0048* 🌐 *www.cohnrestaurants.com* ⏲ *No dinner.*

🎟 Performing Arts

★ Globe Theatres

THEATER | This complex, comprising the Sheryl and Harvey White Theatre, the Lowell Davies Festival Theatre, and the Old Globe Theatre, offers some of the finest theatrical productions in Southern California. Theater classics such as *Into the Woods* and *Dirty Rotten Scoundrels,* and more recent hits like *Bright Star* and *Meteor Shower,* premiered on these famed stages and went on to perform on Broadway. The Old Globe presents a renowned summer Shakespeare Festival with three to four plays in repertory. The theaters, done in a California version of Tudor style, sit between the sculpture garden of the San Diego Museum of Art and the California Tower. ✉ *1363 Old Globe Way, Balboa Park* ☎ *619/234–5623* ⊕ *www.theoldglobe.org* ❂ *Box office closed Mon.*

Activities

Morley Field Sports Complex
GOLF COURSE | FAMILY | In addition to the 2-mile fitness course and ball diamonds, the park's athletic center has a flying-disc golf course where players toss their Frisbees over canyons and treetops to reach the challenging "holes"—wire baskets hung from metal poles. Traditionalists may prefer to tee off at the nearby par 72 Balboa Park Golf Course instead. Morley Field also has a public pool, a velodrome, an archery range, playgrounds, and boccie, badminton, and tennis courts. The website has a downloadable program guide with complete listings and times. The complex is at the northeast corner of Balboa Park, across Park Boulevard and Florida Canyon. ✉ *2221 Morley Field Dr., San Diego* ☎ *619/525–8262* ⊕ *www. sandiego.gov/park-and-recreation/ centers/recctr/morley.*

GOLF
Balboa Park Golf Course
GOLF | San Diego's oldest public course is 5 minutes from Downtown in the heart of Balboa Park and offers impressive views of the city and the bay. The course includes a 9-hole executive course and a challenging 18-hole course that weaves among the park's canyons with some tricky drop-offs. Finish off your round with biscuits and gravy and a mimosa at Tobey's 19th Hole Cafe, a greasy spoon that's also Balboa Park's best-kept secret. ✉ *2600 Golf Course Dr., Balboa Park* ☎ *619/235–1184* ⊕ *www.sandiego.gov* ▱ *$40 weekdays, $50 weekends* ❧ *27 holes, 6339 yards, par 72.*

👜 Shopping

Balboa Park's many gift shops and galleries make it a great place to do some shopping for that unique souvenir. The visitor center gift shop is worth a browse, or stop by any of the museum stores for specialty items related to current and past exhibits. The Zoo Store and Ituri Forest Outpost at the San Diego Zoo carries international crafts, world music, and hats. Don't miss a stroll through the galleries and workshops of the Spanish Village Art Center, with over 200 artists' work on display.

Bankers Hill

The serene neighborhood west of Balboa Park is lined with upscale condos and stately historic homes, many offering stunning vistas of the park and Downtown. This area is defined by the world-famous park, but increasingly it is known for an exceptional contemporary dining scene.

🍴 Restaurants

Bankers Hill is home to some of the city's most enduring restaurants, like the legendary Bertrand at Mister A's. But the eclectic area is also home to several fashionable eateries alongside divey bars and sandwich shops.

★ Azuki Sushi
$$ | SUSHI | Sushi should be a no-brainer when visiting San Diego, especially for tourists from landlocked states who don't often get fresh fish. This menu is based on the seasons, and you'll find innovative sushi, sashimi, and a raw bar, all utilizing the freshest local fish (some is flown in daily from Japan) and produce; there are options for non-sushi fans. **Known for:** reservations recommended; specialty rolls like the R U Kidding Me? (snow crab, diver scallops, tempura asparagus, seared tuna, white truffle oil,

and mixed greens, topped with garlic ponzu and flash-fried leaks); surprising pairings with wine and sake. [$] *Average main: $21* ✉ *2321 5th Ave., Bankers Hill* ☎ *619/238–4760* 🌐 *azukisushi.com* ⏲ *No lunch Sat.–Sun.*

★ Bankers Hill Bar and Restaurant

$$ | **MODERN AMERICAN** | The living wall of succulents, hip warehouse interior, and wine bottle chandeliers suit this vibrant restaurant where good times and great eats meet. An after-work crowd joins residents of this quiet stretch of Bankers Hill for happy hour served from the zinc bar while diners enjoy sophisticated comfort food often with Southwest flair. **Known for:** popular burger with truffle fries; butterscotch pudding topped with shortbread cookies and crème fraîche; living plant wall on the sun-drenched patio. [$] *Average main: $23* ✉ *2202 4th Ave., Bankers Hill* ☎ *619/231–0222* 🌐 *www.bankershillsd.com* ⏲ *No lunch.*

Bertrand at Mister A's

$$$$ | **FRENCH** | For decades, this venerable 12th-floor dining room with panoramic views and polished service, led by the restaurant's namesake Betrand Hug, has reigned as a celebratory fine-dining destination. Chef Stephane Voitzwinkler's California-luxe seasonal cuisine is complemented by a popular happy hour that draws an after-work and pretheater crowd for cocktails and bites. **Known for:** affordable happy hour appetizers; special tasting menus; stunning panoramic bay and city views. [$] *Average main: $41* ✉ *2550 5th Ave., 12th fl., Bankers Hill* ☎ *619/239–1377* 🌐 *www.asrestaurant.com.*

★ Cucina Urbana

$$ | **ITALIAN** | Twentysomethings mingle with boomers in this convivial Bankers Hill dining room and bar, one of the most popular restaurants in town. The open kitchen turns out innovative Italian food with a California sensibility including a selection of small plates and family-style pasta dishes alongside traditional entrées. **Known for:** in-house Wine Shop with reasonably priced bottles and $9 corkage fee; seasonal polenta with ragu; ricotta-stuffed zucchini blossoms. [$] *Average main: $21* ✉ *505 Laurel St., Bankers Hill* ☎ *619/239–2222* 🌐 *www.cucinaurbana.com* ⏲ *No lunch Sat.–Mon.*

Hane Sushi

$$ | **JAPANESE** | An airy room with a sleek red-and-black Japanese aesthetic is the setting for pristine, contemporary sushi by Roger Nakamura, who spent years learning his craft from Yukito Ota of San Diego's beloved Sushi Ota restaurant. Though Hane (pronounced "hah-nay") is trendier than Ota, sushi purists will be happy with special delicacies imported from Japan. **Known for:** Japan-sourced ingredients like kobe beef sashimi; lunch specials; innovative dishes like the crispy eggplant and spicy tuna appetizer or the Diego roll with serrano peppers. [$] *Average main: $27* ✉ *2760 5th Ave., Bankers Hill* ☎ *619/260–1411* ⏲ *Closed Mon. No lunch weekends.*

OLD TOWN AND UPTOWN

Updated by
Claire Deeks Van Der Lee

👁 Sights	🍴 Restaurants	🛏 Hotels	👜 Shopping	🍸 Nightlife
★★★★☆	★★★★★	★★☆☆☆	★★★★☆	★★★★☆

NEIGHBORHOOD SNAPSHOT

GREAT EXPERIENCES

■ **Go back in time:** Experience the early days of San Diego, from its beginnings as a remote military outpost and mission to the development of the first town plaza.

■ **Architectural delights:** Take an architectural journey through San Diego's history. Discover the pueblo- and clapboard-style structures of Old Town and the ornate Victorian gems in Heritage Park. Then head up the hill to view wonderfully preserved early-20th-century homes in Uptown.

■ **Scare yourself silly:** Visit the Thomas Whaley House Museum, "the most haunted house in America," at night.

■ **Tortillas and margaritas:** Enjoy one of Old Town's many Mexican eateries.

■ **Like a local:** Explore the vibrant shopping, dining, and nightlife of Uptown's unique neighborhoods.

GETTING HERE

Old Town and Uptown are northwest and north of Balboa Park, respectively. Access to Old Town is easy thanks to the nearby Old Town Transit Center. Ten bus lines stop here, as do the San Diego Trolley and the Coaster commuter rail line. There are two large parking lots linked to the Old Town Historic Park by an underground pedestrian walkway.

Uptown is best explored by car, although several bus routes do serve the area. Both metered street parking and pay-and-display lots are available.

QUICK BITES

If traveling back in time has left you tired and hungry, Old Town's **Fiesta de Reyes** ⊠ *4016 Wallace St.* has several options for a quick recharge. **La Panaderia** serves sweet and savory empanadas, homemade churros, and hot chocolate. **Old Town Jerky and Root Beer** offers a good selection of snacks and mini sandwiches, and, of course, jerky and root beer. Friday through Sunday look for the booth marked **Street Tacos** for a quick meal.

PLANNING YOUR TIME

■ It takes about two hours to walk through Old Town. Try to time your visit to coincide with one of the daily tours given by costumed park staff. Tours are free and depart at 11:30 and 2 from the Robinson-Rose House Visitor Center. If you go to Presidio Park, definitely consider driving up the steep hill from Old Town.

■ The highlight of an Uptown tour is exploring the hearts of Hillcrest and North Park located at the intersections of University and 5th avenues, and University and 30th St., respectively. Plan to drive or catch a bus between neighborhoods, then explore on foot.

FESTIVALS

■ The Uptown neighborhoods host a variety of events throughout the year. Hillcrest hosts the annual LGBT Pride event every July. In late summer, Cityfest rocks the neighborhood with live music, food stalls, and beer gardens. Old Town celebrates Cinco de Mayo and the Old Town Art and Craft Show held in early fall.

San Diego's Spanish and Mexican roots are most evident in Old Town and the surrounding hillside of Presidio Park. Visitors can experience settlement life in San Diego from Spanish and Mexican rule to the early days of U.S. statehood. Nearby Uptown is composed of several smaller neighborhoods near Downtown and around Balboa Park: the vibrant neighborhoods of Hillcrest, Mission Hills, North Park, and South Park showcase their unique blend of historical charm and modern urban community.

Dense with Mexican eateries, Old Town is the place to be for quick and easy access to house-made tortillas. The neighborhood is also home to historic adobe shops and museums. East of Old Town is Mission Valley, a suburban maze of freeways, shopping centers, and Hotel Circle, where many spacious and inexpensive lodging options are located.

San Diego's Uptown area—Hillcrest, Mission Hills, North Park, South Park, and University Heights—is close to the San Diego Zoo and Balboa Park. There are few hotels, but the area offers pedestrian-friendly shopping—it's known for its mélange of funky bookstores, offbeat gift shops, and nostalgic collectibles and vintage stores—and many of San Diego's venerable craft beer bars and breweries. The diverse communities boast bistros, gastropubs, and ethnic restaurants that range from Afghan and Indian to Russian and Vietnamese.

Hillcrest is a popular area for LGBT nightlife and culture, whereas just a little bit east of Hillcrest, ever-expanding North Park features a diverse range of bars and lounges that cater to a twenty- and thirtysomething crowd, bolstering its reputation as the city's hipster capital. Tucked between Hillcrest and North Park, the charming neighborhood of University Heights is home to several notable bars and restaurants. The thriving nightlife and dining scene continues down Adams Avenue and into neighboring Normal Heights, which is a more laidback alternative. Whichever of these neighborhoods strikes your fancy, a cab from Downtown will run about the same price: $15.

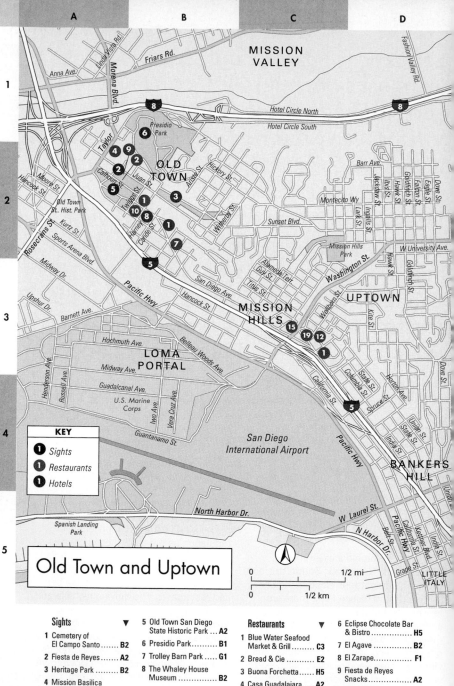

Old Town and Uptown

KEY

- ① Sights
- ① Restaurants
- ① Hotels

0 ___ 1/2 mi
0 ___ 1/2 km

E   F   G   H

Adams Ave.

ADAMS AVENUE

UNIVERSITY HEIGHTS

Madison Ave.

1

Madison Ave.

Monroe Ave.

Monroe Ave.

Maryland St.

Cleveland Ave.

Campus Ave.

North Ave.

Park Blvd.

Georgia St.

Mission Ave.

Florida St.

Alabama St.

Mississippi St.

Louisiana St.

Arizona St.

Hamilton St.

Oregon St.

Idaho St.

Utah St.

Kansas St.

30th St.

Ohio St.

Illinois St.

El Cajon Blvd.

Howard Ave.

163

HILLCREST

Hayes Ave.

Lincoln Ave.

Polk Ave.

North Park Community Park

NORMAL HEIGHTS

2

NORTH PARK

Lincoln Ave.

Cleveland Ave.

University Ave.

University Ave.

Wightman St.

N Park Way

Essex St.

Robinson Ave.

Pennsylvania Ave.

Cypress Ave.

Park Villa Dr.

Arnold Ave.

Villa Terr.

Pershing Ave.

Landis St.

Dwight St.

Grim Ave.

Ray St.

Front

1st Ave.

3rd Ave.

6th Ave.

8th Ave.

Normal St.

Cantle St.

Richmond

Brookes Ave.

Myrtle Ave.

Upas St.

Park Blvd.

Myrtle Ave.

Upas St.

26th St.

30th St.

3

Brookes Ave.

Walnut Ave.

Upas St.

Thorn St.

Spruce St.

5th Ave.

6th Ave.

Balboa Dr.

Cabrillo Freeway

Thorn St.

Redwood St.

Quince St.

Palm St.

Olive St.

MIDDLE-TOWN

Quince Dr.

Palm

Olive

San Diego Zoo

Balboa Park

Maple St.

Laurel St.

SOUTH PARK

Kalmia St.

4

Nutmeg

Albatross St.

Brant St.

1st Ave.

3rd Ave.

4th Ave.

El Prado

Florida Dr.

Pershing Dr.

Balboa Park Municipal Golf Course

Juniper St.

Ivy St.

Hawthorn St.

Grape St.

28th St.

29th St.

30th St.

Date St.

Elm St.

163

Hawthorn St.

Grape St.

Fir St.

Elm St.

5

Date St.

Date St.

Cedar St.

Beech St.

Cedar St.

Pershing Dr.

Wabler Ave.

Bachman Pl.

Bram St.

5

Old Town

As the first European settlement in Southern California, **Old Town** began to develop in the 1820s. However, its true beginnings took place on a nearby hillside in 1769 with the establishment of a Spanish military outpost and the first of California's missions, San Diego de Alcalá. In 1774 the hilltop was declared a *presidio reál*, a fortress built by the Spanish empire, and the mission was relocated along the San Diego River. Over time, settlers moved down from the presidio to establish Old Town. A central plaza was laid out, surrounded by adobe and, later, wooden structures. San Diego became an incorporated U.S. city in 1850, with Old Town as its center. In the 1860s, however, the advent of Alonzo Horton's New Town to the southeast caused Old Town to wither. Efforts to preserve the area began early in the 20th century, and Old Town became a state historic park in 1968.

Today Old Town is a lively celebration of history and culture. The **Old Town San Diego State Historic Park** re-creates life during the early settlement, while San Diego Avenue buzzes with art galleries, gift shops, festive restaurants, and open-air stands selling inexpensive Mexican handicrafts.

◉ Sights

Cemetery of El Campo Santo
CEMETERY | Now a peaceful stop for visitors to Old Town, the old adobe-wall cemetery established in 1849 was, until 1880, the burial place for many members of Old Town's founding families—as well as for some gamblers and bandits who passed through town. Antonio Garra, a chief who led an uprising of the San Luis Rey Indians, was executed at El Campo Santo in front of the open grave he had been forced to dig for himself. Most of the markers give only approximations of where the people named on them are buried; some of the early settlers laid to rest at El Campo Santo actually reside under San Diego Avenue. ⊠ *San Diego Ave. S, between Arista and Ampudia Sts., Old Town.*

★ Fiesta de Reyes
HISTORIC SITE | FAMILY | North of San Diego's Old Town Plaza lies the area's unofficial center, built to represent a colonial Mexican plaza. The collection of more than a dozen shops and restaurants around a central courtyard in blossom with magenta bougainvillea, scarlet hibiscus, and other flowers in season reflects what early California might have looked like from 1821 to 1872. Mariachi bands and folklorico dance groups frequently perform on the plaza stage—check the website for times and upcoming special events. ■ TIP➜ **Casa de Reyes is a great stop for a margarita and some chips and guacamole.** ⊠ *4016 Wallace St., Old Town* ☎ *619/297–3100* ⊕ *www.fiestadereyes. com.*

Heritage Park
BUILDING | A number of San Diego's important Victorian buildings are the focus of this 7.8-acre park on the Juan Street hill near Harney Street. Among the buildings is Southern California's first synagogue, a one-room classical-revival structure built in 1889 for Congregation Beth Israel. The most interesting of the park's six former residences might be the Sherman-Gilbert House, which has a widow's walk and intricate carving on its decorative trim. It was built for real estate dealer John Sherman in 1887 at the then-exorbitant cost of $20,000—indicating just how profitable the booming housing market could be. All the houses, some of which may seem surprisingly colorful, accurately represent the bright hues of the era. The synagogue and the Senlis Cottage are open to visitors daily from 9 to 5; the latter contains a small

Dancers perform during the annual Día de los Muertos celebration at the Fiesta de Reyes plaza in Old Town.

exhibit with information on the history and original locations of the houses. The McConaughy House hosts the Coral Tree Tea House, offering traditional tea service Thursday through Sunday from 11 to 5. Save Our Heritage Organization moved the buildings to this park from their original locations and also restored them. ⊠ *2454 Heritage Park Row, Old Town* ☏ *858/565–3600* ⊕ *www.sdparks. org* ⊠ *Free.*

★ **Old Town San Diego State Historic Park**
HISTORIC SITE | FAMILY | The six square blocks on the site of San Diego's original pueblo are the heart of Old Town. Most of the 20 historic buildings preserved or re-created by the park cluster around **Old Town Plaza,** bounded by Wallace Street on the west, Calhoun Street on the north, Mason Street on the east, and San Diego Avenue on the south. The plaza is a pleasant place to rest, plan your tour of the park, and watch passersby. San Diego Avenue is closed to vehicle traffic here.

Some of Old Town's buildings were destroyed in a fire in 1872, but after the site became a state historic park in 1968, reconstruction and restoration of the remaining structures began. Five of the original adobes are still intact.

Facing Old Town Plaza, the **Robinson-Rose House** was the original commercial center of Old San Diego, housing railroad offices, law offices, and the first newspaper press. The largest and most elaborate of the original adobe homes, the **Casa de Estudillo** was occupied by members of the Estudillo family until 1887 and later gained popularity for its billing as "Ramona's Marriage Place" based on a popular novel of the time. Albert Seeley, a stagecoach entrepreneur, opened the **Cosmopolitan Hotel** in 1869 as a way station for travelers on the daylong trip south from Los Angeles. Next door to the Cosmopolitan Hotel, the **Seeley Stable** served as San Diego's stagecoach stop in 1867 and was the transportation hub of Old Town until 1887, when trains became the favored mode of travel.

Several reconstructed buildings serve as restaurants or as shops purveying wares reminiscent of those that might have been available in the original Old Town. **Racine & Laramie,** a painstakingly reproduced version of San Diego's first cigar store in 1868, is especially interesting.

Pamphlets available at the Robinson-Rose House give details about all the historic houses on the plaza and in its vicinity. Free tours of the historic park are offered daily at 11:30 and 2; they depart from the Robinson-Rose House. ■**TIP→ The covered wagon located near the intersection of Mason and Calhoun streets provides a great photo op.** ✉ *Visitor center (Robinson-Rose House), 4002 Wallace St., Old Town* ☎ *619/220–5422* ⊕ *www.parks.ca.gov* ✇ *Free.*

Presidio Park

HISTORIC SITE | The hillsides of the 50-acre green space overlooking Old Town from the north end of Taylor Street are popular with picnickers, and many couples have taken their wedding vows on the park's long stretches of lawn, some of the greenest in San Diego. The park offers a great ocean view from the top, and more than 2 miles of hiking trails below. It's a nice walk from Old Town to the summit if you're in good shape and wearing the right shoes—it should take about half an hour. You can also drive to the top of the park via Presidio Drive, off Taylor Street.

If you walk, look in at the **Presidio Hills Golf Course** on Mason Street. It has an unusual clubhouse that incorporates the ruins of Casa de Carrillo, the town's oldest adobe, constructed in 1820. At the end of Mason Street, veer left on Jackson Street to reach the **presidio ruins,** where adobe walls and a bastion have been built above the foundations of the original fortress and chapel. Also on-site is the 28-foot-high **Serra Cross,** built in 1913 out of brick tiles found in the ruins. Continue up the hill to find the **Junípero Serra Museum,** built at the sight of the

America's Most Haunted ◉

Built on a former gallows site in 1856, the Whaley House is one of 30 houses designated by the Department of Commerce to be haunted. Legend has it that the house is inhabited by seven spirits, making it the "most haunted house in America." Listen for the sound of heavy footsteps, said to belong to the ghost of Yankee Jim Robinson, a convict hanged on the site in 1852. Less ominous are sightings of the Whaley family's fox terrier scampering about the house.

original Mission San Diego de Alcalá and often mistaken for the mission. Open weekends, the Serra Museum commemorates the history of the site from the time it was occupied by the Kumeyaay Indians through its Spanish, Mexican, and American periods. Then take Presidio Drive southeast to reach the site of **Fort Stockton,** built to protect Old Town and abandoned by the United States in 1848. Plaques and statues also commemorate the Mormon Battalion, which enlisted here to fight in the battle against Mexico. ✉ *Taylor and Jackson Sts., Old Town* ⊕ *www.sdparks.org.*

The Whaley House Museum

HISTORIC SITE | A New York entrepreneur, Thomas Whaley came to California during the gold rush. He wanted to provide his East Coast wife with all the comforts of home, so in 1857 he had Southern California's first two-story brick structure built, making it the oldest double-story brick building on the West Coast. The house, which served as the county courthouse and government seat during the 1870s, stands in strong contrast to the Spanish-style adobe residences that surround the nearby historic plaza and marks an early stage of San Diego's "Americanization." A garden out back includes many varieties of prehybrid roses from before 1867. The place is perhaps most famed, however, for the ghosts that are said to inhabit it. You can tour on your own during the day, but must visit by guided tour after 4:30 pm. The evening tours are geared toward the supernatural aspects of the house. Tours start at 6 pm (5 pm on Saturday) and are offered every half hour, with the last tour departing at 9:30 pm. ✉ *2476 San Diego Ave., Old Town* ☎ *619/297–7511* 🌐 *www.whaley-house.org* 🎟 *$10 before 5 pm; $13 after 5 pm* 🕑 *Closed Sept.–May and Wed.*

🍴 Restaurants

Touristy but fun Mexican food reigns here with giant margaritas and heaping dishes of enchiladas, tacos, and carnitas (slow-cooked pork). You'll also find a few gourmet gems celebrating other cuisines mixed in.

Casa Guadalajara

$ | **MEXICAN** | It's a fiesta at this vibrant Mexican eatery, dotted with folk art, tile fountains, mariachi music, and a 300-year-old pepper tree that holds court on the charming patio. The menu reads like an encyclopedia of familiar favorites, all in hefty portions; wash down your meal with their signature and sizable "Birdbath Margarita" in various fruit flavors or sip on non-alcoholic house-made horchatas. **Known for:** weekday happy hour with complimentary appetizers; traditional Mexican breakfast dishes; nightly mariachi music. [$] *Average main: $16* ✉ *4105 Taylor St., Old Town* ☎ *619/295–5111* 🌐 *www.casaguadalajara.com.*

El Agave

$$$ | **MEXICAN** | Not a typical San Diego taco shop, this Mexican eatery is upstairs in a shopping complex in the middle of a tequila museum with some 2,000 bottles dating from the 1930s. The owners are equally serious about food, calling their cuisine Hispanic-Mexican Gastronomy, which means meat and fish dishes with lots of unusual spicy chilies, herbs, spices, and moles. **Known for:** impressive tequila selection and tequila flights; variety of mole dishes; upscale option in generally casual Old Town. [$] *Average main: $32* ✉ *2304 San Diego Ave., Old Town* ☎ *619/220–0692* 🌐 *www.elagave.com.*

Fiesta de Reyes Snacks

$ | **AMERICAN** | **FAMILY** | If traveling back in time has left you tired and hungry, Old Town's Fiesta de Reyes has several options for a quick recharge. To the right when you enter from the plaza, **La Panaderia** serves sweet and savory empanadas, homemade churros, and hot chocolate. **Old Town Jerky and Root Beer** offers a good selection of snacks and mini sandwiches, fresh lemonade, and, of course, jerky and root beer. [$] *Average main: $10* ✉ *4016 Wallace St., Old Town* ☎ *619/297–3100* 🌐 *www.fiestadereyes.com.*

Harney Sushi

$ | **JAPANESE** | One of San Diego's most popular sushi restaurants is set in a sea of touristy Mexican dining spots in the heart of Old Town. Fans young and old flock to the lively space for refreshing cocktails, sustainable California-style sushi, and modern Asian cuisine. **Known for:** creative sushi rolls like the O'sider #55 with New York strip; specialty edamame in flavors like soy truffle and sesame bacon bonito; live music on Monday and Thursday nights. [$] *Average main: $18* ✉ *3964 Harney St., Old Town* ☎ *619/295–3272* 🌐 *www.harneysushi.com* 🕑 *No lunch Sat.*

Old Town is the place to go for colorful Mexican wares.

🛏 Hotels

Staying in Old Town makes it easy to explore the area on foot, as nearly everything is within walking distance. Old Town is also centrally located between Uptown, Downtown, and the Beaches.

Best Western Plus Hacienda Hotel Old Town

$$ | HOTEL | FAMILY | Perched on a hill in the heart of Old Town, this hotel is known for its expansive courtyards, outdoor fountains, and maze of stairs that connects eight buildings of guest rooms. **Pros:** airport shuttle; well-maintained outdoor areas; excellent location for exploring Old Town. **Cons:** some rooms need renovating; complicated layout; can be noisy in some areas. $ *Rooms from: $219* ✉ *4041 Harney St., Old Town* ☎ *800/888-1991* ⊕ *www.haciendahotel-oldtown.com* ⇨ *200 rooms* ⊙ *No meals.*

The Cosmopolitan Hotel

$ | B&B/INN | With antique furniture, pull-chain toilets, and a veranda overlooking Old Town State Historic Park, the Cosmo offers guests a taste of Victorian-era living. **Pros:** historic charm; huge suites; central location in Old Town State Historic Park. **Cons:** no TVs; limited on-site parking; street noise. $ *Rooms from: $169* ✉ *2660 Calhoun St., Old Town* ☎ *619/297-1874* ⊕ *www.oldtown-cosmopolitan.com* ⇨ *10 rooms* ⊙ *Free Breakfast.*

🍸 Nightlife

Old-timey saloons lure tourists with margaritas, mezcal, and mariachis.

BARS

The Cosmopolitan

BARS/PUBS | The bar at the Cosmopolitan Hotel in Old Town maintains the old-timey aesthetic of the tourist-heavy neighborhood, complete with servers in period garb and game trophies on the walls. The quality of the cocktails and the friendly atmosphere make this a gem among the rest of the old west kitsch. ✉ *2660 Calhoun St., Old Town* ☎ *619/297-1874* ⊕ *www.oldtowncosmopolitan.com/.*

El Agave Tequileria

BARS/PUBS | The bar of this restaurant named for the cactus whose sap is distilled into tequila stocks hundreds of top-shelf brands that are as sip-worthy as the finest cognac. ⊠ *2304 San Diego Ave., Old Town* ☎ *619/220–0692* ⊕ *www. elagave.com.*

🎭 Performing Arts

Cygnet's Old Town Theatre

THEATER | A 246-seat theater operated by Cygnet Theatre Company, this is one of the more interesting small San Diego theater groups. Catch local takes on edgy classics like *Sweeney Todd* and *Little Shop of Horrors.* ⊠ *4040 Twiggs St., Old Town* ☎ *619/337–1525* ⊕ *www.cygnet-theatre.com.*

🛍 Shopping

Tourist-focused Old Town has a festival-like ambience that also makes it a popular destination for locals. It's a must for pottery, ceramics, jewelry, and handcrafted baskets. At Old Town San Diego State Historic Park, you may feel like a time traveler as you visit shops housed in restored adobe buildings. Farther down the street are stores selling Mexican blankets, piñatas, and glassware. Old Town Market offers live entertainment, local artists selling their wares from carts, and a market crammed with unique apparel, home-decor items, toys, jewelry, and food. Dozens of stores sell San Diego logo merchandise and T-shirts at discounted prices, and there are great deals on handcrafted jewelry, art, and leather accessories.

FOOD AND WINE
Cousin's Candy Shop

FOOD/CANDY | Sample homemade fudge and taffy that's been cooked, stretched, and wrapped on-site at this old-fashioned confectionery shop. The old-time candies in nostalgic tins make thoughtful gifts. ⊠ *2711 San Diego Ave., Old Town* ☎ *619/297–2000* ⊕ *www.cousinscandy. net.*

HOME ACCESSORIES AND GIFTS
Tafoya & Son Pottery

CRAFTS | This shop in a historic adobe building specializes in Mexican Talavera pottery and Turkish porcelain. Look for sterling silver jewelry designed by owner Chris Tafoya. ⊠ *2769 San Diego Ave., Old Town* ☎ *619/574–0989* ⊕ *www.tafoyaand-son.com.*

Tienda de Reyes

CERAMICS/GLASSWARE | This festive "store of the kings" stocks Old Town's largest selection of Day of the Dead art, and carries sculpture, handbags, and glassware from Mexico and Peru. ⊠ *2754 Calhoun St., Old Town* ☎ *619/491–0611* ⊕ *www. tiendadereyes.com.*

Ye Olde Soap Shoppe

PERFUME/COSMETICS | The mere scent of Ye Olde's hand-fashioned soaps conjures up a relaxing bath. If you want to craft your own soaps, you'll find a full line of supplies, as well as soaps and lotions from around the world. ⊠ *2497 San Diego Ave., Old Town* ☎ *800/390–9969* ⊕ *www. soapmaking.com.*

JEWELRY
The Diamond Source

GIFTS/SOUVENIRS | Specializing in fashionable diamond and precious gemstone jewelry, this shop showcases the creations of master jeweler Marco Levy. There's a second location in La Jolla. ⊠ *2474 San Diego Ave., Old Town* ☎ *619/299–6900* ⊕ *www.thediamond-source.com* ☉ *Closed Mon.*

MARKETS
Old Town Market

SHOPPING CENTERS/MALLS | The atmosphere is colorful, upbeat, and Mexico-centric at this eclectic market. Local artisans create some of the wares for sale, including everything from dolls and silver jewelry to gourmet foods, home-decor items, and apparel. ✉ *4010 Twiggs St., Old Town* ☎ *619/278–0955* 🌐 *www.oldtownmarketsandiego.com.*

Old Town Saturday Market

SHOPPING CENTERS/MALLS | San Diego's largest weekend artisan market presents live music and local artists selling jewelry, paintings, photography, handblown glass, apparel, pottery, and decorative items. The San Diego Trolley's Old Town stop is two blocks north of the market. ✉ *Harney St. and San Diego Ave., Old Town* ☎ 🌐 *www.oldtownsaturdaymarket.com* 🎫 *Free.*

SHOPPING CENTERS

★ Bazaar del Mundo Shops

SHOPPING CENTERS/MALLS | With a Mexican villa theme, the Bazaar hosts riotously colorful gift shops such as **Ariana,** for ethnic and artsy women's fashions; **Artes de Mexico,** which sells handmade Latin American crafts and Guatemalan weavings; and **The Gallery,** which carries handmade jewelry, Native American crafts, collectible glass, and original silk-screen prints. The **Laurel Burch Gallerita** carries the complete collection of its namesake artist's signature jewelry, accessories, and totes. ✉ *4133 Taylor St., at Juan St., Old Town* ☎ *619/296–3161* 🌐 *www.bazaardelmundo.com.*

Hillcrest

The large retro Hillcrest sign over the intersection of University and 5th avenues makes an excellent landmark at the epicenter of this vibrant section of Uptown. Strolling along University Avenue between 4th and 6th avenues and from Washington Street to Robinson Avenue will reveal a mixture of retail shops and restaurants. National chains such as American Apparel and Pinkberry coexist with local boutiques, bookstores, bars, and coffee shops. A few blocks east, another interesting stretch of stores and restaurants runs along University Avenue to Normal Street. Long established as the center of San Diego's gay community, the neighborhood bustles both day and night with a mixed crowd of shoppers, diners, and partygoers. If you are visiting Hillcrest on Sunday between 9 and 2, be sure to explore the exceptional Hillcrest Farmers Market.

🍴 Restaurants

From brunch to late-night snacks, Hillcrest's lively dining scene has you covered. This is a popular dining neighborhood so reservations are recommended if you don't want to wait during peak times.

Bread & Cie

$ | **CAFÉ** | San Diego's love affair with artisanal bread began when Charles Kaufman, a former New Yorker and a filmmaker, opened this artsy urban bakery and café two decades ago. Ovens imported from France produce irresistible aromas as you choose among classic baguettes and focaccia, delicious assorted pastries and Vienoisserie, and a wide selection of breakfast and lunch specialties. **Known for:** crusty black olive bread; traditional afternoon tea; creamy tomato soup. [$] *Average main: $9* ✉ *350 University Ave., Hillcrest* ☎ *619/683–9322* 🌐 *www.breadandcie.com* 🕒 *No dinner.*

Hash House A Go Go

$$ | **AMERICAN** | **FAMILY** | Big caloric portions and long lines are hallmarks of this southern-accented comfort food destination where hungry regulars from near and far line up for an indulgent meal in the crowded (and sometimes noisy) dining room. Bring an appetite and a friend; sharing plates is a necessity here. **Known for:** decadent sage fried chicken eggs Benedict; huge portions perfect for sharing; inventive and generously garnished cocktails. [$] *Average main: $20* ✉ *3628 5th Ave., Hillcrest* ☎ *619/298–4646* 🌐 *www.hashhouseagogo.com* 🕒 *No dinner Mon.*

Kous Kous Moroccan Bistro

$ | **MOROCCAN** | With one sip of the bubbly "Moroccan Kiss" cocktail in this room lit with lanterns and draped in desert-hued fabrics, diners are transported to chef-owner Moumen Nouri's motherland. The culinary journey continues either à la carte, or by selecting one of the family-style Moroccan feasts, starting at $29.95 per person. **Known for:** traditional tagines with chicken, lamb, or vegetables; "Moroccan feast" menus; interesting cocktails. [$] *Average main: $20* ✉ *3940 4th Ave., Hillcrest* ☎ *619/295–5560* 🌐 *www.kouskousrestaurant.com* 🕒 *No lunch.*

Ortega's Bistro

$$ | **MEXICAN** | **FAMILY** | Seafood lovers have long flocked to Puerto Nuevo, the "lobster village" just south of San Diego in Baja California, Mexico. When a family that operates several Puerto Nuevo restaurants opened Ortega's in Hillcrest, it quickly became a top draw for authentic Baja coastal cuisine, minus the long lines to cross the border. **Known for:** Puerto Nuevo-style lobster; tableside guacamole; daily happy hour including the delicious pomegranate margarita. [$] *Average main: $19* ✉ *141 University Ave., Hillcrest* ☎ *619/692–4200* 🌐 *www.ortegas.com.*

Snooze

$ | **AMERICAN** | Bright "Brady Bunch" decor, plus plenty of sunshine and fresh air pouring through windows and skylights, are cheery wake-ups for diners at this hip neighborhood haunt for pancakes and lattes. Expect long waits for a table, especially on weekends; free coffee helps the time pass while you wait to indulge in made-from-scratch breakfast bliss. **Known for:** pineapple upside-down pancakes; half-order Benedicts; boozy brunch drinks. [$] *Average main: $12* ✉ *3940 5th Ave., Hillcrest* ☎ *619/500–3344* 🌐 *www.snoozeeatery.com* 🕒 *No dinner.*

★ Trust

$$ | **MODERN AMERICAN** | Old-school wood-fire techniques meet modern architecture in this busy bistro where comic book–style art covers the concrete walls and the bottle-lined bar beckons locals and visitors alike. Locally sourced ingredients and smokey, savory flavors feature in the well-balanced menu; be sure to save room for one of the inspired desserts. **Known for:** five-hour braised oxtail raviolini; wood-grilled cauliflower with curry vinaigrette; roomy outdoor patio. [$] *Average main: $22* ✉ *3752 Park Blvd., Hillcrest* ☎ *619/795–6901* 🌐 *www.trustrestaurantsd.com.*

🍸 Nightlife

This is San Diego's most active area for LGBT nightlife.

BARS

Nunu's

BARS/PUBS | This retro-cool hangout with stiff cocktails might be one of the most popular bars in Hillcrest, but don't expect a glitzy facade. The intentionally dated decor sits within the tatty walls of a white-brick box that probably hasn't had a face-lift since the LBJ administration. ✉ *3537 5th Ave., Hillcrest* ☎ *619/295–2878.*

COFFEEHOUSES

★ Extraordinary Desserts

CAFES—NIGHTLIFE | This café lives up to its name, which explains why there's often a line, despite the ample seating. Paris-trained Karen Krasne turns out award-winning cakes, tortes, and pastries of exceptional beauty, while the Japanese-theme patio invites you to linger over yet another coffee drink. ✉ *2929 5th Ave., Hillcrest* ☎ *619/294–2132* 🌐 *www.extraordinarydesserts.com.*

GAY NIGHTLIFE

★ Baja Betty's

BARS/PUBS | Although it draws plenty of gay customers, the festive and friendly atmosphere is popular with just about everyone in the Hillcrest area (and their pets are welcome, too). The bar staff stocks more than 100 brands of tequila and mixes plenty of fancy cocktails. ⊠ *1421 University Ave., Hillcrest* ☎ *619/269–8510* ⊕ *www.bajabettyssd. com.*

Martinis Above Fourth

CABARET | This swank lounge presents live piano, comedy, and cabaret to a friendly crowd. Swill cocktails inside or on the patio, and consider a meal afterward in the restaurant serving contemporary American fare. ⊠ *3940 4th Ave., 2nd fl., Hillcrest* ☎ *619/400–4500* ⊕ *www. ma4sd.com.*

Rich's

DANCE CLUBS | The dancing and music here are some of the best in the city, making Rich's popular not only with gay men but also plenty of lesbians and straight revelers. ⊠ *1051 University Ave., Hillcrest* ☎ *619/295–2195* ⊕ *www.richs-sandiego.com.*

Urban Mo's Bar and Grill

BARS/PUBS | Cowboys gather for line dancing and two-stepping on the wooden dance floor—but be forewarned, yee-hawers, it can get pretty wild on Western nights. There are also Latin, hip-hop, and drag revues but the real allure is in the creative drinks ("Gone Fishing"—served in a fishbowl, for example) and the breezy patio where love (or something like it) is usually in the air. ⊠ *308 University Ave., Hillcrest* ☎ *619/491–0400* ⊕ *www.urbanmos.com.*

⬤ Shopping

The Uptown neighborhood of Hillcrest hosts avant-garde apparel shops alongside gift, thrift, and music stores clustered along University Avenue at 4th and 5th avenues, and again farther down University near 10th Avenue. Hillcrest is also well-known as home to one the city's best weekly farmers' markets.

MARKETS
★ Hillcrest Farmers Market

MARKET | One of the city's best farmers' markets, Hillcrest features 175 vendors that sell farm-fresh produce, handmade clothing, jewelry, and other types of handicrafts every Sunday from 9 am to 2 pm. Browse the market and plan to stay for lunch: there are several vendors selling top-notch ready-to-eat food, from fresh-made crepes and tamales to African and Indian cuisine. ⊠ *3960 Normal St., between Lincoln St. and Normal Ave., Hillcrest* ⊕ *www.hillcrestfarmers-market.com.*

Mission Hills

The route from Old Town to Hillcrest passes through the historic neighborhood of Mission Hills, with its delightful examples of early 20th-century architecture. From the top of Presidio Park, take Presidio Drive into the heart of this residential area. A left on Arista Street and a right on Fort Stockton Drive takes you past wonderfully preserved Spanish Revival, Craftsman, and Prairie-style homes, to name a few. Many local residents fine-tune their green thumbs at the **Mission Hills Nursery** (*1525 Ft. Stockton Dr.*), founded in 1910 by Kate Sessions, the "Mother of Balboa Park." Continuing on Fort Stockton Drive, a right on Goldfinch Street leads you to several popular eateries along the neighborhood's burgeoning restaurant row. From there, a left on University Avenue will take you into the Hillcrest section of Uptown.

⬤ Restaurants

The affluent enclave of Mission Hills offers surprisingly affordable and diverse dining experiences clustered at the bottom of the hill along Washington and India streets, and again near Washington and Goldfinch streets at the top.

Blue Water Seafood Market & Grill

$ | **SEAFOOD** | **FAMILY** | Blame a television segment by Guy Fieri on "Diners, Drive-ins and Dives" for the long lines of fans from around the globe. But it's the fresh seafood cooked to order that keeps them coming back to this no-frills fish market and restaurant. **Known for:** beer-battered cod tacos; classic cioppino plate with mussels and clams, scallops, shrimp, and red snapper; fresh catch cooked to order. [$] *Average main: $17* ✉ *3667 India St., Mission Hills* ☎ *619/497–0914* 🌐 *www.bluewaterseafoodsandiego.com.*

Karina's Ceviche and More

$ | **MEXICAN** | Don't miss the small walk-up window along India Street serving up delicious ceviches, seafood cocktails, and tacos. Outdoor seating is available along the adjacent terrace. **Known for:** Karina's signature spicy ceviche; choice between full-size plates or smaller tostadas; spicy marinades—ask for guidance if you want to order something mild. [$] *Average main: $10* ✉ *3731 India St., Suite B, Mission Hills* ☎ *619/255–5900* 🌐 *karinas-seafood.com.*

Lucha Libre Gourmet Taco Shop

$ | **MEXICAN** | Named for a form of Mexican wrestling, this taco shop with its hot-pink walls and shiny booths was famous mostly for its lack of parking until it appeared on the Travel Channel's "Man v. Food." Then long lines of burrito-crazed fans began forming outside the walk-up window for lunch; their North Park outpost is more spacious. **Known for:** Tap Me Out taco with fried cheese; California burritos with french fries inside; lively and festive interior seating. [$] *Average main: $9* ✉ *1810 W. Washington St., Mission Hills* ☎ *619/296–8226* 🌐 *www.tacosmackdown.com.*

Saffron

$ | **THAI** | Outdoor tables on a narrow sidewalk and inexpensive prices make this a standout. The simple menu by Bangkok-born chef-owner Su-Mei Yu has noodle soups; stir-fried noodles with chicken, beef, pork, or shrimp; and a couple of uncommon Vietnamese and Thai-Indian noodle dishes bathed with aromatic sauces. **Known for:** Thai grilled chicken; health-focused dishes like the Brain-Booster Stir-Fry; fresh noodle dishes. [$] *Average main: $10* ✉ *3731 India St., Mission Hills* ☎ *619/574–7737* 🌐 *www.saffronsandiego.com.*

Nightlife

Take your pick between unpretentious pubs or ultrastylish cocktail grottos.

BARS

Aero Club

BARS/PUBS | Named for its proximity to the airport, this watering hole draws in whiskey lovers for its unbeatable selection. ✉ *3365 India St., Mission Hills* ☎ *619/297–7211* 🌐 *www.aeroclubbar.com.*

Shakespeare Pub & Grille

BARS/PUBS | This Mission Hills hangout captures all the warmth and camaraderie of a traditional British pub—except here you can enjoy consistently sunny weather on the sprawling patio. The bar hands pour from a long list of imported ales and stouts, and the early hours for big matches make this *the* place to watch soccer. ✉ *3701 India St., Mission Hills* ☎ *619/299–0230* 🌐 *www.shakespeare-pub.com.*

★ Starlite

BARS/PUBS | Bar-goers are dazzled by Starlite's award-winning interior design, which includes rock walls, luxe leather booths, and a massive mirror-mounted chandelier. A hexagonal wood-plank entryway leads to a sunken white bar where creative cocktails, such as the signature Starlite Mule served in a copper mug, are mixed. During warmer months, procuring a spot on the outside wood-decked patio is an art form. ✉ *3175 India St., Mission Hills* ☎ *619/358–9766* 🌐 *www.starlitesandiego.com.*

Shopping

The shops and art galleries in Mission Hills have a modern and sophisticated ambience that suits the trendy residents.

CLOTHING AND ACCESSORIES
Le Bel Age Boutique
CLOTHING | A neighborhood staple for more than 30 years, this charming boutique carries maxi dresses, capri pants, and handbags, as well as jewelry designed by the owner, Valerie. Just down the street, sister boutique **Chateau Bel Age** features hard-to-find French designers and exotic-looking kaftans. ⊠ *1607 W. Lewis St., Mission Hills* ☎ *619/297-7080* ⊗ *Closed Sun. and Mon.*

HOME ACCESSORIES AND GIFTS
Maison en Provence
GIFTS/SOUVENIRS | This adorable little shop located in a Mission Hills bungalow is the place for Francophiles to get their French fix in San Diego. The French proprietors Pascal and Marielle Giai stock linen tablecloths and dishes from Provence. There are also fine soaps, antique postcards, and the most elegant of pocket knives. ⊠ *820 Ft. Stockton Dr., Mission Hills* ☎ *619/298-5318* ⊕ *www.everythingprovence.com.*

JEWELRY
Taboo Studio
JEWELRY/ACCESSORIES | This upscale gallery displays and sells the handcrafted jewelry of more than 75 artists from around the world. The stars here are the limited-edition pieces that incorporate precious metals and gemstones. The shop will also repurpose your old jewelry into something new. ⊠ *1615½ W. Lewis St., Mission Hills* ☎ *619/692-0099* ⊕ *www.taboostudio.net* ⊗ *Closed Sun. and Mon.*

MUSIC
M-Theory Music
MUSIC STORES | This locally owned record store in Mission Hills carries new and used vinyl and CDs. They regularly host in-store performances. ⊠ *827 W. Washington St., Mission Hills* ☎ *619/220-0485* ⊕ *www.mtheorymusic.com.*

Mission Valley

Although Mission Valley's charms may not be immediately apparent, it offers many conveniences to visitors and residents alike. One of the area's main attractions is the Fashion Valley Mall, with its mix of high-end and midrange retail stores and dining options, and a movie theater. The Mission Basilica San Diego de Alcalá provides a tranquil refuge from the surrounding suburban sprawl.

Sights

★ Mission Basilica San Diego de Alcalá
HISTORIC SITE | It's hard to imagine how remote California's earliest mission must have once been; these days, however, it's accessible by major freeways (I–15 and I–8) and via the San Diego Trolley. The first of a chain of 21 missions stretching northward along the coast, Mission San Diego de Alcalá was established by Father Junípero Serra on Presidio Hill in 1769 and moved to this location in 1774. In 1775, it proved vulnerable to enemy attack, and Padre Luís Jayme, a young friar from Spain, was clubbed to death by the Kumeyaay Indians he had been trying to convert. He was the first of more than a dozen Christians martyred in California. The present church, reconstructed in 1931 following the outline of the 1813 church, is the fifth built on the site. It measures 150 feet long but only 35 feet wide because, without easy means of joining beams, the mission buildings were only as wide as the trees that

Founded in 1769, Mission Basilica San Diego de Alcalá was the first of California's 21 Catholic missions.

served as their ceiling supports were tall. Father Jayme is buried in the sanctuary; a small museum named for him documents mission history and exhibits tools and artifacts from the early days; there is also a gift shop. From the peaceful, palm-bedecked gardens out back you can gaze at the 46-foot-high *campanario* (bell tower), the mission's most distinctive feature, with five bells. Mass is celebrated on the weekends. ⊠ *10818 San Diego Mission Rd., Mission Valley* ✛ *From I–8 east, exit and turn left on Mission Gorge Rd., then left on Twain Rd.; mission is on right* ☎ *619/281–8449* ⊕ *www.mission-sandiego.com* ✉ *$5.*

Nightlife

BARS

★ Blanco Tacos + Tequila

BARS/PUBS | Get your margarita skinny, spicy, or standard, with house-made sours and fresh-squeezed juices, at this prime new spot within Fashion Valley Mall. Don't miss Margarita Monday ($5 classic margaritas until 6 pm) or Taco Tuesday ($4 happy hour tacos until 6 pm). ⊠ *Fashion Valley Mall, 7007 Friars Rd., Mission Valley* ☎ *619/810–2931* ⊕ *www. blancotacostequila.com.*

Activities

HIKING

A day hike through the canyons and hills of Mission Trails Park is a great way to escape to nature without leaving the city.

Mission Trails Regional Park

HIKING/WALKING | This park 8 miles northeast of Downtown encompasses more than 7,000 acres of wooded hillsides, grasslands, chaparral, and streams. Trails range from easy to difficult; they include one with an impressive view of the city from Cowles Mountain and another along a historic missionary path. The park is also a popular place for rock climbing and camping (the Kumeyaay Lake Campground is open on weekends). Lake Murray is at the southern edge of the park, off Highway 8. ⊠ *1 Father Junípero Serra Trail, Mission Valley* ☎ *619/668–3281* ⊕ *www.mtrp.org.*

🛍 Shopping

Northeast of Downtown near I–8 and Route 163, Mission Valley holds two major shopping centers and a few smaller strip malls. Fashion Valley hosts an impressive roster of high-end department stores—among them Neiman Marcus, Nordstrom, and Bloomingdale's—and a passel of luxury boutiques like Hermès, Gucci, and Fendi. Westfield Mission Valley is home to mainstays like Old Navy, plus bargain-hunter favorites like Marshalls and Nordstrom Rack. The San Diego Trolley and city buses stop at both centers.

SHOPPING CENTERS

★ **Fashion Valley**

SHOPPING CENTERS/MALLS | San Diego's most upscale mall has a contemporary Mission theme, lush landscaping, and more than 200 shops and restaurants. Acclaimed retailers like Nordstrom, Neiman Marcus, Bloomingdale's, and Tiffany & Co. are here, along with boutiques from fashion darlings like Michael Kors, Tory Burch, and Ted Baker. H&M is a favorite of fashionistas in search of edgy and affordable styles. Free wireless Internet service is available throughout the mall. Select "Simon WiFi" from any Wi-Fi–enabled device to log onto the network. ■ **TIP→ If you're visiting from out of state, are a member of the military, or have a AAA membership, you can pick up a complimentary Style Pass at Simon Guest Services (located on the lower level beneath AMC Theaters near Banana Republic), which can get you savings at more than 70 of Fashion Valley's stores and restaurants.** ⊠ *7007 Friars Rd., Mission Valley* ☎ *619/688–9113* ⊕ *www.simon.com/mall/fashion-valley.*

Westfield Mission Valley

SHOPPING CENTERS/MALLS | **FAMILY** | Among the shops at this sprawling outdoor mall, you'll find American Eagle Outfitters, DSW Shoe Warehouse, and Victoria's Secret. ⊠ *1640 Camino del Rio North, Mission Valley* ☎ *619/296–6375* ⊕ *www. westfield.com/missionvalley.*

University Heights, Adams Avenue, and Normal Heights

Tucked between Hillcrest and North Park, the small but charming neighborhood of University Heights is centered on Park Boulevard. The tree-lined street is home to several notable bars and restaurants, as well as the acclaimed LGBT Diversionary Theatre. Kids love the playgrounds at Trolley Barn Park, just around the corner on Adams Avenue. The thriving nightlife and dining scene continues down Adams Avenue and into neighboring Normal Heights.

👁 Sights

Trolley Barn Park

CITY PARK | **FAMILY** | Kids will love the playgrounds at Trolley Barn Park, just around the corner on Adams Ave. The park is also home to free family concerts in the summer. ⊠ *Adams Ave. , between Georgia and Alabama sts., University Heights.*

🍴 Restaurants

On the mesas overlooking Mission Valley, these historic neighborhoods are experiencing a culinary renaissance with new casual ethnic dining and an array of wine bars and brewpubs, many with nightly entertainment.

El Zarape

$ | **MEXICAN** | Don't be fooled by the humble facade—this tiny Mexican taqueria serves up some of the best seafood-focused border food in town. There's almost always a crowd of Uptown locals and savvy travelers here, but orders for burritos, tacos, and combination plates almost fly out of the kitchen. **Known for:** 99¢ fish tacos; seafood dishes; extensive menu. ⓢ *Average main: $8* ✉ *4642 Park Blvd., University Heights* ☎ *619/692–1652.*

Madison

$$ | **MEDITERRANEAN** | The award-winning design of this restaurant and bar is the definition of Southern California chic, as are its patrons. The vaulted wood-clad ceiling and indoor/outdoor space creates a stunning yet inviting backdrop for the inspired cocktails—mixologists incorporate ingredients such as matcha and hemp oil into their featured libations—and SoCal Mediterranean cuisine. **Known for:** dramatic interior design; innovative cocktails; weekend brunch. ⓢ *Average main: $20* ✉ *4622 Park Blvd., University Heights* ☎ *619/269–6566* ⊕ *www.madisononpark.com* ☽ *Closed Mon.; no lunch weekdays.*

ⓨ Nightlife

These low-key uptown neighborhoods house some of San Diego's favorite local watering holes.

BARS

★ Cantina Mayahuel

BARS/PUBS | The well-respected Cantina Mayahuel carries San Diego's largest collection of agave-based Mexican spirits—with tequila flights to boot—and is regularly frequented by local service industry pros. ✉ *2934 Adams Ave., University Heights* ☎ *619/283–6292.*

Park and Rec

BARS/PUBS | Craft cocktails and local beers are served up with a side of fun in this indoor/outdoor bungalow complex featuring live music and classic games from Ping-Pong to pinball. ✉ *4612 Park Blvd., University Heights* ☎ *619/795–9700* ⊕ *www.parkandrecsd.com.*

Polite Provisions

BARS/PUBS | The look of this cocktail lounge on the border of North Park and Normal Heights is drugstore chic, but the drinks themselves—none of which contain vodka—are much more sophisticated fare, shaken or stirred with house-made bitters and sodas. If you're looking to nosh, the adjoining Soda & Swine serves meatballs right to your table, and the $6 drinks during the three-hour Monday–Thursday happy hour are a must for those seeking mixology on a budget. ✉ *4696 30th St., Normal Heights* ☎ *619/269–4701* ⊕ *politeprovisions.com.*

Small Bar

BREWPUBS/BEER GARDENS | True to its name, this University Heights pub is, well, pint-sized, but the beer selection is huge. This means that on any given night the place is packed with aficionados and novices alike vying to try old favorites and new additions. ✉ *4628 Park Blvd., University Heights* ☎ *619/795–7998.*

Sycamore Den

BARS/PUBS | The heavy use of wood and stone, and accents like banjos and rifles, might give Sycamore Den a masculine vibe, but it's a highly specific and kitschy one: '70s dads. Though the hipster-pop concept might seem like it was plucked right out of a Tumblr meme, the drinks here are worth the irony, and the calendar is typically filled with great local, acoustic live bands. ✉ *3391 Adams Ave., Normal Heights* ☎ *619/563–9019* ⊕ *www.sycamoreden.com.*

BREWPUBS

Blind Lady Ale House

BARS/PUBS | There's almost no combination on earth as satisfying as pizza and beer—which just happen to be Blind Lady's specialties. The old world–style pizzas are topped with organic ingredients, like house-made chorizo and avocado, which offer an excellent complement to their extensive beer selection, which is updated on their chalkboard daily. Just be patient waiting for a seat at the popular neighborhood spot, which is decorated in resourced materials such as reclaimed wood floors and glass cases of vintage beer cans. ✉ *3416 Adams Ave., University Heights* ☎ *619/255–2491* 🌐 *www.blindladyalehouse.com.*

COFFEEHOUSES

Lestat's Coffee Shop

CAFES—NIGHTLIFE | One of the few San Diego coffee shops that's open 24 hours a day, this Normal Heights mainstay also has a great selection of baked goods and a neighboring music venue that stages acoustic and comedy acts seven days a week. Lestat's also has locations in University Heights and Hillcrest. ✉ *3343 Adams Ave., Normal Heights* ☎ *619/282–0437* 🌐 *www.lestats.com.*

🎟 Performing Arts

Diversionary Theatre

THEATER | San Diego's premier gay and lesbian company presents a range of original works that focus on LGBT themes. ✉ *4545 Park Blvd., Suite 101, University Heights* ☎ *619/220–0097* 🌐 *www.diversionary.org.*

🛍 Shopping

University Avenue is good for furniture, gift, and specialty stores appealing to college students, singles, and young families.

CLOTHING AND ACCESSORIES

Maven

CLOTHING | Shop hard-to-find clothing, accessories, and home decor at this locally owned store focused on handmade goods. ✉ *2946 Adams Ave., Normal Heights* ☎ *619/280–2474* 🌐 *www.mavensd.com* 🕒 *Closed Sun.*

North Park

Named for its location north of Balboa Park, this evolving neighborhood is home to an exciting array of restaurants, bars, and shops. The stretch of Ray Street near University Avenue is home to several small galleries, as well as the Ray at Night art walk, held the second Saturday of each month. Just around the corner on University Avenue lies the stunning 1920s-era North Park Theatre. With a steady stream of new openings in the neighborhood, North Park is one of San Diego's top dining and nightlife destinations. Beer enthusiasts won't want to miss the breweries and tasting rooms along the 30th St. Beer Corridor, dubbed "Beer Boulevard", for a chance to sample San Diego's famous ales.

🍴 Restaurants

City Tacos

$ | **MEXICAN** | This small space in North Park elevates the traditional taco shop experience with superior ingredients and unique toppings. Several vegan and paleo tacos are offered alongside their seafood and meat selections. **Known for:** unique toppings on traditional tacos; specialty aioli and salsa bar; vegan and paleo tacos. [$] *Average main: $8* ✉ *3028 University Ave., North Park* ☎ *619/296–2303* 🌐 *citytacossd.com.*

URBN North Park

$ | **PIZZA** | **FAMILY** | A 5,000-square-foot brick-and-wood industrial-style dining room and bar attracts hip young locals who chow down on thin-crust New Haven–style pies, fresh salads, cheese boards, and chicken wings. It can get loud and crowded at times, but is always festive for groups—first dates, not so much. **Known for:** mashed-potato pizza; local craft beer selection; desserts cooked in the coal-fired oven. $ Average main: $19 ⊠ 3085 University Ave., North Park ☎ 619/255–7300 ⊕ www.urbnnorth-park.com.

Waypoint Public

$ | **MODERN AMERICAN** | **FAMILY** | Kids romp in their own picket fence–enclosed play area while parents join fellow neighborhood residents in sophisticated meals in this beer-centric casual restaurant. A unique 30-tap system serves up West Coast craft brews; many are suggested as pairings with the seasonal value-priced menu. **Known for:** unique 30-tap craft beer setup; kid-friendly ambience; weekend brunch. $ Average main: $18 ⊠ 3794 30th St., North Park ☎ 619/255–8778 ⊕ www.waypointpublic.com ⊙ No weekday lunch.

ⓨ Nightlife

Young, hip artist types gather to sip craft beer along the 30th Street corridor.

BARS

★ Seven Grand

PIANO BARS/LOUNGES | This whiskey lounge is a swanky addition to an already thriving North Park nightlife scene and a welcome alternative to the neighboring dives and dance clubs. Live jazz, a tranquil atmosphere, and a bourbon-loving craft cocktail list keep locals flocking. ⊠ 3054 University Ave., North Park ☎ 619/269–8820 ⊕ sevengrandbars.com.

Toronado

BARS/PUBS | One of San Diego's favorite gathering spots for hop-heads is named in honor of the San Francisco beer bar of the same name. The beer list—both on tap and by the bottle—is hard to beat.

The place can get noisy, but the food—a mix of burgers and American-style comfort food—more than makes up for it. ⊠ 4026 30th St., North Park ☎ 619/282–0452 ⊕ www.toronadosd.com.

BREWPUBS

Bivouac Ciderworks

BREWPUBS/BEER GARDENS | In a town dominated by beer, craft ciders offer a refreshing alternative to the typical IPA. True to its name, Bivouac's design incorporates an open front and an interior seemingly held together by ropes—the rear table with suspended bench seating is a favorite of larger parties. Cider aficionados and newcomers alike can sample a wide range of styles through customizable flights, while skeptics can stick to the selection of wine, craft beer, and fruit-based cocktails (think brandy). The Filipino-influenced menu, much of it gluten-free and vegan, is as big of a draw as the cider. ⊠ 3986 30th St., North Park ☎ 619/725–0844 ⊕ www.bivouaccider.com ⊙ Closed Mon.

Tiger! Tiger!

BREWPUBS/BEER GARDENS | A communal vibe prevails at this wood, metal, and brick gastropub, where patrons sit at picnic tables to schmooze and sip from one of the dozens of carefully selected craft and microbrews on tap. ⊠ 3025 El Cajon Blvd., North Park ☎ 619/487–0401 ⊕ www.tigertigertavern.com.

COFFEEHOUSES

Caffè Calabria

BARS/PUBS | This longstanding North Park coffee roaster and café expands its evening offerings to include local beer, wine, and Italian-style cocktails. ⊠ 3933 30th St., North Park ☎ ⊕ www.caffecalabria.com ⊙ Closed Mon. and Tues. evenings.

🎭 Performing Arts

Observatory North Park

CONCERTS | Formerly North Park Theatre, the Observatory North Park has 90 years of history inside its ornate and beautiful walls. It's a top-tier destination for touring musical acts, hosting shows several nights a week. ⊠ *2891 University Ave., North Park* ☎ *619/239–8836* ⊕ *www. observatorysd.com.*

🛍 Shopping

North Park, east of Hillcrest, is a hipster's paradise, with resale shops, trendy boutiques, and stores that sell mostly handcrafted items.

CLOTHING AND ACCESSORIES

★ Aloha Beach Club

CLOTHING | This carefully curated boutique with high ceilings and blond-wood accents carries no Billabong or Quiksilver, but make no mistake, this is a surf shop at heart. The store sells handcrafted accessories and apparel from unique labels like Outerknown, Miansai, and the store's own brand of tailored men's clothing designed by co-owner and former pro-surfer Kahana Kalama. ⊠ *3039 University Ave., North Park* ☎ *619/269–9838* ⊕ *www.alohabeachclub.com.*

★ Mimi & Red Boutique

CLOTHING | Laid-back ambience, friendly service, and racks full of moderate to high-end women's fashions have made this shop a favorite with cool San Diegans. Nixon and Everly are here along with RVCA, Free People, and handcrafted bath and body products. ⊠ *3041 University Ave., North Park* ☎ *619/298–7933* ⊕ *www.mimiandred.com.*

Overload

CLOTHING | Get the latest brands of footwear, streetwear, skateboards, and accessories at this edgy skate shop. ⊠ *3827 30th St., North Park* ☎ *619/296–9018* ⊕ *www.shopoverload.com.*

Rufskin

CLOTHING | The flagship menswear boutique for the namesake denim line sells sexy jeans, casual and dress shirts, swimwear, bold accessories, and custom leather items. ⊠ *3944 30th St., North Park* ☎ *619/564–7880* ⊕ *www.rufskin. com* ☾ *Closed Sun.*

HOME ACCESSORIES AND GIFTS

★ Artelexia

GIFTS/SOUVENIRS | Browse the colorful selection of Mexican gifts, cooking supplies, and decor at this inviting local boutique. ⊠ *3803 Ray St., North Park* ☎ *619/501–6381* ⊕ *www.artelexia.com.*

★ Pigment

BOOKS/STATIONERY | This beautifully styled shop carries a wide variety of design-conscious goods for the home, including geometric print pillows, outdoor bistro chairs, and home bar accessories. In Pigment's plant lab, you can build your own terrariums, which make great souvenirs. ⊠ *3801 30th St., North Park* ☎ *619/501–6318* ⊕ *www.shoppigment.com.*

Simply Local

CLOTHING | This shop carries merchandise from more than 55 local artisans, including jewelry, home decor, bath products, and specialty foods like almond butter and local honey. ⊠ *3013 University Ave., North Park* ☎ *619/756–7958* ⊕ *www. simplylocalsandiego.com.*

South Park

The South Park neighborhood is actually on the east side of Balboa Park, but it's south of North Park, hence the name. The tree-lined neighborhood is largely residential but its collection of interesting galleries, boutiques, and restaurants makes for a nice stroll.

🍴 Restaurants

★ Buona Forchetta

$ | **ITALIAN** | **FAMILY** | A golden-domed pizza oven, named Sofia after the owner's daughter, delivers authentic Neapolitan-style pizza to fans who often line up for patio tables at this dog- and kid-friendly Italian restaurant in South Park. Pizzas make a meal or can be shared, but don't miss the equally delicious appetizers, heaping salads, or fresh pastas, and be sure to save room for some dolci. **Known for:** house-made sangria; bubbly Neapolitan-style pizzas; bustling patio. $ Average main: $15 ⊠ 3001 Beech St., South Park ☎ 619/381–4844 ⊕ buonaforchettasd. com ☾ No lunch Mon.

★ Eclipse Chocolate Bar & Bistro

$ | **AMERICAN** | This local bistro and chocolatier sells flavored bars, truffles, cupcakes, and many other confections, as well as breakfast favorites (buttermilk pancakes or avocado Benedict) and mains that are good at any point in the day—pulled pork and grits or mascarpone-stuffed meatballs—plus beer and wine. The owner of this popular brunch spot won a special chocolate episode of Food Network's Guy's Grocery Games in 2017. **Known for:** build-your-own chocolate bar nights; there's a little bit of vanilla, caramel, or cacao worked into every dish; add a chocolate pairing to your glass of wine for $1. $ Average main: $15 ⊠ 2145 Fern St., South Park ☎ 619/578–2984 ⊕ www.eclipsechocolate.com ☾ No dinner Sun.

Kindred

$ | **VEGETARIAN** | Pink paisley wallpaper and marble-topped tables stand among skull prints, Gothic art, and a giant ram head in this busy restaurant-bar—emphasis on the bar. The vegan menu is not what you might expect, and the bold flavors and satisfying portions will please both herbivores and carnivores alike. **Known for:** Memphis BBQ jackfruit sandwich; vegan cheese board; weekend brunch. $ Average main: $12 ⊠ 1503 30th St., South Park ☎ 619/546–9653 ⊕ www.barkindred.com ☾ No lunch weekdays.

Piacere Mio

$ | **ITALIAN** | Fresh homemade pasta served as the diner wants it is the mantra at this cozy Italian restaurant. Opt for indoor seating, which offers a charming, old-world feel, with warm lighting, wood beam ceilings, and exposed brick. **Known for:** make-it-your-own pasta menu; sizable portions; traditional antipasti plates. $ Average main: $17 ⊠ 1947 Fern St., South Park ☎ 619/794–2543 ⊕ www. piaceremiosd.com.

🍸 Nightlife

BARS

★ Hamilton's Tavern

BARS/PUBS | Affectionately known to its loyal crowd of locals as Hammy's, this bar has one of the best beer lists in town. On the ceiling, lights strung between old beer taps twinkle as bright as the eyes of the suds-lovers who flock here. In between pours, grab something from Hammy's kitchen—people come from all over for the wings and burgers. ⊠ 1521 30th St., South Park ☎ 619/238–5460 ⊕ hamiltonstavern.com.

🛍 Shopping

South Park's tree-lined 30th, Juniper, and Fern streets are wonderful for a shopping stroll. Local boutiques have everything from eco-friendly fashions to craft supplies and home decor.

BOOKS

★ The Book Catapult

BOOKS/STATIONERY | FAMILY | This exceptional bookstore offers well-curated local interest materials, bestsellers, and an excellent children's section. Puzzle enthusiasts will appreciate the unique jigsaw selection, guaranteed to keep you challenged. Don't miss the back room with its selection of local clothing and gifts. ✉ *3010-B Juniper St., South Park* ☎ *619/795–3780* ⊕ *thebookcatapult.com* ⊙ *Closed Mon.*

CLOTHING AND ACCESSORIES

Graffiti Beach

CLOTHING | This indie boutique in South Park's historic 30th & Fern building is filled with quirky art, jewelry, gifts, and clothing from emerging designers and artists using recycled or repurposed materials. This is a great place to pick up souvenirs if you're into supporting local: 75% of the designers are from California. ✉ *2220 Fern St., South Park* ☎ *858/433–0950* ⊕ *www.shopgraffitibeach.com.*

HOME ACCESSORIES AND GIFTS

★ Gold Leaf

CERAMICS/GLASSWARE | This home decor shop is run by a husband-and-wife duo. There's furniture, kitchenware, jewelry, greeting cards, and a kids' section. ✉ *2225 30th St., South Park* ☎ *619/738–8120* ⊕ *www.goldleafsouthpark.com.*

Tend Living

GIFTS/SOUVENIRS | This trendy plant shop and boutique stocks succulents, ferns, and cacti that make great home decor gifts. ✉ *1925 30th St., South Park* ☎ *858/876–8363.*

Chapter 6

MISSION BAY AND THE BEACHES

Updated by
Claire Deeks Van Der Lee

👁 Sights   🍴 Restaurants   🛏 Hotels   🛍 Shopping   🍸 Nightlife
★★★★★   ★★★☆☆   ★★★★☆   ★☆☆☆☆   ★★★☆☆

NEIGHBORHOOD SNAPSHOT

GREAT EXPERIENCES

■ **Sun and sand:** With sand stretching as far as the eye can see, Mission and Pacific beaches represent the classic Southern California beach experience.

■ **Bustling boardwalk:** Twentysomethings partying at the bars, families grilling in front of their vacation homes, and kids playing in the sand—take in the scene with a stroll along the Mission Beach boardwalk.

■ **Bayside delights:** A quiet respite from the nearby beaches, Mission Bay is ringed with peaceful pathways, playgrounds, and parks.

■ **Get out on the water:** Catch a wave, paddle a kayak, or rev a Jet Ski at this irresistible water-sports playground.

QUICK BITES

Bao Beach. The Asian poke bowls and fluffy steamed bao "tacos" offer a unique alternative to the typical beach boardwalk fare. With limited seating, this street food shop is best for a quick bite or take-out. **Known for:** filled bao buns or "Asian tacos"; bulgogi street fries; limited seating. ⊠ *3735 Mission Blvd., Mission Beach* ☎ *858/381–0033* ⊕ *www.baobeacheats.com.*

Kono's Cafe. Take in the boardwalk vibe as you wait in line for your breakfast burrito at this legendary spot at the base of Crystal Pier. **Known for:** big breakfasts; surfer vibe; people-watching along the boardwalk. ⊠ *704 Garnet Ave., Pacific Beach* ☎ *858/483–1669* ⊕ *www.konoscafe.com* ⊟ *No credit cards.*

Sportsmen's Seafood. This waterside eatery serves good fish-and-chips, seafood salads, and sandwiches to eat on the inelegant but scenic patio—by the marina, where sportfishing boats depart daily—or to take out to your chosen picnic spot. **Known for:** in the middle of marina action; takeout options; fish-and-chips. ⊠ *1617 Quivira Rd., Mission Bay* ☎ *619/224–3551* ⊕ *www.sportsmensseafood.com* ⊟ *No credit cards.*

GETTING HERE

■ SeaWorld, Mission Bay, and Mission and Pacific beaches are all served by public bus routes 8 and 9. Many local hotels offer shuttle service to and from SeaWorld. There is a free parking lot at Belmont Park, although it can quickly fill during busy times.

PLANNING YOUR TIME

■ You may not find a visit to SeaWorld fulfilling unless you spend at least half a day; a full day is recommended.

■ Belmont Park is open daily, but not all its rides are open year-round.

■ The Mission Beach Boardwalk and the miles of trails around Mission Bay are great for a leisurely bike ride.

■ On foggy days, particularly in late spring or early summer, the beaches can be overcast in the morning with the fog burning off as the day wears on.

MISSION BAY WARNINGS

■ Swimmers at Mission Bay should note signs warning about water pollution; on occasions when heavy rains or other events cause pollution, swimming is strongly discouraged.

Mission Bay and the surrounding beaches are the aquatic playground of San Diego. The choice of activities available is astonishing, and the perfect weather makes you want to get out there and play. If you're craving downtime after all the activity, there are plenty of peaceful spots to relax and simply soak up the sunshine.

Mission Bay welcomes visitors with its protected waters and countless opportunities for fun. The 4,600-acre **Mission Bay Park** is the place for water sports like sailing, stand-up paddleboarding, and water-skiing. With 19 miles of beaches and grassy areas, it's also a great place for a picnic. And if you have kids, don't miss **SeaWorld,** one of San Diego's most popular attractions.

Heading west on Mission Bay Drive to the ocean, the Giant Dipper roller coaster rises into view, welcoming visitors to the **Belmont Park** amusement park and to **Mission Beach.** Mission Boulevard runs north along a two-block-wide strip embraced by the Pacific Ocean on the west and the bay on the east. Mission Beach is a famous and lively fun zone for families and young people both; if it isn't party time at the moment, it will be five minutes from now. The pathways in this area are lined with vacation homes, many for rent by the week or month. Those fortunate enough to live here year-round have the bay as their front yard, with wide sandy beaches, volleyball courts, and—less of an advantage—an endless stream of sightseers on the sidewalk.

North of Mission Beach is the college-packed party town of **Pacific Beach,** or "PB" as locals call it. The laid-back vibe of this surfer's mecca draws in free-spirited locals who roam the streets on skateboards and beach cruisers, in the local uniform of board shorts, bikinis, and baseball caps. Lining the main strip of Grand and Garnet avenues are tattoo parlors, smoke shops, vintage stores, and coffeehouses. The energy level peaks during happy hour, when PB's cluster of nightclubs, bars, and 150 restaurants open their doors to those ready to party.

◉ Sights

Bahia Belle Cruises

LIGHTHOUSE | At the dock of the Bahia Resort Hotel, on the eastern shores of West Mission Bay Drive, you can board this restored stern-wheeler for a sunset cruise of the bay and a party that continues until the wee hours. There's always music on board, and on Friday and Saturday nights the music is live. You can imbibe at the *Belle*'s full bar, but many revelers like to disembark at the Bahia's sister hotel, the Catamaran Resort, and have a few rounds before reboarding; the

Planning a Day at the Beaches and Bay ⊙

A day spent at Mission Bay or the surrounding beaches can be as active or leisurely as you like.

If you want to play in the water, the bay is a great place to kayak, sail, or try some stand-up paddleboarding. If you're into surfing, be sure to check out the waves at **Crystal Pier** in Pacific Beach.

If you want to keep active on land, the Bayside Walk and Bike Path is a great place to jog or ride along the bay. Beach Cruiser bike rentals are widely available. For a more leisurely stroll and some people-watching, head to the **Mission Beach Boardwalk.** At the south end of Mission Beach try your hand at some typically Californian beach volleyball.

If you'd rather take it easy, just find a spot to lay out your towel anywhere along Mission or Pacific Beach and soak up the sun. If you tire of the sand, enjoy a picnic at one of the many grassy spots throughout **Mission Bay Park** or enjoy the view from one of the restaurants at Paradise Point Resort and Spa. As the day winds down, the happy-hour crowd is just heating up along Garnet Avenue in Pacific Beach. Alternatively, head to the Bahia Resort Hotel, where you can catch the Bahia Belle for a cruise around the bay.

If you are traveling with kids, a day at **SeaWorld** should be high on your list. There is plenty of family fun beyond SeaWorld, too. The protected beaches of the bay are popular spots for youngsters. The well-paved, peaceful Bayside Walk and Bike Path winds past picnic tables, grassy areas, and playgrounds, making it an ideal family spot. For a more lively contrast, cross the street to reach the Mission Beach Boardwalk, a classic boardwalk popular with young, hip surfers. At the south end lies **Belmont Park,** which includes an amusement park, restaurants, and the **Giant Dipper** wooden roller coaster.

boat cruises between the two hotels, which co-own it, stopping to pick up passengers every half hour. Most cruises get a mixed crowd of families, couples, and singles, but cruises after 9:30 pm are adults-only. ⊠ *998 W. Mission Bay Dr., Mission Bay* ☎ *858/539–8666* ⊕ *www. bahiahotel.com/bahia-belle* ⊠ *$10 for unlimited cruising; free for guests of Bahia and Catamaran hotels* ⊙ *Closed Dec.–Feb.*

★ **Belmont Park**

AMUSEMENT PARK/WATER PARK | FAMILY | The once-abandoned amusement park between the bay and Mission Beach Boardwalk is now a shopping, dining, and recreation complex. Twinkling lights outline the **Giant Dipper,** an antique wooden roller coaster on which screaming thrill-seekers ride more than 2,600 feet of track and 13 hills (riders must be at least 4 feet, 2 inches tall). Created in 1925 and listed on the National Register of Historic Places, this is one of the few old-time roller coasters left in the United States.

Other Belmont Park attractions include miniature golf, a laser maze, video arcade, bumper cars, a tilt-a-whirl, and an antique carousel. The zip line thrills as it soars over the crowds below, while the rock wall challenges both junior climbers and their elders. ⊠ *3146 Mission Blvd., Mission Bay* ☎ *858/488–1549 for rides* ⊕ *www.belmontpark.com* ⊠ *Unlimited ride day package $32 for 48 inches and taller, $22 for under 48 inches, some attractions not included in price;*

individual ride tickets and other ride/ attraction combo packages are also available.

★ Crystal Pier

BEACH—SIGHT | Stretching out into the ocean from the end of Garnet Avenue, Crystal Pier is Pacific Beach's landmark. A stroll to the end of the pier will likely reveal fishermen hoping for a good catch. Surfers make catches of their own in the waves below. ⊠ *Pacific Beach ✤ At end of Garnet Ave.*

Fiesta Island

NATIONAL/STATE PARK | The most undeveloped area of Mission Bay Park, this is popular with bird-watchers (there's a large protected nesting site for the California tern at the northern tip of the island) as well as with dog owners, because it's the only place in the park where pets can run free. In July the annual Over-the-Line Tournament, a competition involving a unique local version of softball, attracts thousands of players and oglers. ⊠ *Access from East Mission Bay Dr., Mission Bay.*

★ Mission Bay Park

BEACH—SIGHT | San Diego's monument to sports and fitness, this 4,600-acre aquatic park has 27 miles of shoreline including 19 miles of sandy beaches. Playgrounds and picnic areas abound on the beaches and low, grassy hills. On weekday evenings, joggers, bikers, and skaters take over. In the daytime, swimmers, water-skiers, paddleboarders, anglers, and boaters—some in single-person kayaks, others in crowded powerboats—vie for space in the water. ⊠ *2688 E. Mission Bay Dr., Mission Bay ✤ Off I–5 at Exit 22 E. Mission Bay Dr.* ☎ *858/581–7602 park ranger's office* ⊕ *www.sandiego.gov/park-and-recreation* ☞ *Free.*

★ Mission Beach Boardwalk

BEACH—SIGHT | The cement pathway lining the sand from the southern end of Mission Beach north to Pacific Beach is always bustling with activity. Cyclists ping the bells on their beach cruisers to pass walkers out for a stroll alongside the oceanfront homes. Vacationers kick back on their patios, while friends play volleyball in the sand. The activity picks up alongside Belmont Park, where people stop to check out the action at the amusement park and beach bars. ⊠ *Mission Beach ✤ Alongside sand from Mission Beach Park to Pacific Beach.*

SeaWorld San Diego

AMUSEMENT PARK/WATER PARK | **FAMILY** | Spread over 189 tropically landscaped bayfront acres, SeaWorld is one of the world's largest marine-life amusement parks. The majority of its exhibits are walk-through marine environments like **Shark Encounter,** where guests walk through a 57-foot acrylic tube and come face-to-face with a variety of sharks that call the 280,000-gallon habitat home. **Turtle Reef** offers an incredible up-close encounter with the green sea turtle, while the moving sidewalk at **Penguin Encounter** whisks you through a colony of nearly 300 penguins. The park also wows with its adventure rides like the **Electric Eel,** a shocking multi-launch coaster that sends riders twisting forward and backwards 150 feet in the air at speeds reaching 60 mph, and the comparatively milder **Journey to Atlantis,** a water coaster with a heart-stopping 60-foot plunge. Younger children will enjoy the rides, climbing structures, and splash pads at the **Sesame Street Bay of Play**.

SeaWorld is most famous for its large-arena entertainments, but this is an area in transition. The park's latest orca experience features a nature-inspired backdrop and demonstrates orca behaviors in the wild, part of SeaWorld's efforts to refocus its orca program toward education and conservation. Other live-entertainment shows feature dolphins, sea otters, and even household pets. Several upgraded animal encounters are available including the Dolphin Interaction

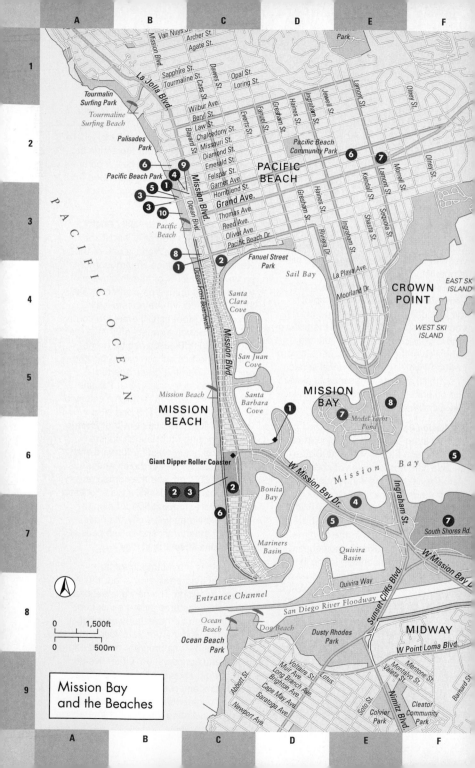

Mission Bay
and the Beaches

6

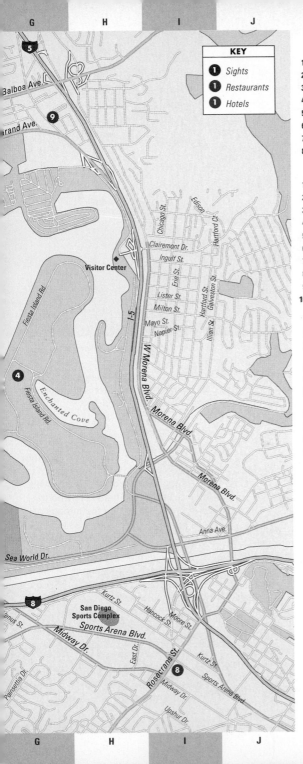

KEY

1 Sights
1 Restaurants
1 Hotels

Sights ▼

1 Bahia Belle Cruises D6
2 Belmont Park...................... C6
3 Crystal Pier B3
4 Fiesta Island G5
5 Mission Bay Park.................. F6
6 Mission Beach Boardwalk C7
7 SeaWorld San Diego.............. F7
8 Vacation Isle E5

Restaurants ▼

1 The Baked Bear.................... B3
2 Cannonball C6
3 Draft South Mission C6
4 JRDN................................ B3
5 Kono's Cafe......................... B3
6 Pacific Beach Fish Shop.......... E2
7 The Patio on Lamont E2
8 Rubio's Coastal Grill I9
9 Sushi Ota G2
10 Waterbar B3

Hotels ▼

1 Blue Sea Beach Hotel............. C3
2 Catamaran Resort
   Hotel and Spa..................... C3
3 Crystal Pier Hotel & Cottages B3
4 The Dana on Mission Bay E7
5 Hyatt Regency Mission Bay
   Spa and Marina................... E7
6 Pacific Terrace Hotel............. B2
7 Paradise Point Resort & Spa...... E6
8 Surfer Beach Hotel................ C3
9 TOWER23.......................... B3

Belmont Park, an amusement park between the bay and Mission Beach Boardwalk, is home to lovely sunsets and the Giant Dipper Roller Coaster.

Program, which gives guests the chance to interact with SeaWorld's bottlenose dolphins in the water. The hour-long program (20 minutes in the water), during which visitors can feed, touch, and give behavior signals, costs $215. ⊠ *500 Sea-World Dr., near west end of I–8, Mission Bay* ☎ *800/257–4268* ⊕ *www.seaworldparks.com* 🖃 *$92 ages 3 and older; advanced purchase discounts available online; parking $22.*

Vacation Isle
BEACH—SIGHT | Ingraham Street bisects this island, providing two distinct experiences for visitors. The west side is taken up by the Paradise Point Resort & Spa, but you don't have to be a guest to enjoy the hotel's lushly landscaped grounds and bay-front restaurants. Boaters and jet-skiers congregate near the launch at **Ski Beach** on the east side of the island, where there's a parking lot as well as picnic areas and restrooms. Ski Beach is the site of the annual Bayfair boat races held every September. At the model yacht pond on the south side of the island,

children and young-at-heart adults take part year-round in motorized miniature boat races. ⊠ *Mission Bay.*

🏖 Beaches

The long expanse of sand running from Mission to Pacific Beach is some of the most popular in San Diego with locals and visitors alike. There is an energetic atmosphere among the throngs of beachgoers—the boardwalks bustle with activity, and surf culture reigns supreme.

The 2-mile stretch of sand that makes up Mission Beach extends north to Belmont Park and draws huge crowds on summer weekends. This is a great place for people-watching along the boardwalk and on the volleyball courts at the southern tip.

Pacific Beach picks up where Mission Beach leaves off and extends north to Crystal Pier. Parking is tough, but the scene on Ocean Front Walk and the party atmosphere may just be worth it. Technically part of Pacific Beach, a portion of **Tourmaline Surfing Park** is designated for

Beach Bonfires 👁

Just because the sun went down doesn't mean it's time to go home. Nothing compares to sitting around a crackling fire as the evening breeze ushers in whiffs of the sea. Fires are allowed only in fire rings, which you can find at Mission Beach and Pacific Beach; they are also available in Ocean Beach and Coronado Beach. Revelers snap up ring slots quickly in summer; stake your claim early by filling one with wood and setting your gear nearby.

surfing only. If you're looking for post-beach drinks, Garnet Street is home to the neighborhood's liveliest bars. College students head to Garnet on Friday and Saturday nights; at other times, it's more laid-back.

Mission Beach

BEACH—SIGHT | FAMILY | With a roller coaster, arcade, and hot dog stands, this 2-mile-long beach has a carnival vibe and is the closest thing you'll find to Coney Island on the West Coast. It's lively year-round but draws a huge crowd on hot summer days. A wide boardwalk paralleling the beach is popular with walkers, joggers, skateboarders, and bicyclists. To escape the crowds, head to South Mission Beach. It attracts surfers, swimmers, and volleyball players, who often play competitive pickup games on the courts near the north jetty. The water near the Belmont Park roller coaster can be a bit rough but makes for good body-boarding and bodysurfing. For free parking, you can try for a spot on the street, but your best bets are the two big lots at Belmont Park. **Amenities:** lifeguards, parking (no fee), showers, toilets. **Best for:** swimming, surfing, walking. ⊠ *3000 Mission Blvd., Mission Bay ✛ Parking near roller coaster at West Mission Bay Dr.* ⊕ *www.sandiego.gov/lifeguards/beaches/mb.shtml.*

Pacific Beach/North Pacific Beach

BEACH—SIGHT | This beach, known for attracting a young college-age crowd and surfers, runs from the northern end of Mission Beach to Crystal Pier. The scene here is lively on weekends, with nearby restaurants, beach bars, and nightclubs providing a party atmosphere. In P.B. (as the locals call it) Sundays are known as "Sunday Funday," and pub crawls can last all day. So although drinking is no longer allowed on the beach, it's still likely you'll see people who have had one too many. The mood changes just north of the pier at North Pacific Beach, which attracts families and surfers. Although not quite pillowy, the sand at both beaches is nice and soft, which makes for great sunbathing and sand-castle building. ■TIP→ **Kelp and flies can be a problem on this stretch, so choose your spot wisely.** Parking at Pacific Beach can also be a challenge. A few coveted free angle parking spaces are available along the boardwalk, but you'll most likely have to look for spots in the surrounding neighborhood. **Amenities:** food and drink, lifeguards, parking (no fee), showers, toilets. **Best for:** partiers, swimming, surfing. ⊠ *4500 Ocean Blvd., Pacific Beach* ⊕ *www.sandiego.gov/lifeguards/beaches/pb.shtml.*

Tourmaline Surfing Park

BEACH—SIGHT | Offering slow waves and frequent winds, this is one of the most popular beaches for surfers. For wind-surfing and kiteboarding, it's only sailable

Talking Tacos 🍴

Even though terms like taco, burrito, enchilada, and tostada are as common as macaroni and cheese to San Diegans, don't count on any residents to agree on where to find the best ones. That's because tacos are as individual as spaghetti sauce and come in endless variations from small, authentic Mexico City–style tacos to Cal-Mex versions in crunchy shells topped with cheddar cheese.

The most traditional style of taco features a small soft corn tortilla pressed from corn masa dough and filled with shredded beef, carne asada (roasted beef), braised tongue in green sauce, spicy marinated pork, or deep-fried fish or seafood. Tortillas made from white flour are out there, too, but they're not nearly as tasty.

Garnishes usually include a drizzle of salsa and a squeeze of tart Mexican lime (a small citrus similar to the Key lime that's juicier than the large lime commonly found in the United States), along with chopped cilantro and onion. Whole radishes topped with lime juice and a sprinkle of salt are served on the side.

with northwest winds. The 175-space parking lot at the foot of Tourmaline Street normally fills to capacity by midday. Just like Pacific Beach, Tourmaline has soft, tawny-colored sand, but when the tide is in the beach becomes quite narrow, making finding a good sunbathing spot a bit of a challenge. **Amenities:** seasonal lifeguards, parking (no fee), showers, toilets. **Best for:** windsurfing, surfing. ✉ *600 Tourmaline St., Pacific Beach.*

🍴 Restaurants

This sprawling area is all about great views of the water, sandy beaches, and relaxation. Most of the restaurants here are casual spots that diners can visit in T-shirts, shorts, and flip-flops. Food is similarly laid-back. Burgers and tacos are easy to find, but so are sushi, Mexican, and Thai food. Many of the restaurants here are bars at heart.

Streets closest to the ocean in Pacific Beach, San Diego's largest beach community, can be party central for visitors and locals who jam-pack a wide range of restaurants and bars reflecting the casual surf and beach culture.

The Baked Bear

$ | BAKERY | FAMILY | This build-your-own ice cream–sandwich shop a block from Pacific Beach is a local favorite thanks to its homemade cookies and diverse array of ice-cream flavors, from birthday cake to peanut butter fudge. **Known for:** Bear Bowls made of cookies; doughnut ice cream sandwiches; long lines on summer evenings. [$] *Average main: $5* ✉ *4516 Mission Blvd., Suite C, Pacific Beach* ☎ *858/886–7433* 🌐 *www.thebakedbear.com.*

Cannonball

$$ | SUSHI | While the panoramic ocean view is the star attraction at this rooftop restaurant next to Belmont Park, the tasty sushi and share plates are a pleasant surprise for such a touristy locale. Lunch and dinner service bookend a popular afternoon happy hour. **Known for:** incredible ocean views; large specialty sushi rolls; summer crowds. [$] *Average main: $21* ✉ *3105 Ocean Front Walk, Mission Beach* ☎ *858/228–9304* 🌐 *www.cannonballsd.com.*

Draft South Mission

$ | **AMERICAN** | Patrons can have their seaside views and craft beer too at this spacious Belmont Park bar and restaurant. The relaxed, boardwalk atmosphere—and giant wall-size television screen—makes it a perfect spot for lounging after riding some waves at Mission Beach, or to cool down after soaking in some sun. **Known for:** burgers—veggie, beef, or bison; huge draft beer selection; people-watching on the boardwalk. $ *Average main: $17* ✉ *3105 Ocean Front Walk, Mission Beach* ☎ *858/228–9305* ⊕ *www.draftsandiego. com.*

JRDN

$$$ | **ECLECTIC** | This chic ocean-facing restaurant (pronounced Jordan), in the boutique Tower23 Hotel, offers a diverse menu including a sushi and raw bar, inspired California cuisine, and a premium steak selection. Lunch and weekend brunch are very popular and on Friday and Saturday the bar is jammed with under-thirty types eager to see and be seen. **Known for:** boozy brunch and lunch with a view; smaller shared plates and family-style entrées including a massive 40-oz. tomahawk steak; upscale option on the beach boardwalk. $ *Average main: $36* ✉ *Tower 23 Hotel, 723 Felspar St., Pacific Beach* ☎ *858/270–5736* ⊕ *www.jrdn.com.*

Kono's Café

$ | **AMERICAN** | **FAMILY** | Surfers, bicyclists, and sun worshippers visiting or living in Pacific Beach line up at the counter of this casual seaside café for hearty breakfasts and lunches. Some chow down inside surrounded by surfing decor, while others watch waves crash from the outdoor patio. **Known for:** huge breakfast portions; local favorite for breakfast burritos; great people-watching along the boardwalk. $ *Average main: $7* ✉ *704 Garnet Ave., Pacific Beach* ☎ *858/483–1669* ⊕ *www.konoscafe.com/* ⊗ *No dinner.*

Pacific Beach Fish Shop

$ | **SEAFOOD** | **FAMILY** | This local fish shop has a customizable menu that lets diners select a type of fish, marinade and preparation style (grilled or fried, and taco, sandwich, salad, or plate) that suits their tastes. You can dine-in on the heated patio, order your food to go, or buy the daily catch to cook at home. **Known for:** serves local beer; daily fresh fish; fish tacos like the TKO Taco. $ *Average main: $15* ✉ *1775 Garnet Ave., Pacific Beach* ☎ *858/483–1008* ⊕ *thefishshoppb.com.*

The Patio on Lamont

$$ | **MODERN AMERICAN** | **FAMILY** | Soft breezes blow through the stylish patio of this modern California bistro that straddles a quiet side street in Pacific Beach. Seated beneath a "green wall" of tropical plants, tourists join locals, many with pets in tow, for breakfast, lunch, and dinner, the popular weekday 3 to 6 happy hour, and weekend brunch. **Known for:** buzzy brunch scene; plant-filled decor; large selection of shared plates. $ *Average main: $25* ✉ *4445 Lamont St., Pacific Beach* ☎ *858/412–4648* ⊕ *www. thepatioonlamont.com.*

Rubio's Coastal Grill

$ | **SEAFOOD** | Credited with popularizing fish tacos in the U.S., Ralph Rubio brought the Mexican staple to San Diego, opening his first restaurant in Pacific Beach where it still stands today. The original beer-battered fish tacos have fried pollock topped with white sauce, salsa, and cabbage atop a corn tortilla. **Known for:** the original fish taco; Taco Tuesday deal—fish taco and a beer for $5; $7 lunch specials. $ *Average main: $10* ✉ *4504 Mission Bay Dr., Pacific Beach* ☎ *858/272–2801* ⊕ *www.rubios. com.*

★ Sushi Ota

$$ | **SUSHI** | One fan called it "a notch above amazing"—an accolade not expected for a Japanese eatery wedged in a strip mall in Pacific Beach. But it's a destination for lovers of high-quality,

superfresh raw fish from around San Diego and abroad; reservations strongly encouraged. **Known for:** velvety hamachi belly; sea urchin specials; chef's omakase tasting menu. [$] *Average main: $25* ✉ *4529 Mission Bay Dr., Pacific Beach* ☎ *858/270–5670* 🌐 *www.sushiota.com* ⏲ *No lunch Sat.–Mon.*

★ Waterbar

$$ | **SEAFOOD** | Occupying a prime oceanfront lot just south of Crystal Pier, the views from the raised dining room are impressive. Throw in an excellent raw bar, a wide selection of shared plates, and a buzzy bar scene and you get Waterbar's "social seafood" concept. **Known for:** late night "Boardwalk hour" oyster specials; boozy weekend brunch; ocean views. [$] *Average main: $24* ✉ *4325 Ocean Blvd., Pacific Beach* ☎ *858/888–4343* 🌐 *www.waterbarsd.com.*

Hotels

Mission Bay, with its beaches, bike trails, boat-launching ramps, golf course, and grassy parks—not to mention SeaWorld—is a haven of hotels and resorts. Smaller hotels, motels, and hostels can be found nearby in Pacific Beach. Mission Beach has fewer hotels but vacation rentals—both houses and apartments—abound.

Blue Sea Beach Hotel

$$$$ | **HOTEL** | **FAMILY** | A modern take on the beachfront motel, the Blue Sea Beach hotel has Pacific Beach's only oceanfront pool. **Pros:** fun lobby; great pool deck; direct beach access. **Cons:** small rooms; can be expensive in peak season; busy location along boardwalk. [$] *Rooms from: $499* ✉ *707 Pacific Beach Dr., Pacific Beach* ☎ *858/488–4780* 🌐 *www.blueseabeachhotel.com* 🛏 *126 rooms* 🍴 *No meals.*

Catamaran Resort Hotel and Spa

$$$$ | **RESORT** | **FAMILY** | Tiki torches light the way through grounds thick with tropical foliage to the six two-story buildings and the 14-story high-rise on Mission Bay. The Polynesian theme continues in the guest rooms while the Catamaran Spa offers Hawaiian-style lomilomi massages, ginger-root detox wraps, and star fruit sugar body scrubs. **Pros:** superb bayfront location; some rooms have bay views; many activities for kids. **Cons:** common areas need renovating; dated room decor; popular wedding and event venue can get busy. [$] *Rooms from: $349* ✉ *3999 Mission Blvd., Mission Beach* ☎ *858/488–1081* 🌐 *www.catamaranresort.com* 🛏 *310 rooms* 🍴 *No meals* ☞ *$25 resort fee.*

Crystal Pier Hotel & Cottages

$$$ | **HOTEL** | **FAMILY** | Rustic little oases with a charm all their own, the beachy cottages may lack some of the amenities of comparably priced hotels, but you're paying for character and proximity to the ocean—these lodgings are literally on the pier. **Pros:** ocean views everywhere you look; historic lodgings; free parking. **Cons:** few amenities; reservations fill up fast; busy foot traffic on pier. [$] *Rooms from: $380* ✉ *4500 Ocean Blvd., Pacific Beach* ☎ *800/748–5894* 🌐 *www.crystalpier.com* 🛏 *30 rooms* 🍴 *No meals.*

The Dana on Mission Bay

$$$ | **RESORT** | **FAMILY** | This waterfront resort, just down the road from SeaWorld, has an ideal location for active leisure travelers. **Pros:** water views; many outdoor activities; shuttle to SeaWorld. **Cons:** expensive resort fee; popular wedding venue; rooms vary in quality and view. [$] *Rooms from: $289* ✉ *1710 W. Mission Bay Dr., Mission Bay* ☎ *619/222–6440, 800/445–3339* 🌐 *www.thedana.com* 🛏 *271 rooms* 🍴 *No meals.*

Hyatt Regency Mission Bay Spa and Marina

$$$ | **RESORT** | **FAMILY** | This modern property has many desirable amenities, including balconies with excellent views of the garden, bay, ocean, or swimming pool courtyard. **Pros:** proximity to water sports; 120-foot waterslides in pools, plus kiddie slide; several suite configurations good for families. **Cons:** daily resort fee; not centrally located; some areas in need of updates. [$] *Rooms from: $299* ✉ *1441 Quivira Rd., Mission Bay* ☎ *619/224–1234, 800/233–1234* 🌐 *www.missionbay.regency.hyatt.com* 🛏 *429 rooms* 🍴 *No meals.*

Pacific Terrace Hotel

$$$$ | **RESORT** | Travelers love this terrific beachfront hotel and the ocean views from most rooms; it's a perfect place for watching sunsets over the Pacific. **Pros:** beach views; large rooms; friendly service. **Cons:** busy and sometimes noisy area; expensive in peak season; resort fee. [$] *Rooms from: $569* ✉ *610 Diamond St., Pacific Beach* ☎ *858/581–3500, 800/344–3370* 🌐 *www.pacificterrace.com* 🛏 *73 rooms* 🍴 *No meals.*

Paradise Point Resort & Spa

$$$ | **RESORT** | **FAMILY** | Minutes from SeaWorld but hidden in a quiet part of Mission Bay, the beautiful landscape of this 44-acre resort offers plenty of space for families to play and relax. **Pros:** water views; five pools; good service. **Cons:** not centrally located; motel-thin walls; parking and resort fees. [$] *Rooms from: $296* ✉ *1404 Vacation Rd., Mission Bay* ☎ *858/274–4630, 800/344–2626* 🌐 *www.paradisepoint.com* 🛏 *462 rooms* 🍴 *No meals.*

Surfer Beach Hotel

$$$ | **HOTEL** | Choose this place for its great location—right on bustling Pacific Beach. **Pros:** beach location; ocean-view rooms; courtyard pool. **Cons:** dated rooms; no air-conditioning; busy location. [$] *Rooms from: $319* ✉ *711 Pacific Beach Dr., Pacific Beach* ☎ *800/820–5772* 🌐 *www.surferbeachhotel.com* 🛏 *69 rooms* 🍴 *No meals.*

TOWER23

$$$$ | **HOTEL** | A neomodern masterpiece with a beachy vibe, this boutique hotel is a favorite of the young and young-at-heart. **Pros:** beach views; central location; hip decor. **Cons:** no pool; busy area; on-site restaurant and bar often crowded. [$] *Rooms from: $409* ✉ *723 Felspar St., Pacific Beach* ☎ *858/270–2323* 🌐 *www.t23hotel.com* 🛏 *44 rooms* 🍴 *No meals.*

Nightlife

Outside of Downtown, some of the most vibrant nightlife activity takes place alongside the coast. It's a great place to glug some suds by the boardwalk after a splash in the Pacific.

Pacific Beach is teeming with activity from happy hour to last call, thanks to a healthy mix of casual hangouts for college students and recent, upscale upgrades to the otherwise dated beach-bum style of the neighborhood. Surfers meet here for happy hour and college students converge to spend their lost weekends.

BARS

★ The Grass Skirt

BARS/PUBS | Accessed through a false freezer door inside Good Time Poke, this speakeasy-styled tiki bar serves a wide selection of rum-based tropical cocktails in delightfully kitsch surroundings. The Polynesian-inspired menu features shareable poke and pupus, but call ahead to reserve a table—this hidden gem is no secret! ✉ *910 Grand Ave., Pacific Beach* ☎ *858/412–5237* 🌐 *www.thegrassskirt.com.*

JRDN

BARS/PUBS | This contemporary lounge (pronounced "Jordan") occupies the ground floor of Pacific Beach's chicest boutique hotel, Tower23, and offers a more sophisticated vibe in what is a very party-happy neighborhood. Sleek walls of windows and an expansive patio overlook the boardwalk. ✉ *723 Felspar St., Pacific Beach* ☎ *858/270–2323* 🌐 *www.t23hotel.com.*

BREWPUBS
Amplified Ale Works

BREWPUBS/BEER GARDENS | Pacific Beach often veers between the trendy and the tawdry, so this genuine craft brewhouse offers a more casual middle ground. Amplified serves more than a dozen in-house-brewed beers at its scenic outdoor beer garden, with breathtaking ocean views. ⊠ *4150 Mission Blvd., No. 208, Pacific Beach* ☎ *858/270–5222* ⊕ *www.amplifiedales.com.*

🛍 Shopping

Mission Boulevard and Grand and Garnet avenues are the big shopping thoroughfares in the beach towns. Souvenir shops are scattered up and down the boardwalk, and along Mission Boulevard there are surf, skate, and bike shops, bikini boutiques, and stores selling hip T-shirts, jeans, sandals, and casual apparel. Garnet Avenue is the hot spot for resale boutiques, thrift stores, and pawn shops.

Gone Bananas Beachwear

CLOTHING | This store can be a bit overwhelming with its more than 15,000 pieces of swimwear lining the walls from floor to ceiling. To make shopping a bit easier, swimsuits have been arranged by color. Browse through mix-and-match pieces from the most fashion-forward swimwear designers like Mikoh, San Lorenzo, and Vitamin A. It's worth taking the time to peruse what is simply San Diego's best swimwear selection. ⊠ *3785 Mission Blvd., Mission Beach* ☎ *858/488–4900* ⊕ *www.gonebananasbeachwear.com.*

★ Pangaea Outpost

GIFTS/SOUVENIRS | This collective houses dozens of local shops under one roof and is a great place to pick up beachy clothing and decor or unique gifts for everyone on your list. ⊠ *909 Garnet Ave., Pacific Beach* ☎ *858/581–0555* ⊕ *www. pangaeaoutpost.com.*

🏃 Activities

BICYCLING

A ride along the Mission Beach Boardwalk is a great way to take in a classic California scene. Keep in mind this route is more for cruising than hardcore cycling, as the gawkers and crowds often slow foot and bike traffic to a crawl. For a leisurely ride, try Mission Bay. It has a 10-mile loop of cement bike/walking paths around Mission Bay and Fiesta Island bordering big green lawns, children's playgrounds, and picnic spots

Cheap Rentals (see Surfing) has bike rentals, including beach cruisers, tandems, hybrids, and two-wheeled baby carriers. Kids bikes are also available. Demand is high during the busy season (May through September), so call to reserve equipment ahead of time.

DIVING AND SNORKELING

The kelp forests and protected marine areas off the San Diego coast are easily accessible and offer divers ample opportunities to explore. Classes are available for beginners, while experienced divers will appreciate the challenges of local wreck and canyon dives. Water temperatures can be chilly, so check with a local outfitter for the appropriate gear before setting out.

The HMCS *Yukon,* a decommissioned Canadian warship, was intentionally sunk off Mission Beach to create the main diving destination in San Diego. A mishap caused the ship to settle on its side, creating a surreal, M.C. Escher–esque diving environment. This is a technical dive and should be attempted only by experienced divers; even diving instructors have become disoriented inside the wreck, and a few have even died trying to explore it.

GOLF
Mission Bay Golf Course and Practice Center

GOLF | Making sure people have fun is the number-one goal at this city-run golf course. San Diego's only night-lighted course, the final tee time is at 8 pm for 9 holes, and the executive course with par 3 and 4 holes isn't too challenging. The golf course's scenic and breezy location next to Mission Bay helps keep it comfortably cool. They also have a foot golf course, in which a player kicks a soccer ball into a cup in as few shots as possible. ⊠ *2702 N. Mission Bay Dr., Mission Bay* ☎ *858/581–7880* ⊕ *www.sandiego.gov/golf* ⌨ *$17 for 9 holes weekdays, $22 weekends; $29 for 18 holes weekdays, $36 weekends* ⚑ *18 holes, 2719 yards, par 58.*

SURFING

If you're a beginner, consider paddling in the waves off Mission Beach, Pacific Beach, and Tourmaline Surfing Park. Several outfitters offer year-round surf lessons as well as surf camp in the summer months and during spring break.

Cheap Rentals

SURFING | One block from the boardwalk, this place has good daily and weekly prices for surfboards, paddleboards, kayaks, snorkel gear, skateboards, coolers, umbrellas, chairs, and bike rentals, including beach cruisers, tandems, hybrids, and two-wheeled baby carriers. Kids bikes are also available. Demand is high during the busy season (May through September) so call to reserve equipment ahead of time. ⊠ *3689 Mission Blvd., Mission Beach* ☎ *858/488–9070, 800/941–7761* ⊕ *www.cheap-rentals.com* ⌨ *From $7/hour.*

WATER SPORTS

Mission Bay and the surrounding beaches provide great access to a variety of water sports, both motorized and nonmotorized. The protected waters of the bay are great for beginners, while the open ocean awaits the adventurous.

Over-the-Line 👁

A giant beach party as much as a sport, Over-the-Line is a form of beach softball played with two teams of just three people each. Every July, over two weekends that include wild beer drinking and partying, the world championships are held on Fiesta Island. Admission is free, but parking is impossible (shuttle buses are available). Check the Old Mission Beach Athletic Club's website (⊕ *www.ombac.org*) for more information.

Rental outfitters are abundant and provide everything from skippered boats to single-person kayaks. Mission Bay has designated open speed areas that are popular with motorboats and Jet Skis, while sailboats and kayakers appreciate the no-wake zones. If you are new to an activity, or just in need of a refresher, consider taking a lesson through the Mission Bay Aquatic Center.

The popularity of stand-up paddleboarding, or SUP, has grown tremendously in recent years. Devotees love the excellent core workout it provides, while newcomers appreciate how much quicker it is to master than traditional surfing. You can paddleboard pretty much anywhere and many local surf breaks are popular for those with experience, but the calmer waters of Mission Bay offer more stability for beginners. Test your communication skills on the latest trend, the Giant SUP, with room for up to five paddlers.

Jet Skis can be launched from most ocean beaches, although you must ride beyond surf lines, and some beaches have special regulations governing their use. In addition to the open speed areas, Mission Bay has two specially designated areas for personal watercraft or Jet Skis. Take note of the speed limit markers when exiting these zones as enforcement is strict and ticketing is common.

Generally speaking, the western portion of Mission Bay is ideal for sailing and kayaking. The aptly named Sail Bay near the Catamaran Resort has seasonal speed restrictions to reduce summertime motorized use of this popular portion of the bay.

Action Sport Rentals

BOATING | From its facility at Bahia Resort Hotel and its sister location, the **Catamaran Resort Hotel** (*3999 Mission Blvd., Mission Beach 858/488–2582*), Action Sport Rentals has paddleboats, kayaks, powerboats, and sailboats from 14 to 22 feet. Thanks to their location on the calm waters of Mission Bay, both are great places for beginners to try paddleboarding. ✉ *998 W. Mission Bay Dr., Mission Bay* ☎ *619/241–4794* ⊕ *www.actionsportrentals.com* ☜ *From $25.*

Mission Bay Aquatic Center

BOATING | **FAMILY** | The world's largest instructional waterfront facility offers lessons in wakeboarding, sailing, surfing, waterskiing, rowing, kayaking, and windsurfing. Equipment rental is also available, but the emphasis is on instruction, and most rentals require a minimum two-hour orientation lesson before you can set out on your own. Reservations are recommended, particularly during the summer. Skippered keelboats and boats for waterskiing or wakeboarding can be hired with reservations. Free parking is available. ✉ *1001 Santa Clara Pl., Mission Beach* ☎ *858/488–1000* ⊕ *www.mbaquaticcenter.com.*

★ Seaforth Boat Rentals

BOATING | The Mission Bay outpost of this popular rental company offers a wide variety of motorized and nonmotorized craft. Jet Skis, SUPs, kayaks, and fishing skiffs are available alongside sailboats and powerboats of all sizes. For added relaxation, charter a skippered pontoon party boat, some with waterslides for added fun. ✉ *1641 Quivira Rd., Mission Bay* ☎ *888/834–2628* ⊕ *www.seaforthboatrental.com.*

LA JOLLA

Updated by
Marlise Kast-Myers

👁 Sights	🍴 Restaurants	🛏 Hotels	🛍 Shopping	🍸 Nightlife
★★★★☆	★★★★☆	★★★★☆	★★★☆☆	★★☆☆☆

LA JOLLA'S BEACHES

La Jolla is synonymous with beautiful vistas.

La Jolla (pronounced La Hoya) means "the jewel" in Spanish and appropriately describes this small, affluent village and its beaches. Some beautiful coastline can be found here, as well as an elegant upscale atmosphere.

Between North County and the Mission and South bays, La Jolla is easily accessible from Downtown San Diego and North County. It's worth renting a car so you can sample the different beaches along the coast. The town's trademark million-dollar homes won't disappoint either—their cliffside locations make them an attractive backdrop to the brilliant views of the sea below. Downtown La Jolla is more commercialized, with high-end stores great for browsing. La Jolla Shores, a mile-long beach, lies in the more residential area to the north. Above all, the beach and cove are La Jolla's prime charms—the cove's seals and underwater kelp beds are big draws for kayakers and nature lovers.

THE CLIFFS AT TORREY PINES

The ocean views from the 300-foot-high sandstone cliffs atop Torrey Pines State Natural Reserve are vast and exquisite. To reach the cliffs, hike one of the short trails that leads from the visitor center. Perch along the sandy edge, and let your legs dangle. You may even see dolphins swimming along the shore or surfers riding a break.

BEST BEACHES

Framed in scenic coves and backed by dramatic cliffs, La Jolla's beaches are legendary. Challenging surf breaks, an underwater marine park, and expansive stretches of sand offer something for everyone. Look out over the sparkling waters to see seals frolicking in the surf, or lie back in the sand and watch hang gliders soar overhead.

Black's Beach. This secluded stretch of sand is considered one of the most beautiful beaches in San Diego. Black's Beach was clothing-optional for many years; although nudity is now prohibited by law, many people still shed their suits whenever the authorities are out of sight.

Children's Pool. This shallow bay was once a great place to bring the kids to swim. Nowadays, it's the best place on the coast to view harbor seals. Good thing kids enjoy that almost as much as playing in the waves.

La Jolla Cove. Truly the jewel of La Jolla, "the Cove" is one of the prettiest spots on the west coast.

La Jolla Shores. One of the most popular beaches in San Diego, La Jolla Shores features a wide sandy beach and calm waves perfect for swimming and beginner surf lessons.

Torrey Pines State Beach. This popular beach is located just below the Torrey Pines State Reserve. Bring your picnic here after an invigorating hike in the reserve.

Windansea Beach. Incredible views, secluded spots, and world-class waves make this a favorite beach for couples and surfers.

(left) La Jolla is synonymous with beautiful vistas. (lower right) The view from Coast Highway 101 in Carlsbad is spectacular. (upper right) Hike down to the beach from Torrey Pines.

7

La Jolla **LA JOLLA'S BEACHES**

LA JOLLA COVE WALK AND SHOP

If you're not keen on dipping your toes in the water (or even the sand, for that matter), head over to La Jolla Cove, an ideal spot for strolling and shopping with a view. Park at any of the available metered spaces on Girard Avenue in Downtown La Jolla and browse the Arcade Building, built in the Spanish Mission style. Make your way toward the cove by following the signs, or simply walk toward any patches of ocean you see.

WATER SPORTS

One of the most popular water activities is kayaking along the caves and snorkeling among the kelp beds near the cove at the Underwater Ecological Reserve. Kayak rental shops offer special outings that include moonlight kayaking and the chance to dive among the leopard sharks that roam La Jolla's waters. Don't worry: the sharks are harmless.

SURFING SAN DIEGO

Head to a San Diego beach on any given day and chances are you'll see a group of surfers in the water, patiently waiting to catch a memorable wave.

Surfing may have originated in Hawaii, but modern surfing culture is inextricably linked to the Southern California lifestyle. From the Malibu setting of *Gidget* to the surf-city sounds of Jan and Dean and the Beach Boys, and TV's *Laguna Beach* and *The OC,* the entertainment industry brought a California version of surfing to the landlocked, and in the process created an enduring mystique.

San Diego surfing in particular is unique. Underwater kelp beds help keep waves intact, preventing the choppiness that surfers bemoan. Santa Ana winds that begin to arrive in fall and throughout early winter bring coveted offshore winds that contribute to morning and evening "glass" (the stillness of the water that encourages smooth waves).

BEST TIME TO GO

The biggest swells usually occur in winter, but good-size waves can form year-round. Generally, swells come from the north in winter and from the south in summer. Certain breaks are better on different swells. In winter, try beaches like Swami's or Black's Beach that can hold large swells without closing out. Summer spots are La Jolla's Windansea and nearby Tourmaline Surfing Park.

La Jollans have long considered their village to be the Monte Carlo of California, and with good cause. Its coastline curves into natural coves backed by verdant hillsides covered with homes worth millions. La Jolla is both a natural and cultural treasure trove. The upscale shops, galleries, and restaurants of La Jolla Village satisfy the glitterati, while secluded trails, scenic overlooks, and abundant marine life provide balance and refuge.

La Jolla

⊙ Sights

Although La Jolla is a neighborhood of the city of San Diego, it has its own postal zone and a coveted sense of class; the ultrarich from around the globe own second homes here and old-money residents maintain friendships with the visiting film stars and royalty who frequent the area's exclusive luxury hotels and private clubs. Development has radically altered the once serene character of the village, but it has gained a cosmopolitan air that makes it a popular vacation resort.

Just off the coast, from La Jolla Cove to La Jolla Shores, lies the 533-acre, world-renowned San Diego–La Jolla [Under]water Park Ecological Preserve.

Birch Aquarium at Scripps

ZOO | FAMILY | Affiliated with the world-renowned Scripps Institution of Oceanography, this excellent aquarium sits at the end of a signposted drive off North Torrey Pines Road with commanding views of La Jolla coastline. More than 60 tanks are filled with colorful saltwater fish, and a 70,000-gallon exhibit on sea kelp and other local sea denizens offers a glimpse of many examples of regional marine life. Besides the fish themselves, the aquarium includes interactive displays based on the institution's ...

[Spaniards called the site Woholle, "the place by white water", referring to the surf breaking on the shoreline. The Spanish referred to La Jolla (same pronunciation) as "the jewel," ... City."]

TYPES OF BREAKS

Beach break: Waves that break over sandbars and the seafloor and are usually tamer and consistently long, thus typically the best type for beginners, with the exception of Black's Beach, which is legendary for its uniquely large, fast, and punchy beach breaks. **La Jolla Shores, Mission Beach,** and **Pacific Beach** are destinations for gentler, more forgiving waves.

Point break: Created as waves that hit a point jutting into the ocean. Surfers then peel down the wave it creates. With the right conditions, this can create very consistent waves. **Swami's** has an excellent point break.

Reef break: Waves break as they hit a reef. It can create great (but dangerous) surf. There's a good chance of getting smashed and scraped over extremely sharp coral or rocks. Many of San Diego's best breaks are at **San Elijo, La Jolla Cove,** and **Windansea.**

SAN DIEGO SURF FINDER

Municipal piers, such as at **Oceanside, Pacific,** and **Mission beaches,** are great places to watch surfers. The high bluffs of **Black's Beach** is also a great spot.

Swami's: Famous for its point break and beautiful water.

Black's Beach: This strand below the cliffs is where to go for beach breaks. Serious surfers carry their boards down the narrow, steep trails to reach the beach.

Windansea Beach: Known for its reef breaks.

Tourmaline Surfing Park: Windsurfers and surfers share Tourmaline's smooth waves.

La Jolla Shores: First-timers head here for more modest waves.

(left) La Jolla Shores is a good beach for beginner surfers. (lower right) Surfer at the end of a good ride. (upper right) Instructors at Surf Diva Surf School cater to women.

SURF SLANG

Barrel: The area created when a wave breaks onto itself in a curl.

Close out: When a wave breaks all at once, rather than breaking steadily in one direction.

Cutback: The most basic turn; executed to maintain position close to the barrel.

Dropping in: A severe breach of etiquette wherein a second surfer joins the wave later and cuts off the original rider.

Goofy foot: Having a right-foot-forward stance on the surfboard.

Grom: An affectionate term for those sun-bleached kids with tiny surfboards.

Hollow: Barrels big enough to create a tube that a surfer can ride within—also called the green room.

Lineup: A group of surfers waiting beyond the whitewash for waves.

Turtle roll: When a surfer rolls over on the surfboard, going underwater and holding the board upside down to bypass the crashing waves.

NEIGHBORHOOD SNAPSHOT

GREAT EXPERIENCES

■ **Promenade above the cove:** The winding pathways above La Jolla Cove offer stunning views of the surf and sea lions.

■ **Shop 'til you drop:** La Jolla's chic boutiques and galleries are San Diego's answer to Rodeo Drive. Watch for celebrities as you browse on Prospect Street and Girard Avenue.

■ **Aquatic adventures:** Grab a kayak or scuba gear to explore the San Diego–La Jolla Underwater Park Ecological Preserve.

■ **Luxe living:** Visit top-notch spas and restaurants, or gawk at multimillion-dollar mansions and their denizens in Ferraris.

■ **Torrey Pines State Beach and Reserve:** Play the links, hike the trails, relax on the beach, or hang glide off the cliffs.

QUICK BITES

Brockton Villa Restaurant. This charming café overlooking La Jolla Cove has indoor and outdoor seating, as well as scrumptious desserts and coffee drinks; the beans are locally roasted. A popular breakfast spot, the café closes at 9 pm. ⊠ 1235 Coast Blvd. ☎ 858/454–7393 ⊕ www.brocktonvilla. com.

The Cheese Shop. Located in the heart of La Jolla Shores, this is a great place to grab a quick lunch or picnic provisions. The sandwiches are excellent, and kids will love the fresh-baked cookies and old-time candy selection. ⊠ 2165 Avenida de la Playa ☎ 858/459–3921 ⊕ www.cheeseshoplajoll...

George's at the Cove. This restaurant com... one of the best-known spots in La Jo... ible views of La Jolla Cove. Althoug... restaurant, **George's California Modern**, is... affair, **Ocean Terrace** on the top level is a gre... for a casual meal. ⊠ 1250 Prospect St. ☎ 858/4... 4244 ⊕ www.georgesatthecove.com.

GETTING HERE

■ If you're traveling north, take the La Jolla Parkway exit off I-5, which veers into Torrey Pines Road, and turn right onto Prospect Street. If you're heading south, take the La Jolla Village Drive exit, which also leads into Torrey Pines Road. For the scenic route, head north from Pacific Beach on La Jolla Boulevard and Camino de la Costa. Signs direct drivers and cyclists past many of La Jolla's famed vistas and coveted homes. As you approach the villa... La Jolla Boulevard turn... into Prospect Street.

PLANNING Y... TIME

■ La Jolla's... be seen i... a visit... and... sc...

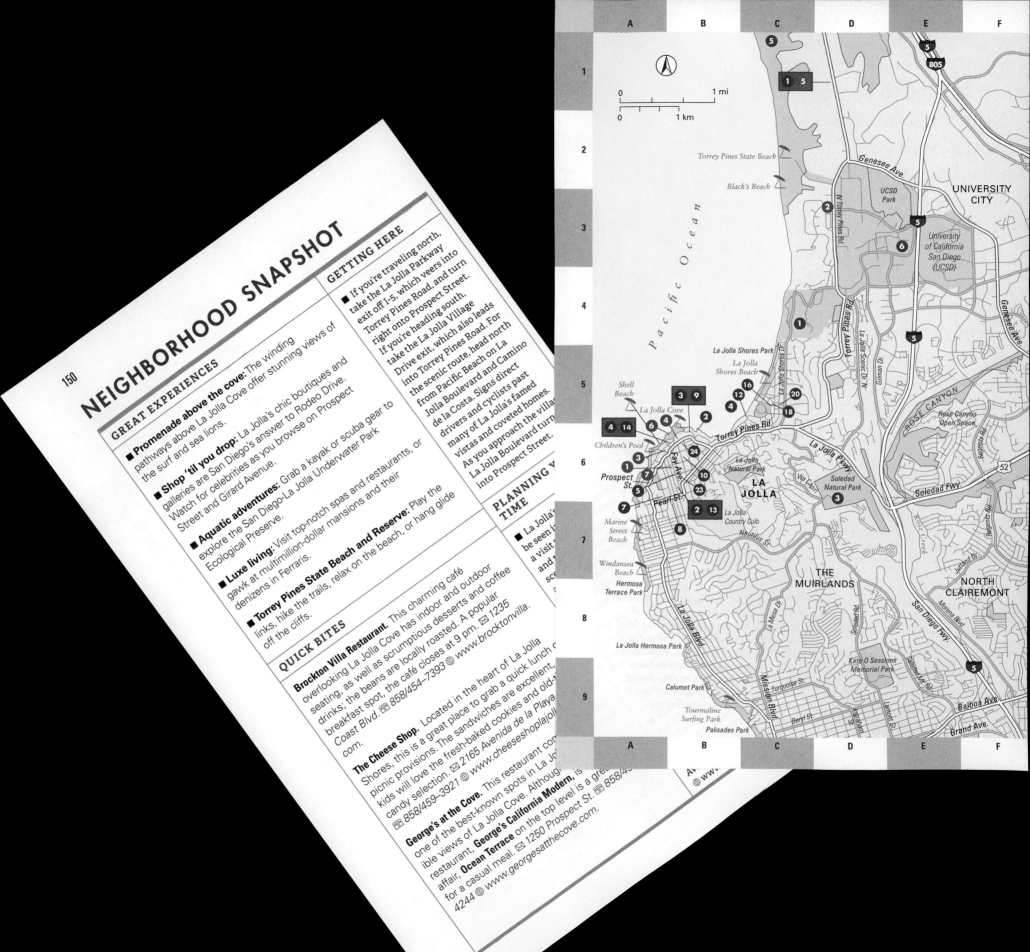

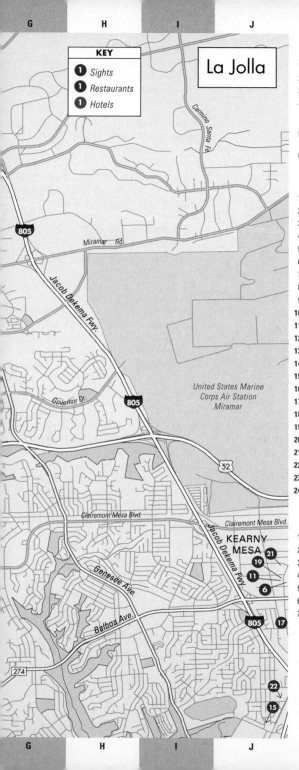

Sights ▼

1 Birch Aquarium at Scripps **C4**
2 La Jolla Caves...................... **B6**
3 Mount Soledad.................... **D7**
4 San Diego - La Jolla
  Underwater Park
  Ecological Reserve............... **B5**
5 Torrey Pines State
  Natural Reserve **C1**
6 University of California
  at San Diego........................ **E3**

Restaurants ▼

1 A.R. Valentien **D1**
2 Bistro du Marché.................. **B6**
3 Brockton Villa **B6**
4 Cody's La Jolla **B6**
5 The Cottage **B6**
6 Dumpling Inn **J8**
7 El Pescador Fish Market.......... **A6**
8 Galaxy Taco **B7**
9 George's at the Cove **B6**
10 Herringbone........................ **B6**
11 j/wata Temaki Bar **J7**
12 The Marine Room....................**C5**
13 Michele Coulon Dessertier....... **B6**
14 NINE-TEN **B6**
15 Original Sab-E-Lee **J9**
16 Osteria Romantica..................**C5**
17 Phuong Trang **J8**
18 Piatti La Jolla........................**C5**
19 RakiRaki...............................**J7**
20 Shorehouse Kitchen.................**C5**
21 Spicy City Chinese...................**J7**
22 Sushi Diner **J9**
23 Trilogy Sanctuary **B6**
24 Whisknladle **B6**

Hotels ▼

1 Empress Hotel....................... **B6**
2 Estancia La Jolla Hotel & Spa.... **D3**
3 Grande Colonial..................... **A6**
4 La Valencia Hotel **B6**
5 The Lodge at Torrey Pines........ **D1**
6 Pantai Inn............................ **B6**
7 Scripps Inn **A6**

☎ *858/534–3474* ⊕ *www.aquarium.ucsd. edu* ✉ *$19.50.*

La Jolla Caves

CAVE | FAMILY | It's a walk of 145 some-times slippery steps down a tunnel to Sunny Jim, the largest of the seven caves in La Jolla Cove and the only one reachable by land. This is a one-of-a-kind local attraction, and worth the time if you have a day or two to really enjoy La Jolla. The man-made tunnel took two years to dig, beginning in 1902; later, a shop was built at its entrance. Today the Cave Store, a throwback to that early shop, is still the entrance to the cave. The shop sells jewelry, postcards, shells, and watercolors by local artists. ✉ *1325 Coast Blvd. S* ☎ *858/459–0746* ⊕ *www. cavestore.com* ✉ *$5.*

Mount Soledad

MOUNTAIN—SIGHT | La Jolla's highest spot can be reached by taking Nautilus Street to La Jolla Scenic Drive South, and then turning left. Proceed a few blocks to the park, where parking is plentiful and the views are astounding, unless the day is hazy. The top of the mountain is an excel-lent vantage point from which to get a sense of San Diego's geography: looking down from here you can see the coast from the county's northern border to the south far beyond downtown. ✉ *6905 La Jolla Scenic Dr. S.*

San Diego-La Jolla Underwater Park Ecological Reserve

BODY OF WATER | Four habitats across 6,000 acres make up this underwater park and ecological reserve. When the water is clear, this is a diver's paradise with reefs, kelp beds, sand flats, and a submarine canyon. Plunge deeper to see guitarfish rays, perch, sea bass, ancho-vies, squid, and hammerhead sharks. Snorkelers, kayakers, and stand-up pad-dleboarders are likely to spot sea lions, seals, and leopard sharks. The Seven La Jolla Sea Caves, 75-million-year-old sandstone caves, are at the park's edge.

■TIP➔ **While the park can be explored on your own, the best way to view it is with a professional guide.** ✉ *La Jolla* ⊕ *La Jolla Cove.*

★ Torrey Pines State Natural Reserve

NATIONAL/STATE PARK | *Pinus torreyana,* the rarest native pine tree in the United States, enjoys a 1,500-acre sanctuary at the northern edge of La Jolla. About 6,000 of these unusual trees, some as tall as 60 feet, grow on the cliffs here. The park is one of only two places in the world (the other is Santa Rosa Island, off Santa Barbara) where the Torrey pine grows naturally. The reserve has several hiking trails leading to the cliffs, 300 feet above the ocean; trail maps are available at the park station. Wildflowers grow profusely in spring, and the ocean panoramas are always spectacular. From December to March, whales can be spot-ted from the bluffs. When in this upper part of the park, respect the restrictions. Not permitted: picnicking, smoking, leav-ing the trails, dogs, alcohol, or collecting plant specimens.

You can unwrap your sandwiches, however, at Torrey Pines State Beach, just below the reserve. When the tide is out, it's possible to walk south all the way past the lifeguard towers to Black's Beach over rocky promontories carved by the waves (avoid the bluffs, however; they're unstable). **Los Peñasquitos Lagoon** at the north end of the reserve is one of the many natural estuaries that flow inland between Del Mar and Oceanside. It's a good place to watch shorebirds. Volunteers lead guided nature walks at 10 and 2 on most weekends and holi-days. ✉ *12600 N. Torrey Pines Rd.* ⊕ *N. Torrey Pines Rd. exit off I–5 onto Carmel Valley Rd. going west, then turn left (south) on Coast Hwy. 101* ☎ *858/755– 2063* ⊕ *www.torreypine.org* ✉ *Parking $15–$20, varies by day of week and by season.*

University of California at San Diego

COLLEGE | The campus of one of the country's most prestigious research universities spreads over 1,200 acres of coastal canyons and eucalyptus groves, where students and faculty jog, bike, and skateboard to class. If you're interested in contemporary art, check out the **Stuart Collection of Sculpture**—18 thought-pro-voking, site-specific works by artists such as Nam June Paik, William Wegman, Niki de St. Phalle, Jenny Holzer, and others arrayed around the campus. UCSD's **Price Center** has a well-stocked, two-level bookstore—the largest in San Diego—and a good coffeehouse, Perks. Look for the postmodern **Geisel Library**, named for longtime La Jolla residents Theodor "Dr. Seuss" Geisel and his wife, Audrey. Bring quarters for the parking meters, or cash or a credit card for the parking structures, because free parking is only available on weekends. ■**TIP→ There are two-hour free campus tours for the public Sunday at 2 pm from Gilman Entrance Information Center; reserve online or by calling (858) 534–4414 before noon on Thursday.** ⊠ *La Jolla ✛ Exit I–5 onto La Jolla Village Dr. going west; take Gilman Dr. off-ramp to right and continue to information kiosk at campus entrance on Gilman Dr.* ☎ *858/534–4414 campus tour information* ∰ *www.ucsd. edu.*

Beaches

Black's Beach

BEACH—SIGHT | The powerful waves at this beach attract world-class surfers, and the strand's relative isolation appeals to nudist nature lovers (although by law nudity is prohibited) as well as gays and lesbians. Backed by 300-foot-tall cliffs whose colors change with the sun's angle, Black's can be accessed from Torrey Pines State Beach to the north, or by a narrow path descending the cliffs from Torrey Pines Glider Port. Beware the city has posted a "do not use" sign there because the cliff trails are unmaintained and highly dangerous so use at your own risk. If you plan to access Black's from the beaches to the north or south, do so at low tide. High tide and waves can restrict access. Strong rip currents are common—only experienced swimmers should take the plunge. Lifeguards patrol the area only between spring break and mid-October. Also keep your eyes peeled for the hang gliders and paragliders who ascend from atop the cliffs. Parking is available at the Glider Port and Torrey Pines State Beach. **Amenities:** none. **Best for:** solitude, nudists, surfing. ⊠ *Between Torrey Pines State Beach and La Jolla Shores ✛ 2 miles south of Torrey Pines State Beach parking lot* ∰ *www.sandie-go.gov/lifeguards/beaches/blacks.shtml.*

Children's Pool

BEACH—SIGHT | **FAMILY** | Due to the groups of harbor seals that have claimed it as their own, this shallow cove, protected by a seawall, is closed to the public for the winter pupping season, December 15 through May 15. People may access its calm, protected waters the other seven months of the year, however, and the beach's small waves make it an ideal place for children to splash and play. Adults will appreciate the view. Because of its location at the tip of La Jolla Peninsula, you can actually look east to get unmatched panoramic views of the coastline and ocean. The area just outside the pool is popular with scuba divers, who explore the offshore reef when the surf is calm. Although you may not be able to go down on the beach during the winter months, it's still worth a peak. It's fun to watch the seals and their pups from above. ■**TIP→ Limited free parking is available along Coast Boulevard. Ameni-ties:** lifeguards, showers, toilets, parking (no fee). **Best for:** walking, scuba diving. ⊠ *850 Coast Blvd.* ∰ *www.sandiego.gov/ lifeguards/beaches/pool.*

Did You Know?

Goldfish Point in La Jolla is named after the garibaldi damselfish, which resemble goldfish, found in these waters. The garibaldi is California's official marine fish.

★ La Jolla Cove

BEACH—SIGHT | FAMILY | This shimmering blue-green inlet surrounded by cliffs is what first attracted everyone to La Jolla, from Native Americans to the glitterati. "The Cove," as locals refer to it, beyond where Girard Avenue dead-ends into Coast Boulevard, is marked by towering palms that line a promenade where people strolling in designer clothes are as common as Frisbee throwers. Ellen Browning Scripps Park sits atop cliffs formed by the incessant pounding of the waves and offers a great spot for picnics with a view. The Cove has beautiful white sand that is a bit course near the water's edge, but the beach is still a great place for sunbathing and lounging. At low tide, the pools and cliff caves are a destination for explorers. With visibility at 30-plus feet, this is the best place in San Diego for snorkeling, where bright-orange Garibaldi fish and other marine life populate the waters of the **San Diego–La Jolla Underwater Park Ecological Reserve.** From above water, it's not uncommon to spot sea lions and birds basking on the rocks, or dolphin fins just offshore. The cove is also a favorite of rough-water swimmers, while the area just north is best for kayakers wanting to explore the Seven La Jolla Sea Caves. **Amenities:** lifeguards, showers, toilets. **Best for:** snorkeling, swimming, walking. ⊠ *1100 Coast Blvd., east of Ellen Browning Scripps Park* ⊕ *www.sandiego.gov/lifeguards/beaches/ cove.*

La Jolla Shores

BEACH—SIGHT | FAMILY | This is one of San Diego's most popular beaches due to its wide sandy shore, gentle waves, and incredible views of La Jolla Peninsula. There's also a large grassy park, and adjacent to La Jolla Shores lies the **San Diego-La Jolla Underwater Park Ecological Reserve,** 6,000 acres of protected ocean bottom and tide lands, bordered by the Seven La Jolla Sea Caves. The white powdery sand at La Jolla Sands is some

Coast Highway 101

The portion of Coast Highway 101 that runs south from North County into La Jolla is one of San Diego's best drives. Start at South Carlsbad beach at Tamarack Avenue and continue through Leucadia, Encinitas, Cardiff, Solana Beach, Del Mar, and, finally, La Jolla. Any turn west will take you toward the beach. The drive offers intermittent glimpses of the sea; views from Carlsbad and Cardiff are especially beautiful. The grand finale is at Torrey Pines, where the waves roll into the misty, high-bluffed beach.

of San Diego's best, and several surf and scuba schools teach here. Kayaks can also be rented nearby. A concrete boardwalk parallels the beach, and a boat launch for small vessels lies 300 yards south of the lifeguard station at Avenida de Playa. Arrive early to get a parking spot in the lot near Kellogg Park at the foot of Calle Frescota. Street parking is limited to one or two hours. **Amenities:** lifeguards, parking (no fee), showers, toilets. **Best for:** surfing, swimming, walking. ⊠ *8200 Camino del Oro, in front of Kellogg Park* ✛ *2 miles north of downtown La Jolla* ⊕ *www.sandiego.gov/lifeguards/ beaches/shores.shtml.*

Shell Beach

BEACH—SIGHT | The small cove north of the Children's Pool remains remarkably under the radar and is typically less crowded than nearby beaches like La Jolla Cove and La Jolla Shores. The secluded beach is accessible by stairs and has clear water and tide pools. The reef comes all the way up to the shore, making it a less-than-ideal spot for swimming, but children love to wade in the shallow water. Step with caution, as rocks can be extremely slippery. As the name would imply, tiny shells make up the sand near the water's edge. It's beautiful but coarse and can be hard on people's feet. Your visit is better spent exploring than sunning. The exposed rocks off the coast have been designated a protected habitat for sea lions; you can watch them frolic in the water. Picnic tables, showers, and toilets are available near the cove. **Amenities:** none. **Best for:** solitude. ✉ *Coast Blvd.* ✣ *North of Children's Pool and south of Ellen Browning Scripps Park.*

★ Torrey Pines State Beach and Reserve
BEACH—SIGHT | With sandstone cliffs and hiking trails adjacent to the beach rather than urban development, Torrey Pines State Beach feels far away from the SoCal sprawl. The beach and reserve encompass 1,500 acres of sandstone cliffs and deep ravines, and a network of meandering trails lead to the wide, pristine beach below. Along the way enjoy the rare Torrey pine trees, found only here and on Santa Rosa Island, offshore. Guides conduct free tours of the nature preserve on weekends and holidays. Torrey Pines tends to get crowded in summer, but you'll find more isolated spots heading south under the cliffs leading to Black's Beach. Smooth rocks often wash up on stretches of the beach making it a challenge, at times, to go barefoot. If you can find a patch that is clear of debris, you'll encounter the nice soft, golden sand San Diego is known for. There is a paid parking lot at the entrance to the park but also look for free angle parking along N. Torrey Pines Road. **Amenities:** lifeguards, parking (fee), showers, toilets. **Best for:** swimming, surfing, walking. ✉ *12600 N. Torrey Pines Rd., San Diego* ☎ *858/755–2063* 🌐 *www.torreypine.org* 🎟 *Parking $15–20 per vehicle.*

★ Windansea Beach
BEACH—SIGHT | With its rocky shoreline and strong shore break, Windansea stands out among San Diego beaches for its dramatic natural beauty. It's one of the best surf spots in San Diego County. Professional surfers love the unusual A-frame waves the reef break here creates. Although the large sandstone rocks that dot the beach might sound like a hindrance, they actually serve as protective barriers from the wind, making this one of the best beaches in San Diego for sunbathing. The beach's palm-covered surf shack is a protected historical landmark, and a seat here at sunset may just be one of the most romantic spots on the West Coast. The name Windansea comes from a hotel that burned down in the late 1940s. You can usually find nearby street parking. **Amenities:** seasonal lifeguards, toilets. **Best for:** sunset, surfing, solitude. ✉ *Neptune Pl. at Nautilus St.* 🌐 *www.sandiego.gov/lifeguards/beaches/windan.shtml.*

🍴 Restaurants

This tony enclave that hugs the ocean from the Bird Rock area to Torrey Pines draws diners from around the world to experience an amazing collection of relaxed fine and casual dining establishments, ranging from classic French bistro fare to California modern cuisine. Ocean-view restaurants along Prospect Street are very popular, but there are many affordable neighborhood favorites that serve tasty food in attractive settings like La Jolla Cove.

★ A.R. Valentien
$$$$ | **AMERICAN** | Champions of in-season, fresh-today produce, the chefs at this cozy room in the luxurious, Craftsman-style Lodge at Torrey Pines have made A.R. Valentin one of San Diego's top fine dining destinations. **Known for:** red-wine braised short rib; creamy chicken liver pâté; smooth dirty martinis. [$] *Average main: $45* ✉ *The Lodge at Torrey Pines, 11480 N. Torrey Pines Rd., La Jolla* ☎ *858/777–6635* 🌐 *www.arvalentien.com.*

The grassy palm-lined park above La Jolla Cove is great for picnics.

Bistro du Marché

$$$ | **MODERN FRENCH** | Bringing Paris to La Jolla, acclaimed chef Jean Michel Diot unveils bistronomie cuisine, a culinary concept that blends bistro favorites with gastronomie techniques. The airy dining room, lined with black-and-white photos of France, is comfortable, if not romantic, an ideal setting for the ever-changing menu that emphasizes fresh ingredients sourced from the Sunday farmers' market that holds court in front of the restaurant. **Known for:** French classics like duck confit; poutine; happy hour cocktails, wine, and beers for under $10. [$] *Average main: $30* ✉ *7437 Girard Ave.* ☎ *858/551–7500* 🌐 *www.bistrodumarche.net* 🕓 *No lunch Sat.–Tues.*

Brockton Villa

$$ | **AMERICAN** | One of the few restaurants with a view that's also worth eating at, Brockton Villa is tucked in an historic cottage on a hillside above La Jolla Cove. Food is served all day, but this dining spot excels at brunch and lunch when ocean views are best. **Known for:** prime ocean views; orange-scented Coast French Toast; the afternoon social hour (Mon.–Thurs., 3–6 pm) is a bottle of wine and artisanal cheese board for $30. [$] *Average main: $20* ✉ *1235 Coast Blvd.* ☎ *858/454–7393* 🌐 *www.brocktonvilla.com.*

Cody's La Jolla

$ | **AMERICAN** | This cozy dining spot in a converted house a block from beautiful La Jolla Cove and Park serves up ocean views and tasty contemporary American fare for well-heeled La Jollans and tourists alike. The atmosphere is laid-back and beach-festive, especially on the front-porch patio cooled by sea breezes. **Known for:** crab cake Benedict; patio with ocean views; breakfast all day. [$] *Average main: $13* ✉ *8030 Girard Ave.* ☎ *858/459–0040* 🌐 *www.codyslj.com* 🕓 *No dinner.*

The Cottage

$ | **AMERICAN** | A cozy beach cottage sets the stage for American comfort food with a California twist at this La Jolla staple.

The restaurant serves lunch and dinner, but it's the well-loved daily breakfast that has locals and visitors happily queuing—sometimes up to two hours on weekends. **Known for:** daily breakfast that people line up for; treats for those waiting in line; great patio seating. [$] *Average main: $14* ✉ *7702 Fay Ave., La Jolla* ☎ *858/454–8409* 🌐 *www.cottagelajolla.com* ⏲ *No dinner Sun. and Mon.*

El Pescador Fish Market

$ | SEAFOOD | This bustling fish market and café in the heart of La Jolla Village has been popular with locals for its super-fresh fish for more than 30 years. Order the char-grilled, locally caught halibut, swordfish, or yellowtail on a toasted torta roll to enjoy in-house or to go for an oceanfront picnic at nearby La Jolla Cove. **Known for:** clam chowder; bustling on-site fish market; daily-caught cuts to go. [$] *Average main: $15* ✉ *634 Pearl St.* ☎ *858/456–2526* 🌐 *www.elpescadorfishmarket.com.*

Galaxy Taco

$$ | MODERN MEXICAN | This casual eatery focuses on high-quality Mexican food like tacos—fish, chicken, mushroom, steak, and avocado—made from non-GMO heirloom corn. Start with shareables like ceviche, birria-steamed clams, or blue corn quesadilla with sweet potato and arugula before choosing from mains that cover tamales, enchiladas, and a wood-grilled carne asada. **Known for:** house-made, high-end blue corn tortillas; smoky mezcal cocktails; Sunday brunch with bottomless mimosas and micheladas. [$] *Average main: $24* ✉ *2259 Av. de la Playa, La Jolla* ☎ *858/228–5655* 🌐 *www.galaxytaco.com.*

★ George's at the Cove

$$$$ | AMERICAN | La Jolla's ocean-view destination restaurant includes three distinct levels: California Modern on the bottom floor, the Level2 bar in the middle, and Ocean Terrace on the roof. At the sleek main dining room, open only for dinner, give special consideration to the legendary "fish tacos" and the six-course chef's tasting menu; for a more casual and inexpensive lunch or dinner option, head to the outdoor-only Ocean Terrace for spectacular views; for unique craft cocktails, like the "La Jolla" chilled with seaweed-laced ice cubes, and a seasonal happy hour with small bites, cocktails, beer, and wine, it's the Level2 lounge. **Known for:** beef tartare with 67-degree egg; excellent ocean views; attention to detail for special occasion dinners. [$] *Average main: $37* ✉ *1250 Prospect St.* ☎ *858/454–4244* 🌐 *www.georgesatthecove.com.*

Herringbone

$$$ | SEAFOOD | If the food doesn't get you, the setting certainly will with its brick courtyard reminiscent of a shipping yard with crates of blowfish, antique canoes, industrial lighting, and a rope-strewn whale skeleton above the oyster bar. Grab a table beside the 150-year-old olive trees and dig into wood-fired flatbreads, oysters on the half shell, or Brussels sprouts with candied pecans. **Known for:** oyster hour; $25 Sunday brunch; Tannin Tuesdays with half-off wine. [$] *Average main: $35* ✉ *7837 Herschel Ave., La Jolla* ☎ *858/459–0221* 🌐 *www.herringboneeats.com.*

The Marine Room

$$$$ | MODERN AMERICAN | It's hard to dine closer to the Pacific than at this venerable La Jolla Shores mainstay. Two-story-tall windows capture beachgoers, kayakers, snorkelers, and swooping gulls, and if the tide is high, waves race across the sand and crash against the glass; they even host a High Tide Breakfast buffet pegged to the event a few times each month. **Known for:** well-priced afternoon happy hours; High Tide breakfast buffet; a fine-dining menu that's sophisticated yet playful. [$] *Average main: $38* ✉ *2000 Spindrift Dr.* ☎ *866/644–2351* 🌐 *www.marineroom.com.*

Michele Coulon Dessertier

$ | **CAFÉ** | **FAMILY** | The desserts are magnificent at this small, charming shop in the heart of La Jolla, where dessertier Michele Coulon confects wonders, using organic produce and imported chocolate. Snack on cookies, cupcakes, brownies, chocolate-dipped strawberries, and mini-desserts, but this is not just a place for dessert as lunch is served Monday through Saturday (the store is open 9 am to 4 pm), and the simple menu includes quiche and salads. **Known for:** Instagram-worthy presentation; the buttercream- and berry-filled Gateau Aileen; gluten-free items usually are available. $ *Average main: $12* ⊠ *7556 Fay Ave., Suite D* ☎ *858/456–5098* ⊕ *www. dessertier.com* ☽ *Closed Sun. No dinner.*

NINE-TEN

$$$ | **AMERICAN** | Accolades continue to roll in for executive chef Jason Knibb—winner of an award of excellence by *Wine Spectator* in 2018—whose seasonal menus for breakfast, lunch, and dinner are magnets for travelers and San Diegans seeking a memorable meal. Located at La Jolla's Grande Colonial Hotel, the space encompasses a cozy ground-floor dining room, bar, and ocean-glimpse covered patio. **Known for:** juicy Jamaican jerk pork belly; breezy patio with La Jolla Village views; half-baked chocolate cake with ice cream of the season. $ *Average main: $34* ⊠ *Grande Colonial Hotel, 910 Prospect St.* ☎ *858/964–5400* ⊕ *www. nine-ten.com* ☽ *No lunch Sun.*

Osteria Romantica

$ | **ITALIAN** | Two guys who grew up in Italy founded this cozy La Jolla Shores eatery in 2004 to bring authentic Italian food to residents and visitors of the walkable neighborhood and its nearby beaches. Friendly servers deliver house-made breads, sauces, and pastas like penne with sausage and bell peppers, pappardelle with braised lamb, and linguine with mussels. **Known for:** tender lamb pappardelle; cozy Italian vibe; half-price wine with the purchase of an entrée on Tuesday. $ *Average main: $17* ⊠ *2151 Av. de la Playa* ☎ *858/551–1221* ⊕ *www. osteriaromantica.com.*

★ Piatti La Jolla

$$ | **MODERN ITALIAN** | **FAMILY** | Blocks from the beach in La Jolla Shores, this comfortably modern dining room and shaded patio hits all the right notes—affordable, polished, and family-friendly. From lunch through close, it bustles with regulars from the neighborhood and visitors from around the world who are guided through the extensive Italian menu by the professional staff, some of whom have worked here for decades. **Known for:** stone-hearth oven pizza; tree-covered patio; house-made ravioli. $ *Average main: $18* ⊠ *2182 Av. de la Playa* ☎ *858/454–1589* ⊕ *www.piatti.com.*

Shorehouse Kitchen

$ | **AMERICAN** | This casual indoor-outdoor eatery in Lo Jolla Shores has a sprawling outdoor patio perfect for leisurely lunches with friends and family. Surfers and well-heeled locals populate the 50-seat patio while enjoying made-to-order organic smoothies and fresh salads, as well as scrumptious breakfast and creative lunch entrées that include flatbreads, soups, sandwiches, and the popular cheeseburger and prime steak frites. **Known for:** mango pancakes; vanilla bean French toast; California K-9 breakfast off the doggie menu. $ *Average main: $15* ⊠ *2236 Av. de la Playa, San Diego* ☎ *858/459–3300* ⊕ *www.shorehouse-kitchen.com* ☽ *No dinner.*

Trilogy Sanctuary

$ | **VEGETARIAN** | Perched on a rooftop in La Jolla, this cafe features mindful menu of bowls, tacos, and other creative entrées that are all 100% organic, vegan, gluten-free, dairy-free, and soy-free. There's also a yoga studio and boutique. **Known for:** plentiful vegetarian and vegan options; juice cleanses via cold-pressed juice; indoor and outdoor yoga studio. $ *Average main: $10* ⊠ *7650 Girard Ave.,*

La Jolla ☎ *858/633–3893* 🌐 *www.trilogy-sanctuary.com.*

Whisknladle

$$$ | **MODERN AMERICAN** | This hip eatery has won national acclaim for its combination of casual comfort and a menu of ever-changing local fare. In nice weather, request a patio table to enjoy the people-watching along with cocktails like the London's Burning with gin, jalapeño, avocado, and lemon or house sangria. **Known for:** brunch served daily; craft cocktails including seasonal mimosas; farm-fresh, from-scratch menu. [$] *Average main: $29* ✉ *1044 Wall St.* ☎ *858/551–7575* 🌐 *www.whisknladle.com* ⏲ *No lunch.*

Hotels

Multimillion-dollar homes line the beaches and hillsides of beautiful and prestigious La Jolla, a community about 20 minutes north of Downtown. La Jolla Shores is a mile-long sandy beach that gets crowded in summer with kayakers, sunbathers, and students in scuba-diving classes. The village—the heart of La Jolla—is chockablock with expensive boutiques, art galleries, restaurants, and a grassy beachfront park that's popular for picnics and weddings.

Empress Hotel

$$$ | **HOTEL** | A few blocks from the ocean and Girard Avenue's upscale shops, the five-story Empress Hotel in La Jolla blends Southern California beach style with a touch of European flair. **Pros:** near shops, restaurants, and beach; quiet street; attention to detail. **Cons:** not exciting for kids; $75 pet fee; small bathrooms. [$] *Rooms from: $233* ✉ *7766 Fay Ave.* ☎ *858/454–3001,* 🌐 *www.empress-hotel.com* 🛏 *73 rooms* 🍴 *Free Breakfast.*

Estancia La Jolla Hotel & Spa

$$$ | **RESORT** | With its rambling California mission–style architecture and brilliant gardens, this resort on what once was a famous equestrian ranch exudes rustic elegance. **Pros:** upscale rooms; nice spa; landscaped grounds. **Cons:** mandatory $30 resort fees; not centrally located; small gym. [$] *Rooms from: $279* ✉ *9700 N. Torrey Pines Rd.* ☎ *858/550–1000* 🌐 *www.estancialajolla.com* 🛏 *210 rooms* 🍴 *No meals.*

★ Grande Colonial

$$$$ | **HOTEL** | This white wedding cake–style hotel in the heart of La Jolla village has ocean views and charming European details that include chandeliers, mahogany railings, a wooden elevator, crystal door knobs, and French doors. **Pros:** great location; superb restaurant; no resort fees. **Cons:** somewhat busy street; no fitness center; valet parking only. [$] *Rooms from: $369* ✉ *910 Prospect St.* ☎ *888/828–5498* 🌐 *www.thegrandecolonial.com* 🛏 *93 rooms* 🍴 *No meals.*

La Valencia Hotel

$$$$ | **HOTEL** | This pink Spanish-Mediterranean confection drew Hollywood film stars in the 1930s and '40s with its setting and views of La Jolla Cove; now it draws the Kardashians. **Pros:** upscale rooms; views; near beach. **Cons:** standard rooms are tiny; lots of traffic outside; strange layout. [$] *Rooms from: $449* ✉ *1132 Prospect St.* ☎ *858/454–0771* 🌐 *www.lavalencia.com* 🛏 *114 rooms* 🍴 *No meals.*

★ The Lodge at Torrey Pines

$$$$ | **RESORT** | Best known for its two 18-hole championship golf courses, this beautiful Craftsman-style lodge sits on a bluff between La Jolla and Del Mar with commanding coastal views, excellent service, a blissful spa, and the upscale A. R. **Pros:** spacious upscale rooms; remarkable service; adjacent the famed Torrey Pines Golf Course; warm decor with Craftsman accents and hardwoods. **Cons:** not centrally located; expensive; $30 daily parking fee. [$] *Rooms from: $379* ✉ *11480 N. Torrey Pines Rd.* ☎ *858/453–4420, 888/826–0224* 🌐 *www.lodgetorreypines.com* 🏌 *Two 18-hole*

championship golf courses ⇌ *170 rooms* ⏺ *No meals.*

Pantai Inn

$$$$ | **HOTEL** | Located along La Jolla coastline with ocean views from almost every corner, this sophisticated, Bali-inspired inn offers a mix of studios, one- and two-bedroom suites, and cottages. **Pros:** spacious rooms; ocean views; free parking and breakfast. **Cons:** no pool; no fitness center; not good for kids. $ *Rooms from: $380* ✉ *1003 Coast Blvd.* ☎ *858/224–7600, 855/287–2682* ⊕ *www.pantai.com* ⇌ *30 rooms* ⏺ *Free Breakfast.*

Scripps Inn

$$$$ | **B&B/INN** | You'd be wise to make reservations well in advance for this small, quiet inn tucked away on Coast Boulevard atop Whale Watch Point; its popularity with repeat visitors ensures that it's booked year-round. **Pros:** beach access; intimate feel; rooms spacious and clean. **Cons:** daily resort fee; a three-night minimum is required in the summer; no a/c. $ *Rooms from: $355* ✉ *555 S. Coast Blvd.* ☎ *858/454–3391, 888/976–2912* ⊕ *www.scrippsinn.com* ⇌ *14 rooms* ⏺ *Free Breakfast.*

🍸 Nightlife

Just a little north of Pacific Beach, the bar tab increases considerably in the chi-chi clime of La Jolla, home to many of San Diego's wealthiest residents, and for that matter, the bars with the best ocean views. It's not all bank-breaking martini lounges, however; there's enough diversity in the options here to appease both the day-trippers and the residents alike.

BARS

Cusp

BARS/PUBS | The stone walls and modern metal accents along the bar give the impression of Cusp being a dark, intimate lounge, but the panoramic views of La Jolla shores brighten up this chic spot on the 11th floor of Hotel La Jolla.

Sip on one of their signature cocktails during their daily happy hour from 4 to 6. ✉ *7955 La Jolla Shores Dr.* ☎ *858/551–3620* ⊕ *www.cusprestaurant.com.*

George's Level 2

BARS/PUBS | Located on the middle level of George's at the Cove, this hip, casual, and somewhat more affordable hangout is always buzzing with activity—especially on weekends. Stop in for craft cocktails or bar snacks that rank among La Jolla's best, and with gorgeous ocean views to boot. ✉ *1250 Prospect St.* ☎ *858/454–4244* ⊕ *www.georgesatthecove.com/level2.*

Manhattan of La Jolla

PIANO BARS/LOUNGES | Lovingly referred to as the "Manhattan Lounge" by locals, this underrated and largely undiscovered bar neighbors the Italian steak house inside the Empress Hotel. It feels like the type of place that the Rat Pack would have frequented, thanks to a dark, old-school interior that's perfect for sipping martinis and live jazz Wednesday–Saturday. ✉ *7766 Fay Ave.* ☎ *858/459–0700* ⊕ *www.manhattanoflajolla.com.*

The Spot

BARS/PUBS | Nightlife can be kind of sleepy in affluent La Jolla, but in-the-know locals keep this tavern buzzing on any given night thanks to powerful cocktails and bar grub that's served late into the evening—one of the few spots that's open in La Jolla in the wee hours. ✉ *1005 Prospect St.* ☎ *858/459–0800* ⊕ *www.thespotonline.com.*

COFFEEHOUSES

Living Room Coffeehouse

GATHERING PLACES | La Jolla's outpost of this local coffee chain is open until midnight and sports a full bar, which means that customers can spend a pleasant evening sipping a true-blue Irish coffee complete with whiskey at one of the many tables or couches. ✉ *1010 Prospect St.* ☎ *858/459–1187* ⊕ *www.livingroomusa.com.*

COMEDY AND CABARET
The Comedy Store La Jolla
CABARET | Like its sister establishment in Hollywood, this club hosts some of the best national touring and local talent. Cover charges range from nothing on open-mike nights to $20 or more for national acts. Seating is at bistro-style tables, and a two-drink minimum applies for all shows. ⊠ *916 Pearl St.* ☎ *858/454–9176* ⊕ *www.thecomedystore.com/la-jolla* ☞ *Closed Mon. and Tues.*

🎭 Performing Arts

MUSIC
La Jolla Athenaeum Music & Arts Library
MUSIC | The Athenaeum is a membership-supported, nonprofit library with an exceptional collection of books, periodicals, CDs, and other media related to arts and music. It also hosts classes, exhibits, lectures, and intimate jazz, chamber music, and the occasional folk concert throughout the year. ⊠ *1008 Wall St.* ☎ *858/454–5872* ⊕ *ljathenaeum.org* ☞ *Closed Sun. and Mon.*

The Loft at UCSD
CONCERTS | This quaint, comfortable performance space inside the Price Center on the University of California San Diego campus hosts intimate music concerts, spoken word programs, film screenings, and culinary events. ⊠ *Price Center East, 9500 Gilman Dr., 4th fl.* ☎ *858/678–0922* ⊕ *theloft.ucsd.edu* ☞ *Closed weekends.*

THEATER
More than a few Tony-winning Broadway productions have been launched at San Diego theaters; La Jolla Playhouse is one of the stars in the city's large ensemble.

★ La Jolla Playhouse
THEATER | Under the artistic direction of Christopher Ashley, the playhouse presents exciting and innovative plays and musicals on three stages. Many Broadway shows—among them *Memphis, Come From Away, Tommy,* and *Jersey Boys*—have previewed here before their East Coast premieres. Its Without Walls program also ensures that the productions aren't limited to the playhouse, having put on site-specific shows in places like outdoor art spaces, cars, and even the ocean. ⊠ *University of California at San Diego, 2910 La Jolla Village Dr.* ☎ *858/550–1010* ⊕ *www.lajollaplayhouse.org.*

🏃 Activities

BICYCLING
Bike & Kayak Tours
BICYCLING | This bike and kayak outfitter, with locations in La Jolla and on Coronado, is your one-stop shop for biking and kayaking fun. It offers bike rentals and tours like La Jolla Freefall tour that starts at Mt. Soledad, La Jolla's highest point, and continues down the mountain, past mansions, and along the coastline. Bike & Kayak Tours also offers a hotel delivery service, via which they drop off bikes right at your doorstep. ⊠ *2158 Ave. De La Playa* ☎ *858/454–1010* ⊕ *www.bikeandkayaktours.com* 🎟 *Tours from $49; bike rentals from $29.*

Hike Bike Kayak Adventures
BICYCLING | This outfitter offers guided bike tours for all biking abilities, through coastal La Jolla to many of San Diego's most famous landmarks. Tours last 2 hours. The company also rents kayaks, surfboards, paddleboards, and snorkel gear. ⊠ *2222 Av. de la Playa* ☎ *858/551–9510* ⊕ *www.hikebikekayak.com* 🎟 *From $45.*

Route S21 (*Coast Highway 101*)
BICYCLING | On many summer days, Route S21, more commonly known as "the 101," from La Jolla to Oceanside looks like a freeway for cyclists. About 24 miles long, it's easily the most popular and scenic bike route around, never straying far from the beach. Although the terrain is fairly easy, the long, steep Torrey Pines grade is famous for weeding out the weak. Another Darwinian

Torrey Pines Golf Course has fantastic views to go along with its challenging holes.

challenge is dodging slow-moving pedestrians and cars pulling over to park in towns like Encinitas and Del Mar. ⊠ *La Jolla.*

DIVING
Scuba San Diego

SCUBA DIVING | This center is well regarded for its top-notch instruction and certification programs, as well as for guided dive tours. Scuba Adventure classes for non-certified divers are held daily in Mission Bay, meeting near Mission Point. Trips for certified divers depart from La Jolla and include dives to kelp reefs in La Jolla Cove, and night diving at La Jolla Canyon. They also have snorkeling tours to La Jolla's Sea Caves. ⊠ *San Diego Hilton Hotel, 1775 E. Mission Bay Dr., Mission Bay* ☎ *619/260–1880* ⊕ *www. scubasandiego.com* ⊠ *From $70* ☞ *Scuba Adventure meeting point is 2615 Bayside Lane in South Mission Bay, near Mission Point.*

GOLF
★ Torrey Pines Golf Course

GOLF | Due to its clifftop location overlooking the Pacific and its classic championship holes, Torrey Pines is one of the best public golf courses in the United States. The course was the site of the 2008 U.S. Open and has been the home of the Farmers Insurance Open since 1968. The par-72 South Course, redesigned by Rees Jones in 2001, receives rave reviews from touring pros; it is longer, more challenging, and more expensive than the North Course. Tee times may be booked from 8 to 90 days in advance (*858/552–1662*) and are subject to an advance booking fee ($45). ⊠ *11480 N. Torrey Pines Rd.* ☎ *858/452–3226, 800/985–4653* ⊕ *www.torreypinesgolf-course.com* ⊠ *South: $202 weekdays, $252 weekends. North: $110 weekdays, $138 weekends; $40 for golf cart* 🏌 *South: 18 holes, 7227 yards, par 72. North: 18 holes, 7258 yards, par 72.*

HANG GLIDING AND PARAGLIDING

Torrey Pines Gliderport

HANG GLIDING/PARAGLIDING/PARASAILING
| Perched on the cliffs overlooking the ocean north of La Jolla, this is one of the most spectacular spots to hang glide in the world. It's for experienced pilots only, but hang gliding and paragliding lessons and tandem rides for inexperienced gliders are available. Those who'd rather just watch can grab a bite at the Cliffhanger Cafe, which offers incredible views of the Pacific and of the paragliders taking off. During the summer, there's live music on weekends. ⊠ *2800 Torrey Pines Scenic Dr.* ☎ *858/452–9858* ⊕ *www.flytorrey. com* ✈ *From $175.*

HIKING

Los Peñasquitos Canyon Preserve

HIKING/WALKING | Trails at this inland park north of Mira Mesa accommodate equestrians, runners, walkers, and cyclists as well as leashed dogs. Look at maps for trails specific to bikes and horses. A 7-mile loop passes a small waterfall among large volcanic rock boulders—it's an unexpected oasis amid the arid valley landscape. ⊠ *12020 Black Mountain Rd., Rancho Peñasquitos* ✛ *From I–15, exit Mercy Rd., and head west to Black Mountain Rd.; turn right then left at first light; follow road to Ranch House parking lot* ☎ *858/484–7504* ⊕ *www.sdparks.org.*

Torrey Pines State Reserve

HIKING/WALKING | Hikers and runners will appreciate this park's many winning features: switchback trails that descend to the sea, an unparalleled view of the Pacific, and a chance to see the Torrey pine tree, one of the rarest pine breeds in the United States. The reserve hosts guided nature walks as well. Dogs and food are prohibited at the reserve. Parking is $15–$20, depending on day and season. ⊠ *12600 N. Torrey Pines Rd.* ✛ *Exit I–5 at Carmel Valley Rd. and head west toward Coast Hwy. 101 until you reach N. Torrey Pines Rd.; turn left.* ☎ *858/755–2063* ⊕ *www.torreypine.org* ✈ *Parking $15–$20.*

KAYAKING

There are several places to kayak throughout San Diego. You can spend an especially memorable afternoon exploring the Seven Caves off La Jolla Cove, where you can often see seals, sea lions, and even dolphins, or the Underwater Park and Ecological Reserve at the cove.

Everyday California

KAYAKING | This action-on-the-water sports company also has its own clothing line offering beach casual styles inspired by La Jolla. Tours with expert guides, many of which are former college-level athletes, include a sunset kayak tour, where wildlife to see includes sea lions, seals, pelicans, and dolphins; the tour combines kayaking and snorkeling. Leopard shark migration tours are offered May–August, and whale-watching tours December–March. If you'd rather go out on your own, Everyday California rents kayaks, stand-up paddleboards, surfboards, snorkel equipment, and bodyboards. ⊠ *2261 Av. de la Playa* ☎ *858/454–6195* ⊕ *www. everydaycalifornia.com* ✈ *From $40.*

Hike Bike Kayak Adventures

KAYAKING | This shop offers several kayak tours, from easy excursions in La Jolla Cove that are well suited to families and beginners to more advanced jaunts. Tours include kayaking the caves off La Jolla coast, and whale-watching (from a safe distance) December through March. Tours last two to three hours and require a minimum of four people. ⊠ *2222 Av. de la Playa* ☎ *858/551–9510* ⊕ *www. hikebikekayak.com* ✈ *From $50.*

La Jolla Kayak

KAYAKING | This family-owned company offers kayak tours of the Seven Caves of La Jolla as well as snorkel and biking adventures. Several guides have extensive backgrounds in marine biology and ecology. ⊠ *2199 Av. de la Playa* ☎ *858/459–1114* ⊕ *www.lajollakayak.com* ⌨ *From $39.*

SURFING

Menehune Surf School

SURFING | This surf school provides surf lessons as well as paddleboard and surfboard rentals. Private or family lessons can be arranged (from $65 per person for one hour). Menehune Surf also offers popular surf camps for kids every summer from June through August at La Jolla Shores and Del Mar. ⊠ *La Jolla Shores Beach* ✛ *Blue canopy at La Jolla Shores Beach located north of parking lot at Kellogg Park in front of 4th–5th house on sand as you walk toward Scripps Pier* ☎ *858/663–7299* ⊕ *www.menehunesurf. com* ⌨ *From $65.*

★ Surf Diva Surf School

SURFING | Check out clinics, surf camps, and private lessons especially formulated for girls and women. Most clinics and trips are for women only, but there are some coed options. Guys can also book group or private lessons from the nationally recognized staff. Surf Diva is also home to a boutique that sells surf and stand-up paddleboard equipment. They also offer surf retreats in Costa Rica. ⊠ *2160 Ave. de la Playa* ☎ *858/454–8273* ⊕ *www.surfdiva.com* ⌨ *Group lessons $65; private lessons $90.*

🛍 Shopping

San Diego's answer to Rodeo Drive in Beverly Hills, La Jolla has chic boutiques, art galleries, and gift shops lining narrow, twisty streets that attract well-heeled shoppers and celebrities. Prospect Street and Girard Avenue are the primary shopping stretches, and North Prospect is packed with art galleries *(see Performing Arts for information on art galleries).* The Upper Girard Design District stocks home decor accessories and luxury furnishings. Store hours vary widely so it's wise to call in advance, though most shops on Prospect Street stay open until 10 pm on weeknights to accommodate evening strollers. If you're driving, there's free parking in the La Jolla Cove or garages along Prospect Street, between Wall and Silverado, or along Herschel, Girard, and Fay. Rates range from $1.50 for 20 minutes to a maximum of $15 per day. After 4 pm, there's a flat rate of $10.

La Jolla's chic boutiques offer a more intimate shopping experience, along with some of the classiest clothes, jewelry, and shoes in the county. The new La Plaza La Jolla is an open-air shopping center with boutiques and galleries in a Spanish-style building overlooking the cove.

BOOKS

Warwick's

BOOKS/STATIONERY | This family-owned-and-operated bookstore has been a La Jolla fixture since 1939, and often hosts big-name author signings. They also carry stationery, calendars, and other gifts. ⊠ *7812 Girard Ave., La Jolla* ☎ *858/454–0347* ⊕ *www.warwicks.com.*

CLOTHING AND ACCESSORIES

Ascot Shop

CLOTHING | The classic Ivy League look is king in this traditional haberdashery that sells menswear by Saxx, Robert Talbott, and Peter Miller. In-house same-day tailoring is available. ⊠ *7750 Girard Ave., La Jolla* ☎ *858/454–4222* ⊕ *www.ascot-shop.com* ☾ *Closed Sun.*

Fresh Produce

CLOTHING | Sunny and spirited Fresh Produce sells beach-inspired clothing made with comfy fabrics. The boutique's easy-to-wear pieces are perfect for vacations and weekend getaways. ⊠ *1147 Prospect St., La Jolla* ☎ *858/456–8134* ⊕ *www. freshproduceclothes.com.*

La Jolla Surf Systems

CLOTHING | One block from La Jolla Shores beach, this local institution stocks hip beach and resort wear, plus top-brand surfboards, bodyboards, and wet suits. The shop also rents surf and stand-up paddleboards, beach chairs, umbrellas, kayaks, and snorkel gear. ⊠ *2132 Av. de la Playa, La Jolla* ☎ *858/456–2777.*

Rangoni Firenze

CLOTHING | The shoe shop carries its own house brand of Valentina Rangoni footwear, as well as handbags. ⊠ *7870 Girard Ave., La Jolla* ☎ *858/459–4469* ⊕ *www. rangonistore.com.*

Sauvage Swimwear

CLOTHING | This luxurious boutique sells sexy and sophisticated swimsuits, beachwear, jewelry, and accessories for women, as well as swim trunks, surf shorts, and workout gear for men. ⊠ *1025 Prospect St., Suite 140, La Jolla* ☎ *858/729–0015* ⊕ *www.sauvageswimwear.com.*

GALLERIES

The Stuart Collection at UCSD

ART GALLERIES—ARTS | Less a gallery than an open-air scavenger hunt for some of the city's most impressive works of visual art, the Stuart Collection—located on campus at UCSD—boasts a number of must-see, and sometimes massive, pieces by some of the biggest names in contemporary art, including Jenny Holzer, John Baldessari, and Robert Irwin. ⊠ *UCSD, 9500 Gilman Dr.* ⊕ *stuartcollection.ucsd.edu.*

Thumbprint Gallery

ART GALLERIES—ARTS | This quaint little gallery brings a little edge to otherwise sleepy La Jolla, showing off some of the best lowbrow and street artists in the city. This is a great place to purchase something truly unique for a low price. ⊠ *920 Kline St.* ☎ *858/354–6294* ⊕ *www. thumbprintgallerysd.com* ☞ *Closed Mon.–Thurs.*

HOME ACCESSORIES AND GIFTS

Africa and Beyond

ART GALLERIES | This La Jolla art gallery has been selling traditional and contemporary African art for more than 30 years. Find Shona stone sculptures and ceremonial masks as well as ceramics, textiles, fair trade gifts, and furniture. While most of the items come from Africa, look for oceanic art from Papua New Guinea, and sterling and gold-plated jewelry from across the world. ⊠ *1250 Prospect St., La Jolla* ☎ *858/454–9983* ⊕ *www. africaandbeyond.com.*

La Jolla Cove Gifts

GIFTS/SOUVENIRS | Located one block from the ocean, this gift shop sells T-shirts, souvenirs, seashells, jewelry, and nautical items. ⊠ *8008 Girard Ave., No. 120, La Jolla* ☎ *858/454–2297* ⊕ *www.lajollacovegifts.com.*

JEWELRY

CJ Charles

JEWELRY/ACCESSORIES | An exquisitely appointed shop selling designer and estate jewelry, CJ Charles specializes in Bulgari watches, Cartier, and Patek Philippe, along with stunning fine jewelry, Baccarat crystal, and gift items. ⊠ *1135 Prospect St.* ☎ *858/454–5390* ⊕ *www. cjcharles.com.*

Pomegranate

JEWELRY/ACCESSORIES | In La Jolla for nearly 40 years, Pomegranate pairs contemporary and antique jewelry with edgy and artistic fashions by American, European, and Asian designers. ⊠ *1152 Prospect St.* ☎ *858/459–0629* ⊕ *www.pomegranatelajolla.com.*

TOYS

Geppetto's Toys

TOYS | FAMILY | This family-run toy shop has been in business for more than 40 years. With 10 locations throughout San Diego, the store offers classic toys and games as well as the newest must-haves. It's a great place to wander with kids or pick up something to take home. ⊠ *7850 Girard Ave., La Jolla* ☎ *858/456–4441* ⊕ *www.geppettostoys.com.*

SHOPPING MALLS

Westfield UTC

SHOPPING CENTERS/MALLS | This popular outdoor mall on the east side of I–5 has more than 150 shops and 40 eateries, plus an ArcLight Cinemas and a children's play area. **Nordstrom and Macy's** anchor the center, and specialty stores of note include **Madewell** (*858/458–0012*) for high-quality basics; **Pottery Barn Kids** (*858/ 824–9079*) for children's bedding and accessories; **Crate & Barrel** (*858/558–4545*) for kitchenware, china dishes, and furniture; and an **Apple Store** (*858/795–6870*) for the latest igadget. One of the country's greenest shopping centers, UTC has lush gardens, open-air plazas, and pedestrian-friendly walkways. Additional eco-friendly cred: Tesla Motors shows off its latest electric vehicles here. ✉ *4545 La Jolla Village Dr., between I–5 and I–805, La Jolla* ☎ *858/546–8858* 🌐 *www.westfield.com/utc.*

Northern San Diego: Clairemont and Kearny Mesa

Located inland from La Jolla and north of Mission Valley, the neighborhoods of Clairemont and Kearny Mesa often fly under the radar of most visitors to San Diego. The shopping centers and restaurants of this area serve as a hub for San Diego's sizeable and diverse Asian population, especially along Convoy Street between Clairemont Mesa Boulevard and Aero Drive. Though these neighborhoods aren't traditional tourist destinations, those who do venture here will be rewarded as they dine at myriad authentic Asian restaurants, relax with a reflexology foot massage, or peruse the aisles of specialty grocery stores.

Clairemont

Centered on Tecolote Canyon, this suburban neighborhood occupies a series of mesas, many with views of Mission Bay. Heading inland, Balboa Avenue serves as the area's commercial hub.

🍴 Restaurants

This postwar bedroom community offers adventurous diners numerous affordable and authentic mom-and-pop ethnic restaurants and grocery stores. The setting may be simple, and the service minimal, but the food can be unforgettable.

Original Sab-E-Lee

$ | **THAI** | Opened since 2008, Original Sab-E-Lee may be a bit out of the way and lacking in ambience, but the northeastern Thai dishes featured on the menu—noodles, curry, and the spicy larb (think meat salad), which comes with pork, chicken, beef, catfish, or duck—make the trip worth it. **Known for:** cash-only; spicy food; authentic northeastern Thai cuisine. [$] *Average main: $9* ✉ *6925 Linda Vista Rd., San Diego* ☎ *858/650–6868* 🌐 *originalsab-e-lee.webs.com* ⏲ *Closed Mon.* 💳 *No credit cards.*

Sushi Diner

$ | **SUSHI** | With Rastafari flags, surfer videos on loop, and Bob Marley–inspired sushi rolls, chef/owner Daisuke makes it clear that this is a place to chill. The tiny and always bustling restaurant has a loyal following of locals who don't mind waiting for tables because of the friendly service, inexpensive sushi, and tasty island-inspired extras like Spam fried rice. **Known for:** affordable menu; crunchy roll; vegetarian options. [$] *Average main: $10* ✉ *7530 Mesa College Dr., Clairemont* ☎ *858/565–1179* 🌐 *www.sushidiner1.com* ⏲ *Closed Sun. No lunch Sat.*

Kearny Mesa

Farther inland, Kearny Mesa is less residential than neighboring Clairemont. The bustling shopping centers lining Convoy Street are home to many popular Asian restaurants, supermarkets, and probably the best ramen you'll have outside of Japan.

🍴 Restaurants

Kearny Mesa, considered the city's "Asian Restaurant Row," is definitely off the tourist radar but offers a host of small family-owned eateries serving superb authentic Chinese, Vietnamese, Thai, Japanese, Korean, and Filipino food—all within a stone's throw of one another.

Dumpling Inn
$ | **CHINESE** | Lovers of traditional Northern Chinese food drive for hundreds of miles to sample this value-packed menu, overlooking frequent long waits outside, crowded seating, and lack of in-house restrooms. The tiny establishment loads its 10 or so tables with bottles of aromatic and spicy condiments for the boiled, steamed, and fried dumplings that are the house specialty—the pork and chive are particularly good. **Known for:** huge portions; spicy chow mein; soup dumplings. [$] *Average main: $9* ✉ *4619 Convoy St., #F, Kearny Mesa* ☎ *858/268–9638* 🌐 *www.dumplinginn.menutoeat.com* 🕒 *Closed Mon.*

★ **j/wata Temaki Bar**
$ | **SUSHI** | For an interactive dining experience, snag a seat at j/wata Temaki Bar for made-to-order hand rolls filled with premium fish—best eaten immediately. Don't miss the blue crab and bay scallop temaki. **Known for:** sushi hand rolls; set menu—no substitutions or splitting; to-go options available. [$] *Average main: $10* ✉ *4646 Convoy St., Ste. 103, Kearny Mesa* ☎ *858/251–4071* 🌐 *www.j-wata.com.*

When the Grunions Run

A generations-old San Diego tradition is heading to the beach during certain high tides—preferably when the moon is full—to hunt grunion. These small, barely edible fish come ashore during mating periods and "run" on the beach, causing great excitement among spectators. As the fish flop across the sand in search of adventure (as it were), bold individuals chase them down and scoop up a few with their hands—catching them by any other means is illegal. Beach-area businesses and eateries often know the date of the next run.

Phuong Trang
$ | **VIETNAMESE** | This much-praised, popular Vietnamese restaurant offers such a mind-numbing selection of dishes that choosing a meal here can be difficult. Waiters steer diners to familiar tasty offerings like traditional pho, kung pao chicken, garlic butter–fried chicken wings, and fresh pork or shrimp spring rolls. **Known for:** garlic butter chicken wings; fried lobster; oven-roasted catfish. [$] *Average main: $10* ✉ *4170 Convoy St., Kearny Mesa* ☎ *858/565–6750* 🌐 *www.phuongtrangrestaurant.com.*

RakiRaki
$ | **JAPANESE** | The line out the door is the first sign you're at San Diego's best ramen spot, and the sight of thick handcrafted noodles soaking in deep pots of tonkotsu broth and garlic oil is sure to seal the deal. Original, red, or black-edition ramen are local go-tos, each topped with cabbage, bean sprouts, pickled egg, wakame seaweed, garlic chips, and crushed sesame. **Known for:** charcoal-fired yakitori; lunch specials;

sake and beer. $ Average main: $15
⊠ 4646 Convoy St, #102-A, Kearny Mesa
☎ 858/573–2400 ⊕ www.rakirakiramen.
com.

Spicy City Chinese

$ | SICHUAN | Get bold Sichuan flavors
with loads of chili peppers at this
restaurant, where food is served family
style, and "not spicy" is not an option.
Known for: affordable prices; extremely
quick service; authentic Sichuan cuisine.
$ Average main: $9 ⊠ 4690 Convoy St.,
Kearny Mesa ☎ 858/278–1818.

🍸 Nightlife

Beer-snob heaven is situated between
ramen houses and car dealerships.

BARS

Common Theory

BARS/PUBS | More than 30 craft beers
on tap, elevated pub-style food, and a
killer weekday happy hour (3-6 pm) make
this Kearny Mesa brewery a magnet
for beer aficionados. Depending on the
day of the week, last call hits between
11 pm and 1 am, meaning you can curl
up in the unique living room setting
and make yourself right at home for the
night. ⊠ 4805 Convoy St., Kearny Mesa
☎ 858/384–7974 ⊕ www.commontheo-
rysd.com.

POINT LOMA PENINSULA

Updated by
Marlise Kast-Myers

👁 **Sights**
★★★☆☆

🍴 **Restaurants**
★★★☆☆

🛏 **Hotels**
★★★☆☆

🛍 **Shopping**
★★★☆☆

🍸 **Nightlife**
★☆☆☆☆

CABRILLO NATIONAL MONUMENT

Cabrillo National Monument marks the site of the first European visit to San Diego, made by 16th-century Spanish explorer Juan Rodríguez Cabrillo on September 15, 1542. Cabrillo called the spot San Miguel. Today the 166-acre preserve is one of the most frequently visited national monuments.

Catching sight of a whale from the cliffs of Cabrillo National Monument can be a highlight of a wintertime visit to San Diego. More accessible sea creatures can be seen in the tide pools at the foot of the monument's western cliffs.

Trails lead down the hillside through sagebrush and cactus, and overlook points at 430 feet offer unobstructed views of the desert mountains, Downtown, and beyond.

■TIP→ **Restrooms and water fountains are plentiful, but, except for the Visitor Center's vending machines, there's no food. Exploring the grounds consumes time and calories; pack a picnic to enjoy with the views.**

SERVICE INFORMATION

The informative Visitor Center, located next to the statue of Cabrillo, and the lighthouse give a historical perspective to this once-remote promontory. The center presents films and lectures about Cabrillo's voyage, the sea-level tide pools, and migrating gray whales.

1800 Cabrillo Memorial Dr., Point Loma ☎ 619/557–5450 ⊕ www.nps.gov/cabr $15 per car, $5 per person entering on foot or by bicycle, admission good for 7 days. Park daily 9–5.

A HALF DAY AT CABRILLO NATIONAL MONUMENT

A **statue of Cabrillo** overlooks downtown from a windy promontory, where people gather to admire the stunning panorama over the bay, from the snowcapped San Bernardino Mountains, 130 miles north, to the hills surrounding Tijuana to the south. The stone figure standing on the bluff looks rugged and dashing, but he is a creation of an artist's imagination—no portraits of Cabrillo are known to exist.

The moderately steep **Bayside Trail,** 2½ miles round-trip, winds through coastal sage scrub, curving under the cliff-top lookouts and taking you ever closer to the bay-front scenery. You cannot reach the beach from this trail and must stick to the path to protect the cliffs from erosion and yourself from thorny plants and snakes—including rattlers. You'll see prickly pear cactus and yucca, fragrant sage, and maybe a lizard, rabbit, or hummingbird. The climb back is long but gradual, leading up to the old lighthouse.

Old Point Loma Lighthouse's oil lamp was first lighted in 1855 and was visible from the sea for 25 miles. Unfortunately, it was too high above the cliffs to guide navigators trapped in Southern California's thick offshore fog. In 1891 a new lighthouse was built 400 feet below. The restored old lighthouse is open to visitors. An exhibit in the Assistant Keepers Quarters next door tells the story of the Old Lighthouse, the daily lives of the keepers, how lighthouses work, and the role they played in the development of early maritime commerce along the West Coast. On the edge of the hill near the old lighthouse sits a refurbished radio room containing displays of U.S. harbor defenses at Point Loma used during World War II.

(left) Point Loma from the water, as Cabrillo would have seen it in 1542. (lower right) Old Point Loma Lighthouse stood watch for 36 years. (upper right) Cabrillo's statue adorns the visitor center.

WHALE-WATCHING

The western and southern cliffs of Cabrillo National Monument are prime whale-watching territory. A sheltered **viewing station** has wayside exhibits describing the great gray whales' yearly migration from Baja California to the Bering and Chukchi seas near Alaska. High-powered telescopes and binoculars—available from the Visitor Center—help you focus on the whales' waterspouts. Whales are visible on clear days from late December through early March, with the highest concentration in January and February. Note that when the whales return north in spring, they are too far out in the ocean to be seen from the monument.

TIDE POOLS

When the tide is low you can walk on the rocks around saltwater pools filled with starfish, crabs, anemones, octopuses, and hundreds of other sea creatures and plants. Tide pooling is best when the tide is at its lowest, so call ahead or check tide charts online before your visit. Exercise caution on the slippery rocks.

NEIGHBORHOOD SNAPSHOT

GREAT EXPERIENCES

■ **Boating paradise:** San Diego's picturesque marinas are filled with sportfishing charters and ultraluxury yachts.

■ **Military might:** From the endless rows of white headstones at Fort Rosecrans National Cemetery to the roar of fighter jets over North Island Naval Air Station, San Diego's strong military ties are palpable.

■ **Peninsula hopping:** The thin strips of land that make up Harbor and Shelter Islands pack in restaurants, hotels, marinas, and parks, all with a water view.

■ **Taste of Liberty:** Point Loma's Liberty Station is home to galleries, museums, restaurants, breweries, and the bustling culinary hub, Liberty Public Market.

QUICK BITES

The Cravory. San Diego's best cookies come in crowd-pleasing flavors such as birthday cake, red velvet, and pancakes and bacon. There's also craft sodas, Cravory flavored milks, edible cookie dough, ice cream, and cold brew to round out your snack. **Known for:** amazing cookies; cookie-of-the-month club; ships anywhere. ⊠ *3960 W. Point Loma Blvd., Suite G, Point Loma* ✛ *next to Souplantation* ☎ *619/795–9077* ⊕ *thecravory.com.*

Liberty Public Market. The city's former Naval Training Center is now home to more than 30 vendors so even the pickiest of diners will be pleased. Options include tacos and quesadillas at Cecilia's Taqueria; fried rice, pad Thai, and curries at Mama Made Thai; artisan cheeses and charcuteries at Venissimo; lavender lattes from Westbean Coffee Roasters; more than a dozen Argentinian empanadas at Parana Empanadas; and croissants, eclairs, and macarons at Le Parfait Paris. **Known for:** cuisines from around the world; lively kid- and dog-friendly patio; the best regional foods under one roof. ⊠ *2820 Historic Decatur Rd., Liberty Station* ☎ *619/487–9346* ⊕ *www.libertypublicmarket.com.*

GETTING HERE

■ West of downtown San Diego, you'll find Point Loma Peninsula accessible from the I-5 at Sea World Drive. Take exit 21 and continue on Sea World Drive to Nimitz Boulevard. This thoroughfare splits to Harbor Island, Shelter Island, and Point Loma by way of Catalina Boulevard. Bus 84 has routes that pass near Point Loma.

PLANNING YOUR TIME

■ The best way to take in the entire peninsula is by car or bike, with afternoon excursions set aside for strolling Liberty Station, Harbor Island, Shelter Island, Sunset Cliffs, the Old Point Loma Lighthouse, and a few other noteworthy sites in between. Active travelers can spend a day biking the trails that run along the marinas to America's Cup Harbor. For a challenging climb, the views from Cabrillo National Monument often reward with an occasional whale-spotting. If museums, galleries, and theaters are on your itinerary, add in an extra day. Generally, two to three days are enough to soak in the Point Loma attractions and still have time for an afternoon on the water followed by fresh seafood at a local market.

Point Loma protects the San Diego Bay from the Pacific's tides and waves. Here you'll find sandy beaches, private marinas, and prominent military installations. Nestled between Coronado and Point Loma, Harbor and Shelter islands owe their existence to dredging in the bay.

Point Loma is a low-key community that caters to sailing enthusiasts, trading the bar-hopping culture of Pacific Beach for a few select locales, like the clean and artsy look of Modern Times Brewing, or the mid-century cool of the Pearl. Yet in neighboring Ocean Beach, it's a different world, where an inescapable hippie culture bleeds into the kitschy and earnestly earthy dives along Newport Avenue allowing it to retain its bohemian beach town vibe. Shelter Island's best watering holes boast campy tiki-theme decor; it's also home to revered concert destination Humphrey's Concerts by the Bay, which is famous for its great sound, scenic location, and kayaking passersby.

Bays, beaches, and cliffs are the stars of these diverse coastal communities, where low-key seafood spots mingle with romantic eateries, quaint bistros, and lively beer bars. The bars and restaurants of Harbor and Shelter islands are great places to take in the views of downtown across the bay. Although the water view is always lovely during the day, the lights of the city make the scene come alive at night. Every December, over 80 boats are lavishly illuminated for the festive, San Diego Bay Parade of Lights.

Point Loma

The hilly peninsula of **Point Loma** curves west and south into the Pacific and provides protection for San Diego Bay. Its high elevations and sandy cliffs provide incredible views, and make Point Loma a visible local landmark. Its maritime roots are evident, from its longtime ties to the U.S. Navy to its bustling sportfishing and sailing marinas. The funky community of **Ocean Beach** coexists alongside the stately homes of **Sunset Cliffs** and the honored graves at **Fort Rosecrans National Cemetery**.

◉ Sights

★ Cabrillo National Monument
LIGHTHOUSE | **FAMILY** | This 166-acre preserve marks the site of the first European visit to San Diego, made by 16th-century Spanish explorer Juan Rodríguez Cabrillo when he landed at this spot on September 15, 1542. Today the site, with its rugged cliffs and shores and outstanding overlooks, is one of the most frequently visited of all the national monuments. There's a good visitor center and useful interpretive stations along the cliffside walkways. Higlights include the moderately difficult Bayside Trail, the Old Point

8

Sights ▼

1 Cabrillo Naitonal Monument D9
2 Fort Rosecrans
  National Cemetery.................C7
3 Ocean Beach Pier B2
4 Visions Art Museum...............F3
5 Women's Museum of California... F3

Restaurants ▼

1 Azucar C2
2 Bali Hai............................E5
3 BO-beau kitchen + bar.............C2
4 Coasterra G4
5 Con Pane Rustic
  Breads & Cafe F3
6 The Cravory E1
7 Hodad's C2
8 Island Prime and C Level G4
9 Jimmy's Famous
  American Tavern E4
10 Liberty Public Market F3
11 The Little Lion B3
12 Phil's BBQ F3
13 Pisco Rotisserie & Cevicheria.....E3
14 Plzza Port...........................C2
15 Point Loma Seafoods..............E4
16 Raglan Public House B2
17 Slater's 50/50 ....F3
18 Soda & Swine......................F3
19 South Beach Bar & Grille.........B2
20 Stone Brewing World Bistro
   and Gardens.......................F3
21 3rd Corner Wine Shop
   and Bistro..........................C2
22 Tom Ham's Lighthouse F4

Hotels ▼

1 Best Western Plus Island Palms
  Hotel & Marina..................... D5
2 Courtyard Marriott
  San Diego Airport
  Liberty Station......................E4
3 Holiday Inn San Diego Bayside ... E4
4 Homewood Suites
  San Diego Airport
  Liberty Station......................E4
5 Kona Kai Resort & Spa............ D5
6 The Pearl Hotel D4

Point Loma Peninsula

Loma Lighthouse, and the tide pools. There's also a sheltered viewing station where you can watch the gray whales' yearly migration from Baja California to Alaska (including high-powered telescopes). ⊠ *1800 Cabrillo Memorial Dr., Point Loma* ☎ *619/557–5450* ⊕ *www. nps.gov/cabr* ⊠ *$15 per car, $5 per person on foot/bicycle, entry good for 7 days.*

Fort Rosecrans National Cemetery

CEMETERY | In 1934, 8 of the 1,000 acres set aside for a military reserve in 1852 were designated as a burial site. More than 100,000 people are now interred here; it's impressive to see the rows upon rows of white headstones that overlook both sides of Point Loma just north of the Cabrillo National Monument. Some of those laid to rest here were killed in battles that predate California's statehood; the graves of the 17 soldiers and one civilian who died in the 1874 Battle of San Pasqual between troops from Mexico and the United States are marked by a large bronze plaque. Perhaps the most impressive structure in the cemetery is the 75-foot granite obelisk called the Bennington Monument, which commemorates the 66 crew members who died in a boiler explosion and fire on board the USS *Bennington* in 1905. The cemetery, visited by many veterans, is still used for burials. ⊠ *Cabrillo Memorial Dr., Point Loma* ☎ *619/553–2084* ⊕ *www. cem.va.gov.*

Visions Art Museum

MUSEUM | This three-room museum pays tribute to textile artists and the quilting community with impressive fabric works on display. An on-site shop is stocked with jewelry, baskets, books, textile hangings, and other items related to fabric art. Monthly needlepoint workshops are hosted regularly. ⊠ *2825 Dewey Rd., Suite 100, Liberty Station* ☎ *619/546–4872* ⊕ *www.visionsartmuseum.org* ⊠ *$7* ⊗ *Closed Mon.*

Women's Museum of California

MUSEUM | Dedicated to the history and advocacy of women's rights, this small museum in Liberty Station hosts monthly exhibits, educational programs, and community events to educate visitors on women's experiences and contributions. Permanent displays focus on the suffrage movement and women in the military. ⊠ *2730 Historic Decatur Rd., Suite 103, Liberty Station* ☎ *619/233–7963* ⊕ *www. womensmuseumca.org* ⊠ *$5* ⊗ *Closed Mon. and Tues.*

🏖 Beaches

Sunset Cliffs

BEACH—SIGHT | As the name would suggest this natural park near Point Loma Nazerene University is one of the best places in San Diego to watch the sunset thanks to its cliff-top location and expansive ocean views. Some limited beach access is accessible via an extremely steep stairway at the foot of Ladera Street. Beware of the treacherous cliff trails and pay attention to warning signs. The cliffs are very unstable and several fatalities have occurred over the last few years. If you're going to make your way to the narrow beach below, it's best to go at low tide when the southern end, near Cabrillo Point, reveals tide pools teeming with small sea creatures. Farther north the waves lure surfers, and Osprey Point offers good fishing off the rocks. Keep your eyes peeled for migrating California gray whales during the winter months. Check WaveCast (*www.wavecast.com/ tides*) for tide schedules. **Amenities:** parking (no fee). **Best for:** solitude, sunset, surfing. ⊠ *Sunset Cliffs Blvd., between Ladera St. and Adair St., Point Loma* ⊕ *www.sunsetcliffs.info.*

🍴 Restaurants

Once a neighborhood of tuna-fishing families, this famous peninsula is now a wealthy enclave where residents enjoy charming neighborhood restaurants, and new upscale dining spots clustered in walkable Liberty Station, and Harbor and Shelter islands. Although there's some fine dining here, most eateries are casual and cater to laid-back locals, sun-loving tourists, and sailing enthusiasts.

Con Pane Rustic Breads & Cafe

$ | **CAFÉ** | **FAMILY** | The scent of fresh-baked bread whets the appetite of customers at this Liberty Station bakery and café seeking rustic scones or raisin brioche cinnamon rolls for breakfast, or one of the hearty lunch sandwiches like almost grilled cheese with melted brie and gorgonzola on warm rosemary olive oil bread. All can be enjoyed inside or on the sunny patio with hot or cold drinks including the house-made lemonade. **Known for:** fluffy raisin brioche cinnamon rolls; sandwiches served in half portions. [$] *Average main: $8* ✉ *2750 Dewey Rd., Point Loma* ☎ *619/224–4344* 🕒 *Closed Tues. and Wed.*

★ The Cravory

$ | **BAKERY** | San Diego's best cookies come in crowd-pleasing flavors such as birthday cake, red velvet, and pancakes and bacon. There's also craft sodas, Cravory flavored milks, edible cookie dough, ice cream, and cold brew to round out your snack. **Known for:** amazing cookies; cookie-of-the-month club; ships anywhere. [$] *Average main: $5* ✉ *3960 W. Point Loma Blvd., Suite G, Point Loma* ✥ *next to Souplantation* ☎ *619/795–9077* 🌐 *thecravory.com.*

Jimmy's Famous American Tavern

$$ | **AMERICAN** | Tucked bayside between Harbor and Shelter islands, Jimmy's (JFAT for short) draws hungry boaters and sea-lovers with its marina views and elevated backyard BBQ faves. The interior blends lots of varnished wood with industrial-chic I-beams and garage-style doors, plus there's a patio with a fire pit. **Known for:** Bloody Marys during weekend brunch; nine types of burgers; Monday specials like burger and draft beer for $15. [$] *Average main: $21* ✉ *4990 N. Harbor Dr., Point Loma* ☎ *619/226–2103* 🌐 *www.j-fat.com.*

★ Liberty Public Market

$ | **INTERNATIONAL** | **FAMILY** | The city's former Naval Training Center is now home to more than 30 vendors so even the pickiest of diners will be pleased. Options include tacos and quesadillas at Cecilia's Taqueria; fried rice, pad Thai, and curries at Mama Made Thai; artisan cheeses and charcuteries at Venissimo; lavender lattes from Westbean Coffee Roasters; more than a dozen Argentinian empanadas at Parana Empanadas; and croissants, eclairs, and macarons at Le Parfait Paris. **Known for:** cuisines from around the world; lively kid- and dog-friendly patio; the best regional foods under one roof. [$] *Average main: $10* ✉ *2820 Historic Decatur Rd., Liberty Station* ☎ *619/487–9346* 🌐 *www.libertypublicmarket.com.*

Phil's BBQ

$ | **BARBECUE** | During peak hours at San Diego's most popular barbecue, lines can be long for diners craving heaping portions of fall-off-the-bone baby-back ribs, moist pulled pork, or huge, crispy onion rings. Don't be discouraged by the line; it moves quickly. **Known for:** Toro tri-tip sandwich; tender baby back ribs and hand-cut fries; secret recipe BBQ sauce. [$] *Average main: $15* ✉ *3750 Sports Arena Blvd., Point Loma* ☎ *619/226–6333* 🌐 *www.philsbbq.net.*

Pisco Rotisserie & Cevicheria

$$ | **PERUVIAN** | At this rotisserie and cevicheria, modern Peruvian cuisine prevails with indigenous influences and traditional dishes that shine even brighter with a pisco cocktail. Chef Emmanuel Piqueras brings Lima to San Diego with crisp yucca croquettes, spicy pulled lamb with sweet potato, and ceviche in leche de tigre (tiger's milk) marinade. **Known for:** Taco Tuesday; pisco cocktails; signature rotisserie chicken marinated for 48 hours. [$] *Average main: $22* ✉ *2401 Truxtun Rd.,*

#102, Liberty Station ☎ *619/222–3111* 🌐 *www.piscorotisserie.com* 🕓 *Closed Mon.*

★ Point Loma Seafoods
$ | SEAFOOD | FAMILY | When fishing boats unload their catch on-site, a seafood restaurant and market earns the right to boast that they offer "The Freshest Thing in Town." At first, mostly sport fishermen came here, but word got out about the just-caught fried fish on San Francisco–style sourdough bread and now locals and visitors come to enjoy bay views, sunshine, and a greatly expanded menu of seafood dishes. A friendly efficient crew takes orders for food and drinks at the counter, keeping the wait down even on the busiest days. **Known for:** San Francisco-style seafood on sourdough; dockside bay views; seafood so fresh it's right from the boat. [$] *Average main: $15* ✉ *2805 Emerson St., Point Loma* ☎ *619/223–1109* 🌐 *www.pointlomaseafoods.com.*

Slater's 50/50
$ | BURGER | FAMILY | Bacon is king at this lively burger, beer, and sports bar in Liberty Station. Founder Scott Slater's signature "designer" patty, half beef and half ground bacon, is topped with a fried egg and cheese, and sauced with chipotle adobo mayonnaise. **Known for:** half-beef and half-ground bacon burgers; extensive craft beer selection; pet-friendly patio with dog menu. [$] *Average main: $13* ✉ *2750 Dewey Rd., Point Loma* ☎ *619/398–2600* 🌐 *www.slaters5050.com.*

Soda & Swine
$ | BURGER | Meatballs get a trendy spin at S&S, where the decor blends a gold-wrapped bar and geometric stools with old-time touches like a bakery area fashioned after a vintage storefront. First select a meatball type (pork, chorizo, beef, chicken, quinoa, or sietan) before choosing the style—sliders, with spaghetti, or in a skillet. **Known for:** mix-and-match meatball menu; house-made pies paired with soft serve; cozy space that's the perfect spot to indulge in comfort food with a twist. [$] *Average main: $8* ✉ *2750 Dewey Rd., Liberty Station* ☎ *619/501–9989* 🌐 *www.sodaandswine.com.*

★ Stone Brewing World Bistro and Gardens
$$ | ECLECTIC | FAMILY | This 50,000 square-foot monument to beer and good food is a crowd-pleaser, especially for fans of San Diego's nationally known craft beer scene. The global menu features dishes like the Bavarian pretzel and Korean-style BBQ ribs that pair perfectly with on-tap and bottled beers from around the world and Stone's famous IPAs. **Known for:** massive outdoor patio; brew-friendly eats; Meatless Mondays. [$] *Average main: $22* ✉ *2816 Historic Decatur Rd., Liberty Station* ☎ *619/269–2100* 🌐 *www.stonelibertystation.com.*

🛏 Hotels

Point Loma is a hilly community that's home to Cabrillo National Monument, a naval base, and a growing destination for shopping, dining, and art called Liberty Station. The central location near the San Diego airport has made Point Loma a popular spot for chain hotels.

Courtyard Marriott San Diego Airport Liberty Station
$$$ | HOTEL | FAMILY | Close to the restaurants and shops of Liberty Station, this family-friendly hotel spares travelers the extra fees charged by most downtown and coastal lodgings. **Pros:** modern rooms; free airport shuttle; no resort fees. **Cons:** limited views; not much charm or personality; family-friendly might not appeal to you. [$] *Rooms from: $279* ✉ *2592 Laning Rd., Point Loma* ☎ *619/221–1900, 888/236–2427* 🌐 *www.marriott.com/sanal* 🛏 *200 rooms* 🍴 *No meals.*

Holiday Inn San Diego Bayside
$$ | HOTEL | FAMILY | If SeaWorld and the San Diego Zoo aren't enough to sap kids

of their energy, the outdoor activities at this hotel across from San Diego Bay fishing docks should do the trick. **Pros:** great for kids; close to airport; happy hour at the on-site Bayside Bar. **Cons:** not centrally located; confusing layout; might be too kid-friendly for some. *$ Rooms from: $216 ⊠ 4875 N. Harbor Dr., Point Loma ☎ 619/224–3621, 800/662–8899 ⊕ www.holinnbayside.com ⇨ 291 rooms ◯| No meals.*

★ Homewood Suites San Diego Airport Liberty Station

$$$ | HOTEL | FAMILY | Families and business travelers will benefit from the space and amenities at this all-suites hotel. **Pros:** outstanding central location near attractions; close to paths for joggers and bikers; complimentary airport shuttle. **Cons:** breakfast area can get crowded; far from nightlife. *$ Rooms from: $249 ⊠ 2576 Laning Rd., Point Loma ☎ 619/222–0500 ⊕ www.home-woodsuites.com ⇨ 150 suites ◯| Free Breakfast.*

★ The Pearl Hotel

$$$ | HOTEL | This 1960s Sportsman's Lodge received a mid-century modern makeover, turning it into a retro-chic hangout decorated with kitschy lamps and original, in-room art by local children. **Pros:** near marina; hip bar/restaurant on-site (dinner only, except for seasonal specials); "Oysters and Bubbles" Mondays with $1 oysters and $7 bubbly. **Cons:** not centrally located; one bed in rooms; noise on movie night. *$ Rooms from: $233 ⊠ 1410 Rosecrans St., Point Loma ☎ 619/226–6100 ⊕ www.thepearlsd.com ⇨ 23 rooms ◯| No meals.*

ⓨ Nightlife

Point Loma is a low-key community, trading the bar-hopping culture of Pacific Beach for a few select locales, like the clean and artsy look of The Lomaland Fermentorium, or the mid-century cool of The Pearl Hotel.

BARS

Charles and Dinorah

PIANO BARS/LOUNGES | Paying tribute to Charles and Dinorah, the property's original owners, this hotel bar is like stepping back into late '60s Palm Springs, with shag carpet, clean lines, and lots of wood accents. The lobby bar is almost as fabulous as the outdoor pool area, where inflatable balls bob in illuminated water and vintage flicks show on a huge screen. And feel free to drink to excess: after 10 pm, when the bar closes, you can stay over at a discounted $79 "play and stay" rate if there are any rooms available. ⊠ *The Pearl Hotel, 1410 Rosecrans St., Point Loma ☎ 619/226–6100 ⊕ www.thepearlsd.com.*

BREWPUBS

Modern Times Beer

BREWPUBS/BEER GARDENS | Fondly referred to as the Lomaland Fermentorium, California's first employee-owned brewery lives up to its name with innovative design—including a mural made entirely of Post-It notes—simple and stylish take-home six-packs, and a rotating cast of beers on tap with the diversity to please every type of palate. ⊠ *3725 Greenwood St., Point Loma ☎ 619/546–9694 ⊕ www.moderntimesbeer.com.*

ⓟ Performing Arts

Arts District Liberty Station

ART GALLERIES—ARTS | FAMILY | The former Naval Training Center at Liberty Station has been transformed into an eclectic and family-friendly alternative to the more avant-garde arts scene in San Diego. This hub for arts and culture is home to over 120 tenants, including artists, galleries, museums, and nonprofits. ⊠ *2750 Historic Decatur Rd., Point Loma ☎ 619/573–9300 ⊕ www.NTCLibertyStation.com.*

Malashock Dance

DANCE | The city's esteemed modern dance company presents edgy, intriguing works at venues throughout the city; Malashock has often collaborated on performances with the San Diego Opera, the San Diego Symphony, and other major cultural institutions. ✉ *2650 Truxtun Rd., Suite 104, Point Loma* ☎ *619/260–1622* ⊕ *www.malashockdance.org.*

San Diego Dance Theater

DANCE | The company has earned serious kudos for its diverse company and provocative programming, including Mexican waltzes and its annual "Trolley Dances," which take place at various trolley stops throughout San Diego. Other performances are held at venues around the city. ✉ *2650 Truxtun Rd., Suite 108, Liberty Station* ☎ *619/225–1803* ⊕ *www.sandiegodancetheater.org.*

🏃 Activities

FISHING

Pier fishing doesn't offer as much excitement, but it's the cheapest ocean fishing option available. No license is required to fish from a public pier, which includes those at Ocean Beach.

Fisherman's Landing

FISHING | You can book space on a fleet of luxury vessels from 57 feet to 124 feet long and embark on multiday trips in search of yellowfin tuna, yellowtail, and other deep-water fish. Half-day fishing is also available. ✉ *2838 Garrison St., Point Loma* ☎ *619/221–8500* ⊕ *www.fishermanslanding.com* 🔖 *From $50.*

H&M Landing

FISHING | Join one of the West's oldest sportfishing companies for year-round fishing trips, or whale-watching excursions from December through March. ✉ *2803 Emerson St., Point Loma* ☎ *619/222–1144* ⊕ *www.hmlanding.com* 🔖 *From $24.*

HIKING

★ Bayside Trail at Cabrillo National Monument

HIKING/WALKING | Driving here is a treat in itself, as a vast view of the Pacific unfolds before you. The view is equally enjoyable on Bayside Trail (2 miles round-trip), which is home to the same coastal sagebrush that Juan Rodriguez Cabrillo saw when he first discovered the California coast in the 16th century. After the hike, you can explore nearby tide pools, the monument statue, and the Old Point Loma Lighthouse. Don't worry if you don't see everything on your first visit; your entrance receipt ($15 per car) is good for 7 days. ✉ *1800 Cabrillo Memorial Dr., Point Loma* ✛ *From I–5, take Rosecrans exit and turn right on Canon St. then left on Catalina Blvd. (also known as Cabrillo Memorial Dr.); follow until end* ☎ *619/557–5450* ⊕ *www.nps.gov/cabr* 🔖 *Parking $15.*

🛍 Shopping

The laid-back Point Loma Peninsula offers incredible views of downtown San Diego, and some great shopping away from the large crowds often seen in downtown and at Fashion Valley. In the former Naval Training Center, the Liberty Station shopping area has art galleries, restaurants, and home stores.

Liberty Station

SHOPPING CENTERS/MALLS | FAMILY | San Diego's former Naval Training Center is now a mixed-use development with shops, restaurants, and art galleries. With its large grassy areas and Spanish colonial revival–style architecture, it's a great place to take a stroll. The section on Truxton Road between Womble and Roosevelt includes a **Trader Joe's, Vons,** and restaurants like **Pisco Rotisserie & Cevicheria** . To the north are more locally owned businesses lining the arcades in the area known as the Arts District. **Moniker General** sells homewares, custom furniture, and craft beer and coffee; and

Banyan Kitchen carries handmade Chi Chocolates and truffles. New in 2016, **Liberty Public Market** is San Diego's only food hall, open daily with over 30 eclectic vendors selling artisanal goods. If you're in town on the first Friday of the month, check out Liberty Station's **Friday Night Liberty** (5 to 9 pm), a free art walk featuring refreshments and entertainment. ✉ *2640 Historic Decatur Rd., Point Loma* ☎ *619/573–9300* ⊕ *www.libertystation. com.*

Ocean Beach

At the northern end of Point Loma lies the chilled-out, hippyesque town of Ocean Beach, commonly referred to as "OB." The main thoroughfare of this funky neighborhood is dotted with dive bars, coffeehouses, surf shops, and 1960s diners. OB is a magnet for everyone from surfers to musicians and artists. Newport Avenue, generally known for its boisterous bars, is also home to San Diego's largest antiques district. Fans of OB applaud its resistance to "selling out" to upscale development, whereas detractors lament its somewhat scruffy edges.

◉ Sights

Ocean Beach Pier
MARINA | This T-shaped pier is a popular fishing spot and home to the Ocean Beach Pier Café and a small tackle shop. Constructed in 1966, it is the longest concrete pier on the West Coast and a perfect place to take in views of the harbor, ocean, and Point Loma Peninsula. Surfers flock to the waves that break just below. ✉ *1950 Abbott St., Ocean Beach.*

⊕ Beaches

Ocean Beach
BEACH—SIGHT | This mile-long beach south of Mission Bay's channel is the place

to get a slice of vintage SoCal beach culture. It's likely you'll see VW vans in the parking lot near the Ocean Beach Pier. The wide beach is popular with volleyball players, sunbathers, and surfers. The municipal pier at the southern end extends a ½ mile out to sea where you can fish without a valid California fishing license. There's a café about halfway out, and taco shops, bars, and restaurants can be found on the streets near the beach. Swimmers should beware of strong rip currents around the main lifeguard tower, where lifeguards are on duty year-round. One of Ocean Beach's most popular features is the Dog Beach at the northern end, where canines can run freely and splash in the waves 24 hours a day. For shade, picnic areas with barbecues, and a paved path, check out Robb Field, across from Dog Beach. **Amenities:** lifeguards, parking (no fee), showers, toilets. **Best for:** surfing, swimming, walking. ✉ *Newport Ave. at Abbott St., Ocean Beach* ⊕ *7 miles from Downtown San Diego* ⊕ *www.sandiego.gov.*

🍴 Restaurants

One of the last "real" California beach towns, OB, as locals know it, has one foot in its hippie past and another in gentrified coastal living, which explains why it's home to an eclectic group of bars and restaurants, everything from charming wine bars and bistros to Cuban cafés and burger joints.

★ Azucar
$ | **CUBAN** | For a taste of Cuba in San Diego, head to this colorful Ocean Beach bakery where owner Vivian Hernandez Jackson combines her Cuban heritage, Miami childhood, and London culinary training in breakfast and lunch offerings. Morning specialties like raspberry scones with passion fruit icing, a traditional guava and cheese puff pastry, and ham and spinach quiche can be savored with café con leche, a sweet Cuban espresso with hot milk. **Known for:** tangy, citrus-centric

desserts; traditional Cuban pastries; a quick bite before shopping or hitting the beach. $ *Average main: $7* ✉ *4820 Newport Ave., Ocean Beach* ☎ *619/523–2020* ⊕ *www.iloveazucar.com* ⊗ *No dinner.*

BO-beau kitchen + bar

$$ | BISTRO | Ocean Beach is a slightly eccentric beach town, not a place diners would expect to find this warm, romantic bistro that evokes a French farmhouse. The satisfying French-inspired menu of soups, woodstone-oven flatbreads, mussels, and other bistro classics is served in cozy dining rooms and a rustic outdoor patio. **Known for:** popular crispy Brussels sprouts with pancetta; Tuesday date night special; happy hour; featured on Anthony Bourdain's No Reservations. $ *Average main: $22* ✉ *4996 W. Point Loma Blvd., Ocean Beach* ☎ *619/224–2884* ⊕ *www.cohnrestaurants.com/bobeaukitchenbar* ⊗ *No lunch.*

★ Hodad's

$ | BURGER | FAMILY | Surfers with big appetites chow down on huge, messy burgers, fries, onion rings, and shakes at this funky, hippie-beach joint adorned with beat-up surf boards and license plates from almost every state. Don't be put off by lines out the door, they move quickly and the wait is worth it. **Known for:** legendary bacon-cheeseburgers and thick-cut onion rings; surf-shack vibe; a little sass with your burger. $ *Average main: $9* ✉ *5010 Newport Ave., Ocean Beach* ☎ *619/224–4623* ⊕ *www.hodadies.com.*

★ The Little Lion

$$ | MODERN AMERICAN | Amid surf shacks and hippie beach bars, this restaurant perched on stunning Sunset Cliffs feels like a hidden European bistro. The sisters who run the show come from a long line of successful local restaurateurs and have brought their passed-down expertise to the simple, healthy menu and thoughtful service. **Known for:** light, healthy breakfast fare; cozy bistro setting; flash-fried cauliflower. $ *Average*

main: $20 ✉ *1424 Sunset Cliffs Blvd., Ocean Beach* ☎ *619/756–6921* ⊕ *www.thelittlelioncafe.com* ⊗ *Closed Mon.; no dinner Tues., Wed., and Sun.*

Pizza Port

$ | PIZZA | Rows of picnic tables, surfboard decor, and beer-brewing on-site have made this funky, friendly brewpub a block from the beach a locals' favorite. The nearly 40 brews on tap include a namesake pour and other craft beers that have made San Diego a beer-drinkers destination. **Known for:** namesake Pizza Port beer; beer-friendly menu items; the place to be on warm summer days. $ *Average main: $18* ✉ *1956 Bacon St., Ocean Beach* ☎ *619/224–4700* ⊕ *www.pizzaport.com.*

Raglan Public House

$ | BURGER | Inspired by the grass-fed burgers they sampled in New Zealand, the founders of this convivial eatery set out to replicate those same high-quality 'wiches in their Ocean Beach spot. The interior nods to the outdoor-oriented Kiwi country, with surfboards turned into light fixtures, rugby photos, and bodyboards as wall art. **Known for:** grass-fed beef burgers; exceptional handmade cocktails and great daily specials; great local craft beer. $ *Average main: $13* ✉ *1851 Bacon St., Ocean Beach* ☎ *619/794–2304* ⊕ *www.raglanpublichouse.com.*

South Beach Bar & Grille

$ | SEAFOOD | This two-story-tall restaurant and bar in Ocean Beach looks like a typical sports bar from the outside, but inside is the place to eat what many consider to be the best fish tacos in San Diego. Grab a seat at the bar and choose from an ever-changing array of fresh grilled fish from lobster to mahi. **Known for:** mahi mahi fish taco; great sunset and ocean views; Taco Tuesday specials. $ *Average main: $10* ✉ *5059 Newport Ave. #104, Ocean Beach* ☎ *619/226–4577* ⊕ *www.southbeachob.com.*

3rd Corner Wine Shop and Bistro

$$ | WINE BAR | Enthusiasts from around the world laud this combined wine shop, bar, and cozy California bistro. Available from lunch until after midnight Tuesday to Saturday, the American bistro fare starts with baked Brie or chicken-liver mousse, moves on to savory short-rib sliders and seafood risotto, and ends with apple-almond galette or goat's milk cheesecake. **Known for:** amazing array of nicely discounted wines can be purchased to go or enjoyed on premises; bottomless mimosa weekend brunch; knowledgeable staff who can offer bottle recommendations. ⓢ *Average main: $20* ✉ *2265 Bacon St., Ocean Beach* ☎ *619/223–2700* ⊕ *www. the3rdcorner.com* ⊘ *Closed Mon.*

Nightlife

Ocean Beach's nightlife is a world away from Point Loma. There's not a dress code in sight, and an inescapable hippie culture bleeds into the kitschy and earnestly earthy dives along Newport Avenue.

PAC Shores Cafe

BARS/PUBS | This bar isn't going for classy with its acid-trip mermaid mural and underwater theme but hey, it's OB—a surf town populated by leftovers from the '60s, man. A laid-back but see-and-be-seen crowd congregates here for relatively inexpensive drinks (no beers on tap, though), pool games, and pop and rock tunes on the jukebox. ✉ *4927 Newport Ave., Ocean Beach* ☎ *619/223–7549.*

Shopping

ANTIQUES
The Corner Store

ANTIQUES/COLLECTIBLES | Get in on the chalk-paint craze with furniture-painting workshops, and plenty of vintage and antique pieces ranging from cottage and beachy to industrial and shabby chic. ✉ *4873 Newport Ave., Ocean Beach*

☎ *619/222–1911* ⊕ *www.thecornerstore-ob.com.*

Vignettes

ANTIQUES/COLLECTIBLES | Expect a pleasant culture shock when you step from the bohemian Newport Avenue into this French-inspired antique shop with time-worn pieces with a rich history. Over 30 vendors showcase vintage and antique collectibles and fascinating oddities. ✉ *4828 Newport Ave., Ocean Beach* ☎ *619/222–9244* ⊕ *www.vignettesdecor. com.*

HOME ACCESSORIES AND GIFTS
Ocean Gifts & Shells

GIFTS/SOUVENIRS | This huge beach-themed store is filled with seashells of every size and shape, nautical decor items, wind chimes, T-shirts, swimwear, accessories, toys, and souvenirs. ✉ *4934 Newport Ave., Ocean Beach* ☎ *619/224–6702* ⊕ *www.oceangiftsandshells.com.*

Often Wander at NOON

BOOKS/STATIONERY | Affordable handmade jewelry and American-made home accessories like tea towels, candles, and glassware fill the shelves at this whimsical boutique and design studio in Ocean Beach. NOON also stocks fresh-smelling soaps, lotions, and perfumes, as well as letterpress greeting cards. ✉ *4993 Niagara Ave., #105, Ocean Beach* ☎ *619/523–1744* ⊕ *www.noondesignshop.com.*

MARKETS
Ocean Beach Farmers' Market

MARKET | Every Wednesday from 4 to 8 pm, this bustling market features live music, fresh produce, samples from local restaurants, crafts, and more. Other popular offerings include handmade apparel and accessories, holistic products, and fresh flowers. ✉ *4900 Newport Ave., between Cable and Bacon Sts., Ocean Beach* ⊕ *oceanbeachsandiego.com/attractions/annual-events/ farmers-market-wednesdays.*

Shelter Island is home to several marinas and resorts like Kona Kai Resort & Spa, as well as the Polynesian-themed restaurant Bali Hai.

Shelter Island

In 1950 San Diego's port director decided to raise the shoal that lay off the eastern shore of Point Loma above sea level with the sand and mud dredged up during the course of deepening a ship channel in the 1930s and '40s. The resulting peninsula, **Shelter Island,** became home to several marinas and resorts, many with Polynesian details that still exist today, giving them a retro flair. Shelter Island is the center of San Diego's yacht-building industry, and boats in every stage of construction are visible in its yacht yards. A long sidewalk runs past boat brokerages to the hotels and marinas that line the inner shore, facing Point Loma. On the bay side, fishermen launch their boats and families relax at picnic tables along the grass, where there are fire rings and permanent barbeque grills. Within walking distance is the huge Friendship Bell, given to San Diegans by the people of Yokohama, Japan, in 1958 and the Tunaman's Memorial, a statue commemorating San Diego's once-flourishing fishing industry.

🍴 Restaurants

Countless yachts and sailboats are berthed at marinas and hotels along this bayfront spit of land where visitors and locals come to picnic, enjoy concerts, and dine at a variety of casual bayside restaurants specializing in fresh seafood.

Bali Hai

$$ | **HAWAIIAN** | For more than 50 years, generations of San Diegans and visitors have enjoyed this Polynesian-themed icon with its stunning bay and city skyline views. The menu is a fusion of Hawaiian and Asian cuisines with standouts like the Hawaiian tuna poke, Mongolian lamb with pad Thai, and wok-fried bass. **Known for:** potent Bali Hai mai tais; Sunday brunch buffet with a DIY sundae bar; Hawaiian and Asian-themed menu. [$] *Average main: $25* ✉ *2230 Shelter Island Dr., Shelter Island* ☎ *619/222–1181* 🌐 *www.balihairestaurant.com* 🕒 *No lunch Sun.*

Hotels

One of two man-made peninsulas between Downtown and Point Loma, Shelter Island has grassy parks, tree-lined paths, and views of Downtown.

Best Western Plus Island Palms Hotel & Marina

$ | HOTEL | FAMILY | With tennis courts, two pools, jogging paths, and complimentary bike rentals, this waterfront hotel is a natural fit for fitness enthusiasts. **Pros:** near water; great room views; private marina. **Cons:** confusing layout; can be noisy; $15 daily parking fee. [$] *Rooms from: $159* ✉ *2051 Shelter Island Dr., Shelter Island* ☎ *619/222–0561, 800/922–2336* 🌐 *www.islandpalms.com* 🛏 *227 rooms* 🍴 *No meals.*

Kona Kai Resort & Spa

$$$$ | RESORT | A $30-million-dollar renovation in 2018 took this Shelter Island resort up a notch, with remodeled rooms, a new pool, spa, gym, and lobby—making the marina view an added bonus rather than the main focus. **Pros:** quiet area; near marina; water views. **Cons:** not centrally located; resort fees; popular for business meetings and weddings. [$] *Rooms from: $329* ✉ *1551 Shelter Island Dr., Shelter Island* ☎ *619/221–8000, 800/566–2524* 🌐 *www.resortkonakai.com* 🛏 *170 rooms* 🍴 *No meals.*

Nightlife

Shelter Island's best watering holes boast campy tiki-themed decor; it's also home to revered concert destination Humphrey's Concerts by the Bay, which is famous for its great sound, scenic location, and kayaking passersby.

LIVE MUSIC

Humphrey's Concerts by the Bay

MUSIC CLUBS | From June through September this dining and drinking oasis surrounded by water hosts the city's best outdoor jazz, folk, and light-rock concert series and is the stomping ground of such musicians as the Cowboy Junkies, Kenny G, and Chris Isaak. The rest of the year the music moves indoors for first-rate jazz, blues, and more. ✉ *2241 Shelter Island Dr., Shelter Island* ☎ *619/224–3577* 🌐 *www.humphreysconcerts.com.*

Harbor Island

Following the successful creation of Shelter Island, in 1961 the U.S. Navy used the residue from digging berths deep enough to accommodate aircraft carriers to build **Harbor Island,** a 1½-mile-long peninsula adjacent to the airport. Restaurants and high-rise hotels dot the inner shore while the bay's shore is lined with pathways, gardens, and scenic picnic spots. On the west point, the restaurant **Tom Ham's Lighthouse** has a U.S. Coast Guard–approved beacon shining from its tower and a sweeping view of San Diego's bayfront.

Restaurants

The man-made peninsula across from the airport, with its bayside parks, marinas, and hotels, is a popular dining destination for lunches and dinners served with stunning views of San Diego Bay and the city skyline.

Coasterra

$$$ | MODERN MEXICAN | It took eight years to bring this massive waterfront destination to fruition, but with one of the best skyline views in the city, Coasterra was worth the wait—the space is swathed in murals, intricate light fixtures, breezy outdoor seating, and a cushy interior. The menu veers toward modern Mexican with starters like tableside guacamole and plantain taquitos and cocktails like organic margaritas, tequila-spiked watermelon fresca, and various agave-based libations. **Known for:** extraordinary skyline views; happy hour appetizers; Sunday brunch with tres leches French toast.

$ *Average main: $33* ✉ *880 Harbor Island Dr., Harbor Island* ☎ *619/814–1300* ⊕ *www.cohnrestaurants.com/coasterra.*

Island Prime and C Level

$$$$ | MODERN AMERICAN | Two restaurants in one share this enviable spot on the shore of Harbor Island: the splurge-worthy Island Prime steak house and the relaxed C Level with a choice terrace. Both venues tempt with unrivaled views of downtown San Diego's skyline. **Known for:** sunset views; popovers served with jalapeño jelly butter; waterfront dining. $ *Average main: $39* ✉ *880 Harbor Island Dr., Harbor Island* ☎ *619/298–6802* ⊕ *www.cohnrestaurants.com/island-prime* ⊗ *No lunch at Island Prime.*

Tom Ham's Lighthouse

$$$ | SEAFOOD | It's hard to top this longtime Harbor Island restaurant's incredible views across San Diego Bay to the Downtown skyline and Coronado Bridge. Now a new alfresco dining deck and a contemporary seafood-focused menu ensure the dining experience at this working lighthouse doesn't take a back seat to the scenery. **Known for:** bottomless mimosa Sunday brunch; alfresco dining deck with skyline and Coronado bridge views; fresh seafood and beer-battered cod. $ *Average main: $30* ✉ *2150 Harbor Island Dr., Harbor Island* ☎ *619/291–9110* ⊕ *www.tomhamslighthouse.com* ⊗ *No lunch Sun.*

🏃 Activities

Harbor Sailboats

BOATING | You can rent sailboats from 22 to 45 feet long here for open-ocean adventures. The company also offers skippered charter boats for whale-watching, sunset sails, and bay tours. ✉ *2040 Harbor Island Dr., Harbor Island* ☎ *619/291–9568* ⊕ *www.harborsailboats.com* 🚤 *From $75.*

Chapter 9

CORONADO

Updated by
Jeff Terich

👁 **Sights**
★★★☆☆

🍴 **Restaurants**
★★★★☆

🛏 **Hotels**
★★★★☆

🛍 **Shopping**
★★★☆☆

🍸 **Nightlife**
★★☆☆☆

NEIGHBORHOOD SNAPSHOT

GREAT EXPERIENCES

■ **The Hotel Del:** As the grande dame of San Diego, the historic Hotel Del Coronado charms guests and visitors alike with her graceful architecture and ocean-front setting.

■ **Sandy beaches:** The long stretches of sand on Coronado are family-friendly.

■ **Small town charm:** Though just across the bay from San Diego, Coronado has the quaint charm of a more intimate seaside small town.

■ **History:** From the Hollywood history at the Del and *Wizard of Oz* creator L. Frank Baum to the island's naval history, including an actual sunken ship, there's a lot to discover in Coronado's past.

GETTING HERE

■ Coronado is accessible via the arching blue 2.2-mile-long San Diego–Coronado Bay Bridge, which offers breathtaking views of the harbor and downtown. Alternatively, pedestrians and bikes can reach Coronado via the popular ferry service. Bus 904 meets the ferry and travels as far as Silver Strand State Beach. Bus 901 runs daily between the Gaslamp Quarter and Coronado.

QUICK BITES

Clayton's Coffee Shop. A classic diner with bar-seating in a circle, Clayton's is a great lunch or breakfast spot with a menu that ranges from classic American fare to Mexican-inspired dishes like their popular breakfast burrito. Just don't forget dessert! **Known for:** bottomless coffee; breakfast burrito; gooey cinnamon roll sundae. ⊠ *979 Orange Ave., Coronado* ☎ *619/435–5425.*

Mootime Creamery. For a deliciously sweet pick-me-up, check out the rich ice cream, frozen yogurt, and sorbet made fresh daily on the premises. Dessert nachos made from waffle-cone chips are an unusual addition to an extensive sundae menu. Just look for the statue of Elvis on the sidewalk in front. ⊠ *1025 Orange Ave., Coronado* ☎ *619/435–2422* ⊕ *www. mootime.com* ▭ *No credit cards.*

Night & Day Cafe. Easy to spot from its red neon sign perched above the front door, Night & Day Cafe offers simple, hearty Mexican food with countertop service and ample portions. **Known for:** Coronado breakfast burrito (with hash browns inside); the iconic red sign; friendly service. ⊠ *847 Orange Ave., Coronado* ☎ *619/435–9776* ⊕ *www.coronadondcafe. com* ⊗ *Closed Mon.*

PLANNING YOUR TIME

■ A leisurely stroll through Coronado takes at least an hour, more if you stop to shop or walk along the family-friendly beaches. If you're a history buff, you might want to visit on Tuesday, Thursday, or Saturday, when you can combine the tour of the historic homes that departs from the Glorietta Bay Inn at 11 am with a visit to the Coronado Museum of History and Art, open daily. Whenever you come, if you're not staying overnight, remember to get back to the dock in time to catch the final ferry out at 9:30 (10:30 on weekends).

Although Coronado is actually an isthmus, easily reached from the mainland if you head north from Imperial Beach, it has always seemed like an island and is often referred to as such. Coronado has stately homes, sandy beaches, private marinas, and prominent military installations.

As if freeze-framed in the 1950s, Coronado's quaint appeal is captured in its old-fashioned storefronts, well-manicured gardens, and charming **Ferry Landing Marketplace.** The streets of Coronado are wide, quiet, and friendly, and many of today's residents live in grand Victorian homes handed down for generations. Naval Air Station North Island was established in 1911 on Coronado's north end, across from Point Loma, and was the site of Charles Lindbergh's departure on the transcontinental flight that preceded his famous solo flight across the Atlantic. Coronado's long relationship with the U.S. Navy has made it an enclave for military personnel; it's said to have more retired admirals per capita than anywhere else in the United States.

◉ Sights

Coronado Ferry Landing

STORE/MALL | FAMILY | This collection of shops at Ferry Landing is on a smaller scale than the Embarcadero's Seaport Village, but you do get a great view of the Downtown San Diego skyline. The little bayside shops and restaurants resemble the gingerbread domes of the Hotel Del Coronado. ⊠ 1201 1st St., at B Ave., Coronado ⊕ www.coronadoferrylanding.com.

Coronado Museum of History and Art

HISTORIC SITE | The neoclassical First Bank of Commerce building, constructed in 1910, holds the headquarters and archives of the Coronado Historical Association, a museum, the Coronado Visitor Center, and the Coronado Museum Store. The museum's collection celebrates Coronado's history with photographs and displays of its formative events and major sights. A guided tour of the area's architecturally and historically significant buildings departs from the museum lobby on Wednesday mornings at 10:30 and costs $15 (reservations required). Alternatively, pick up a self-guided tour in the museum's shop. ⊠ 1100 Orange Ave., at Park Pl., Coronado ☎ 619/435–7242, 619/437–8788 walking tour reservations ⊕ www.coronadohistory.org ⊠ Free.

★ Hotel Del Coronado

BEACH—SIGHT | The Del's distinctive red-tile roofs and Victorian gingerbread architecture have served as a set for many movies, political meetings, and extravagant social happenings. It's speculated that the Duke of Windsor may have first met the Duchess of Windsor Wallis Simpson here. Eleven presidents have been guests of the Del, and the film *Some*

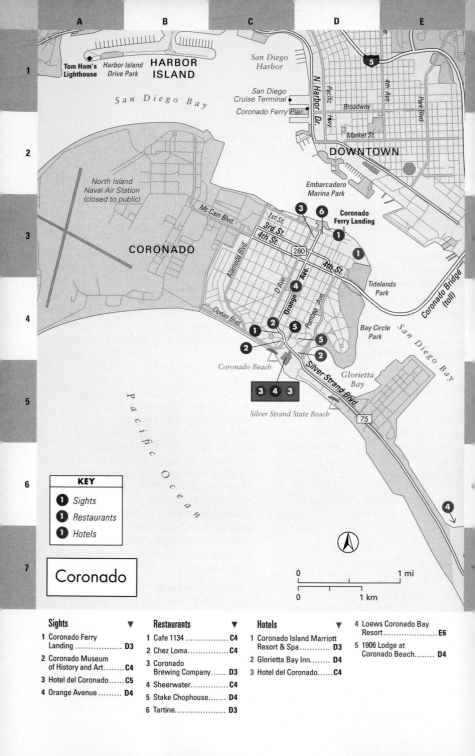

Coronado

KEY

- ① Sights
- ① Restaurants
- ① Hotels

Sights ▼	Restaurants ▼	Hotels ▼
1 Coronado Ferry Landing **D3**	1 Cafe 1134 .... **C4**	1 Coronado Island Marriott Resort & Spa **D3**
2 Coronado Museum of History and Art **C4**	2 Chez Loma **C4**	2 Glorietta Bay Inn **D4**
3 Hotel del Coronado **C5**	3 Coronado Brewing Company **D3**	3 Hotel del Coronado **C4**
4 Orange Avenue **D4**	4 Sheerwater **C4**	
	5 Stake Chophouse **D4**	4 Loews Coronado Bay Resort **E6**
	6 Tartine **D3**	5 1906 Lodge at Coronado Beach **D4**

Early morning fog occasionally meets surfers off the waters of Coronado.

Like It Hot—starring Marilyn Monroe, Jack Lemmon, and Tony Curtis—used the hotel as a backdrop.

The Hotel Del, as locals call it, was the brainchild of financiers Elisha Spurr Babcock Jr. and H. L. Story, who saw the potential of Coronado's virgin beaches and its view of San Diego's emerging harbor. It opened in 1888 and has been a National Historic Landmark since 1977. The History Gallery displays photos from the Del's early days, and books elaborating on its history are sold, along with logo apparel and gifts, in the hotel's 15-plus shops.

Although the pool area is reserved for hotel guests, several surrounding dining patios make great places to sit back and imagine the scene during the 1920s, when the hotel rocked with good times. Behind the pool area, an attractive shopping arcade features a classic candy shop as well as several fine clothing and accessories stores. A lavish Sunday brunch is served in the Crown Room. During the holidays, the hotel hosts Skating by the Sea, an outdoor beach-front ice-skating rink open to the public. ■ TIP→ **Whether or not you're staying at the Del, enjoy a drink at the Sun Deck Bar and Grill in order to gaze out over the ocean—it makes for a great escape.**

Tours of the Del are $40 per person and take place daily at 10 am. Tours are free for children ages 5 and under. ⊠ *1500 Orange Ave., at Glorietta Blvd., Coronado* ☎ *619/435–6611* ⊕ *www.hoteldel.com.*

★ **Orange Avenue**

NEIGHBORHOOD | Comprising Coronado's business district and its village-like heart, this avenue is surely one of the most charming spots in Southern California. Slow-paced and very "local" (the city fights against chain stores), it's a blast from the past, although entirely up to date in other respects. The military presence—Coronado is home to the U.S. Navy Sea, Air, and Land (SEAL) forces—is reflected in shops selling military gear and places like **McP's Irish Pub,** at No. 1107. A family-friendly stop for a good, all-American meal, it's the unofficial SEALs headquarters. Many clothing boutiques, home-furnishings stores, and upscale restaurants cater to visitors with deep pockets, but you can buy plumbing supplies, too, or get a genuine military haircut at **Crown Barber Shop,** at No. 947. If you need a break, stop for a latte at the sidewalk café of **Bay Books,** San Diego's largest independent bookstore, at No. 1029. ✉ *Orange Ave., near 9th St., Coronado.*

Beaches

★ Coronado Beach

BEACH—SIGHT | **FAMILY** | This wide beach is one of San Diego's most picturesque thanks to its soft white sand and sparkly blue water. The historic Hotel Del Coronado serves as a backdrop, and it's perfect for sunbathing, people-watching, and Frisbee tossing. The beach has limited surf, but it's great for bodyboarding and swimming. Exercisers might include Navy SEAL teams or other military units that conduct training runs on beaches in and around Coronado. There are picnic tables, grills, and popular fire rings, but don't bring lacquered wood or pallets. Only natural wood is allowed for burning. There's also a dog beach on the north end. There's free parking along Ocean Boulevard, though it's often hard to snag a space. **Amenities:** food and drink, lifeguards, showers, toilets. **Best for:** walking, swimming. ✉ *Ocean Blvd., between S. O St. and Orange Ave., Coronado* ✣ *From the San Diego–Coronado bridge, turn left on Orange Ave. and follow signs.*

Silver Strand State Beach

BEACH—SIGHT | **FAMILY** | This quiet beach on a narrow sand-spit allows visitors a unique opportunity to experience both the Pacific Ocean and the San Diego Bay. The 2½ miles of ocean side is great for surfing and other water sports while the bay side, accessible via foot tunnel under Highway 75, has calmer, warmer water and great views of the San Diego skyline. Lifeguards and rangers are on duty year-round, and there are places for biking, volleyball, and fishing. Picnic tables, grills, and firepits are available in summer, and the Silver Strand Beach Cafe is open Memorial Day through Labor Day. The beach is close to Loews Coronado Bay Resort and the Coronado Cays, an exclusive community popular with yacht owners. You can reserve RV sites ($65 beach; $50 inland) online (*www.reserveamerica.com*). Three day-use parking lots provide room for 800 cars. **Amenities:** food and drink, lifeguards, parking (fee), showers, toilets. **Best for:** walking, swimming, surfing. ✉ *5000 Hwy. 75, Coronado* ✣ *4½ miles south of city of Coronado* ☎ *619/435–5184* 🌐 *www.parks.ca.gov/silverstrand* 🎫 *Parking $10, motor home $30.*

Restaurants

The home of charming, but pricey, vintage houses, the famous Hotel Del Coronado, and historic North Island Naval Station offers visitors a great variety of tourist-oriented bars and eateries—a few of them very good. While most of the dining options are recommended for the view (it's hard to beat), there are a number of excellent restaurants that range from family-friendly and casual to glamorous and upscale.

Cafe 1134

$ | **CAFÉ** | Locals flock to this hip mini-bistro to start the day with flavorful omelettes or fresh pastries and coffee. Lunch and dinner patrons enjoy a variety of classic deli sandwiches and salads in a relaxed and friendly atmosphere. **Known for:** hearty breakfast; fresh sandwiches and salads for lunch; friendly service. [$] *Average main: $5* ✉ *1134 Orange Ave., Coronado* ☎ *619/437–1134* 🌐 *www.cafe1134.net* 💳 *No credit cards.*

Chez Loma

$$ | **FRENCH** | French meets Southern Californian cuisine at this charming historic Victorian home in the heart of Coronado. A favorite of locals and guests at nearby Hotel Del Coronado, the romantic bistro offers French favorites like boeuf bourguignonne and moules marinière as well as California standbys like rockfish ceviche in tomatillo sauce. **Known for:** eclectic Sunday brunch; solid dessert selection; romantic atmosphere. [$] *Average main: $25* ✉ *1132 Loma Ave., Coronado* ☎ *619/435–0661* ⏲ *No lunch.*

Coronado Brewing Company

$ | **AMERICAN** | **FAMILY** | Perfect for beer lovers with kids, this popular, laid-back Coronado brewpub offers a menu that features large portions of basic bar food like burgers, sandwiches, pizza, and salads. Enjoy a brew at a pair of sidewalk terraces or belly up to the bar and a new batch being made such as the Islander Pale Ale (IPA) or Mermaid's Red Ale. **Known for:** a good selection of house-crafted beers; kids' menu; more strollers than bar stools. [$] *Average main: $12* ✉ *170 Orange Ave., Coronado* ☎ *619/437–4452* 🌐 *www.coronadobrewing.com.*

Sheerwater

$$$ | **AMERICAN** | The menu at this casual but pricey all-day dining room offers a local take on all-American fare that's split between meat and seafood entrées. A spacious, breeze-swept terrace offers extraordinary ocean views, while the indoor room can be on the noisy side, especially when families are present. **Known for:** all-day dining; primary restaurant at Hotel Del Coronado; standard kids' menu options. [$] *Average main: $28* ✉ *Hotel Del Coronado, 1500 Orange Ave., Coronado* ☎ *619/522–8490* 🌐 *www.hoteldel.com.*

Stake Chophouse

$$$$ | **STEAKHOUSE** | A recent addition to the Orange Avenue dining scene, this chophouse is a more modern alternative to the vintage steak house. Stake features high-quality cuts of beef along with fresh seafood, oysters, hand-cut fries, and an award-winning wine list. **Known for:** Australian Wagyu rib eye; extensive wine offerings; the "Baked California" dessert. [$] *Average main: $42* ✉ *1309 Orange Ave., Coronado* ☎ *619/522–0077* 🌐 *www.stakechophouse.com.*

Tartine

$ | **FRENCH** | **FAMILY** | Dine any time of day at this French-inspired café a block from San Diego Bay, as breakfast commences at 6 am with house-made granola, quiche, and just-baked coffee cakes and croissants. Sandwiches, salads, and soups round out the daytime menu, while dinner highlights include the catch of the day; just be sure be sure to save room for the Paris-pretty desserts. **Known for:** Coronado's best bet for casual but satisfying fare; in-house pastries and desserts; quiche any time of the day. [$] *Average main: $15* ✉ *1106 1st St., Coronado* ☎ *619/435–4323* 🌐 *www.tartinecoronado.com.*

Hotels

Occupying its own strip of land across the bay from San Diego, Coronado doesn't boast the overwhelming number of hotels as its neighboring city, but most of the properties on the island offer luxurious accommodations. None more so than the iconic Hotel del Coronado, a historic beachside hotel with more than 100 years of history that attracts a large number of tourists, if only sometimes for a beachside drink. At Loews Coronado, visitors can expect more modern upscale accommodations, while the 1906 Lodge offers more of an intimate, yet very comfortable, bed-and-breakfast-type stay.

★ **Coronado Island Marriott Resort & Spa**

$$$$ | **RESORT** | **FAMILY** | Near San Diego Bay, this snazzy hotel has rooms with great Downtown skyline views. **Pros:** spectacular views; on-site spa; close to

water taxis. **Cons:** not in downtown Coronado; resort fee; expensive self-parking. $ *Rooms from: $329* ✉ *2000 2nd St., Coronado* ☎ *619/435–3000* ⊕ *www.marriott.com/hotels/travel/sanci-corona-do-island-marriott-resort-and-spa* ➔ *300 rooms* ⦿ *No meals.*

Glorietta Bay Inn
$$ | **HOTEL** | **FAMILY** | The main building on this property is an Edwardian-style mansion built in 1908 for sugar baron John D. Spreckels, who once owned much of Downtown San Diego. **Pros:** great views; friendly staff; close to beach. **Cons:** mansion rooms are small; lots of traffic nearby; due for a renovation. $ *Rooms from: $179* ✉ *1630 Glorietta Blvd., Coronado* ☎ *619/435–3101, 800/283–9383* ⊕ *www.gloriettabayinn.com* ➔ *100 rooms* ⦿ *Free Breakfast.*

★ Hotel Del Coronado
$$$$ | **RESORT** | **FAMILY** | As much of a draw today as it was when it opened in 1888, the Victorian-style "Hotel Del" is always alive with activity, as guests—including U.S. presidents and celebrities—and tourists marvel at the fanciful architecture and ocean views. **Pros:** 17 on-site shops; on the beach; well-rounded spa. **Cons:** some rooms are small; expensive dining; hectic public areas. $ *Rooms from: $425* ✉ *1500 Orange Ave., Coronado* ☎ *800/468–3533, 619/435–6611* ⊕ *www.hoteldel.com* ➔ *757 rooms* ⦿ *No meals.*

Loews Coronado Bay Resort
$$$$ | **RESORT** | **FAMILY** | You can park your boat at the 80-slip marina of this romantic retreat set on a secluded 15-acre peninsula on the Silver Strand. **Pros:** great restaurants; lots of activities; all rooms have furnished balconies with water views. **Cons:** far from anything; confusing layout; not ideal for couples. $ *Rooms from: $349* ✉ *4000 Coronado Bay Rd., Coronado* ☎ *619/424–4000, 800/815–6397* ⊕ *www.loewshotels.com/coronado-bay-resort* ➔ *439 rooms* ⦿ *No meals.*

★ 1906 Lodge at Coronado Beach
$$$$ | **B&B/INN** | Smaller but no less luxurious than the sprawling beach resorts of Coronado, this lodge—whose name alludes to the main building's former life as a boardinghouse built in 1906—welcomes couples for romantic retreats two blocks from the ocean. **Pros:** most suites feature Jacuzzi tubs, fireplaces, and porches; historic property; free underground parking. **Cons:** too quiet for families; no pool; limited on-site dining options. $ *Rooms from: $329* ✉ *1060 Adella Ave., Coronado* ☎ *619/437–1900, 866/435–1906* ⊕ *www.1906lodge.com* ➔ *17 rooms* ⦿ *Free Breakfast.*

🎭 Performing Arts

Coronado Playhouse
THEATER | This cabaret-type theater near the Hotel Del Coronado stages regular dramatic and musical performances. ✉ *1835 Strand Way, Coronado* ☎ *619/435–4856* ⊕ *www.coronadoplayhouse.com.*

Lamb's Players Theatre
THEATER | The theater's regular season of five mostly uplifting productions runs from February through November. It also stages an original musical, *Festival of Christmas,* in December. The company has two performance spaces: the one used for most productions in Coronado, and the Horton Grand Theatre in the Gaslamp Quarter. ✉ *1142 Orange Ave., Coronado* ☎ *619/437–6000* ⊕ *www.lambsplayers.org.*

🏃 Activities

BICYCLING
Holland's Bicycles
BICYCLING | This is a great bike rental source on Coronado Island, so you can ride the Silver Strand Bike Path on an electric bike, beach cruiser, road bike, or tandem. ✉ *977 Orange Ave., Coronado* ☎ *619/435–3153* ⊕ *www.hollandsbicycles.com* 💲 *From $25.*

GOLF
★ Coronado Municipal Golf Course

GOLF | Spectacular views of Downtown San Diego and the Coronado Bridge as well as affordable prices make this public course one of the busiest in the world. Bordered by the bay, the trick is to keep your ball out of the water. Wind can add some difficulty, but otherwise this is a leisurely course and a good one to walk. It's difficult to get on unless you reserve a tee time 3 to 14 days in advance. The course's Bayside Grill restaurant is well-known for its Thursday and Sunday night prime rib dinner. Reservations are recommended. ⊠ *2000 Visalia Row, Coronado* ☎ *619/522–6590* ⊕ *www.golfcoronado. com* ⊠ *$37 weekdays, $42 weekends* ⚑ *18 holes, 6590 yards, par 72.*

JET SKIING
Seaforth Boat Rentals

JET SKIING | You can rent Yamaha WaveRunners and explore San Diego Bay or Mission Bay from Seaforth Boat Rentals' four different San Diego locations. On most Fridays and weekends you can join a two-hour WaveRunner tour of La Jolla's coast, departing from the Mission Bay location (April–September only). ⊠ *1715 Strand Way, Coronado* ☎ *888/834–2628* ⊕ *www.seaforthboatrental.com* ⊠ *From $99.*

KAYAKING
Bike & Kayak Tours

KAYAKING | While La Jolla's outpost of Bike & Kayak Tours offers a Leopard Shark Encounter snorkeling tour ($39 per person), where adventuresome travelers can see the shy spotted creatures up close, the Coronado location has you embarking on a kayak tour ($49 per person) underneath the Coronado Bridge at dusk to enjoy incredible views of Downtown San Diego. The Coronado branch also offers stand-up paddleboards for as little as $29 per person. ⊠ *1201 1st St., #215, Coronado* ☎ *858/454–1010* ⊕ *www. bikeandkayaktours.com* ⊠ *From $39.*

SAILING AND BOATING
BOAT CHARTERS
California Cruisin'

BOATING | Contact California Cruisin' for sailboat or powerboat charter excursions and dinner cruises. The company also provides dockside accommodations aboard a private luxury yacht or houseboat on San Diego Bay. ⊠ *1450 Harbor Island Dr., Harbor Island* ☎ *619/296–8000* ⊕ *www.californiacruisin.com* ⊠ *From $350.*

The Gondola Company

BOATING | You don't have to travel to Venice to be serenaded by a gondolier. This company features authentic Venetian gondola rides that depart daily from the picturesque Coronado Cays. ⊠ *503 Grand Caribe Causeway,, Suite C, Coronado* ☎ *619/429–6317* ⊕ *www.gondolacompany.com* ⊠ *From $95 for 2 people.*

BOAT RENTALS
Seaforth Boat Rentals

BOATING | You can book charter tours and rent kayaks, Jet Skis, fishing skiffs, powerboats and sailboats at Seaforth's five locations around town. The outfitter also can hook you up with a skipper for a deep-sea fishing trip. Seaforth also rents paddleboards at their Mission Bay and Coronado locations. ⊠ *1715 Strand Way, Coronado* ☎ *888/834–2628* ⊕ *www. seaforthboatrental.com* ⊠ *From $25.*

🛍 Shopping

Coronado's resort hotels attract tourists in droves, but somehow the town has managed to avoid being overtaken by chain stores. Instead, shoppers can browse through family-owned shops, dine at sidewalk cafés along Orange Avenue, stroll through the historic Hotel del Coronado, and take in the specialty shops at Coronado Ferry Landing. Friendly shopkeepers make the boutiques lining Orange Avenue, Coronado's main drag, a good place to browse for clothes, home decor, gift items, and gourmet foods.

Hotel del Coronado's iconic red-roofed turret houses the resort's ballroom.

BOOKS
Bay Books
BOOKS/STATIONERY | FAMILY | This independent bookstore is the spot to sit, read, and sip coffee on an overcast day by the sea. Great for international travelers, there's a large selection of foreign-language magazines and newspapers, and for youngsters, there's a section in the back devoted to children's books and games. Because of its close proximity to the Navy bases on Coronado, the shop has a large stock of books dedicated to military history. Bay Books also has regular book-signing events; it has hosted a wide array of authors, from Newt Gingrich to Captain Chesley "Sully" Sullenberger. ⌧ *1029 Orange Ave., Coronado* ☎ *619/435–0070* ⊕ *www.baybookscoronado.com.*

FOOD AND WINE
Coronado Taste of Oils
FOOD/CANDY | The walls are lined, front-to-back, with countless flavors of olive oils and balsamic vinegars, from more standard fare to creative infusions. Some of the varied choices include lemon and lime, chilies, currants, garlic, harissa (hot chili pepper paste), chipotle, and herbs de Provence, all of which are available to sample with bread inside the shop. ⌧ *954 Orange Ave., Coronado* ☎ *619/522–0098* ⊕ *www.tasteofoils.com.*

Wine A Bit
FOOD/CANDY | Part store and part wine bar, the popular Wine A Bit carries hundreds of boutique wines, along with craft beers, appetizers, and decadent desserts. Cigars, gifts, and wine-related accessories are also for sale. ⌧ *928 Orange Ave., Coronado* ☎ *619/365–4953* ⊕ *www.wineabitcoronado.com.*

HOME ACCESSORIES AND GIFTS
Celtic Corner Scottish Treasures
GIFTS/SOUVENIRS | Get in touch with your Celtic roots with imported apparel, gifts, tableware, and jewelry from Ireland, Scotland, England, and Wales. You can rent or order a custom-made kilt. ⌧ *916 Orange Ave., Coronado* ☎ *619/435–1880* ⊕ *www.celticcorner.net.*

Seaside Papery

BOOKS/STATIONERY | Customize your correspondence with products from Seaside Papery, including high-end wedding invitations, greeting cards, luxury personal stationery, and wrapping papers. ⊠ *1162 Orange Ave., Coronado* ☎ *619/435–5565* ⊕ *www.seasidepapery.com.*

JEWELRY
D Forsythe Jewelry

JEWELRY/ACCESSORIES | Stepping into D Forsythe is like taking a quick spin around the world. The one-of-a-kind jewelry sold here features sapphires, emeralds, moonstones, and baroque pearls from such faraway places as Denmark, Cambodia, Turkey, Bali, India, England, and Thailand. ⊠ *1136 Loma Ave., Coronado* ☎ *619/435–9211* ⊕ *www.dforsythe.com* ⊗ *Closed Sun. and Mon.*

SHOPPING CENTERS
Coronado Ferry Landing

SHOPPING CENTERS/MALLS | A staggering view of San Diego's Downtown skyline across the bay and a dozen boutiques make this a delightful place to shop while waiting for a ferry. **La Camisa** (*619/435–8009*) is a fun place to pick up kitschy souvenirs, T-shirts, fleece jackets, and postcards. **The French Room** (*619/889–4325*) specializes in comfy women's shoes and affordable casual wear. **House of Soles & Shades** (*619/437–0546*) sells sandals and designer eyewear. There's a farmers' market every Tuesday 2:30–6, and some restaurants offer a daily late-afternoon happy hour. ⊠ *1201 1st St., Coronado* ☎ *619/435–8895* ⊕ *www. coronadoferrylanding.com.*

★ Hotel Del Coronado

SHOPPING CENTERS/MALLS | At the gift shops within the peninsula's main historic attraction, you can purchase sportswear, designer handbags, jewelry, and antiques. **Babcock & Story Emporium** carries an amazing selection of home decor items, garden accessories, and classy gifts. **Blue Octopus** is a children's store featuring creative toys, gifts, and apparel. **Spreckels Sweets & Treats** offers old-time candies, freshly made fudge, and decadent truffles. **Kate's** has designer fashions and accessories, while **Brady's for Men,** with its shirts and sport coats, caters to well-dressed men. **Crown Jewels Coronado** features fine jewelry, some inspired by the sea. ⊠ *1500 Orange Ave., Coronado* ☎ *619/435–6611* ⊕ *www. hoteldel.com/coronado-shopping.*

Chapter 10

NORTH COUNTY AND AROUND

Updated by
Marlise Kast-Myers

👁 Sights	🍽 Restaurants	🛏 Hotels	🛍 Shopping	🍸 Nightlife
★★★★☆	★★★☆☆	★★★☆☆	★★☆☆☆	★★☆☆☆

WELCOME TO NORTH COUNTY AND AROUND

TOP REASONS TO GO

★ **Talk to the animals:** Get almost nose to nose with giraffes, lions, tigers, and rhinos at the San Diego Zoo Safari Park in Escondido.

★ **Build a dream at LEGOLAND California Resort:** Explore model cities built with LEGO bricks, including New Orleans, Washington, D.C., and New York City.

★ **Be a beach bum:** Surf Swami's for towering blue-water breaks, tiptoe through the sand at Moonlight Beach, cruise the coast in a sailboat, or spot a whale spouting.

★ **Tour SoCal-style wineries:** Savor the red and white wines while touring in Temecula, home to more than 35 wineries as well as boutique lodging and elegant restaurants.

★ **Step back in time:** Sink your teeth into sweet apple pie in the historic mining town of Julian where the Cuyamuca Mountains meet the Colorado Desert.

1 Del Mar. The coastal town is the location of the Del Mar Fairgrounds and the famed Del Mar Thoroughbred Club.

2 Solana Beach. Adjacent to Del Mar and Encinitas, the area is known for shopping—antiques, collectibles, and contemporary artwork—and the Cedros Design District.

3 Rancho Santa Fe. Affluent town east of I–5 where you'll find the Inn at Rancho Santa Fe and the Rancho Valencia Resort & Spa.

4 Encinitas. The surfer town encompasses Cardiff-by-the-Sea, Leucadia, and Olivenhain. It's one of the largest flower-producing areas in the world, and is home to the longboarding favorite, Swami's beach.

5 Carlsbad. Famous for LEGOLAND, the Carlsbad Outlets, and the Flower Fields at Carlsbad Ranch.

6 Oceanside. Surf shops, casual dining options, a museum, a great boardwalk, and some of the best surfing beaches.

7 Rancho Bernardo. Straddling I–15 between San Diego and Escondido, the town is home to Rancho Bernardo Inn and Bernardo Winery.

8 Escondido. Home to the San Diego Zoo Safari Park and the California Center for the Arts.

9 Temecula. A darling Old Town and the center of the wine-making industry in Temecula Valley.

10 Julian. The historic mining town of Julian is famous for its apple pies, B&Bs, and Fourth of July parade.

11 Ramona. Golf at two highly rated courses (Barona Creek Golf Club and Mount Woodson Golf Club), the Barona casino, and a budding winery scene.

12 Anza-Borrego Desert State Park. This is desert at its best: vast, mostly untracked wilderness where you can wander and camp; a huge repository of prehistoric beasts, illustrated by a large collection of life-size sculptures along desert roadsides; and the best wildflower display in Southern California in the springtime.

13 Borrego Springs. Set in the heart of the Anza-Borrego Desert State Park, this is an emerging destination for desert lovers.

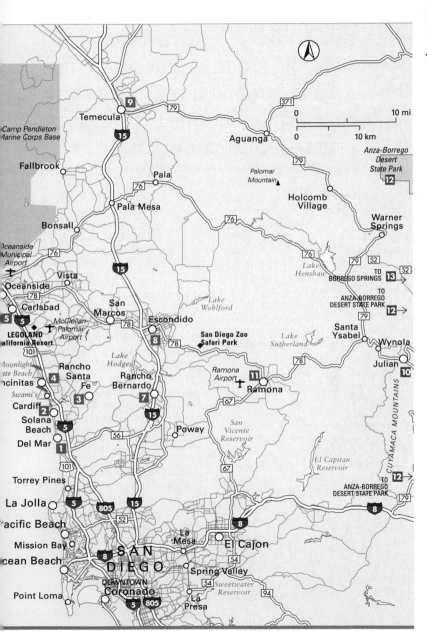

Temecula **15** **9**

79

371

0   10 mi

0   10 km

Camp Pendleton Marine Corps Base

Fallbrook

Aguanga

79

Anza-Borrego Desert State Park **12**

Pala

76

Palomar Mountain▲

Pala Mesa

Holcomb Village

Bonsall

76

76

Warner Springs

Oceanside Municipal Airport

76

Vista

15

Lake Henshaw

79 S2

TO BORREGO SPRINGS **13** S2

Oceanside

78

Carlsbad

San Marcos

78

Escondido

Lake Wohlford

TO ANZA-BORREGO DESERT STATE PARK **12** →

LEGOLAND California Resort

5 **5**

McClellan-Palomar Airport

8

78

San Diego Zoo Safari Park

Lake Sutherland

Santa Ysabel

Wynola

Julian **10**

101

Moonlight State Beach

Encinitas **4**

Rancho Santa Fe

Lake Hodges

Rancho Bernardo

7

Ramona Airport

11

78

Swami's

Cardiff **2** **3**

Ramona

CUYAMACA MOUNTAINS

Solana Beach **5**

15

67

Del Mar **1**

56

Poway

San Vicente Reservoir

101

Torrey Pines

El Capitan Reservoir

TO ANZA-BORREGO DESERT STATE PARK **12** →

67

79

La Jolla **5**

805 **15**

52

Pacific Beach

La Mesa

El Cajon

8

Mission Bay

Ocean Beach **8**

SAN DIEGO

La Mesa

El Cajon

54

Spring Valley

Point Loma

DOWNTOWN Coronado

5 **805**

La Presa

54 Sweetwater Reservoir

94

A whole world of scenic grandeur, fascinating history, and scientific wonder lies just beyond San Diego's city limits. If you travel north along the coast, you'll encounter the great beaches for which the region is famous, along with some sophisticated towns, fine restaurants, great galleries, and museums.

What these towns shared was at least a half-century's worth of Southern California beach culture—think Woodies (wood-bodied cars), surfing, the Beach Boys, alternate lifestyles—and the road that connected them. That was U.S. Highway 101, which nearly passed into oblivion when I–5 was extended from Los Angeles to the Mexican border. If you venture off the freeway and head for the ocean, you can discover remnants of the old beach culture surviving in the sophisticated towns of Del Mar, Solana Beach, Cardiff-by-the-Sea, Encinitas, Leucadia, Carlsbad, and Oceanside, where the arts, fine dining, and elegant lodgings also now rule. As suburbanization continues, the towns are reinventing themselves—Carlsbad, for instance, has morphed from a farming community into a tourist destination with such attractions as LEGOLAND California, several museums, and an upscale outlet shopping complex.

If you travel east, you'll find art hubs and organic farms in Escondido, the San Diego Zoo Safari Park, a pair of world-class destination spas, a selection of challenging golf courses, and nightlife in bucolic settings. Inspiring mountain scenery plus beautiful places to picnic and hike can be found in the Cuyamaca Mountains and in the surrounding areas near the historic gold-rush-era town of Julian (known for its apple pies). Just beyond the county limits in Temecula you can savor Southern California's only developed wine country, where dozens of wineries offer tastings and tours.

MAJOR REGIONS

Once upon a time, to say that the **North Coast** of San Diego County was different from the city of San Diego would have been an understatement. From the northern tip of La Jolla up to Oceanside, a half-dozen small communities developed separately from urban San Diego—and from one another. **Del Mar,** because of its 2 miles of wide beaches, splendid views, and Thoroughbred horse-racing complex, was the playground of the rich and famous. The affluent town of **Rancho Santa Fe** was also a haunt of Old Hollywood with the likes of Bette Davis and Bing Crosby hanging out at the Inn at Rancho Santa Fe. Up the road, agriculture played a major role in the development of **Solana Beach** and **Encinitas**.

Carlsbad, too, rooted in the old Mexican rancheros, has agriculture in its past, as well as the entrepreneurial instinct of a late 19th-century resident, John Frazier, who promoted the area's water as a cure for common ailments and constructed a replica of a European mineral-springs resort. **Oceanside** was a beachside getaway for inland families in the 19th century; today it's home to one of the longest wooden piers on the West Coast (its first pier was built in the 1880s), and the city promotes its beach culture with a yacht harbor and beachside resort hotels. It's also the location of Camp Pendleton, a Marine Corps training base during World War II that's still in use today.

Long regarded as San Diego's beautiful backyard, replete with green hills, quiet lakes, and citrus and avocado groves, **Inland North County** is home to some of Southern California's fastest growing areas. Subdivisions, many containing palatial homes, now fill the hills and canyons around **Escondido** and **Rancho Bernardo.** Growth notwithstanding, the area still has such natural settings as the San Diego Zoo Safari Park and the destination spas like the renowned Golden Door Spa and Cal-a-Vie Health Spa.

As the premium winemaking region of Southern California, **Temecula** produces award-winning blends, ideal for those who want to tour local vineyards after a stroll through historic Old Town center or a round of golf on any one of Temecula's championship courses.

The area known as **The Backcountry** contains the Cuyamaca and Laguna mountains to the east of Escondido, which are favorite weekend destinations for hikers, bikers, nature lovers, stargazers, and apple-pie fanatics. Most of the latter group head to **Julian,** a historic mining town now better known for apple pie than for the gold once extracted from its hills. But golfers will want to head to **Ramona** for two highly rated courses (Barona Creek Golf Club and Mount Woodson Golf Club), and there's also the Barona casino, and a budding winery scene.

In most spring seasons the stark desert landscape east of the Cuyamaca Mountains explodes with colorful wildflowers. The beauty of this spectacle, as well as the natural quiet and blazing climate, lures many tourists and natives each year to **Anza-Borrego Desert State Park**, about a two-hour drive from central San Diego. It's best visited from October through May to avoid the extreme summer temperatures. Winter temperatures are comfortable, but nights (and sometimes days) are cold, so bring a warm jacket.

Planning

GETTING HERE AND AROUND
BUS AND TRAIN TRAVEL
The Metropolitan Transit System covers the city of San Diego up to Del Mar.

Buses and trains operated by North County Transit District (NCTD) serve all coastal communities in San Diego County, going as far east as Escondido; the NCTD Sprinter runs a commuter service between Oceanside and Escondido. Routes are coordinated with other transit agencies serving San Diego County. Amtrak stops in Solana Beach, Oceanside, and Downtown San Diego.

Coaster operates commuter rail service between San Diego and Oceanside, stopping en route in Old Town, Sorrento Valley, Solana Beach, Encinitas, and Carlsbad. The last Coaster train leaves San Diego at about 7 each night. NCTD's bus system, Breeze, serves North County; for on-demand service they offer Flex, and door-to-door paratransit service on Lift.

BUS AND TRAIN CONTACTS Amtrak.
✉ *235 S. Tremont St., Oceanside* ☎ *760/722–4622 in Oceanside, 800/872–7245* ⊕ *www.amtrak.com* **Coaster.** ☎ *760/966–6500* ⊕ *www.gonctd.com.* **Metropolitan Transit System.** ☎ *619/233–3004* ⊕ *www.sdmts.com.* **North County Transit District.** ☎ *760/966–6500* ⊕ *www. gonctd.com.*

CAR TRAVEL

Interstate 5 is the main freeway artery connecting San Diego to Los Angeles, passing just east of the beach cities from Oceanside south to Del Mar. Running parallel west of I–5 is Route S21, also known and sometimes indicated as historic Highway 101, Old Highway 101, or Coast Highway 101, which never strays too far from the ocean. An alternate, especially from Orange and Riverside counties, is I–15, the inland route through Temecula, Escondido, and eastern San Diego County.

A loop drive beginning and ending in San Diego is a good way to explore the backcountry and Julian area. You can take the S1, the Sunrise National Scenic Byway (sometimes icy in winter) from I–8 to Route 79 and return through Cuyamaca Rancho State Park (also sometimes icy in winter). If you're only going to Julian (a 75-minute trip from San Diego in light traffic), take either the Sunrise Byway or Route 79, and return to San Diego via Route 78 past Santa Ysabel to Route 67; from here I–8 heads west to Downtown.

Escondido sits at the intersection of Route 78, which heads east from Oceanside, and I–15, the inland freeway connecting San Diego to Riverside, which is 30 minutes north of Escondido. Route 76, which connects with I–15 north of Escondido, veers east to Palomar Mountain. Interstate 15 continues north to Temecula.

RESTAURANTS

Dining in North County tends to reflect the land where the restaurant is located. Along the coast, for example, there is one fine-dining spot after another. Most have dramatic water views and offer platters of exquisite fare created by graduates of the best culinary schools. Right next door you can wander into a typical beach shack or diner for the juiciest hamburger you've ever tasted. Locally sourced food can be found at restaurants throughout the area, although a few chefs have adopted molecular gastronomic techniques. Farm-to-table cuisine is most common in Rancho Sante Fe, Del Mar, and Escondido. Backcountry cuisine east of Escondido toward Julian is generally served in huge portions and tends toward home-style cooking, steak and potatoes, burgers, and anything fried. Several casinos near Temecula and Valley Center are famous for their all-you-can-eat seafood buffets.

HOTELS

Like the restaurants, hotels in the North County reflect the geography and attractions where they are set. There are a number of luxury resorts that offer golf, tennis, entertainment, and classy service. For those who want the ultimate pampered vacation, North County holds two world-class spas: Cal-a-Vie and the Golden Door. Along the beach, there are quite a few stand-alone lodgings that attract the beach crowd; while some lack in appeal and service, they still charge a big price in summer. Lodgings in the Carlsbad area are family-friendly, and close to beaches and LEGOLAND. In Temecula, some of the best and most delightful lodgings are tied to wineries; they offer a whole experience: accommodations, spa, dining, and wine. One-of-a-kind bed-and-breakfasts are the rule in the Julian area. Some hotels charge resort fees up to $35 per night.

For expanded hotel reviews, facilities, and current deals, visit Fodors.com.

WHAT IT COSTS

	$	$$	$$$	$$$$
RESTAURANTS				
	under $18	$18–$27	$28–$35	over $35
HOTELS				
	under $161	$161–$230	$231–$300	over $300

FLOWERS

The North County is a prolific flower-growing region. Nurseries, some open to the public, line the hillsides on both sides of I–5 in Encinitas, Leucadia, and Carlsbad. Most of the poinsettias sold in the United States get their start here. If you're visiting in spring, don't miss the ranunculus bloom at the Flower Fields at Carlsbad Ranch.

San Diego Botanic Gardens in Encinitas displays native and exotic plants year-round. The gardens at the San Diego Zoo Safari Park attract nearly as many people as the animals do.

VISITOR INFORMATION San Diego Tourism Authority. *☎ 619/232–3101 ⊕ www. sandiego.org.*

Del Mar

23 miles north of Downtown San Diego on I–5, 9 miles north of La Jolla on Rte. S21.

Del Mar comprises two sections: the small historic village adjacent to the beach west of I–5 and a growing business center surrounded by multimillion-dollar tract housing east of the freeway. Tiny Del Mar village, the smallest incorporated city in San Diego County, holds a population of 4,500 tucked into a 2.1-square-mile beachfront. It's known for its quaint half-timbered Tudor-style architecture, 2 miles of accessible beaches, and the Del Mar racetrack and San Diego County Fairgrounds complex. The village attracted rich and famous visitors from the beginning; they still come for seclusion and to watch the horses run. The Del Mar Gateway business complex has high-rise hotels and fast-food outlets east of the interstate at the entrance to Carmel Valley. Both Del Mars, old and new, hold expensive homes belonging to staff and scientists who work in the biotech industry and at UC San Diego in adjacent La Jolla. Access to Del Mar's beaches is from the streets that run east–west off Coast Boulevard; access to the business complex is via Highway 56.

TOUR OPTIONS

San Diego Air Tours conducts excursions aboard restored 1920s-vintage open-cockpit biplanes. Flights are from Montgomery Field and start at $199 per couple for 20 minutes. Civic Helicopters gives whirlybird tours of the area along the beaches, starting at $300 for 30 minutes aboard a Robinson R-44.

TOUR CONTACTS Civic Helicopters. ✉ *2206 Palomar Airport Rd., Suite H, Carlsbad ☎ 760/438–8424 ⊕ www. civichelicopters.com.* **San Diego Air Tours.** ✉ *3750 John J. Montgomery Dr., Suite D, San Diego ☎ 760/930–0903, 800/359–2939 ⊕ www.sandiegoairtours.com.*

◉ Sights

Del Mar Fairgrounds

FAIRGROUND | FAMILY | The Spanish Mission–style fairground is the home of the **Del Mar Thoroughbred Club** (*www. dmtc.com*). Crooner Bing Crosby and his Hollywood buddies—Pat O'Brien, Gary Cooper, and Oliver Hardy, among others—organized the club in the 1930s, and the racing here (usually July through September, Wednesday through Monday, post time 2 pm) remains a fashionable affair. Del Mar Fairgrounds hosts more than 500 different events each year, including the San Diego County Fair, the Del Mar National Horse Show in April and May, the KAABOO Musical Festival in September, and the fall Scream Zone that's popular with local families. ✉ *2260 Jimmy Durante Blvd. ☎ 858/755–1161 ⊕ www.delmarfairgrounds.com.*

Del Mar Plaza

STORE/MALL | Along with its collection of high-end shops, the tiered plaza contains outstanding restaurants and fountain courtyards with Pacific views. Some businesses validate parking, which is

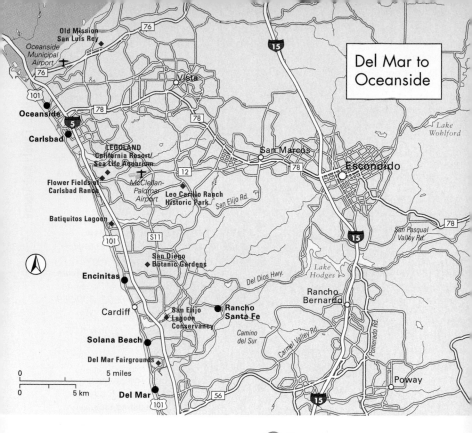

underground. ⊠ *1555 Camino del Mar* ⊕ *www.delmarplaza.com*.

Free Flight Exotic Bird Sanctuary

ZOO | FAMILY | This small exotic-bird aviary adjacent to the Del Mar Fairgrounds houses a collection of parrots and other exotic birds—a guaranteed child pleaser. ⊠ *2132 Jimmy Durante Blvd.* ☎ *858/481–3148* ⊕ *www.freeflightbirds.org* ⌨ *$7.*

Seagrove Park (*Powerhouse Park*)

CITY PARK | Picnics and weddings make this coastal park popular on weekends. For free summer evening concerts and beach access, head to Powerhouse Park at the north end of this small stretch of grass overlooking the ocean. ⊠ *15th St. and Coast Blvd.* ☎ *858/755–1524* ⊕ *www.delmar.ca.us*.

🛆 Beaches

Del Mar Beach

BEACH—SIGHT | FAMILY | This famously clean 2-mile-long beach is the perfect place for long barefoot walks and sunbathing due to its extremely fine, soft sand and lack of seaweed and other debris. Del Mar Beach is also a great place for families. It has year-round lifeguards and areas clearly marked for swimming and surfing. Depending on the swell, you may see surfers at the 15th Street surf break, right below two coastal parks, Powerhouse and Seagrove; volleyball players love the courts at the beach's far north end. The section of beach south of 15th is lined with cliffs and tends to be less crowded than Main Beach, which extends from 15th north to 29th. Leashed dogs are permitted on most sections of the beach, except Main

Beach, where they are prohibited from June 15 through the Tuesday after Labor Day. For the rest of the year, dogs may run off leash at North Beach, just north of the River Mouth, also known locally as Dog Beach. Food, shopping, and hotels including L'Auberge Del Mar, are near Del Mar Beach. Parking costs from $1.50 to $3 per hour at meters and pay lots on Coast Boulevard and along Camino Del Mar. **Amenities:** food and drink, lifeguards, parking (fee), showers, toilets. **Best for:** swimming, walking. ✉ *Main Beach, 1700 Coast Blvd., North Beach 3200–3300 Camino Del Mar* ☎ *858/755–1556* 🌐 *www.delmar.ca.us/203/Beaches-Parks.*

🍴 Restaurants

The neighborhood just north of La Jolla is well-known for its posh, ocean-view homes and the famed Del Mar racetrack. It's also known for the numerous restaurants that line the main drag of Camino Del Mar; there's even a few worthwhile spots tucked into upscale shopping centers and beachside locales.

★ Addison

$$$$ | FRENCH | Indulge in the finer things in life at this AAA 5-Diamond restaurant by acclaimed chef William Bradley who serves up haute French flavors in his 4- and 10-course prix-fixe dinners. Beyond the swanky bar and wine cave is a sophisticated Tuscan-style dining room with intricately carved dark-woods, marble pillars, and arched windows draped in red velvet. **Known for:** decadent tasting menus; the ultimate fine-dining experience; impeccable service; the only 5-star restaurant in San Diego. [$] *Average main: $110* ✉ *5200 Grand Del Mar Way* ☎ *858/314–1900* 🌐 *www.addisondelmar.com* 🕒 *Closed Sun. and Mon. No lunch.*

CUCINA enoteca

$$ | MODERN ITALIAN | An off-shoot of Bankers Hill's Cucina Urbana, Enoteca occupies a grand two-story space in the Flower Hill Promenade shopping center and is as notable for its whimsical decor—antler chandeliers, burlap-wrapped chairs, and more than 400 horse figurines honor the restaurant's proximity to the Thoroughbred Club—as it is for its beloved Italian food. There are many familiar favorites from Cucina Urbana like the creamy polenta board and pizzas, as well as unique Enoteca plates, including a charred octopus, Sicilian puttanesca, and heirloom carrot risotto. **Known for:** wines at retail; daily deals 4:30–6; garden-like second-floor seating area;. [$] *Average main: $25* ✉ *Flower Hill Promenade, 2730 Via de la Valle* ☎ *858/704–4500* 🌐 *www.cucinaenoteca.com* 🕒 *No lunch Mon.*

Flower Child

$ | MODERN AMERICAN | FAMILY | Fast-casual takes a healthy spin at this cheery spot—think Technicolor peace sign, floral wallpaper in the bathroom, and yoga mat "parking" for those dining postworkout. The menu evokes the same colorful vibe with salads mixed with fresh ingredients like organic kale, lemon tahini vinaigrette, and proteins that include sustainable salmon, grass-fed steak, and organic, non-GMO tofu. **Known for:** kid-friendly ambience; rotating house-made lemonades; mix-and-match healthy sides. [$] *Average main: $11* ✉ *Flower Hill Promenade, 2690 Via De La Valle* ☎ *858/314–6818* 🌐 *www.iamaflowerchild.com.*

> **Did You Know?**
>
> San Diego County consists of 18 incorporated cities and several unincorporated communities, and is about the same size as the state of Connecticut.

Jake's Del Mar

$$$ | AMERICAN | Situated next to grassy Powerhouse Park, Jake's feels like Southern Californian dining at its best—a beachfront location coupled with beautiful ocean views and the freshest ingredients. Starters include ocean-inspired fare like crab cakes with tamarind aioli and pineapple salsa, while the main menu is split "by garden," "by sea," and "by land," with options like curry- and cumin-crusted ahi; Double Ranch rib eye; an avocado-topped sirloin-brisket burger; and shrimp ravioli. **Known for:** prime beachfront location; iconic Hula Pie dessert, a thick wedge of macadamia nut ice cream on a chocolate cookie crust that's topped with chocolate fudge, whipped cream, and more macadamia nuts; Sunday brunch. $ *Average main: $29* ⊠ *1660 Coast Blvd.* ☎ *858/755–2002* ⊕ *www.jakesdelmar.com.*

★ Market Restaurant + Bar

$$$ | AMERICAN | Carl Schroeder, one of California's hottest young chefs, draws well-heeled foodies to his creative and locally sourced California fare, much of it with an Asian influence from his time in Japan. The menu changes regularly depending upon what's fresh, but might include carrot-ginger soup or crispy duck confit with candied kumquats. **Known for:** succulent short ribs; award-winning chef; seasonal menu. $ *Average main: $30* ⊠ *3702 Via de la Valle* ☎ *858/523–0007* ⊕ *www.marketdelmar.com* ☽ *No lunch.*

Pacifica Del Mar

$$$ | SEAFOOD | The view of the shimmering Pacific from this lovely restaurant perched atop Del Mar Plaza is one of the best along the coast, and complements the simply prepared, beautifully presented seafood. The highly innovative menu is frequently rewritten to show off such creations as barbecue sugar-spice salmon with mustard sauce and mustard catfish with Yukon Gold potato–corn succotash. **Known for:** incredible views of the Pacific; ever-changing, creative seafood

menu; Sunday brunch. $ *Average main: $30* ⊠ *Del Mar Plaza, 1555 Camino del Mar* ☎ *858/792–0476* ⊕ *www.pacificadelmar.com.*

Sbicca

$$$ | AMERICAN | The menu at this American bistro changes quarterly but the clientele is here to stay, especially during summer months when people-watching becomes a sport. Grab a seat on the terrace if you're lucky to enjoy such magical cocktails like a cucumber crush of grapefruit, vodka, and elderflower, and menu mainstays such as buttermilk-fried Jidori chicken, braised short ribs, and seared ahi tuna. **Known for:** half-off wine Tuesday and Thursday; Sunday and Monday no corkage fee; ahi tacos. $ *Average main:* ⊠ *215 15th St., Del Mar* ☎ *858/481–1001* ⊕ *www.sbiccadelmar.com.*

🛏 Hotels

★ Fairmont Grand Del Mar

$$$$ | RESORT | FAMILY | Mind-blowing indulgence in serene surroundings, from drop-dead gorgeous guest accommodations to myriad outdoor adventures, sets the opulent Mediterranean-style Fairmont Grand Del Mar apart from any other luxury hotel in San Diego. **Pros:** ultimate luxury; secluded, on-site golf course; enormous rooms; has most acclaimed fine-dining restaurant in San Diego. **Cons:** floor plan may be confusing; 6 miles from the coast; $150 pet fee. $ *Rooms from: $415* ⊠ *5200 Grand Del Mar Ct.* ☎ *858/314–2000, 855/314–2030* ⊕ *www.fairmont.com/san-diego* ⋆ *Greens fees $250; 18 holes, 7160 yards, par 72* ⟿ *249 rooms* ﺓ *No meals.*

Hilton Garden Inn San Diego Del Mar

$ | HOTEL | The corporate crowd—and anyone wanting to reach San Diego's attractions within 15 minutes—select this Hilton property conveniently located where three highways (5, 805, and 56) merge. **Pros:** great location—beach is 5 miles away; remarkable service;

hassle-free benefits include free Wi-Fi, self-parking, and a New York-style deli. **Cons:** parking lot views; no in-room safes; a drive to the beach. $ *Rooms from: $159* ✉ *3939 Ocean Bluff Ave.* ☎ *858/720–9500* ⊕ *www.sandiegodelmar.hgi.com* 🛏 *84 rooms* ⫯❑ *No meals.*

L'Auberge Del Mar

$$$$ | **HOTEL** | Each room at this ocean-front luxury hotel is reminiscent of an airy beach cottage with plantation shutters, a fireplace, and vintage coastal artwork; balconies face the ocean and pool where guests lounge in private cabanas. **Pros:** tennis courts, a fitness center, and shuttle service to neighboring beaches, shops, and restaurants; excellent service; dogs welcomed with gift bags. **Cons:** occasional train noise; adult atmosphere; ground-level rooms have no privacy. $ *Rooms from: $450* ✉ *1540 Camino del Mar* ☎ *858/259–1515, 800/245–9757* ⊕ *www.laubergedelmar.com* 🛏 *121 rooms* ⫯❑ *No meals.*

🏃 Activities

HORSE RACING

Del Mar Racetrack (*Del Mar Thorough-bred Club*)

HORSE RACING/SHOW | The racetrack attracts the best horses and jockeys in the country—Seabiscuit even won a much-talked-about race here in 1938. Spectators can enjoy 11 weeks of racing annually at the historic Del Mar Race-track. The summer season starts in mid-July and runs through early September and includes a summer concert series and opening and closing-day celebrations. The fall season lasts for a month starting in November. The track, which opened in 1937, was founded in part by singer and actor Bing Crosby. ✉ *2260 Jimmy Durante Blvd.* ⊹ *Take I–5 north to Via de la Valle exit* ☎ *858/755–1141* ⊕ *www.dmtc.com* 🎟 *From $10.*

👜 Shopping

In Del Mar, browse the cute boutiques in Del Mar Village or head to Flower Hill Promenade, an outdoor shopping center that has become one of San Diego's most thriving retail destinations with an eclectic mix of locally owned retailers. If you're headed to the Del Mar Racetrack, be sure to pick up a glamorous hat to wear while cheering on the ponies—a racetrack tradition.

Flower Hill Promenade

SHOPPING CENTERS/MALLS | At first glance, this open-air shopping center anchored by a **Whole Foods Market** (*858/436–9800*) might look like your typical upscale SoCal mall, but take a closer look, because there's way more to it than meets the eye. There's not only some great shopping—much of it locally owned and eco-minded—but also some of San Diego's best restaurateurs like Tracy Borkum and Steven Molina have opened restaurants here (CUCINA enoteca and Flower Child, respectively). **Sweetpea** (*858/481–0683*) stocks children's clothing from brands like Catimini, Magnolia Baby, and Petit Bateau. **Van de Vort** (*858/720–1059*) sells the latest boho-chic fashions, including floral prints, fringe, and maxi dresses. ✉ *2720 Via De La Valle, Del Mar* ☎ *858/481–2904.*

Solana Beach

1 mile north of Del Mar on Rte. S21, 25 miles north of Downtown San Diego on I–5 to Lomas Santa Fe Dr. west.

Once-quiet Solana Beach is *the* place to stroll with a latte and look for collectibles, artwork, and contemporary fashions. The Cedros Design District, occupying four blocks south of the Amtrak station, contains shops, galleries, designers' studios, restaurants, and a popular music venue, the Belly Up Tavern. The town is known for its excellent restaurants, but most area lodging is in adjacent Del Mar and Encinitas.

Beaches

Fletcher Cove

BEACH—SIGHT | Most of the beaches in the little city of Solana Beach are nestled under cliffs, and access is limited to private stairways. However, at the west end of Lomas Santa Fe Drive, where it turns into Plaza Street, there's an entrance to this small beach, along with parking lot, picnic area, playground, and restrooms. The softest sand can be found by the cliffs and it gets a bit courser as you near the water's edge. During low tide it's an easy walk under the cliffs to nearby beaches, but high tide can make some of the beach impassable. At the northern end of town there are also restrooms, a pay lot, and easy beach access. The City of Solana Beach and the Belly Up Tavern often host free summer concerts at Fletcher Cove (*www.cityofsolanabeach.org*) and there are plenty of great restaurants nearby on Highway 101 and on Cedros Avenue. Tides and surf conditions are posted at a kiosk by this parking lot. **Amenities:** lifeguards, parking (no fee), showers, toilets. **Best for:** surfing, solitude, swimming, walking. ✉ *Plaza St. at S. Sierra Ave.*

Restaurants

The Fish Market

$$ | **SEAFOOD** | **FAMILY** | In 1976, a fisherman and captain teamed up to deliver fresh, quality seafood at a decent price. Today, they run six restaurants across California including this North County branch that lacks an ocean view but makes up for it with perfectly cooked fish and simple preparations from a menu that changes daily. **Known for:** delicious clam chowder and crisp fish-and-chips; oyster bar; happy hour 11–4 on weekends. [$] *Average main: $25* ✉ *640 Via de la Valle* ☎ *858/755–2277* 🌐 *www.thefishmarket.com.*

Pamplemousse Grille

$$$$ | **FRENCH** | One of North County's best restaurants, across the street from the Del Mar Fairgrounds and racetrack, offers French cuisine with California flare. Chef-proprietor Jeffrey Strauss brings a caterer's sensibilities to the details, like a mix-or-match selection of sauces—such as wild mushroom, grain mustard, or peppercorn—to complement the simple but absolutely top-quality grilled meats and seafood. **Known for:** exceptional service; comprehensive wine list; traditional French sauces to accompany entrées. [$] *Average main: $36* ✉ *514 Via de la Valle, Suite 100* ☎ *858/792–9090* 🌐 *www.pgrille.com* 🕒 *No lunch Sat.–Thurs.*

Pizza Port

$ | **PIZZA** | **FAMILY** | Local families flock here for great pizza and handcrafted brews. Pick a spot at one of the long picnic-type tables, choose traditional or whole-grain beer crust for your pie and any original topping—such as the Monterey, with pepperoni, onions, mushrooms, and artichoke hearts—and tip back a brew from one of the longest boutique lists in San Diego. **Known for:** handcrafted beer and whole-grain beer crust; popular post-work spot; family-friendly dining. [$] *Average main: $17* ✉ *135 N. Hwy. 101* ☎ *858/481–7332* 🌐 *www.pizzaport.com.*

Red Tracton's

$$$ | **STEAKHOUSE** | Across the street from the Del Mar racetrack, this classic old-fashioned steak and seafood house is a high-roller's heaven and a perennial favorite with jockeys celebrating their wins. The food is simple but good, and the menu highlights roasted prime rib in addition to filet mignon, panfried scallops, and such starters as lobster bisque and "jumbo" shrimp on ice. **Known for:** lively piano music; juicy steaks, prime rib, and shrimp; supper club atmosphere. [$] *Average main: $40* ✉ *550 Via de la Valle* ☎ *858/755–6600* 🌐 *www.redtractonssteakhouse.com* 🕒 *Closed Sun.*

Nightlife

Belly Up

MUSIC CLUBS | A fixture on local papers' "best of" lists, Belly Up has been drawing crowds since it opened in 1974. Its longevity attests to the quality of the eclectic entertainment on its stage. Within converted Quonset huts, critically acclaimed artists play everything from reggae and folk to—well, you name it. ☒ 143 S. Cedros Ave. ☎ 858/481–8140 ⊕ www.bellyup.com.

 Performing Arts

North Coast Repertory Theatre (*North Coast Rep*)

THEATER | A diverse mix of comic and dramatic works is shown in the 194-seat space. The emphasis is on contemporary productions, but the theater has been known to stage some classics, too. ☒ 987 Lomas Santa Fe Dr., Suite D ☎ 858/481–1055 ⊕ www.northcoastrep.org.

 Activities

BIKING

Lomas Santa Fe Drive

BICYCLING | Experienced cyclists follow this route in Solana Beach east into Rancho Santa Fe, perhaps even continuing east on Del Dios Highway, past Lake Hodges, to Escondido. These roads can be narrow and winding in spots.

 Shopping

Aaron Chang Ocean Art Gallery

ART GALLERIES | On the south end of Cedros Design District, the Ocean Art Gallery features works by award-winning surf photographer, Aaron Chang. On display are photographic prints with ocean themes and several striking surfboard sculptures. ☒ 415 S. Cedros Ave., No. 110 ☎ 858/345–1880 ⊕ www.aaronchang.com.

Cedros Design District

SHOPPING NEIGHBORHOODS | FAMILY | A collection of more than 85 shops, along a two-block stretch of S. Cedros Avenue, this district specializes in interior design, apparel, jewelry, and gifts. You won't find chain restaurants here, as they are not allowed, but you will find local chefs shopping at the Sunday Farmers' Market (1 to 5 pm). There's also free parking along this dog-friendly strip. ☒ District office, 444 S. Cedros Ave. ⊕ www.cedrosavenue.com.

House Vintage

ANTIQUES/COLLECTIBLES | Inside this tiny 1920s cottage are funky, handmade treasures including repurposed furniture and craft kits for DIY projects. The owner also hosts monthly on-site art classes like furniture painting 101 and DIY paint class. ☒ 315 S. Cedros Ave. ☎ 858/222–2989 ⊕ www.debisdesigndiary.com ☉ Closed Mon.–Wed.

Solo

BOOKS/STATIONERY | Operated by nine creative women, this upscale collective is a highlight of Cedros. Shoppers are lured in by the restored warehouse and won over by antiques, artwork, home furnishings, greeting cards, and books on cooking, industrial design, and everything in between. ☒ 309 S. Cedros Ave. ☎ 858/794–9016 ⊕ www.solocedros.com.

Rancho Santa Fe

4 miles east of Solana Beach on Rte. S8, Lomas Santa Fe Dr., 29 miles north of Downtown San Diego on I–5 to Rte. S8 east.

Groves of huge, drooping eucalyptus trees cover the hills and valleys of this affluent and exclusive town east of I–5. Rancho Santa Fe and the surrounding areas are primarily residential, where there are mansions at every turn. It's also common to see entire families riding horses on the many trails that crisscross the hillsides.

Modeled after a Spanish village, the town was designed by Lilian Rice, one of the first women to graduate with a degree in architecture from the University of California. Her first structure, a 12-room house built in 1922, evolved into the Inn at Rancho Santa Fe, which became a gathering spot for celebrities such as Bette Davis, Errol Flynn, and Bing Crosby in the 1930s and 1940s. The challenging Rancho Santa Fe Golf Course, the original site of the Bing Crosby Pro-Am, is considered one of the best courses in Southern California.

🍴 Restaurants

Mille Fleurs

$$$$ | FRENCH | Wealthy regulars who have dined at this elegant Rancho Santa Fe eatery since 1978 got a pleasant surprise when young surfer chef Sean McCart took over the kitchen in 2018, bringing a modern twist to the familiar menu. Devotees can still enjoy Mille Fleurs favorites like Wiener schnitzel and lobster salad, but new highlights include seasonal dishes prepared with ingredients from neighboring Chino Farms like handmade ravioli stuffed with pumpkin and sage, or crispy-skin salmon with chanterelle mushrooms and tarragon mustard sauce. **Known for:** fresh produce from neighboring Chino Farms; authentic French desserts; soft jazz in the piano bar Wednesday–Saturday. ⓢ Average main: $35 ⌂ Country Squire Courtyard, 6009 Paseo Delicias ☎ 858/756–3085 ⊕ www. millefleurs.com ⊙ No lunch Sat.–Wed.

Morada

$$$ | AMERICAN | Loyal locals frequent this classy farm-to-fork restaurant, where black-and-white photos of Santa Fe's history provide a glimpse into the storied past of The Inn at Rancho Santa Fe. Cozy up to the fireplace and partake of locally sourced California cuisine that leans

heavily on comfort food like root vegetable potpie, baked macaroni-and-cheese, and fried chicken with buttermilk biscuits. **Known for:** elevated comfort food; divine desserts like doughnut holes with apple cider caramel or olive oil cake with lemon gelato; happy hour (Mon.–Thurs. 3–5:30 pm) and live music (Fri. and Sat. 6–10 pm). ⓢ Average main: $33 ⌂ The Inn at Rancho Santa Fe, 5951 Linea Del Cielo ☎ 858/381–8289 ⊕ www.theinnatrsf.com.

Veladora

$$$$ | MEDITERRANEAN | Setting the stage for your dining journey at Veldora are open wood beams, iron chandeliers, and a Damien Hirst butterfly wing art piece valued at over $1 million—this place is refined without being stuffy. Executive Chef Jarrod Moiles delivers a coastal ranch menu that changes seasonally and there are nearly 900 wines and 120 tequilas giving you more than enough options to pair with the iberico bellota tartare or oysters on the half shell. **Known for:** attentive service; extensive wine list; menu for small dogs; house-made veal bacon. ⓢ Average main: $41 ⌂ 5921 Valencia Circle ☎ 858/756–1123 ⊕ www. ranchovalencia.com ⊙ Closed Mon.

🛏 Hotels

The Inn at Rancho Santa Fe

$$$ | HOTEL | Understated elegance is the theme of this genteel old resort, designed in 1923 by Lilian Rice, who was known for her architectural works reflecting Spanish colonial style. **Pros:** charming historic hotel; excellent service; country comfort. **Cons:** dim lighting in the rooms; cold pool; some rooms close to the road. ⓢ Rooms from: $275 ⌂ 5951 Linea del Cielo ☎ 858/756–1131, 800/843–4661 ⊕ www.theinnatrsf.com ⤳ 80 rooms ⊙ No meals.

★ Rancho Valencia Resort & Spa

$$$$ | RESORT | FAMILY | Elegant, two-level, hacienda-style casitas—appointed with

corner fireplaces, luxurious bathrooms, and shuttered French doors leading to private patios—are nestled among 45 acres in one of Southern California's most affluent neighborhoods. **Pros:** one of the few properties in the U.S. with both 5-star spa and resort; impeccable personalized service; use of minibar, fitness classes, Porsches, and tennis clinic included in rate; one of nation's top tennis resorts. **Cons:** $30 daily resort fee; very expensive; far from San Diego attractions. $ *Rooms from: $868* ⊠ *5921 Valencia Circle* ☎ *858/756–1123, 866/233–6708* ⊕ *www.ranchovalencia. com* ⊃ *49 suites* ⦿ *No meals.*

🛍 Shopping

The Country Friends

GIFTS/SOUVENIRS | Operated by a nonprofit foundation, The Country Friends is a great place for unusual gifts and carries collectibles, silver, furniture, and antiques donated or consigned by community residents. ⊠ *6030 El Tordo* ☎ *858/756–1192* ⊕ *www.thecountryfriends.org* ⊙ *Closed Sun. and Mon.*

The Spa at Rancho Valencia

SPA/BEAUTY | The Spa at Rancho Valencia Resort invites couples (and everyone else) to relax, romance, and renew. Massages include Thai, relaxation, deep tissue, hot stone, and prenatal, but the Lovers Ritual begins with a couple's bath, followed by a Duet Massage in a cabana for two. Treatment rooms have private Jacuzzis, fireplaces, and outdoor showers. Day access to the spa amenities—plunge circuit, sauna, relaxation room, saline pool, fitness classes—is included when you book a treatment. Discounted rates are offered Monday–Thursday. **Price:** Massages $190–$390; manicures $60–$200; facials $200–$350; body therapies $200–$375; couples $380–$750. ⊠ *5921 Rancho Valencia Cir.* ☎ *858/759–6490* ⊕ *www.ranchovalencia.com.*

Vegetable Shop at Chino Farm

FOOD/CANDY | This is the place to buy the same premium (and very expensive) fruits, micro greens, edible flowers, and rare vegetables that the Chino Family Farm grows for many of San Diego's upscale restaurants, and for such famed California eateries as Chez Panisse in Berkeley and George's in La Jolla. ⊠ *6123 Calzada del Bosque* ☎ *858/756–3184* ⊕ *www.chinofamilyfarm.com* ⊙ *Closed Mon.*

Encinitas

6 miles north of Solana Beach on Rte. S21, 7 miles west of Rancho Santa Fe on Rte. S9, 28 miles north of Downtown San Diego on I–5.

Flower breeding and growing has been the major industry in Encinitas since the early part of the 20th century. The city, which encompasses the coastal towns of Cardiff-by-the-Sea and Leucadia as well as inland Olivenhain, is home to Paul Ecke Poinsettias (open only to the trade), and today is the largest producer and breeder of the Christmas blossom in the world. The golden domes of the Self-Realization Fellowship Retreat mark famed Swami's Beach and the southern entrance to downtown Encinitas.

The vibe is laid-back, with surfing and yoga as top priorities for residents. Expect to see flip-flop-clad locals crossing the boulevard with surfboards in tow, and signs of historic California alive and well. Lining the main drag are plenty of cafés, bars, and restaurants to hold your attention, as well as the 1928 La Paloma Theater that still shows cult classics, foreign films, and music performances nightly.

GETTING HERE AND AROUND

From San Diego, head north on I–5. If you're already on the coast, drive along Route S21. Lodgings, restaurants, and the beach pop up along Route S21 (Old

Highway 101) west of the freeway. The San Diego Botanic Gardens lie to the east of the freeway.

👁 Sights

San Diego Botanic Gardens

GARDEN | FAMILY | More than 4,000 rare, exotic, and endangered plants are on display on 37 landscaped acres. Displays include plants from Central America, Africa, Australia, the Middle East, the Mediterranean, the Himalayas, Madagascar, and more; the most diverse collection of bamboo in North America; California native plants; and subtropical fruits. The park contains the largest interactive children's garden on the West Coast, where kids can roll around in the Seeds of Wonder garden, explore a baby dinosaur forest, discover a secret garden, or play in a playhouse. An Under the Sea Garden displays rocks and succulents that uncannily mimic an underwater environment. ⊠ *230 Quail Gardens Dr.* ☎ *760/436–3036* ⊕ *www.sdbgarden.org* ⊠ *$18.*

San Elijo Lagoon Conservancy

NATURE PRESERVE | FAMILY | Between Solana Beach and Encinitas, this is the most complex of the estuary systems in San Diego North County. A 7-mile network of trails surrounds the 979-acre reserve, where more than 700 species of plants, fish, and birds (many of them migratory) live. Be sure to stop by the San Elijo Lagoon Nature Centre. The center, open 9 to 5 daily, offers museum-quality exhibits about the region and a viewing deck overlooking the estuary. Docents offer free public walks every Saturday at 10 am. ⊠ *2710 Manchester Ave., Cardiff-by-the-Sea* ☎ *760/436–3944 conservancy, 760/634–3026 nature center* ⊕ *www.sanelijo.org* ⊠ *Free.*

Self-Realization Fellowship Temple
(*Self-Realization Gardens*)

RELIGIOUS SITE | Founded in 1920 as a retreat and place of worship, the center also offers one of the best views along the Pacific Coast, a sweeping seascape extending north and south as far as the eye can see. Paramahansa Yogananda, author of the classic *Autobiography of a Yogi,* created two beautiful meditation gardens that are open to the public. The gardens are planted with flowering shrubs and trees and contain a series of koi ponds connected by miniature waterfalls. Swami's Point at the south end of the gardens is a popular surfer's break. ⊠ *215 W. K St., between 2nd and 3rd Sts.* ✥ *Off 1150 S. Coast Hwy. 101* ☎ *760/753–5353* ⊕ *www.encinitastemple.org* ⊠ *Free* ☾ *Closed Mon.*

🏖 Beaches

Moonlight State Beach

BEACH—SIGHT | FAMILY | Its large parking areas, many facilities, and proximity to the quaint coastal town of Encinitas make this beach tucked into a break in the cliffs a great getaway; it's perfect for families with young kids. The volleyball courts on the northern end attract many competent players, and professionals can be spotted surfing the break known locally as "D Street." Moonlight is easily accessible from the Encinitas Coaster train station and Coast Highway 101, which runs right through town and is lined with great shops, restaurants, and bars; there's a large free parking lot near the corner of 3rd and B Street. **Amenities:** food and drink, lifeguards, parking (no fee), showers, toilets. **Best for:** sunset, surfing, swimming. ⊠ *399 C St.* ✥ *To get to beach from I–5, take Encinitas Blvd. west until it ends* ⊕ *www.parks.ca.gov.*

★ Swami's

BEACH—SIGHT | The palms and the golden lotus-flower domes of the nearby Self-Realization Fellowship temple and ashram earned this picturesque beach, also a top surfing spot (it's one of the few spots that can hold a massive winter swell), its name. Extreme low tides expose tide pools that harbor anemones, starfish, and other sea life. The only access is by a long stairway leading down from the cliff-top Swami's Seaside Park, where there's free parking. A shower is at the base of the steps. On big winter swells, the bluffs are lined with gawkers watching the area's best surfers take on—and be taken down by—some of the county's best big waves. The beach has flat, packed sand and can accumulate seaweed and some flies, so if laying out is your main objective you might want to head north to Moonlight Beach. Offshore, divers do their thing at North County's underwater park, Encinitas Marine Life Refuge. The small park next to the Swami's parking lot offers shade trees, picnic tables, barbecues, and clean bathrooms. Across the street is the cheerful Swami's Cafe, where surfers refuel postsurf. **Amenities:** lifeguards, parking (no fee), showers, toilets. **Best for:** snorkeling, surfing, swimming. ⊠ *1298 S. Coast Hwy. 101 (Rte. S21)* ⊹ *1 mile north of Cardiff.*

🍴 Restaurants

★ Fish 101

$ | SEAFOOD | The line out the door—especially during happy hour—is a clear sign you're at the best place in North County to find locally sourced, sustainably caught fish at a great price. Owned by surfers-divers-fishermen, John Park and Ray Lowe, the vibe is SoCal at its best, with a chill staff serving fresh-shucked oysters, thick clam chowder, and fish sandwiches grilled to perfection; a chalkboard menu displays the day's catch and what's been shucked on ice. **Known for:** happy hour with $1 oysters, $3 tacos, and $4 beers; fresh and healthy seafood; seasonal, sustainable ingredients. $ *Average main: $13* ⊠ *1468 N. Coast Hwy. 101* ☏ *760/943–6221* ⊕ *fish101restaurant.com* ☾ *Closed Mon.*

Ki's Restaurant

$$ | VEGETARIAN | Veggies with a view could be the subtitle for this venerable Cardiff-by-the-Sea restaurant that grew from a simple juice shack. Ki's is well known for heart-healthy, gluten-free, vegan, locally sourced, ovo-lacto, vegetarian-friendly dishes like huevos rancheros, filling tofu scrambles, taco plates, chopped salads with feta and nuts, watermelon juice, and carrot ice-cream smoothies. **Known for:** healthy vegan and gluten-free menu; yummy Asian-inspired dishes; popular post-surfing spot across from the beach. $ *Average main: $20* ⊠ *2591 S. Coast Hwy. 101, North County* ☏ *760/436–5236* ⊕ *www.kisrestaurant.com.*

Las Olas

$ | MEXICAN | FAMILY | One of the best oceanfront Mexican restaurants in North County, Las Olas is right across the street from the beach at Cardiff. Grab a margarita or some fish tacos before heading off to view surfers awaiting their next wave. **Known for:** fish tacos; authentic Mexican food; local craft beers. $ *Average main: $10* ⊠ *2655 S. Coast Hwy. 101, Cardiff-by-the-Sea* ☏ *760/942–1860* ⊕ *www.lasolasmex.com* ▭ *No credit cards.*

Pacific Coast Grill

$$$$ | SEAFOOD | This casual beachy-style eatery offers sweeping ocean views and seasonal Pacific Coast fare that reflects California's Mexican and Asian influences with dishes like lobster tacos and kung pao shrimp. Evenings are a scene, as attractive beachy types sip microbrews and well-priced wines along with morsels from the sushi bar; lunch in the spacious dining room or on the dog-friendly sunny patio brings sashimi ahi salad with greens, seaweed, and mango, or plum-ginger–braised short ribs washed down with a margarita that sings with fresh lime and lemon juice. **Known for:** romantic waterfront dining; fresh oysters, sushi rolls, and black mussels; stunning sunsets; rich lobster carbonara. $ *Average main: $37* ⊠ *2526 S. Hwy. 1010, Cardiff-by-the-Sea* ☏ *760/479–0721* ⊕ *www.pacificcoastgrill.com.*

Solace & The Moonlight Lounge

$$ | AMERICAN | The modern American cuisine, patio overlooking historic Highway 101, and industrial setting—garage doors that retract on sunny days and exposed spiral ductwork— at this downtown Encinitas restaurant draws a beach-fresh clientele. Cocktails like the grapefruit mule pair well with the warm cheddar-and-chive biscuit topped with orange honey butter, or the $1 oysters served daily 3–6. **Known for:** weekend brunch and live music on Sunday night; stellar vegetarian options; cocktails and $1 oysters. $ *Average main: $24* ⌧ *25 East E St.* ☎ *760/753–2433* ⊕ *www.eatatsolace.com.*

Activities

GOLF
Encinitas Ranch Golf Course

GOLF | See the Pacific Ocean from virtually every vantage point at this course on bluffs in North County. Local golfers love it because low scores aren't that hard to come by. It's a forgiving course with wide-open fairways. Encinitas Ranch also has a 6,000-square-foot clubhouse with a bar and café. The adjoining patio has a stone fireplace and great ocean views. ⌧ *1275 Quail Gardens Dr.* ☎ *760/944–1936* ⊕ *www.jcgolf.com* ⌧ *$82 Mon.–Thurs., $88 Fri., $104 weekends (cart included)* ⅄ *18 holes, 6587 yards, par 72.*

Shopping

Souvenir items are sold at shops along South Coast Highway 101 and in the Lumberyard Shopping Center.

Encinitas Seaside Bazaar

OUTDOOR/FLEA/GREEN MARKETS | For art, clothing, jewelry, antiques, and leather goods, this open-air craft market on Highway 101 has more than 30 booths selling quirky crafts at reasonable prices. It's open weekends 9–5. ⌧ *459 S. Coast Hwy. 101* ☎ *760/753–1611* ⊕ *www.seasidebazaar.co* ⊗ *Closed weekdays.*

Hansen's

SPORTING GOODS | One of San Diego's oldest surfboard manufacturers is owned by Don Hansen, surfboard shaper extraordinaire, who came here from Hawaii in 1962. The store stocks a full line of surf, snowboard, and ski gear and apparel. They also have entire departments dedicated to wet suits and footwear. ⌧ *1105 S. Coast Hwy. 101* ☎ *800/480–4754, 760/753–6596* ⊕ *www.hansensurf.com.*

Carlsbad

6 miles from Encinitas on Rte. S21, 36 miles north of Downtown San Diego on I–5.

Once-sleepy Carlsbad, lying astride I–5 at the north end of a string of beach towns extending from San Diego to Oceanside, has long been popular with beachgoers and sunseekers. On a clear day in this village you can take in sweeping ocean views that stretch from La Jolla to Oceanside by walking the 2-mile-long sea walk running between the Encina Power Station and Pine Street. En route, you can get closer to the water via several stairways leading to the beach; quite a few benches are here as well.

East of I–5 is LEGOLAND California and other attractions like two of the San Diego area's most luxurious resort hotels, one of the last remaining wetlands along the Southern California coast, a discount shopping mall, golf courses, the cattle ranch built by movie star Leo Carrillo, and colorful spring-blooming Flower Fields at Carlsbad Ranch. Until the mid-20th century, when suburban development began to sprout on the hillsides, farming was the main industry in Carlsbad, with truckloads of vegetables shipped out year-round. Some agriculture remains. Area farmers develop and grow new varieties of flowers, including the ranunculus that transform a hillside into a rainbow each spring. Carlsbad strawberries are among the sweetest in Southern California; in spring you can pick them yourself in fields on both sides of I–5.

GETTING HERE AND AROUND

LEGOLAND California Resort, off Cannon Road east of I–5, is surrounded by the Flower Fields, hotels, and the Museum of Making Music. On the west side of the freeway is beach access at several points and quaint Carlsbad village shops.

ESSENTIALS

VISITOR INFORMATION Carlsbad Visitors Center. ✉ *400 Carlsbad Village Dr.* ☎ *760/434–6093, 800/227–5722* ⊕ *www.visitcarlsbad.com.*

 Sights

Batiquitos Lagoon

NATURE PRESERVE | While development destroyed many of the saltwater marsh wildlife habitats that once punctuated the North County coastline, this 610-acre lagoon was restored in 1997 to support fish and bird populations. Today, there are 200 species of birds here. A stroll along the 2-mile trail from the Batiquitos Lagoon Foundation Nature Center along the north shore of the lagoon reveals nesting sites of the red-winged blackbird; lagoon birds such as the great blue heron, the great egret, and the snowy egret; and life in the mud flats. This wheelchair-accessible trail is a quiet spot for contemplation or a picnic. ✉ *7380 Gabbiano La.* ✛ *Take Poinsettia La. exit off I–5, go east, and turn right onto Batiquitos Dr., then right again onto Gabbiano La.* ☎ *760/931–0800* ⊕ *www.batiquitos-foundation.org.*

★ Flower Fields at Carlsbad Ranch

GARDEN | **FAMILY** | The largest bulb-production farm in Southern California has hillsides abloom here each spring, when thousands of Giant Tecolote ranunculus produce a stunning 50-acre display of color against the backdrop of the blue Pacific Ocean. Other knockouts include the rose gardens—with examples of

every All-American Rose Selection award-winner since 1940—and a historical display of Paul Ecke poinsettias. Peak flower season is mid-March through mid-April. Open to the public during this time, the farm offers family activities that include wagon rides, panning for gold, and a kids' playground. ✉ *5704 Paseo del Norte, east of I–5* ☎ *760/431–0352* ⊕ *www.theflowerfields.com* 🎫 *$18* ☾ *Closed mid-May–Feb.*

★ LEGOLAND California Resort

AMUSEMENT PARK/WATER PARK | **FAMILY** | The centerpiece of a development that includes resort hotels, a designer discount shopping mall, an aquarium, and a water park, LEGOLAND has rides and diversions geared to kids ages 2 to 12. Fans of *Star Wars*, and building Legos in general, should head straight to *Star Wars* **Miniland,** where you can follow the exploits of Yoda, Princess Leia, Obi-Wan, Anakin, R2, Luke, and the denizens of the *Star Wars* films. There's also **Miniland U.S.A.**, which features a miniature, animated, interactive collection of U.S. icons that were constructed out of 34 million LEGO bricks! **LEGO Heartlake City,**

features LEGO Friends and Elves, and you can test your ninja skills in **LEGO NINJAGO WORLD**.

If you're looking for rides, **NINJAGO The Ride** uses hand gesture technology to throw fireballs, shock waves, ice, and lightning to defeat villains in this interactive 4-D experience. Journey through ancient Egyptian ruins in a desert roadster, scoring points as you hit targets with a laser blaster at **Lost Kingdom Adventure.** Or, jump on the **Dragon Coaster,** an indoor/outdoor steel roller coaster that goes through a castle. Don't let the name frighten you—the motif is more humorous than scary. Kids ages 6 to 13 can stop by the **Driving School** to drive speed-controlled cars (not on rails) on a miniature road; driver's licenses are awarded after the course. Junior Driving School is the pint-size version for kids 3 to 5.

Bring bathing suits—there are lockers at the entrance and at Pirate Shores—if you plan to go to **Soak-N-Sail**, which has 60 interactive features, including a pirate shipwreck–theme area. You'll also need your swimsuit for **LEGOLAND Water Park,** where an additional $30 gives you access to slides, rides, rafts, and the CHIMA Water Park, as well as Surfer's Bay with competitive water raceways and a "spray ground" with water jets.

Be sure to try Granny's Apple Fries, Castle Burgers, and Pizza Mania for pizzas and salads. The Market near the entrance has excellent coffee, fresh fruit, and yogurt. The LEGOLAND Hotel is worth a visit even if you're not staying overnight. There are activities and a LEGO pit in the lobby that will entertain kids while parents recover with a cocktail. ■TIP→ **The best value is one of the Hopper Tickets that give you one admission to LEGOLAND plus Sea Life Aquarium and/or the LEGOLAND Water Park for $119. These can be used on the same day or on different days. Purchase tickets online for discounted pricing. Go midweek to avoid the crowds.** ⊠ 1

Legoland Dr. ⊕ Exit I–5 at Cannon Rd. and follow signs east ¼ mile ☎ 760/918–5346 ⊕ www.legoland.com/california ⊠ LEGOLAND $103 adults, $89 children; parking $20; water park additional $30; hopper ticket $119 ⊙ Closed Tues. and Wed. Sept.–Feb.

Leo Carrillo Ranch Historic Park

HISTORIC SITE | This was a real working ranch with 600 head of cattle owned by actor Leo Carrillo, who played Pancho in the *Cisco Kid* television series in the 1950s. Before Carrillo bought the spread, known as Rancho de Los Kiotes, in 1937, the rancho was the home of a band of Luiseno Indians. Carrillo's hacienda and other buildings have been restored to reflect the life of the star when he hosted his Hollywood friends for long weekends in the country. Four miles of trails take visitors through colorful native gardens to the cantina, washhouse, pool and cabana, barn, and stable that Carrillo used. You can tour these buildings on weekends when guided tours are offered twice daily. After Carrillo's death in 1961, the ranch remained in the family until 1979, when part of the acreage was acquired by the city for a park. ⊠ 6200 Flying Leo Carrillo La. ☎ 760/476–1042 ⊕ www.carrillo-ranch.org ⊠ Free ⊙ Closed Mon. ☞ Guided tours Sat. 11 am and 1 pm; Sun. noon and 2 pm.

Museum of Making Music

MUSEUM | FAMILY | Take an interactive journey through 100 years of popular music with displays of more than 500 vintage instruments and samples of memorable tunes from the past century. Hands-on activities include playing a digital piano, drums, guitar, and more. ⊠ 5790 Armada Dr., east of I–5 ☎ 760/438—5996 ⊕ www.museumofmakingmusic.org ⊠ $10 ⊙ Closed Mon.

Sea Life Aquarium

AMUSEMENT PARK/WATER PARK | FAMILY | Offering an educational and interactive underwater experience, the walk-through exhibits focus on creatures found in

The spring blooms at the Flower Fields at Carlsbad Ranch are not to be missed.

local waters including California lakes and streams and the cold water marine animals that live along the California coast. Other exhibits include an underwater acrylic tunnel that affords a deep sea (but dry) look at sharks, fish, and invertebrates. There's a seahorse kingdom, interactive tide pools, jelly fish discovery, and a chance for kids to build a LEGO coral reef. This park has a separate admission from LEGOLAND, although two-day tickets including both venues are available. ⊠ *1 LEGOLAND Dr.* ☏ *760/918–5346* ⊕ *www.visitsealife. com/california* 🎟 *$22* ☞ *Strollers not permitted June–Aug.*

🏊 Beaches

South Carlsbad State Beach/Carlsbad State Beach

BEACH—SIGHT | There are fine street- and beach-level promenades at Carlsbad State Beach, where people come to surf and swim at Ponto and Tamarack beaches. On the bluff, there's overnight camping for self-contained RVs

(*800/444–7275*) and tents (from $35). Farther north at the foot of Tamarack Avenue is Carlsbad State Beach. You can't camp here, but there's fishing and jogging trails and the beach has separate swimming and surfing sections. In summer, the south swell creates good surf when other San Diego beaches are bereft. The cement walkway that borders the beach continues into downtown Carlsbad, which has plenty of restaurants. Carlsbad State Beach has a paid parking lot on Tamarack Avenue and at South Ponto. **Amenities:** lifeguards, parking (fee), showers, toilets. **Best for:** walking, swimming, surfing. ⊠ *South Carlsbad Beach, 7201 Carlsbad Blvd., Carlsbad Beach; Tamarack Ave. at Carlsbad Blvd.* ☏ *760/438-3143* ⊕ *www.parks.ca.gov* 🎟 *$15 per vehicle.*

🍴 Restaurants

★ Campfire

$$ | **BARBECUE** | Paying tribute to community around the campfire, it's all about connecting here, both with the cool crowd and with the distinctive cocktail and dinner menus. Throughout the restaurant, subtle hints of the camping theme—canvas-backed booths, servers in flannels, leather menus branded with the Campfire log—are visible, but it's the food that will leave you setting up camp, as chefs work their magic behind glass walls grilling, roasting, and smoking almost every dish including the shrimp with pumpkin chili butter. **Known for:** smoky cocktails; wood-fired American fare. $ *Average main: $23* ✉ *2725 State St.* ☎ *760/637–5121* ⊕ *www.thisiscampfire.com* ☾ *No lunch Mon.*

Vigilucci's Cucina Italiana

$$$ | **ITALIAN** | Restaurateur Roberto Vigilucci's fell in love with San Diego in the '80s and decided to bring Milan to North County with four eateries that are fine-dining experiences without the stuffiness. While each has its own character, Vigilucci's on historic State Street has an authenticity that's hard to beat, right down to its street-side patio, bustling servers with thick Italian accents, and wine list that will leave you appreciating "la bella vita." Roasted artichokes are blanketed in melted mozzarella, and paper-thin Carpaccio is topped with a mound of peppery arugula. **Known for:** classic Italian menu; live music on the outdoor patio; extensive wine list. $ *Average main: $31* ✉ *2943 State St., Carlsbad* ☎ *760/434–2500* ⊕ *www.vigiluccis.com.*

🛏 Hotels

★ Beach Terrace Inn

$$$ | **HOTEL** | One of only four SoCal hotels directly on the sand, this former 1960s Best Western was remodeled in 2011 as a boutique inn with plantation shutters, luxurious linens, and open floor plans. **Pros:** direct beach access; no resort fees; enormous rooms. **Cons:** lots of stairs; no kitchenettes; no restaurant or bar. $ *Rooms from: $269* ✉ *2775 Ocean St.* ☎ *760/729–5951* ⊕ *www.*

beachterraceinn.com ⇨ *48 rooms* ⦿ *Free Breakfast.*

Cape Rey Carlsbad

$$ | **HOTEL** | **FAMILY** | Sea and sand loom large at this Hilton property, where the fitness center has an ocean view and guest rooms have sitting areas so you can easily enjoy the sea views and breezes when you're not exploring South Carlsbad State Park nearby. **Pros:** afternoon coastal breezes; 150 steps from the beach; shuttle service to nearby sites. **Cons:** on main highway; resort fee $25; some rooms face the parking lot. $ *Rooms from: $229* ✉ *1 Ponto Rd.* ☎ *760/602–0800* ⊕ *www.caperey.com* ⇨ *215 rooms* ⦿ *No meals.*

Carlsbad Inn Beach Resort

$$$ | **HOTEL** | **FAMILY** | On the main drag and with direct access to the beach, this sprawling inn and time-share condominium complex is popular with families and has a variety of rooms, ranging from cramped to large, including many with ocean views, balconies, and kitchenettes, and some with fireplaces and Jacuzzis. **Pros:** on the beach; walking distance to shops and restaurants; warm ambience. **Cons:** lots of kids; can be noisy; tiny pool. $ *Rooms from: $269* ✉ *3075 Carlsbad Blvd.* ☎ *760/434–7020, 800/235–3939* ⊕ *www.carlsbadinn.com* ⇨ *61 rooms* ⦿ *No meals.*

LEGOLAND Hotel

$$ | **HOTEL** | **FAMILY** | This is the place for the family that eats, sleeps, and lives LEGOS; check out the neighboring Castle Hotel with rooms themed around knights, dragons, wizards, and royal princesses. **Pros:** guests get early admission to the park; dive-in movies at the pool; tempting hands-on activities throughout the hotel. **Cons:** frequently sells out; no romance here; small rooms. $ *Rooms from: $179* ✉ *5885 The Crossings Dr.* ☎ *888/690–5346* ⊕ *www.legoland.com/california* ⇨ *250 rooms* ⦿ *Free Breakfast.*

LEGOLAND California's Miniland U.S.A. has scenes from San Francisco, Washington, D.C., New Orleans, New York, and Las Vegas.

★ Ocean Palms Beach Resort

$$ | **HOTEL** | **FAMILY** | Just 40 steps from the sand, bring your kids (furry or not) to this delightful pet- and family-friendly hotel where the staff go out of their way to please guests. **Pros:** no resort fees; helpful staff; full kitchens; near shops and restaurants. **Cons:** some rooms face the street; inconsistent Wi-Fi in some rooms; no refunds on cancelled reservations. [$] *Rooms from: $169* ✉ *2950 Ocean St.* ☎ *760/729–2493* 🌐 *www.oceanpalms.com* 🛏 *52 rooms* 🍴 *Free Breakfast.*

Omni La Costa Resort & Spa

$$$$ | **RESORT** | **FAMILY** | This chic Spanish colonial oasis on 400 tree-shaded acres has ample guest rooms, two golf courses, and is known for being family-friendly, with plenty of kids' activities (including a kids' club, a game room, eight swimming pools, three waterslides, and a water play zone). **Pros:** adult-only pool; excellent kids' facilities; spa under the stars. **Cons:** very spread out, making long walks necessary; lots of kids; $33 daily resort fee; self parking $24. [$] *Rooms from: $349* ✉ *2100 Costa del Mar Rd.* ☎ *760/438–9111, 800/439–9111* 🌐 *www.lacosta.com* 🛏 *650 rooms* 🍴 *No meals.*

★ Park Hyatt Aviara Resort

$$$$ | **RESORT** | **FAMILY** | This retreat is one of the most luxurious hotels in San Diego, boasting an Arnold Palmer–designed golf course, a tennis club, two pools, six restaurants, and views overlooking Batiquitos Lagoon and the Pacific among its 250 acres. **Pros:** unbeatable location; best golf course in San Diego; surrounding nature trails. **Cons:** $25 resort fee and $35 parking; expensive; breakfast not included. [$] *Rooms from: $309* ✉ *7100 Aviara Resort Dr.* ☎ *800/233–1234, 760/448–1234* 🌐 *www.parkhyattaviara.com* 🕒 *Greens fee $255; 18 holes, 7007 yards, par 72* 🛏 *327 rooms* 🍴 *No meals.*

Pelican Cove Inn

$ | **B&B/INN** | Close to the beach and surrounded by palm trees and mature colorful gardens with secluded nooks, this two-story B&B has spacious rooms with gas fireplaces, canopied feather beds, and private entrances. **Pros:** welcoming host; attractive rooms; electric car charger. **Cons:** limited facilities; no a/c; often booked. $ *Rooms from: $160* ✉ *320 Walnut Ave.* ☎ *888/735–2683, 760/434–5995* 🌐 *www.pelican-cove.com* 🛏 *10 rooms* 🍴 *Free Breakfast.*

West Inn and Suites

$$ | B&B/INN | FAMILY | Coastal luxury meets Cape Cod practicality at this warm and friendly inn near the beach. **Pros:** full buffet breakfast; great service; guest shuttle service for Carlsbad area; near beaches. **Cons:** adjacent to railroad tracks and freeway; no water views; no in-room dining. $ *Rooms from: $189* ✉ *4970 Av. Encinas* ☎ *760/448–4500, 866/431–9378* 🌐 *www.westinnandsuites.com* 🛏 *86 rooms* 🍴 *Free Breakfast.*

Activities

GOLF

Omni La Costa Resort and Spa

GOLF | One of the premier golf resorts in Southern California, La Costa over the years has hosted many of the best professional golfers in the world as well as prominent politicians and Hollywood celebrities. The Dick Wilson–designed Champions course has Bermuda fairways and bunkers. The more spacious Legends Course has wide, paspalum-grass fairways and a challenging par-4 15th hole with tough shots around wetlands. After a day on the links you can wind down with a massage, steam bath, and dinner at the resort. ✉ *2100 Costa del Mar Rd.* ☎ *760/438–9111* 🌐 *www.omnihotels.com* 🎟 *$155 Mon.–Thurs., $175 Fri.–Sun.* ⛳ *Champions: 18 holes, 6747 yards, par 72. Legends: 18 holes, 6587 yards, par 72.*

★ Park Hyatt Aviara Golf Club

GOLF | This golf course consistently ranks as one of the best in California and is the only course in San Diego designed by Arnold Palmer. The course features gently rolling hills dotted with native wildflowers and views of the protected adjacent Batiquitos Lagoon and the Pacific Ocean. There are plenty of bunkers and water features for those looking for a challenge, and the golf carts, included in the cost, come fitted with GPS systems that tell you the distance to the pin. The two-story Spanish colonial clubhouse has full-size lockers, lounge areas, a bar, and a steak house. ✉ *7447 Batiquitos Dr.* ☎ *760/603–6900* 🌐 *www.golfaviara.com* 🎟 *$240 Mon.–Thurs., $260 Fri.–Sun.* ⛳ *18 holes, 7007 yards, par 72.*

WATER SPORTS

California Watersports

JET SKIING | FAMILY | Waveless Carlsbad Lagoon, east of the intersection of Tamarack Avenue and I–5, is easy to reach from this water recreation center, which has a private beach and landing ramp. You can rent ski boats, WaveRunners, Jet Skis, canoes, aqua cycles, and stand-up paddleboards. ✉ *4215 Harrison St.* ☎ *760/434–3089* 🌐 *www.carlsbadlagoon.com* 🎟 *From $20.*

Shopping

The Big Shop (☎ *760/918–5346*) at LEGOLAND is great for collectors and collectors-in-training, with the largest selection of LEGO sets in the nation. ⇨ *For more information about LEGOLAND, see the Carlsbad Sights section.*

Aviara Spa

SPA/BEAUTY | With its soothing sauna, steam room, Jacuzzi, and relaxation lounge, simple elegance defines the spa at Park Hyatt Aviara. Signature treatments include the couple's massage with champagne and chocolate-covered strawberries, and Nurture at the Park—a holistic therapy including a scrub, foot treatment, scalp ritual, and massage. The five-hour Ultimate Escape for two, with a massage, scrub, facial, and lunch, goes for $1,200. Guests of the resort can use spa facilities for $30; all others must book a treatment. ✉ *7100 Aviara Resort*

Dr. ☎ 760/603–6902 ⊕ www.golfaviara. com/spa ⚲ Spa day pass $30; massages and facials from $85.

Carlsbad Premium Outlets
OUTLET/DISCOUNT STORES | FAMILY | This outdoor shopping center contains more than 90 outlet stores, including designer brands like Barneys New York, Coach, Kate Spade, Michael Kors, and Nike. ⊠ *5620 Paseo Del Norte* ☎ *760/804– 9000, 888/790–7467* ⊕ *www.premiu- moutlets.com/carlsbad.*

Oceanside

8 miles north of Carlsbad on Rte. S21, 37 miles north of Downtown San Diego on I–5.

The beach culture is alive and well in Oceanside with surf shops, casual restaurants, museums, and a boardwalk that leads to the pier and harbor where surfers line up to catch the next wave. Numerous hotels are within walking distance of the city's best swimming and surfing beaches: Harbor Beach, brimming with beach activities and fun, and Buccaneer Beach, home to some of the best surfing in North County. And Camp Pendleton, the sprawling U.S. Marine base, lies at the north end of the city. ■**TIP→ If you'd like to see the base, visitors must be sponsored and vetted, with forms filled out four days in advance.**

Oceanside is also home to Mission San Luis Rey, the largest and one of the best-preserved California missions. The town's history extends back to the 1700s, when the Spanish friars walked along the California coast founding missions as they went. Today it celebrates its historic culture with the regionally exciting Oceanside Museum of Art, which displays the works of San Diego area artists. Residents and visitors gather weekly at the farmers' market and Sunset Market on Main Street, where

shopping for fresh-picked produce is a pleasant pastime.

GETTING HERE AND AROUND
The northernmost of the beach towns, Oceanside, lies 8 miles north of Carlsbad via I–5; exit the freeway on Mission Avenue. If you go west, you'll come to the redeveloped downtown and harbor where you'll find most of the restaurants, lodgings, and attractions. Downtown Oceanside is quite walkable from the Transportation Center, where Amtrak, the Coaster, and Sprinter stop. Buses and taxis are also available at the Transportation Center.

ESSENTIALS
VISITOR INFORMATION California Welcome Center, Oceanside. ⊠ *928 N. Coast Hwy., Suite A* ☎ *760/721–1101, 800/350– 7873* ⊕ *www.visitoceanside.org.*

◉ Sights

California Surf Museum
MUSEUM | A large collection of surfing memorabilia, going back to the earliest days of the sport, is on display here, along with old black-and-white photos, vintage boards, apparel, and accessories. ⊠ *312 Pier View Way* ☎ *760/721–6876* ⊕ *www.surfmuseum.org* ⚲ *$5; 1st Tues. of month $1.*

Oceanside Harbor
MARINA | With 1,000 slips, this is North County's fishing, sailing, and water-sports center. On the south end of the harbor, the Oceanside Harbor Village has oyster bars, fish-and-chip shops, and an ice cream parlor where you can linger and watch the boats coming and going. If you fancy a day at sea, Helgren's Sportfishing can arrange whale-watching and harbor tours. ⊠ *1540 Harbor Dr. N* ☎ *760/435– 4000* ⊕ *www.oceansideharborvillage. com.*

Oceanside Museum of Art
MUSEUM | Housed in side-by-side buildings designed by two Southern California

modernist architects—Irving Gill and Frederick Fisher—the museum showcases contemporary art exhibitions including paintings, photography, sculptures, furniture, quilts, and architectural glass by San Diego area artists. ✉ *704 Pier View Way* ☎ *760/435–3720* 🌐 *www.oma-online.org* 🎟 *$8; free 1st Sun. of every month* 🕒 *Closed Mon.*

Oceanside Pier

MARINA | At 1,954 feet, this is one of the longest piers on the West Coast. The water surrounding it is known for its surf breaks and good fishing. A restaurant, Ruby's Diner, stands at the end of the wooden pier's long promenade. ✉ *Pier View Way.*

★ Old Mission San Luis Rey

RELIGIOUS SITE | **FAMILY** | Known as the King of the Missions, the 18th, the largest, and the most prosperous of California's missions was built in 1798 by Franciscan friars under the direction of Father Fermin Lasuen to help educate and convert local Native Americans. The *sala* (parlor), the kitchen, a friar's bedroom, a weaving room, and a collection of religious art and old Spanish vestments convey much about early mission life. A special behind-the-scenes tour starts at 1 pm on Saturday and Sunday, and Mass is held at noon weekdays. ✉ *4050 Mission Ave.* ☎ *760/757–3651* 🌐 *www.sanluisrey.org* 🎟 *$7.*

Beaches

Oceanside City Beach

BEACH—SIGHT | This long, straight beach is popular with swimmers, surfers, and U.S. Marines from nearby Camp Pendleton. The impressive wooden Oceanside Pier extends a quarter of a mile into the ocean, and there's a '50s-style diner called Ruby's at the end. The sand here is a bit coarse, and smaller rocks can be found in some sections, but due to its width (a quarter mile from street to surf near 1200 N. Pacific Street) nice patches can almost always be found. There is surfing around the pier, but the waves are faster and usually better just north at Oceanside Harbor, which gets a south swell in the summer. Pay lots and meters are located around the pier and also in the Oceanside Harbor area. A free two-hour lot can be found east of the pay lots on Harbor Drive South. There are plenty of shops and restaurants along Oceanside Harbor Village. Families love the kid-friendly Buccaneer Beach, just south of the pier across from Buccaneer Beach Park. This area has free parking, a café, restrooms, showers, and lifeguards on duty in summer. **Amenities:** seasonal lifeguards, food and drink, parking (fee), toilets, showers. **Best for:** surfing, swimming, walking. ✉ *200 N. the Strand* 🎟 *$5 parking.*

Restaurants

★ Flying Pig Pub & Kitchen

$$ | **AMERICAN** | **FAMILY** | This meat-focused eatery fills bellies with farm-to-table artisanal cuisine like braised octopus, bacon mac-and-cheese, and a 12-ounce pork chop topped with apple-raisin chutney and served over house grits. Add a sunny-side-up farm egg to your burger, chop, shank, or house-made pasta, and if you're into sauces, chef is on-point with lick-your-plate gravies based with garlic, onions, and herbs. **Known for:** rustic American cuisine; craft beers on tap; house-made pasta, bread, and bacon; natural prime-grade steaks seared in cast-iron skillet. [$] *Average main: $18* ✉ *626 S. Tremont St.* ☎ *760/453–2940* 🌐 *flyingpig.pub* 🕒 *No breakfast or lunch.*

Harbor Fish & Chips

$ | **SEAFOOD** | Pick up a basket of fresh-cooked fish-and-chips at this dive and you're in for a treat. The shop has been serving clam chowder, shrimp cocktail, and fish sandwiches since 1969. **Known for:** crunchy, battered fish tacos piled high with coleslaw and secret sauce; great prices; affordable daily specials.

$ *Average main: $12* ✉ *276 S. Harbor Dr.* ☎ *760/722–4977* ⊕ *www.harborfishand-chips.net.*

Hello Betty Fish House

$ | SEAFOOD | FAMILY | Overlooking the water in Oceanside, this beachside restaurant serves oysters, clam chowder, fish tacos, and several fresh catch options, which can be enjoyed from their rooftop lounge. **Known for:** classic Baja SoCal food like margaritas and fish tacos; rooftop deck; Taco Tuesday 3–6 pm. $ *Average main: $17* ✉ *211 Mission Ave.* ☎ *760/722–1008* ⊕ *hellobettyoceanside.com.*

101 Cafe

$ | AMERICAN | FAMILY | A diner dating back to 1928 is both a local hangout and the headquarters of the historic Highway 101 movement. Find all kinds of Highway 101 memorabilia here along with old-school ambience, prompt service, and great prices. **Known for:** headquarters of the historic Highway 101 movement; all-day breakfast; thick milkshakes. $ *Average main: $12* ✉ *631 S. Coast Hwy.* ☎ *760/722–5220* ⊕ *www.101cafe.net.*

333 Pacific

$$$ | SEAFOOD | Directly across from Oceanside Pier, Oceanside's most upscale restaurant specializes in seafood dishes and upscale comfort food in an elegant, art-deco setting; it's worth visiting for the ocean views and appetizers and sides like charred Brussels sprouts and lamb lollipops. If you're thirsty, start with a drink from the menu of more than 120 vodkas that make up exotic cocktails like the Spicy Pineapple, Pear Blossom, and Cali Mango. **Known for:** martinis; weekly dinner specials; ocean views. $ *Average main: $35* ✉ *333 N. Pacific St.* ☎ *760/433–3333* ⊕ *www.333pacific.com* ☽ *No lunch Mon.–Thurs.*

🛏 Hotels

★ Courtyard Marriott Oceanside

$ | HOTEL | Close proximity to the beach and train, coupled with plenty of modern amenities, make this SoCal-style Marriott Oceanside's best lodging. **Pros:** convenient location; two wheelchair-accessible rooms; helpful and friendly staff. **Cons:** breakfast not included; no ocean views; a drive to the beach. $ *Rooms from: $139* ✉ *3501 Seagate Way* ☎ *760/966–1000* ⊕ *www.courtyardoceanside.com* ⤺ *142 rooms* ⊖ *No meals.*

🏃 Activities

HIKING
San Luis Rey River Trail

BICYCLING | Paralleling the San Luis Rey River, this 7.2-mile (one-way) paved trail starts in Oceanside and ends at the beach near the Harbor. Void of traffic lights and motorized traffic, the path is relatively flat and is a fun way to reach the coast for bikers, walkers, and in-line skaters. ✉ *North Santa Fe Ave. and Hwy. 76.*

FISHING
Helgren's Sportfishing

FISHING | Your best bet in North County, Helgren's offers fishing and whale-watching trips from Oceanside Harbor. ✉ *1395 1/2 North Harbor Dr.* ☎ *760/722–2133* ⊕ *www.helgrensportfishing.com* ☽ *From $40.*

SURFING
San Diego Surfing Academy

SURFING | Choose from private and group lessons and customizable surf camps for teens, kids, adults, and families. Instructional videos are also available online. The academy, which has been running since 1995, is based near Oceanside Harbor and meets for lessons near Tower 10. Students are given a keepsake GoPro video of their surf lesson. Owner Pat Weber is known throughout the community for his dedication to coaching top contenders in the World Adaptive Surfing Championships. ⊠ *Oceanside* ⚓ *Near Oceanside Harbor at Tower 10* ☎ *760/230–1474, 800/447–7873* ⊕ *www.sandiegosurfingacademy.com* 💲 *From $90.*

🛍 Shopping

Sunset Market

OUTDOOR/FLEA/GREEN MARKETS | Every Thursday night 5–9 pm, Oceanside's Main Street comes alive with food stalls, a farmers' market, live music, and an arts and crafts fair. ⊠ *316 Mission Ave.* ⚓ *Corner of Pier View Way and S. Tremont St.* ☎ *760/754–4512* ⊕ *www.mainstreetoceanside.com.*

Rancho Bernardo

23 miles northeast of Downtown San Diego on I–15.

Rancho Bernardo straddles a stretch of I–15 between San Diego and Escondido and is technically a neighborhood of San Diego. Originally sheep- and cattle-grazing land, it was transformed in the early 1960s into a planned suburban community, one of the first, and a place where many wealthy retirees settled down. It's now home to a number of high-tech companies, the most notable of which is Sony. If you want to spend some time at the nearby San Diego Zoo Safari Park, this community, home of the Rancho Bernardo resort, makes a convenient and comfortable headquarters for a multiday visit.

🍴 Restaurants

★ AVANT

$$$ | **AMERICAN** | The appropriately named AVANT—meaning stylistically advanced and original—delivers contemporary California cuisine—duck, lobster, lamb, fish, or the pride of AVANT, Snake River Farms Wagyu beef—in an upscale setting. Dark

woods, leather chairs, and pillar-candle chandeliers adorn the mission-style dining room, and the upper-level bar shakes up handcrafted pear martinis and margaritas with their own double-barrel reposado tequila. **Known for:** local, sustainable, and seasonal ingredients; their own double-barrel reposado tequila; live music Friday and Saturday nights. 💲 *Average main: $35* ⊠ *Rancho Bernardo Inn, 17550 Bernardo Oaks Dr.* ☎ *866/990–6845* ⊕ *www.avantrestaurant.com* 🕐 *No breakfast or lunch.*

The Barrel Room

$$ | **EUROPEAN** | A refined wine bar ambience and a European-inspired menu set the tone for the unpretentious creations of chef Trevor Chappell. Shareable plates and innovative sides complement an impressive new-world wine list that includes more than 250 blends, plus four of their own beers on tap from Mason Ale Works. **Known for:** wine-tasting events second Saturday of month; plates to share; Sunday brunch. 💲 *Average main: $24* ⊠ *The Plaza, 16765 Bernardo Center Dr.* ☎ *858/673–7512* ⊕ *www.tbrsd.com.*

🛏 Hotels

Rancho Bernardo Inn

$$$ | **RESORT** | **FAMILY** | The gorgeous, flower-decked 265-acre grounds draw a sophisticated clientele looking for a golf and spa getaway. **Pros:** excellent service; popular golf course; website offers great packages and specials. **Cons:** walking required in spacious grounds; sections of hotel are showing signs of age; $60 day use of spa amenities. 💲 *Rooms from: $289* ⊠ *17550 Bernardo Oaks Dr.* ☎ *858/675–8500, 888/476–4417* ⊕ *www.ranchobernardoinn.com* 🏌 *Greens fee $103; 18 holes, 6631 yards, par 72* 🛏 *287 rooms* 🍽 *No meals.*

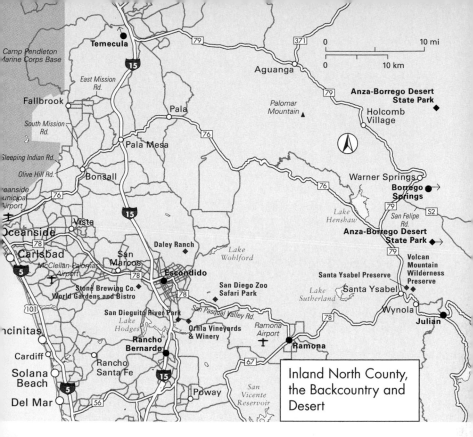

Inland North County, the Backcountry and Desert

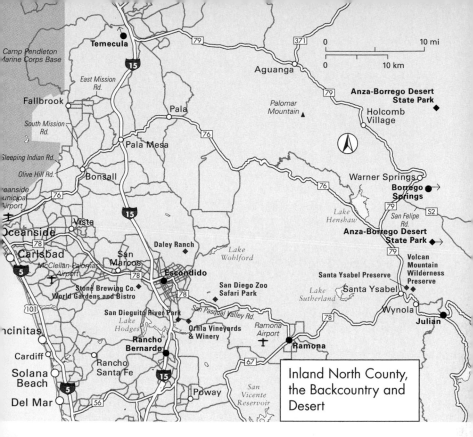 Activities

GOLF

Rancho Bernardo Inn Golf Course

GOLF | Designed by William Francis Bell in 1962, this 18-hole course has a traditional layout, but regular upgrades keep it feeling fresh and new. The course has hosted both PGA and LPGA events and offers an oasis in Rancho Bernardo, with its tree-lined fairways and various water features. A challenging 18th hole requires an approach shot over a creek. Located at the esteemed Rancho Bernardo Inn, the property offers great amenities like a spa and several restaurants, including AVANT, where gourmet mustards are served on tap. ⊠ *17550 Bernardo Oaks Dr.* ☎ *858/675–8470* ⊕ *www.ranchobernardoinn.com/golf* ⊠ *$105 Mon.–Thurs., $119 Fri., $144 weekends* ⅄ *18 holes, 6631 yards, par 72.*

🛍 Shopping

Bernardo Winery

WINE/SPIRITS | A trip to the oldest operating winery in Southern California, founded in 1889 and run by the Rizzo family since 1928, feels like traveling back to early California days; some of the vines on the former Spanish land-grant property have been producing grapes for more than 100 years. Most of the grapes now come from other wine-growing regions. A collection of quaint shops surrounds the winery. Manzanita Roasting Company has coffee and fresh pastries, and The Kitchen serves lunch daily except Monday. Shops sell cold-pressed olive oil and other gourmet goodies, as well as apparel, home-decor items, and arts and crafts. A farmers' market is held Friday 9 am–1 pm, and there's live music on the Tasting Room Patio Sunday 2–5 pm.

☒ *13330 Paseo Del Verano N* ☎ *858/487–1866* ⊕ *www.bernardowinery.com* 🍷 *Winery free, tastings $10.*

Escondido

8 miles north of Rancho Bernardo on I–15, 31 miles northeast of Downtown San Diego on I–15.

Escondido and the lovely rolling hills around it were originally a land grant bestowed by the governor of Mexico on Juan Bautista Alvarado in 1843. The Battle of San Pasqual, a bloody milestone in California's march to statehood, took place just east of the city. For a century and a half, these hills supported citrus and avocado trees, plus large vineyards. The rural character of the area began to change when the San Diego Zoo established its Safari Park in the San Pasqual Valley east of town in the 1970s. By the late 1990s suburban development had begun to transform the hills into housing tracts. The California Center for the Arts, opened in 1993, now stands as the downtown centerpiece of a burgeoning arts community that includes a collection of art galleries along Grand Avenue. On Friday nights (April–September), downtown is lined with pre-1970s vintage cars that slowly cruise Grand Avenue. Despite its urbanization, Escondido still supports several pristine open-space preserves that attract nature lovers, hikers, and mountain bikers. And, the area's abundant farms are slowly luring award-winning chefs who are taking the lead on opening farm-to-fork establishments.

ESSENTIALS
VISITOR INFORMATION Visit Escondido. ☒ *235 E. Grand Ave.* ☎ *760/839–4777* ⊕ *www.VisitEscondido.com.*

◉ Sights

California Center for the Arts
MUSEUM | FAMILY | An entertainment complex with two theaters, an art museum, and a conference center, the center presents operas, musicals, plays, dance performances, and symphony and chamber-music concerts. Performers conduct free workshops for children; check the website for dates. The museum, which focuses on 20th-century art, occasionally presents blockbuster exhibits that make a side trip here worthwhile. ☒ *340 N. Escondido Blvd.* ☎ *800/988–4253 box office, 760/839–4138 museum* ⊕ *www.artcenter.org* 🍷 *Museum $10* ⊘ *Closed Mon.–Wed.*

Daley Ranch
NATIONAL/STATE PARK | FAMILY | A 3,058-acre conservation area and historic ranch site is laced with more than 20 miles of multipurpose trails for hikers, mountain bikers, and equestrians. The 2.4-mile Boulder Loop affords sweeping views of Escondido, and the 2.5-mile Ranch House Loop passes two small ponds, the 1928 Daley family ranch house, and the site of the original log cabin. Private cars are prohibited on the ranch, but there's free parking just outside the entrance. From the main trailhead, you can access Dixon Lake, a popular fishing and camping spot. Free naturalist-guided hikes are offered on a regular basis; call for schedule. Leashed dogs permitted. ☒ *3024 La Honda Dr.* ☎ *760/839–4680* ⊕ *www.daleyranch.org* 🍷 *Free.*

Escondido Arts Partnership Municipal Gallery
MUSEUM | This gallery showcases works by local artists, with regular exhibitions and year-round special events. ☒ *262 E. Grand Ave.* ☎ *760/480–4101* ⊕ *www.escondidoarts.org* 🍷 *Free* ⊘ *Closed Sun., Mon., and Wed.*

Escondido History Center
MUSEUM | This outdoor museum adjacent to the California Center for the Arts

in Grape Day Park consists of several historic buildings moved here to illustrate local development from the late 1800s, when grape growing and gold mining supported the economy. Exhibits include the 1888 Santa Fe Depot, Escondido's first library, the Bandy Blacksmith shop, a furnished 1890 Victorian house, and other 19th-century buildings. Free 90-minute walking tours take place the second Saturday of every month, beginning at 10 am on the southeast corner of Broadway and Grand; no reservations necessary. ■TIP→ **Download their app, Explore Escondido, for a self-guided tour of the historic district, organic farms, wineries, museums, and more.** ⊠ *321 N. Broadway* ☎ *760/743–8207* ⊕ *www.escondidohistory.com* ⊠ *$3 suggested donation* ☉ *Closed Fri., Sun., and Mon.*

Orfila Vineyards & Winery
WINERY/DISTILLERY | Visitors here can taste award-winning Syrah, Sangiovese, and Viognier produced from grapes harvested from the 10,000-acre vineyard. The Rose Arbor has a picnic area, and there's a gift shop with wine-related merchandise. There's also a tasting room on Main Street in Julian. ⊠ *13455 San Pasqual Rd.* ☎ *760/738–6500* ⊕ *www.orfila.com* ⊠ *Tastings $15.*

Queen Califia's Magical Circle
PUBLIC ART | **FAMILY** | The last work by sculptor Niki de Saint Phalle (1930–2002), this sculpture garden designed for entertaining children consists of nine totemic figures up to 21 feet tall. Adorned with stylized monsters, animals, protective deities, geometric symbols, and crests, the pieces evoke ancient tales and legends. Youngsters can climb on the giant fanciful figures. ⊠ *Kit Carson Park, Bear Valley Pkwy. and Mary La.* ☎ *760/839–4000* ⊕ *www.queencalifia.org* ⊠ *Free* ☉ *Closed Mon., Wed., and Fri.–Sun.*

★ San Diego Zoo Safari Park
ZOO | **FAMILY** | A branch of the San Diego Zoo, 35 miles to the north, the 1,800-acre preserve in the San Pasqual Valley is designed to protect endangered species from around the world. Exhibit areas have been carved out of the dry, dusty canyons and mesas to represent the animals' natural habitats in various parts of Africa and Asia.

The best way to see these preserves is to take the 25-minute, 2½-mile Africa tram safari, included with admission. More than 3,500 animals of more than 400 species roam or fly above the expansive grounds. Predators are separated from prey by deep moats, but only the elephants, tigers, lions, and cheetahs are kept in enclosures. Good viewpoints are at the Elephant Viewing Patio, African Plains Outlook, and Kilmia Point. The park's newest project is the **Tull Family Tiger Trail**, a Sumatran tiger habitat opened in 2014, where you can get face-to-face (with a glass between) with the gorgeous cats. The 5-acre exhibit features a waterfall and swimming hole, and addresses poaching and other environmental threats to the species. ■TIP→ **In summer, when the park stays open late, the trip is especially enjoyable in the early evening, when the heat has subsided and the animals are active and feeding. When the tram travels through the park after dark, sodium-vapor lamps illuminate the active animals. Photographers with zoom lenses can get spectacular shots of zebras, gazelles, and rhinos.**

For a more focused view of the park, you can take one of several other safaris that are well worth the additional charge. You can choose from several behind-the-scenes safaris, fly above it all via the zip-line safari, or get up close to giraffes and rhinos on a Caravan safari.

The park is as much a botanical garden as a zoo, serving as a "rescue center" for rare and endangered plants. Unique gardens include cacti and succulents from Baja California, a bonsai collection, a fuchsia display, native plants, and protea.

The gift shops are well worth a visit for their limited-edition items. There are lots of restaurants, snack bars, and some picnic areas. Rental lockers, strollers, and wheelchairs are available. You can also arrange to stay overnight in the park in summer on a Roar and Snore Sleepover ($140 and up, plus admission).

✉ *15500 San Pasqual Valley Rd.* ✥ *Take I–15 north to Via Rancho Pkwy. and follow signs for 6 miles* ☎ *760/747–8702* 🌐 *www.sdzsafaripark.org* 🎟 *$56 one-day pass including Africa tram ride; multipark and multiday passes are available; special safaris are extra starting at $54 per person; parking $15.*

San Dieguito River Park

TRAIL | **FAMILY** | The park maintains several hiking and walking trails in the Escondido area. These are part of an intended 70-mile-long Coast to Crest Trail that will eventually link the San Dieguito Lagoon near Del Mar with the river's source on Volcan Mountain, north of Julian. Among the existing trails are three that circle Lake Hodges: the **North Shore Lake Hodges Trail;** the **Piedras Pintadas Trail,** which informs about native American Kumeyaay lifestyles and uses for native plants; and the **Highland Valley Trail,** the first mile of which is the Ruth Merrill Children's Walk. Three trails in **Clevenger Canyon** lead to sweeping views of the San Pasqual Valley. **■ TIP→ Visit the website for a list of upcoming free guided hikes and pay attention to signs warning against leaving valuables in your car.** ✉ *18372 Sycamore Creek Rd.* ☎ *858/674–2275* 🌐 *www.sdrp.org* 🎟 *Free.*

Stone Brewing World Gardens and Bistro

WINERY/DISTILLERY | **FAMILY** | One of the fastest-growing companies in the United States, Stone staked out a hilltop overlooking Escondido to create, brew, and sell its beloved craft beer. It's a gorgeous, solar-run facility, filled with massive stainless steel tanks used in beer-making. You can take a tour ($8 includes four tastings and a souvenir glass) to see how the beer is made and get a taste, dine on farm-to-table fare at the on-site bistro, and purchase signature items in the company store. Thirty-six craft and specialty beers are always on tap in the tasting bar and the bistro, which has indoor and garden seating for lunch and dinner. The ingenious menu features honey Sriracha quail knots, hemp seed pretzels, and the plant-based Impossible Burger. Save room for a real beer float. **■ TIP→ Check their website for weekly events, including live music on Thursdays during summer months.** ✉ *1999 Citracado Pkwy.* ☎ *760/294–7866* 🌐 *www.stonebrewing.com* 🎟 *Tours $8.*

🍴 Restaurants

It might not have coastal views and ocean breezes, but Escondido has recently lured several top chefs capitalizing on the surrounding farms in this untapped market. Don't be surprised to find an elegant French restaurant next to a hole-in-the-wall taco stand, along with a clientele as mixed as the area's cuisine. Despite the inland location, Grand Avenue has a string of charming downtown eateries, with local chefs serving farm-to-table dishes at a fraction of what you'd pay along the coast.

Bellamy's Restaurant

$$$ | **FRENCH FUSION** | Live piano music, crystal chandeliers, and leather tufted chairs set the stage at this fine-dining restaurant by Chef Jonathan Freyberg for a delectable menu that includes market oysters, scallops with fennel purée, duck with braised endive, and rack of lamb with fingerling potatoes. For a sweet conclusion, try the bread pudding made from flaky croissants, or the decadent chocolate ganache with gold leaf and caramel ice cream. **Known for:** California-French cuisine; upscale dining; heavenly desserts. [$] *Average main: $28* ✉ *417 W. Grand Ave.* ☎ *760/747–5000* 🌐 *www.bellamysdining.com* 🕒 *Closed Sun. and Mon.*

Vincent's

$$$ | **FRENCH** | This French restaurant is an excellent choice for dinner before an event at the nearby California Center for the Arts. Original paintings decorate the walls and crisp white tablecloths cover the tables, adorned with fresh flowers. **Known for:** half-off wine Wednesdays; weekly prix-fixe menu; braised veal shanks; warm artisanal breads with rich sauces. [$] *Average main: $32* ✉ *113 W. Grand Ave.* ☎ *760/745–3835* 🌐 *www.vincentsongrand.com* ⏲ *Closed Sun. and Mon. No lunch.*

Vintana

$$$ | **MODERN AMERICAN** | Don't let its location above the Lexus dealership dissuade you; this swanky restaurant is part of the Cohen Restaurant empire and it's designed as three restaurants in one: a formal glass-walled dining room; a lively patio with firepits and cabanas; and the lobby bar with leather couches and a wine shop. No matter where you dine, try the macadamia-crusted sea bass or the skirt steak with blue cheese quesadillas, followed with a cocktail using one of the more than 140 vodkas. **Known for:** weekend brunch; nightly specials; large portions. [$] *Average main: $30* ✉ *The Centre at Lexus Escondido, 1205 Auto Park Way* ☎ *760/745–7777* 🌐 *www.dinevintana.com.*

★ The Wooden Spoon

$$ | **AMERICAN** | Former fine-dining chef Jesse Paul—who oversaw kitchens at Four Seasons Aviara, L'Auberge Del Mar, and Via Italia Trattoria—left it all behind to bring redefined comfort food to Escondido. In this casual mom-and-pop restaurant, it starts with seasonal produce gathered daily from six local farms, followed by preparation and service from a tight-knit family-like staff; the menu changes daily, which might be problematic if you're craving a repeat from a previous visit, and nearly everything is made in-house, including kimchi, dressings, sauerkraut, pickles, and ketchup. **Known for:** comfort food; supporting local farms; Thurday–Sunday brunch. [$] *Average main: $20* ✉ *805 E. Valley Pkwy.* ☎ *760/745–0266* 🌐 *www.woodenspoonsd.com* ⏲ *Closed Mon. and Tues.*

🛏 Hotels

With the exception of the Welk Resort, which is now primarily a time-share property, Escondido has little to offer in the way of accommodations. The neighboring towns of Vista and San Marcos are home to two of the most luxurious destination spas in the nation.

Cal-a-Vie Health Spa

$$$$ | **RESORT** | At this destination spa—celebrities like Julia Roberts and Oprah Winfrey escape here for some serious R&R—you'll feel like you've died and gone to a pampering Provençal village heaven. **Pros:** exclusive spa haven; on 500 private acres; customized to health and fitness goals. **Cons:** no children under 16; three-day minimum stay; no TVs or alcohol might be an issue for some. [$] *Rooms from: $4,675* ✉ *29402 Spa Havens Way, Vista* ☎ *760/945–2055* 🌐 *www.cal-a-vie.com* 🔑 *32 rooms* 🍴 *All meals.*

★ Golden Door

$$$$ | **RESORT** | Considered by many to be the world's best destination spa, the venerable Golden Door takes you on a journey to tranquillity, transformation, and self-realization during a seven-night stay; day passes are available. **Pros:** peaceful sanctuary; customized programs; luxury camp forms sisterhood; largest collection of Japanese art in the country. **Cons:** no alcohol, sugar, or salt; mostly appeals to women; expensive. [$] *Rooms from: $8,850* ✉ *777 Deer Springs Rd., San Marcos* ☎ *760/744–5777* 🌐 *www.goldendoor.com* 🔑 *40 rooms* 🍴 *All meals.*

Welk Resort

$$$$ | **RESORT** | **FAMILY** | Built by bandleader Lawrence Welk in the 1960s, the

With more than 40 wineries, most along Rancho California Road, Temecula is Southern California's premier winemaking region.

property sprawls over 600 acres of rugged, oak-studded hillside and is family-friendly, with abundant children's activities. **Pros:** excellent theater; popular golf course; near the Safari Park. **Cons:** located outside the city; very spread out; rooms may not always be available due to time-sharing; time-share pitch. [$] *Rooms from: $301* ✉ *8860 Lawrence Welk Dr.* ☎ *760/749–3000, 800/932–9355* 🌐 *www.welkresorts.com* 🛏 *714 rooms* 🍴 *No meals.*

Activities

FISHING

There are three freshwater lakes—Dixon, Hodges, and Wohlford—that surround the North County city of Escondido.

California Department of Fish and Game

FISHING | A fishing license, available at most bait-and-tackle and sporting-goods stores, is required for fishing from the shoreline. Nonresidents can purchase an annual license or a 10-day, 2-day, or 1-day short-term license. Licenses can also be purchased online through the department's website or at the San Diego headquarters. Children younger than 16 do not need a license. Note that some city reservoirs no longer sell snacks, drinks, bait, or fishing licenses, nor do they rent pedal boats or electric motors. They also accept payment by credit card or check (no cash) for day-use fees. Make sure to check updated concession availability for your specific destination, or obtain a fishing license in advance. **■TIP→ You do not need a license to fish from public piers. Any lobster or crab taken on hook and line must be returned to the water immediately.** ✉ *3883 Ruffin Rd., San Diego* ☎ *858/467–4201* 🌐 *www.wildlife.ca.gov.*

HIKING

San Dieguito River Park

HIKING/WALKING | This corridor begins at the mouth of the San Dieguito River in Del Mar and heads from the riparian lagoon area through coastal sage scrub and mountain terrain to end in the desert; eventually the Coast to Crest Trail will connect 70 miles to Volcan Mountain. It's open to hikers, bikers, and horses. The expansive park is also home to the Sikes Adobe Farmhouse, an 1880s farmstead that was almost completely destroyed by wildfire in 2007. After painstaking restoration it reopened in 2010 and is now home to a museum. The restored adobe creamery reopened in 2014. ✉ *18372 Sycamore Creek Rd.* ☎ *858/674–2270* ⊕ *www.sdrp. org* 🅿 *Adobe parking $3.*

🛍 Shopping

Although farmland began to give way to suburbs in the 1990s, and the area's fruit, nut, and vegetable bounty has diminished, you can still find overflowing farm stands in the San Pasqual Valley and in Valley Center, just east of the city.

The San Diego Zoo Safari Park's Bazaar (☎ *760/738–5055*) sells authentic African artifacts, books, home-decor items, and apparel. ⇨ *For more information on the Safari Park, see the Escondido Sights Section.*

Bates Nut Farm
FOOD/CANDY | FAMILY | Home of San Diego's largest pumpkin patch each fall, this family farm is where you might find a 200-pound squash. It also sells locally grown pecans, macadamia nuts, and almonds. On the 100 acres, there's a farm zoo, a picnic area, and a gift shop. ✉ *15954 Woods Valley Rd., Valley Center* ☎ *800/642–0348* ⊕ *www.batesnut-farm.biz* ☞ *$5 parking fee in Oct. on weekends.*

Brick n Barn
ANTIQUES/COLLECTIBLES | Dating back to 1872, this former homestead of baking legend Betty Crocker opens its gates monthly for antique shows hosted in a massive white barn. Step inside for themed events, unveiling a range of inventory including mid-century, industrial, vintage, rustic, primitive, and French country items. You'll often find homemade baked goods and gourmet coffee to enjoy on the manicured grounds.

Go Fish 🏃

The California Department of Fish and Game (⊕ *www.wildlife.ca.gov*) issues "Fishing Passports" showing 150 different species of fresh and saltwater fish and shellfish found throughout the state. In San Diego County fishing aficionados can catch (and, hopefully, release) many of the species listed, receiving a stamp for each species caught.

Check their website for show dates and other events. ✉ *29200 Miller Rd., Valley Center* ☎ *760/651–2635* ⊕ *www. bricknbarn.com* ⊙ *Open one weekend a month, 10–5 pm.*

VinKlectic
CLOTHING | This eclectic boutique packs the racks with trendy fashions and accessories ranging from bohemian trends to leather bags crafted by local artisans. ✉ *157 E. Grand Ave.* ☎ *760/975–3552* ⊕ *www.shopvinklectic.com.*

Temecula

29 miles from Escondido, 60 miles from San Diego on I–15 north to Rancho California Rd. east.

Once an important stop on the Butterfield Overland Stagecoach route and a market town for the huge cattle ranches surrounding it, Temecula (pronounced teh-*mec*-yoo-la) is now a developed wine region, designated the South Coast region, which also includes some wineries in San Diego County. Known for its gently rolling hills, the region is studded with ancient oak trees and vernal pools. French and Italian grapes thrive in the valley's hot climate, which has turned Temecula's wine route into a tourist attraction and weekend escape for San Diegans. Today there are more than 40 wineries open to the pubic. Winemakers are creating luscious blended reds and whites that resemble rich Rhônes and Tuscan vintages. Because most of the wineries sell their bottles only at the wineries, it pays to stock up if you find something you especially enjoy.

Most of the wineries that line both sides of Rancho California Road offer tours and tastings (for a fee) daily and have creatively stocked boutiques, picnic facilities, and restaurants on the premises. Some wineries have opened luxury boutique lodgings and fine-dining restaurants. For shopping, restaurants, and museums, Old Town runs along historic Front Street on the west side of I–15. In addition to its visitor appeal, Temecula is also a suburban bedroom community for many who work in San Diego's North County. Between hot-air balloon rides over vineyards and wine tours by horse-drawn carriage, this romantic destination has plenty to offer for the wine lover, and everyone else.

TOUR OPTIONS

Several companies offer individual and group tours of the Temecula wine country with departures from San Diego and Temecula. Some include lunch or refreshments as part of the package.

LIMOUSINE TOURS Destination Temecula. ⊠ 28475 Old Town Front St., Suite F 📞 951/695–1232, 800/584–8162 ⊕ www. destem.com. **Grapeline Wine Tours.** ⊠ Office, 27286 Via Industria, Suite A 📞 951/693–5755 ⊕ www.gogrape.com. **Temecula Carriage Company.** 📞 858/205–9161 ⊕ www.temeculacarriageco.com.

ESSENTIALS

VISITOR INFORMATION Temecula Valley Winegrowers Association. ⊠ 29377 Rancho California Rd., Suite 203 📞 951/699–6586, 800/801–9463 ⊕ www.temeculawines.org. **Visit Temecula Valley.** ⊠ 28690 Mercedes St., Suite A 📞 951/491–6085 ⊕ www.visittemeculavalley.com.

◉ Sights

★ Old Town Temecula

TOWN | Once a hangout for cowboys, Old Town has been updated and expanded to include boutique shops, good restaurants, a children's museum, and a theater, while retaining its Old West appearance. A walking tour put together by the **Temecula Valley Historical Society,** starting at the Temecula Valley Museum, covers some of the old buildings; most are identified with bronze plaques. ∎**TIP→ Free maps can be downloaded from their website (www.temeculahistoricalsociety.org). Guided walking tours are hosted every Saturday (10 am–noon; $5) by the Temecula Valley Museum.** ⊠ Temecula ⊕ www.oldtowntemecula.com.

Pennypickle's Workshop (Temecula Children's Museum)

MUSEUM | **FAMILY** | This is the imaginary home of Professor Phineas Pennypickle, where kids accompanied by parents enter a time machine that carries them through 11 rooms of interactive exhibits demonstrating perception and illusion, music making, flight and aviation, chemistry and physics, plus power and electricity. The shop stocks an array of educational toys, games, and books. Reservations are not taken, so be sure to get their early, especially during school vacations. ⊠ 42081 Main St. 📞 951/308–6376 ⊕ www.pennypickles.org 🎟 $5 🕙 Closed Mon.

Santa Rosa Plateau Ecological Reserve

NATURE PRESERVE | **FAMILY** | This 9,000-acre wooded preserve provides a glimpse of what this countryside was like back in the day, with bunch-grass prairies frequented by mule deer, golden eagles, and other wildlife. Trails wind through ancient oak forests and past seasonal, vernal pools and rolling grassland. A visitor and operations center has interpretive displays and maps; some of the reserve's hiking trails begin here. There are designated trails for leashed dogs, horses, and mountain bikers. ✉ *39400 Clinton Keith Rd., Murrieta* ✛ *Take I–15 south to Clinton Keith Rd. exit and head west 5 miles* 🕾 *951/677–6951* ⊕ *www.rivcoparks.org/santa-rosa-plateau-ecological-reserve* 🔁 *$4 per person; $1 for each horse or dog* ⊙ *Visitor Center closed Mon.*

Temecula Valley Museum

MUSEUM | **FAMILY** | Adjacent to Sam Hicks Monument Park, this museum focuses on Temecula Valley history, including early Native American life, Butterfield stage routes, and the ranchero period. A hands-on interactive area for children holds a general store, photographer's studio, and ride-a-pony station. Outside there's a playground and picnic area. ∎**TIP**➔ **A walking tour ($5) of Old Town Temecula is given every Saturday 10–noon.** ✉ *28314 Mercedes St.* 🕾 *951/694–6450* ⊕ *www. temeculavalleymuseum.org* 🔁 *$5 suggested donation.*

Europa Village

WINERY/DISTILLERY | You'll find three tasting rooms here, reflecting three European-style wineries: French Cabernet Sauvignon; Spanish Tempranillo; and Italian Pinot Grigio. You can walk through lush gardens and enjoy live music every Sunday 1–4 pm. The Inn at Europa Village, perched on an adjacent hilltop, offers 10 guest rooms. ✉ *3347 La Serena Way* 🕾 *951/216–3380* ⊕ *www.europavillage.com* 🔁 *Tastings $20.*

Hart Family Winery

WINERY/DISTILLERY | A perennial crowd-pleaser, this winery specializes in well-crafted red wines made by Jim Hart, whose father and mother, Joe and Nancy, started the winery in the 1970s. Syrah, Cabernet Franc, and Cabernet Sauvignon are among the stars, but Hart Family also works with little-known varietals like Aleatico, used in a marvelous dessert wine. ✉ *41300 Ave. Biona, off Rancho California Rd.* 🕾 *951/676–6300* ⊕ *www.hartfamilywinery.com* 🔁 *Tasting $5.*

Leoness Cellars

WINERY/DISTILLERY | Bordeaux and Rhône blends are the specialties of this 20-acre hilltop estate with magnificent views of Cabernet Sauvignon vines. If it's available, try the winemaker's pride and joy, the Mélange de Reves (Blend of Dreams), made from the traditional Rhône combo of Grenache, Syrah, and Mourvèdre. Winery tours take in the vineyards and the wine-making areas. The tours require a reservation, as do wine-and-food pairing sessions that might include fruits and cheeses or, in the case of dessert wines, chocolates. Leoness's popular French-inspired restaurant is open daily. ✉ *38311 De Portola Rd.* 🕾 *951/302–7601* ⊕ *www.leonesscellars. com* 🔁 *Tasting $18–$22; tours with tasting $40–$90.*

Miramonte Winery

WINERY/DISTILLERY | Temecula's hippest winery sits high on a hilltop. Rhône-style whites (including the Four Torch Blanc blend of Grenache Blanc) and reds like the estate Syrah and Opulente blend of Grenache, Syrah, and Mourvèdre are the strong suits, though the Tempranillo and rosé have their partisans. Taste inside at the casual bistro, outside on the deck, perhaps with an artisanal cheese plate. On Friday and Saturday night from 6 to 9, the winery goes into party mode with tastings of wine and beer, live music, and dancing that spills into the vineyards. ✉ *33410 Rancho California Rd.* 🕾 *951/506–5500* ⊕ *www.miramontewinery.com* 🔁 *Tastings $17–$20, tours $75 (reservations required).*

Mount Palomar Winery

WINERY/DISTILLERY | One of the original Temecula Valley wineries, opened in 1969, Mount Palomar introduced Sangiovese, a varietal that has proven perfectly suited to the region's soil and climate. New owners have transformed the homey winery into a grand Mediterranean villa with acres of gardens and trees, turning it into an award-winning wedding and event venue. The Sangiovese is worth a try, as are the Solera Cream Sherry (ask how it's made) and the popular Cloudbreak, an inky red blend with a Petit Verdot base. Annata Bistro/Bar is open daily for lunch and dinner. ✉ *33820 Rancho California Rd.* ☎ *951/676–5047* 🌐 *www.mountpalomar.com* 🎫 *Tastings Mon.–Thurs. $16, Fri.–Sun. $20.*

Wiens Family Cellars

WINERY/DISTILLERY | A visit to this serious winery can be an enlightenment; request information cards for a full description of each vintage you taste, combinations of Cabernet Sauvignon, Cabernet Franc, Petite Syrah, Zinfandel, and Pinot Noir. The winery is known for its so-called Big Reds, which include Crowded, a four-grape blend; lighter Infinite Perspective, a three-grape blend; and a jammy Zinfandel. ✉ *35055 Via Del Ponte* ☎ *951/694–9892* 🌐 *www.wienscellars.com* 🎫 *Tastings $20.*

Wilson Creek Winery & Vineyards

WINERY/DISTILLERY | One of Temecula's busiest tasting rooms sits amid inviting, park-like grounds. Wilson is known for its Almond sparkling wine, but the winery also produces appealing still wines. Among these the Petite Sirah, Viognier, reserve Syrah, reserve Zinfandel, and late-harvest Zinfandel all merit a taste. The on-site gluten-free Creekside Grill Restaurant serves sandwiches, salads, vegetable potpie, and seasonal seafood. ✉ *35960 Rancho California Rd.* ☎ *951/699–9463* 🌐 *www.wilsoncreekwinery.com* 🎫 *Tasting $20.*

🍴 Restaurants

Café Champagne

$$$ | **CONTEMPORARY** | With its flowering trellises and vineyard views, the spacious patio at Thornton Winery's café is the perfect place to lunch on a sunny day. The kitchen, which faces the French-country–style dining room, turns out pan-seared New York steak, chicken with pesto risotto, sandwiches, and other hearty fare. **Known for:** bacon cheeseburger; Sunday brunch; live music on Friday night. [$] *Average main: $32* ✉ *Thornton Winery, 32575 Rancho California Rd.* ☎ *951/699–0099* 🌐 *www.thorntonwine.com.*

★ The Goat & Vine

$ | **MEDITERRANEAN** | At this vintage-meets-industrial style restaurant, don't be surprised to see a line outside the door, as patrons wait to partake of Mediterranean–Italian–American dishes made from scratch in the stone-hearth kitchen. Nearly everything is produced in-house, including the sauces, dressings, and breads baked with a sourdough starter dating back 120 years. **Known for:** stone-hearth kitchen; house sangria; sourdough pretzels. [$] *Average main: $13* ✉ *41911 5th St.* ☎ *951/695–5600* 🌐 *www.thegoatandvine.com* ⏲ *No breakfast.*

Trattoria Toscana

$$ | **TUSCAN** | California native Blythe Wilson and Sardinian-born chef Pietro Cinus met while Wilson was exploring the Tuscan countryside and together they brought all things Italian to Temecula. Grab a seat at a wooden table—built by the chef—and try gnocchi, ravioli, and soft breads all made by hand; the bustling scratch kitchen integrates spicy sausage and aged pecorino imported from Italy. **Known for:** dishes from Tuscany and Sardinia; special three-course dinners; tiramisu and panna cotta with citrus coulis made with lemons from chef's garden. [$] *Average main: $20* ✉ *Palm Plaza, 26485 Ynez Rd., between Overland and Winchester Dr.* ☎ *951/296–2066* 🌐 *www.trattoriatoscanaintemecula.com* ⏲ *Closed Tues.*

🛏 Hotels

★ Carter Estate Winery and Resort

$$$ | **HOTEL** | Enter by way of a long driveway lined with olive trees, past the automatic gates, and suddenly you're in a Mediterranean-inspired neighborhood of freestanding bungalows that overlook the vineyards and mountains. **Pros:** all rooms have vineyard views with patio; complimentary in-room breakfast; use of facilities at South Coast Winery Resort. **Cons:** slow Wi-Fi; no on-site restaurant; rose gardens attract bees. $ *Rooms from: $250* ✉ *34450 Rancho California Rd.* ☎ *844/851–2138* ⊕ *www.cart-erestatewinery.com* ⇲ *60 rooms* ❍ *Free Breakfast.*

The Inn at Europa Village

$$ | B&B/INN | Offering a lovely hillside setting for an escape to the wine country, this 10-room B&B delights guests with old-world charm and modern amenities, while providing the perfect spot to unplug (there are no TVs) and watch the world—and hot-air balloons—go by. **Pros:** privacy and scenery; delicious home-cooked breakfast; 2-for-1 wine tasting at Europa Village. **Cons:** long walk to wineries; no TVs; two-night minimum stay on weekends. $ *Rooms from: $220* ✉ *33350 La Serena Way* ☎ *877/676–7047* ⊕ *www.europavillage.com/inn* ⇲ *10 rooms* ❍ *Breakfast.*

★ Ponte Vineyard Inn

$$$$ | HOTEL | Comfortable and relaxed digs offer vineyard and garden views and have an Old California feel, with lots of dark wood, leather furnishings, and open spaces. **Pros:** firepits in garden; excellent service; live music on weekends. **Cons:** many weekend weddings; rather pricey; tasting room can get crowded. $ *Rooms from: $380* ✉ *35001 Rancho California Rd.* ☎ *951/587–6688* ⊕ *www.pontevine-yardinn.com* ⇲ *90 rooms* ❍ *No meals.*

South Coast Winery Resort & Spa

$$ | HOTEL | At Temecula's largest winery, this full-service resort offers richly appointed and highly private rooms surrounded by 38 acres of vineyards. **Pros:** elegantly appointed rooms; full-service resort; pool and spa. **Cons:** spread out property requires lots of walking; poor

service; $19 resort fee. $ *Rooms from: $199* ✉ *34843 Rancho California Rd.* ☎ *951/587–9463, 866/994–6379* ⊕ *www.southcoastwinery.com* ⇲ *132 rooms* ❍ *No meals.*

Temecula Creek Inn

$$ | RESORT | Most of the rooms at this property that sprawls over 360 acres have private patios or balconies overlooking the championship golf course. **Pros:** beautiful grounds; top golf course; course views from most rooms. **Cons:** $75 pet fee; often busy; location away from Old Town and wineries. $ *Rooms from: $209* ✉ *44501 Rainbow Canyon Rd.* ☎ *951/694–1000, 888/976–3404* ⊕ *www.temeculacreekinn.com* ⦚ *Greens fee $80–$100; 27 holes, 6800 yards, par 36* ⇲ *130 rooms* ❍ *No meals.*

🏃 Activities

BALLOONING

California Dreamin'

BALLOONING | Head here for hot-air balloon rides; the company specializes in Temecula wine country flights. ✉ *33133 Vista del Monte Rd.* ☎ *800/373–3359* ⊕ *www.californiadreamin.com* ✉ *weekdays $140; weekends $188.*

A Grape Escape Balloon Adventure

BALLOONING | Enjoy a morning hot-air balloon lift-off from Europa Village Winery. ✉ *33475 La Serena Way* ☎ *951/699–9987, 800/965–2122* ⊕ *www.hotairtours.com* ✉ *weekdays $139; weekends $159.*

🛍 Shopping

Temecula Lavender Co.

SPA/BEAUTY | Owner Jan Schneider offers an inspiring collection of the herb that fosters peace, purification, sleep, and longevity. Bath salts, hand soaps, essential oil, even dryer bags to freshen up the laundry—she's got it all. ✉ *28561 Old Town Front St.* ☎ *951/676–1931* ⊕ *www.temeculalavenderco.com* ⊗ *Closed Mon.*

Temecula Olive Oil Company

FOOD/CANDY | FAMILY | Ranch tours and complimentary tastings of locally pressed olive oil are offered at the Temecula Olive Oil Company, where you can find a selection of oils seasoned with garlic, herbs, and citrus. This Old Town shop has dipping and cooking oils, locally crafted oil-based soaps and bath products, and a selection of preserved and stuffed olives. ⊠ 28653 Old Town Front St. ☎ 951/693–4029 ⊕ www.temeculaoliveoil.com.

Julian

62 miles from San Diego to Julian, east on I–8 and north on Rte. 79.

Gold was discovered in the Julian area in 1869, and gold-bearing quartz a year later. More than $15 million worth of gold was taken from local mines in the 1870s. Many of the buildings along Julian's Main Street and the side streets today date back to the gold-rush period; others are reproductions.

When gold and quartz became scarce, the locals turned to growing apples and pears. During the fall harvest season you can buy fruit, sip apple cider (hard or soft), eat apple pie, and shop for local original art, antiques, and collectibles. But spring is equally enchanting (and less congested), as the hillsides explode with wildflowers—thousands of daffodils, lilacs, and peonies. More than 50 artists have studios tucked away in the hills surrounding Julian; they often show their work in local shops and galleries. The Julian area comprises three small crossroads communities: Santa Ysabel, Wynola, and historic Julian. You can find bits of history, shops, and dining options in each community. Most visitors come to spend a day in town, but the hillsides support small B&B establishments for those who want to linger longer.

It's worth a side trip to Cuyamaca Rancho State Park, 15 miles south of Julian.

Spread over more than 25,000 acres of meadows and forests, the park offers a beautiful outdoor experience with a lake, camps, picnic areas, and more than 100 hiking trails. For an inspirational desert view, stop at the lookout about 2 miles south of Julian on Route 79. The Sunrise Highway, passing through the Cleveland National Forest, is the most dramatic approach to Julian.

ESSENTIALS

VISITOR INFORMATION Julian Chamber of Commerce. ⊠ Town Hall, 2129 Main St. ✛ Corner of Washington and Main ☎ 760/765–1857 ⊕ www.visitjulian.com.

◉ Sights

California Wolf Center

NATURE PRESERVE | FAMILY | This center, just outside Julian, is one of the few places in North America where you can get an up-close view of the gray wolves that once roamed much of the continent. The center participates in breeding programs and houses several captive packs, including some rare Mexican grays, a subspecies of the North American gray wolf that came within seven individuals of extinction in the 1970s. The animals are kept secluded from public view in 3-acre pens, but some may be seen by visitors during educational tours by appointment. The dirt road here is rough, so it's best to have a high clearance vehicle. ⊠ Hwy. 79 at KQ Ranch Rd. ☎ 760/765–0030 ⊕ www.californiawolfcenter.org ⊠ $20, reservations required ⊗ Closed Tues.–Thurs. ☞ Tours Mon. at 10 am, Fri. at 2 pm, weekends at 10 and 2.

★ Eagle Mining Company

MINE | FAMILY | Five blocks east of the center of Julian you can take an hour-long tour of an authentic family-owned gold mine from 1870. Displays along the route include authentic tools and machinery, gold extraction process, and gold quartz-bearing veins. A small rock shop and gold-mining museum are also on the

Hot-air ballooning is available daily, year-round, in Temecula and flights typically last 60–75 minutes.

premises. ✉ *2320 C St.* ☎ *760/765–0036* ⊕ *www.theeaglemining.com* 🎟 *$10.*

Julian Pioneer Museum

MUSEUM | FAMILY | When the gold mines in Julian played out, the mobs of gold miners who had invaded it left, leaving behind discarded mining tools and empty houses. Today the Julian Pioneer Museum, a 19th-century brewery, displays remnants of that time, including pioneer clothing, a collection of old lace, mining tools, and original photographs of the town's historic buildings and mining structures. ✉ *2811 Washington St.* ☎ *760/765–0227* ⊕ *julianpioneermuseum. org* 🎟 *$3* ⊗ *Closed Mon.–Thurs.*

Observer's Inn

OBSERVATORY | FAMILY | One of the best ways to see Julian's star-filled summer sky is by taking a sky-tour at Mike and Caroline Leigh's observatory, with research-grade telescopes. The hosts guide you through the star clusters and galaxies, pointing out planets and nebulae. The guides also offer solar tours at 11 am, when you can get a good look at the sun using a telescope designed for this purpose. It's also an inn, if you wish to stay the night. Reservations are necessary for tours and lodging. ✉ *3535 Hwy. 79* ☎ *760/765–0088* ⊕ *www. observersinn.com* 🎟 *$30* ⚓ *Reservations essential.*

Santa Ysabel Preserve

NATURE PRESERVE | Three Native American tribes operate small farms in this valley, which looks pretty much the way the backcountry appeared a century ago, with sweeping meadows surrounded by oak-studded hillsides. The San Dieguito River (Santa Ysabel Creek) emerges from Volcan Mountain here and winds its way 65 miles to San Dieguito Lagoon at Del Mar along the Coast to Crest Trail. An 8-mile trail follows the river from Farmer Road in Julian to the East Entrance of Santa Ysabel Preserve. Legacy oak trees shade the trail, waterfalls provide a background sound, there are spectacular views along the way, and picnic tables abound. The trail is best explored in the fall. ✉ *Hwy. 79* 🕾 *760/765–4098* ⊕ *www. sdparks.org.*

Volcan Mountain Wilderness Preserve

NATURE PRESERVE | The San Diego County Parks and Recreation manage this 3,000-acre preserve, where hikes challenge your stamina and views are stunning. A 5-mile trail through the preserve passes through Engelmann oak forest, native manzanita, and rolling mountain meadows to a viewpoint where the panorama extends north all the way to Palomar Mountain. On a clear day you can see Point Loma in San Diego. At the entrance you pass through gates designed by James Hubbell, a local artist known for his ironwork, wood carving, and stained glass. You can see splendid views from the Volcan Summit. Guided hikes on the Sky Island Trail and the Five Oaks Trail are offered regularly. ✉ *1209 Farmer Rd. (trailhead), north of Julian Town* ⊹ *From Julian take Farmer Rd. to Wynola Rd., go east a few yards, and then north on continuation of Farmer Rd.* 🕾 *760/765–4098* ⊕ *www.volcanmt.org* ✉ *Free.*

🍽 Restaurants

Apple Alley Bakery

$ | **BAKERY** | This bakery tucked down a narrow alley proves there's no such thing as too many pie shops in Julian. After mastering the apple-to-crust ratio, they took on lunch specials by offering a soup–sandwich–pie combo for $11. **Known for:** apple pie; lunch specials; gluten-free and vegan options. Ⓢ *Average main: $11* ✉ *2122 Main St.* 🕾 *760/765–2532.*

★ Jeremy's on the Hill

$$ | **MODERN AMERICAN** | **FAMILY** | Julian's most upscale restaurant has gained a solid reputation thanks to the chef's commitment to quality cuisine reflected in the farm-to-table menu. Although the menu features grilled steak and locally grown pork and veggies, the stars are rack of lamb, bison meat loaf, and some

of the best burgers around. **Known for:** live music weekend nights; flash-fried Brussels sprouts; on-site sommelier; family run. Ⓢ *Average main: $27* ✉ *4354 Hwy. 78* 🕾 *760/765–1587* ⊕ *www. bestrestaurantinjulian.com.*

Julian Pie Company

$ | **CAFÉ** | The apple pies that made Julian famous come from the Smothers family bakery in a one-story house on Main Street. In pleasant weather you can sit on the front patio and watch the world go by while savoring a slice of hot pie—from Dutch apple to apple mountain berry crumb—topped with homemade cinnamon ice cream. **Known for:** sweet Dutch apple pie; frozen uncooked pies to go; flaky crust. Ⓢ *Average main: $8* ✉ *2225 Main St.* 🕾 *760/765–2449* ⊕ *www. julianpie.com.*

Julian Tea & Cottage Arts

$$ | **CAFÉ** | **FAMILY** | Sample finger sandwiches, scones topped with whipped cream, and lavish sweets, which are served during afternoon tea inside the Clarence King House, built by Will Bosnell in 1898. Regular sandwiches, soups, salads, and a children's tea are also available. **Known for:** homemade

lemon curd and scones; bottomless tea; charming turn-of-the-century home. [$] *Average main: $27* ✉ *2124 3rd St.* ☎ *760/765–0832, 866/765–0832* 🌐 *www.juliantea.com* 🕘 *Closed Tues. and Wed. No dinner.*

★ Moms Pie House

$ | **BAKERY** | **FAMILY** | In 1984, "Mom" (aka Anita Nichols) opened her first pie shop in the old Julian Café building. People lined the streets for a slice of the guilty pleasure, known for its buttery crust, not-too-sweet filling with local apples, and commitment to quality. **Known for:** pressed apple cider; cinnamon ice cream; baking classes; cream pies. [$] *Average main: $8* ✉ *2119 Main St.* ☎ *760/765–2472* 🌐 *www.momspiesjulian.com* 🕘 *No dinner.*

Romano's Restaurant

$$ | **SICILIAN** | This is a casual, red-checked-tablecloth kind of place, where you can dine outside in good weather. Huge portions of antipasto, pizza, pasta, sausage sandwiches, and seafood await you. **Known for:** thin crust pizza; cozy setting; old-school Italian cooking. [$] *Average main: $20* ✉ *2718 B St.* ☎ *760/765–1003* 🌐 *www.romanosrestaurantjulian.com.*

Soups and Such Cafe

$ | **CAFÉ** | It's worth the wait for breakfast or lunch at this cozy café, where everything is fresh and made to order. The breakfast standout is eggs Benedict, both classic and vegetarian. **Known for:** combo soup, salad, and sandwich for $12; great BLT; homemade soups. [$] *Average main: $15* ✉ *2000 Main St.* ☎ *760/765–4761* 🕘 *No dinner.*

Wynola Pizza & Bistro

$ | **PIZZA** | **FAMILY** | Locals and San Diegans come to this quaint and casual indoor-outdoor restaurant for delicious, single-portion pies, such as pesto pizza, Thai chicken pizza, vegan pizza, and pulled pork pizza. Other items include chili, lasagna, seared Cajun salmon, and a killer fire-roasted artichoke dip served with homemade buffalo crackers. **Known for:** gourmet wood-fired pizza; cold craft beer; weekday specials. [$] *Average main: $15* ✉ *4355 Hwy. 78, Santa Ysabel* ☎ *760/765–1004* 🌐 *www.wynolapizza.com.*

Hotels

Butterfield Bed & Breakfast

$ | **B&B/INN** | This beautifully landscaped inn on a 3-acre hilltop is cordial and romantic, with knotty-pine ceilings, Laura Ashley accents, and rooms with nice touches, such as fireplaces or woodstoves and private entrances. **Pros:** great food that's dietary-need friendly; helpful hosts live next door; breakfast and afternoon refreshments are included. **Cons:** half a mile from town; no room phones; ornate and frilly rooms are not for everyone. [$] *Rooms from: $135* ✉ *2284 Sunset Dr.* ☎ *760/765–2179, 800/379–4262* 🌐 *www.butterfieldbandb.com* 🛏 *5 rooms* 🍴 *Free Breakfast.*

★ Eaglenest Bed & Breakfast

$$ | **B&B/INN** | If the plush beds, country breakfast, homemade desserts, and tranquil location weren't enough, you've also got unparalleled hospitality. **Pros:** one block above Main Street; personalized service; lovely breakfast served in the tower. **Cons:** two-night stay requested; five dogs might be too much for some; family-style breakfast means dining with strangers. [$] *Rooms from: $175* ✉ *2609 D St.* ☎ *888/345–6378, 760/765–1252* 🌐 *www.eaglenestbnb.com* 🛏 *4 rooms* 🍴 *Free Breakfast.*

Julian Gold Rush Hotel

$ | **B&B/INN** | Built in 1897 by freed slave Albert Robinson and his wife, Margaret, this old hotel is Julian's only designated national landmark and offers antiques-filled rooms and cottage accommodations with private entrances and fireplaces. **Pros:** genuine historic hotel; convivial atmosphere; afternoon tea.

Cons: small rooms; no TV; no in-room phones. [$] *Rooms from: $160* ✉ *2032 Main St.* ☎ *760/765–0201, 800/734–5854* 🌐 *www.julianhotel.com* 🛏 *16 rooms* 🍴 *Free Breakfast.*

Julian Lodge
$ | HOTEL | Near shops, this small hotel renovated in 2018 is a replica of the late 19th-century Washington Hotel. **Pros:** in-town location; free parking; reasonable rates and online promotions. **Cons:** simple appointments; mediocre breakfast; no view. [$] *Rooms from: $125* ✉ *2720 C St.* ☎ *760/765–1420, 800/542–1420* 🌐 *www.julianlodge.com* 🛏 *23 rooms* 🍴 *Free Breakfast.*

Orchard Hill Country Inn
$$ | B&B/INN | On a hill above town, this inn with a lodge and five Craftsman-style cottages offers luxurious accommodations decorated with antiques, original art, and handcrafted quilts, complemented by sweeping views of the countryside; some of the cottage suites have see-through fireplaces, whirlpool tubs, and private patios or balconies. **Pros:** most luxurious digs in Julian; good food; lovely views. **Cons:** limited amenities; not recommended for young children; management can be curt. [$] *Rooms from: $225* ✉ *2502 Washington St.* ☎ *760/765–1700, 800/716–7242* 🌐 *www.orchardhill.com* 🛏 *23 rooms* 🍴 *Free Breakfast.*

Wikiup Bed and Breakfast
$$ | B&B/INN | Best known for its herd of llamas, this cedar-and-brick inn is decorated with romantic furnishings and offers themed guest rooms with fireplaces and outdoor hot tubs for stargazing. **Pros:** private entrances; pleasant surroundings; full breakfast, afternoon dessert, and snacks are included. **Cons:** limited facilities; strict 4 pm check-in; two-night minimum. [$] *Rooms from: $165* ✉ *1645 Whispering Pines Dr.* ✣ *1-mile outside of town* ☎ *800/694–5487* 🌐 *www.wikiupbnb.com* 🛏 *5 rooms* 🍴 *Free Breakfast.*

Nightlife

Julian Beer Company
BREWPUBS/BEER GARDENS | FAMILY | Although lights are out by 11 pm, this brewery might be the closest thing to nightlife in Julian. On tap are craft farmhouse-style beers along with small plates and bar bites when you need to sober up. As the largest venue on Main Street, they have live music, games, events, and plenty of indoor–outdoor seating for you and your crew. ✉ *2307 Main St.* ☎ *760/765–3757* 🌐 *www.julianbeercompany.com* ☞ *Closed Mon.*

Nickel Beer Company
BREWPUBS/BEER GARDENS | Some of the best brew in San Diego is served at this little beer bar that occupies an old jail in Julian. Owner Tom Nickel is considered one of the most creative brewers in the region and is always cooking up new recipes that win accolades from judges and fans. There are 16 taps and contents change regularly. If you're having trouble making your pick, go for the flight of six beers for $12. The patio is dog-friendly. ✉ *1485 Hollow Glen Rd.* ☎ *760/765–2337* 🌐 *www.nickelbeerco.com.*

Shopping

The Julian area has a number of unique shops that are open weekends, but midweek hours vary considerably. In autumn locally grown apples, pears, nuts, and cider are available in town and at a few roadside stands. The best apple variety produced here is a Jonagold, a hybrid of Jonathan and Golden Delicious.

The Barn Vintage Marketplace
ANTIQUES/COLLECTIBLES | Between Julian and Santa Ysabel, "The Barn" goes beyond standard antiques with one-of-a-kind vintage home decor, spanning industrial, primitive, rustic, and more. Be sure to greet the resident emus, Daisy and Duke. ✉ *4559 Hwy. 78, Santa Ysabel*

☎ 760/310–8587 ⊘ Closed Tues. and Wed.

The Cider Mill

FOOD/CANDY | Family-owned and operated for more than 30 years, this small cider-pressing factory sells honey, nuts, candy, apples, preserves, and, of course, fresh local cider. Don't ask how they make their pumpkin butter and homemade fudge—both are crafted from a secret recipe. ✉ 2103 Main St. ☎ 760/765–1430 ⊕ www.juliancidermillinc.com.

Julian Mercantile

JEWELRY/ACCESSORIES | With three stores on Main Street, it's easy to see why this gift shop dominates Julian, with its crafts, carvings, soaps, jewelery, leather, and other imports from Bali, Mexico, Brazil, and Ecuador. ✉ 2111A Main St. ☎ 760/765–0280 ⊕ www.julianimports.net.

The Mountain Gypsy

JEWELRY/ACCESSORIES | This shop is popular for its extensive collection of jewelry, apparel, and shoes for men and women. ✉ 2007 Main St. ☎ 760/765–0643 ⊕ www.themountaingypsy.com.

Santa Ysabel Art Gallery

ART GALLERIES | On display here are works of fine art, including paintings, stained glass, sculptures, fiber, and other creations by local artists, including James Hubbell and Joe Garcia. Many of the rotating works focus heavily on landscape and wildlife. ✉ 30352 Hwy. 78, Santa Ysabel ☎ 760/765–1676 ⊕ www.santaysabelartgallery.com ⊘ Closed Tues. and Wed.

Ramona

For many heading into the San Diego mountains or desert, Ramona is the last stop. It's where drivers fill up with gas (sometimes less expensive than in the city), pick up provisions at one of several supermarkets (there are none farther east), and have a bite to eat. Increasingly, visitors are spending time in Ramona for a couple of reasons: to play golf at two highly rated courses and to drop some cash at the Barona casino, located along a country road a few miles south of town. Ramona's history is intertwined with Julian's, the town 22 miles east, where a gold rush drew argonauts in the 1870s. Descendants of those settlers still run cattle on ranches extending from Ramona to Julian. Today Ramona is a growing unincorporated area of about 28,000 residents, most of whom have ranches. There's a budding wine-making industry with more than 30 wineries now open to the public on weekends. The main thoroughfare also houses the largest selection of antiques shops in the backcountry. With the exception of the Barona Resort, lodging and dining fall into the simple and comfortable category. Don't come here if you're looking for luxury.

◉ Sights

Milagro

WINERY/DISTILLERY | **FAMILY** | For quality wine and an enjoyable wine-tasting experience, Milagro leads the long list of wineries in Ramona. Overseeing production is Hugo D'Acosta, who trained in Bordeaux and is considered one of Mexico's preeminent winemakers. The classy tasting room is tucked inside a copse of ancient oak trees, surrounded by vineyards, fruit trees, and local animals. Since 2008, winemaker Jim Hart has captured awards from important competitions, including best in San Diego for his luscious fruity Sauvignon Blanc. Other highly rated wines are Barbera and Sangiovese. ✉ 18750 Littlepage La. ☎ 760/787–0738 ⊕ www.milagrowinery.com 🍷 $12 tastings (6 tastes and a glass) ⊘ Closed weekdays.

🍴 Restaurants

Barona Oaks Steakhouse

$$$ | **STEAKHOUSE** | The elegant, dinner-only restaurant at Barona Resort is one of the few fine-dining venues east of San Diego. It caters to high rollers whose culinary choice often involves steak, thus the menu here lists a large selection of USDA Prime, including dry-aged porterhouse and buffalo rib eye, but there are seafood options, too. **Known for:** dry-aged steaks; live piano music; remarkable rack of lamb. [$] *Average main: $35* ✉ *1932 Wildcat Canyon Rd.* ☎ *619/443–2300* 🌐 *www.barona.com* 🕓 *Closed Mon. No lunch.*

🛏 Hotels

Barona Resort & Casino

$$ | **HOTEL** | Attracting players who want to spend a couple of days in the casino, and lobster lovers looking for an affordable meal, this resort also has golf and a small but appealing day spa for those who want to be pampered. **Pros:** well-appointed rooms; gameside dining; eight restaurant options. **Cons:** isolated; not good for families; casino focused. [$] *Rooms from: $179* ✉ *1932 Wildcat Canyon Rd.* ☎ *619/443–2300* 🌐 *www.barona.com* 🛏 *432 rooms* 🍽 *No meals.*

San Vicente Golf Resort

$ | **RESORT** | Accommodations in this three-story resort popular with golfers are clean, pleasant, and have mountain or golf-course views from balconies or patios. **Pros:** scenic location; free parking; great-value golf packages. **Cons:** limited amenities (but there are great jogging and nature trails); casual service; breakfast not included. [$] *Rooms from: $115* ✉ *24157 San Vicente Rd.* ☎ *760/789–3788, 800/776–1289* 🌐 *www.sanvicenteresort.com* 🛏 *28 rooms* 🍽 *No meals.*

🏃 Activities

GOLF

★ Barona Creek Golf Club

GOLF | Rated among the top five courses nationwide, this 7,392-yard course won accolades from day one for its challenging slopes, strategically placed boulders, and native grass landscaping. Barona Creek offers four tees to accommodate golfers of all skills and abilities. For those looking to be challenged at the expert level, the course provides a championship layout with four T configurations. ✉ *1000 Wildcat Canyon Rd.* ☎ *619/328–3742* 🌐 *www.barona.com* 🎟 *$120 weekdays, $160 weekends* 🏌 *Black: 18 holes, 7092 yards, par 72. Gold: 18 holes, 6632 yards, par 72. Silver: 18 holes, 6231 yards, par 72. Burgundy: 18 holes, 5296 yards, par 70.*

Mount Woodson Golf Club

GOLF | This beautiful, heavily wooded club in a hilly area off Highway 67 is set amid a grove of ancient oak trees and granite boulder-strewn hillsides with spectacular views of the historic Woodson Castle, a private residence built in 1921 that is now one of San Diego's most popular wedding venues. The course features some challenging holes like the par 5 Windinface, a deep, three-tiered green, where accuracy is a must. The course also features wooden bridges and good views, particularly from Hole 17. There is a pro shop and a small café. This is a popular local tournament site. ✉ *16422 N. Woodson Dr.* ☎ *760/788–3555* 🌐 *www.mtwoodsongolfclub.com* 🎟 *$40 weekdays, $60 weekends* 🏌 *18 holes, 6004 yards, par 70.*

HIKING

Mount Woodson Trail

HIKING/WALKING | Due to San Diego's varied terrain, a range of hiking trails is accessible for any skill level. Aptly nicknamed the Potato Chip Rock hike, Mount Woodson is best known for a picturesque rock formation that juts out of the mountainside—providing a timely photo op for hikers. It's not uncommon for people to wait in line to climb up on the rock and have their photo taken, since the trail can get crowded on weekends. This steep hike located between Poway and Ramona isn't for the faint of heart, taking most people about three hours to complete the 8-mile loop. But if for no other reason, do it for the Insta-worthy photo. ✉ lake Poway Recreation Area, 14644 Lake Poway Rd., Poway ☎ 858/668–4772 ⊕ poway.org/502/Trails-Hiking ☞ parking $10.

Anza-Borrego Desert State Park

88 miles from downtown San Diego (park border due west of Borrego Springs).

GETTING HERE AND AROUND
You'll need a car to visit the Anza-Borrego Desert and Borrego Springs, which is totally surrounded by wilderness. The trip from San Diego is about 88 scenic miles, and it takes around two hours. Once there be prepared to drive on dusty roads as there is no public transportation. The best route to Borrego Springs is via I–8 east out of San Diego; exit east on Highway 79 and take the scenic drive through the Cuyamaca Mountains to Julian, where Highway 79 intersects with Highway 78 going east. Follow Highway 78 into the desert to Yaqui Pass Road, turn left and follow the signs to Borrego Springs Christmas Circle. Take Borrego Palm Canyon west to reach the Anza-Borrego Desert State Park headquarters.

TOUR OPTIONS
California Overland Desert Excursions offers day tours and overnight excursions into hard-to-reach scenic desert destinations using climate-controlled and open-air, military-transport vehicles.

Typical destinations include Font's Point, the Badlands, and Split Mountain.

TOUR INFORMATION California Overland Desert Excursions. ✉ *1233 Palm Canyon Dr., Borrego Springs* ☎ *760/767–1232* ⊕ *www.californiaoverland.com.*

ESSENTIALS
VISITOR INFORMATION Anza-Borrego Desert State Park. ✉ *200 Palm Canyon Dr., Borrego Springs* ☎ *760/767–5311* ⊕ *www.parks.ca.gov* **State Park Reservations.** ☎ *800/444–7275* ⊕ *www. reserveamerica.com.*

◉ Sights

Anza-Borrego State Park
NATIONAL/STATE PARK | Today more than 1,000 square miles of desert and mountain country are included in the Anza-Borrego Desert State Park, one of the few parks in the country where you can follow a trail and pitch a tent wherever you like. There are 110 miles of hiking and riding trails that allow you to explore canyons, capture scenic vistas, tiptoe through fields of wildflowers in spring, and possibly see wildlife—the park is home to rare Peninsula bighorn sheep, mountain lions, coyotes, black-tailed jackrabbit, and roadrunners. State Highway 78, which runs north and south through the park, has been designated the Juan Bautista de Anza National Historic Trail, marking portions of the route of the Anza Colonizing Expedition of 1775–76 that went from northern Mexico to the San Francisco Bay area. In addition, 28,000 acres have been set aside in the eastern part of the desert near Ocotillo Wells for off-road enthusiasts. General George S. Patton conducted field training in the Ocotillo area to prepare for the World War II invasion of North Africa.

Many of the park's sites can be seen from your vehicle, as 500 miles of paved and dirt roads traverse the park—note that you are required to stay on them so as not to disturb the park's ecological

Spring Wildflowers

Southern California's famous climate has blessed this corner of the continent with an ever-changing, year-round palette of natural color. It's hard to find a spot anywhere around the globe that produces as spectacular a scene as San Diego in spring—from native plant gardens found tucked away in mountain canyons and streambeds to carpets of wildflowers on the desert floor. You'll have to see it yourself to believe just how alive the deceptively barren desert really is.

When to Go

Spring debuts in **late February or early March.** Heavy winter rains always precede the best bloom seasons. And good blooms also bring even more beauty—a bounty of butterflies. A further boon: here in this generally temperate climate, the bloom season lasts nearly all year.

Some drought-tolerant plants rely on fire to germinate, and the years following wildfires generally produce a profusion of plant life not normally seen.

What to See

Look for rare western redbud trees erupting into a profusion of crimson flowers, sometimes starting as early as February. Native California lilacs (ceanothus) blanket the hillsides throughout the backcountry with fragrant blue-and-white blossoms starting in May and showing until August.

Native varieties of familiar names show up in the mountain canyons and streambeds. A beautiful white western azalea would be the star in anyone's garden. A pink California rose blooms along streambeds in spring and summer. Throughout the year three varieties of native dogwood show off white blooms and beautiful crimson fall foliage. The **Cuyamaca Mountains** usually put on a display of fall color as the native oaks turn gold and red. By winter the rare toyon, known as the California Christmas tree, lights up the roadside with its red berries.

Farther east in the **Anza-Borrego Desert State Park,** the spring wildflower display can be spectacular: carpets of pink, purple, white, and yellow verbena and desert primrose as far as the eye can see. Rocky slopes yield clumps of beavertail cactus topped with pink blossoms, clumps of yellow brittlebush tucked among the rocks, and crimson-tip ocotillo trees. For an introduction to desert vegetation, explore the visitor center demonstration garden, adjacent to the park's underground headquarters.

To seee the blooms, take I–8 east to Route 79, go north to Julian, and then east on Route 78 into Anza-Borrego park.

balance. On dirt roads it's easy to sink up to your wheel covers in dry sand, so rangers recommend using four-wheel-drive vehicles on the dirt roads. Also, carry the appropriate supplies: shovel and other tools, flares, blankets, and plenty of water. Canyons are susceptible to flash flooding; inquire about weather conditions before entering.

Wildflowers, which typically begin to bloom in January and are at their peak in mid-March, attract thousands of visitors each spring. A variety of factors, including rainfall and winds, determine how extensive the bloom will be in a particular year. However, good displays of low-growing sand verbena and white evening primrose can usually be found along Airport Road and DiGeorgio Road. Following wet winters, spectacular displays fill the dry washes in Coyote Canyon and along Henderson Canyon Road.

■TIP→ **The best light for photography is in early morning or late afternoon.**

Erosion Road is a self-guided, 18-mile auto tour along Route S22 on the way to the Salton Sea. The **Southern Emigrant Trail** follows the route of the Butterfield Stage Overland Mail, the route used by half of the argonauts heading for the gold fields in Northern California.

At **Borrego Palm Canyon,** a few minutes west of the visitor information center is a 1½-mile trail that leads to a small oasis with a waterfall and palms. The Borrego Palm Canyon and Tamrisk Grove—12 miles southeast of Borrego Palm Canyon—are the only campgrounds with flush toilets and showers in the park. (Day use is $10 and camping is $25 in high season, $35 with hookup.)

Geology students from all over the world visit the Fish Creek area of Anza-Borrego to explore a famous canyon known as **Split Mountain** (*Split Mountain Rd. south from Rte. 78 at Ocotillo Wells*), a narrow gorge with 600-foot perpendicular walls that was formed by an ancestral stream. Fossils in this area indicate that a sea covered the desert floor at one time. Wind Caves Trail, a 2-mile nature trail west of Split Mountain, rewards hikers with a good view of shallow caves created by erosion. Dogs are not permitted on any of the hiking trails in the park. ⊠ *200 Palm Canyon Dr., Borrego Springs* ☎ *760/765–5311* ⊕ *www.parks.ca.gov.*

INFO CENTER |Visitor Information Center. Rangers and displays at this excellent visitor center can point you in the right direction. Most of the desert plants

Unburied Treasure ◉

The Anza-Borrego Desert is one of North America's most geologically active spots and a repository of paleontological treasure. Beneath the desert's surface are fossil-bearing sediments that provide clues to past geological activity, from climate change to tectonic activity and up-thrust. Reading the fossil record, scientists have learned that the badlands here were once a wonderland of green and home of saber-toothed tigers, flamingos, zebras, camels, and a flying bird with a 16-foot wingspan.

also can be seen in the demonstration desert garden here. ⊠ *200 Palm Canyon Dr., Borrego Springs* ☎ *760/767–4205, 760/767–4684 wildflower hotline* ⊕ *www. parks.ca.gov* ⊗ *Closed weekdays June–Sept.*

Borrego Springs

31 miles from Julian, east on Rte. 78 and Yaqui Pass Rd., and north on Rte. S3.

A quiet town with a handful of year-round residents, Borrego Springs is set in the heart of the Anza-Borrego Desert State Park and is emerging as a destination for desert lovers. From September through June, temperatures hover in the 80s and 90s, and you can enjoy activities such as hiking, nature study, golf, tennis, horseback riding, and mountain-bike riding. Even during the busier winter season, Borrego Springs feels quiet. There are several golf resorts, B&B, and a community of winter residents, but the laid-back vibe prevails. If winter rains cooperate, Borrego Springs puts on the best wildflower displays in the low desert.

ESSENTIALS

VISITOR INFORMATION Borrego Springs Chamber of Commerce. ✉ *786 Palm Canyon Dr.* ☎ *760/767–5555, 800/559–5524* ⊕ *www.borregospringschamber.com.*

Sights

★ Galleta Meadows

PUBLIC ART | FAMILY | At Galleta Meadows, camels, llamas, saber-toothed tigers, tortoises, and monumental gomphotherium (a sort of ancient elephant) appear to roam the earth again. These life-size bronze figures are of prehistoric animals whose fossils can be found in the Borrego Badlands. The collection of more than 130 sculptures created by Ricardo Breceda was commissioned by the late Dennis Avery, who installed the works of art on property he owned for the entertainment of locals and visitors. Maps are available from Borrego Springs Chamber of Commerce. ✉ *Borrego Springs Rd., from Christmas Circle to Henderson Canyon* ☎ *760/767–5555* 💲 *Free.*

Restaurants

Carlee's Place

$$ | AMERICAN | This local watering hole seems to collect characters ranging from hippies to mountain men and is the place to go any night of the week. A large, dimly lighted room houses the bar and dining tables, and the menu lists pasta and pizza in addition to old-fashioned entrées such as liver and onions, ribs and steaks, and a mixed grill. **Known for:** classic entrées; long-standing roadhouse; extensive menu; good buffalo wings. 💲 *Average main: $21* ✉ *660 Palm Canyon Dr.* ☎ *760/767–3262* ⊕ *www. carleesplace.com.*

Carmelita's Mexican Grill and Cantina

$ | MEXICAN | A friendly family-run eatery tucked into a back corner of what is called "The Mall," Carmelita's draws locals and visitors all day whether it's for a hearty breakfast, a cooked-to-order

enchilada or burrito, or a brew at the bar. The menu lists typical combination plates (enchiladas, burritos, tamales, and tacos). **Known for:** reasonably priced menu; large portions; festive cantina. 💲 *Average main: $14* ✉ *575 Palm Canyon Dr.* ☎ *760/767–5666.*

Red Ocotillo

$ | AMERICAN | For inexpensive comfort food, this desert diner serves sandwiches, burgers, and chicken-fried steak with thick fries. This is the area's best breakfast joint, with menu highlights including cinnamon French toast and smoked salmon eggs Benedict. **Known for:** smoked salmon eggs Benedict; flavorful rosemary potatoes; hearty biscuits and gravy; pet-friendly patio. 💲 *Average main: $12* ✉ *721 Ave. Sureste, off Christmas Circle* ☎ *760/767–7400* ⊕ *www.redocotillo.com.*

Hotels

Borrego Springs Resort, Golf Club & Spa

$$ | RESORT | The large rooms at this quiet resort set around a swimming pool and with golf, tennis, and golf options come with either a shaded balcony or a patio with desert views. **Pros:** golf, tennis, and bikes available; good desert views from most rooms; close to sculpture gardens. **Cons:** rooms slightly dated; average service; breakfast not included. 💲 *Rooms from: $182* ✉ *1112 Tilting T Dr.* ☎ *760/767–5700, 888/826–7734* ⊕ *www. borregospringsresort.com* 🛏 *100 rooms* 🍽 *No meals.*

★ Borrego Valley Inn

$$$ | B&B/INN | Those looking for desert landscapes and some stargazing—guests must be 21 or older—may enjoy the adobe Southwestern-style buildings here that house spacious rooms, which boasts plenty of natural light, original art, pine beds, and corner fireplaces. **Pros:** swim under the stars in the clothing-optional pool; exquisite desert gardens; breakfast included. **Cons:** no kids and no

Day Trip to Tijuana

Just 18 miles (29 km) south of San Diego, Tijuana is an easy day trip, but gone are the days when Americans could cross into Mexico and return by simply showing their driver's license. For the last decade, U.S. Customs and Border Protection has required Americans to show a valid passport (or passport card) to return to the U.S.

Getting To the Border

There are several options for getting to the border at San Ysidro, but the easiest is via the trolley. Check the CBP Border Wait Times mobile app for estimated wait times.

The trip on I–5 takes a half hour (no traffic) to an hour or more (rush hour). Leave your **car** on the U.S. side at one of the border parking lots ($8–$15 per day), and then cross on foot or by bus. Border Station Parking ⊕ *borderstationparking.com*, a 24-hour guarded lot at Camino de la Plaza, next to the Las Americas Premium Outlets, is a reliable choice; they also have shuttle service to and from Tijuana. To get there, take the last U.S. exit off I–5 (marked "Last US Exit, Camino de la Plaza"), turn right at the stoplight, and follow the signs for the lot.

A **taxi** ride from downtown San Diego to the border at San Ysidro will cost about $55. Uber and Lyft are also options; expect to pay about $20–25.

The **San Diego Trolley** travels from the Santa Fe Depot in San Diego, at Kettner Boulevard and Broadway. You'll take the blue line to the last stop, San Ysidro/Tijuana, which is within 100 feet of the border. The blue line runs approximately every 15 minutes from 5 am to 1 am. The 45-minute trip costs $5.

Crossing the Border

The most common way to cross the border is on **foot,** and the experience—going through a metal turnstile amid the throngs of people—is in many ways a more memorable one than any other. Don't expect much of a hassle when crossing into Mexico, but allow extra time on your way back and expect random inspections. To reach the border from the San Ysidro trolley stop (a five-minute walk) or any of the border parking garages, just follow the crowds.

Once you've crossed the border, you'll be inundated with taxi drivers, who will take you to downtown Tijuana for about $7. However, it's an easy ½-mile walk to downtown (follow the crowds).

You can avoid the turnstyle conjestion by taking the **bus.** If you arrive by trolley, take a shuttle from the San Ysidro trolley terminal to the Tijuana Tourist Terminal on Avenida Revolución between 6th and 7th streets.

When You're There

Avenida Revolución is lined with restaurants, bars, cafés, and stores selling everything from tequila to Tiffany-style lamps. The shopping area spreads across Calle 2 to a pedestrian walkway leading from the border. Beware of fake goods, and above all, beware of higher prices offered to gringos. The best bargains can be closer to the border; pick up your piñatas and serapes on your way out of town. Between Calles 1 and 8, Avenida Revolución is lined with crafts and curios.

Playas de Tijuana is Tijuana's beach neighborhood; Rosarito and Ensenada are thought to be the best.

pets; rooms could use sprucing up; service inconsistent. $ *Rooms from: $285* ✉ *405 Palm Canyon Dr.* ☎ *760/767–0311, 800/333–5810* ⊕ *www.borregovalleyinn. com* ⇄ *15 rooms* ❍ *Free Breakfast.*

★ La Casa del Zorro

$ | RESORT | FAMILY | Even though it's changed hands multiple times since it was first built in 1933, Casa del Zorro is still a secret desert hideaway for those looking for spacious and comfortable accommodations—many with private pools, surrounded by gorgeous desert mountains. **Pros:** colorful gardens; summer stargazing; amenities such as fitness center, spa, and pools. **Cons:** expensive restaurant; huge campus; spotty service. $ *Rooms from: $129* ✉ *3845 Yaqui Pass Rd.* ☎ *760/767–0100* ⊕ *www.lacasadel-zorro.com* ⇄ *66 rooms* ❍ *No meals.*

The Palms at Indian Head

$$ | B&B/INN | Spectacular desert views can be had from this small, 1950s hotel that displays an authentic mid-century look, with handcrafted, Southwest lodge-pole furniture and original art by local artists. **Pros:** quiet, oasis-like atmosphere; breakfast included in rate; great views. **Cons:** somewhat remote location; simple decor; no room phones. $ *Rooms from: $189* ✉ *2220 Hoberg Rd.* ☎ *760/767–7788* ⊕ *www.thepalmsatindianhead.com* ⇄ *12 rooms* ❍ *Free Breakfast.*

🏃 Activities

Borrego Springs Resort and Spa

GOLF | Midwinter, when you can expect cool breezes, is the best time for a round of golf at the Borrego Springs Resort and Spa. The public course here is fairly flat and dotted with palm trees. Rates vary from winter to summer, and packages are available. The course is open November 15 through July 1. ✉ *1112 Tilting T Dr.* ☎ *760/767–3330* ⊕ *www.borregosprings-resort.com* ⌷ *$75* ⛳ *18 holes, 6760 yards, par 71* ☉ *Closed Sept.–mid-Nov.* ☞ *Facilities: putting green, driving range, pitching area, golf carts; rental clubs, pro shop, lessons, restaurant, bar.*

Roadrunner Golf and Country Club

GOLF | Adjacent to the Springs at Borrego course and with some shared facilities, this club has an 18-hole par-3 golf course. Though the course has views of the Santa Rosa, San Ysidro, and Vallecito Mountains and Indian Head Mountain, the terrain is relatively flat. Another bonus: there's rarely a wait for a tee time. ✉ *1010 Palm Canyon Dr.* ☎ *760/767–5374* ⊕ *www.roadrunnerclub.com* ⌷ *$40* ⛳ *18 holes, 2445 yards, par 3.*

Index

Photo Credits

Notes

Notes

Notes

Notes

Notes

Notes

Notes

Notes

Fodor's SAN DIEGO

Publisher: Stephen Horowitz, *General Manager*

Editorial: Douglas Stallings, *Editorial Director*; Margaret Kelly, Jacinta O'Halloran, Amanda Sadlowski, *Senior Editors*; Kayla Becker, Alexis Kelly, Teddy Minford, Rachael Roth, *Editors*

Design: Tina Malaney, *Design and Production Director*; Jessica Gonzalez, *Graphic Designer*; Mariana Tabares, *Design & Production Intern*

Production: Jennifer DePrima, *Editorial Production Manager*; Carrie Parker, *Senior Production Editor*; Elyse Rozelle, *Production Editor*; Jackson Pranica, *Editorial Production Assistant*

Maps: Rebecca Baer, *Senior Map Editor*; David Lindroth, Mark Stroud (Moon Street Cartography), *Cartographers*

Photography: Jill Krueger, *Director of Photo*; Namrata Aggarwal, Ashok Kumar, Carl Yu, *Photo Editors*; Rebecca Rimmer, *Photo Intern*

Business & Operations: Chuck Hoover, *Chief Marketing Officer*; Robert Ames, *Group General Manager*; Tara McCrillis, *Director of Publishing Operations*; Victor Bernal, *Business Analyst*

Public Relations and Marketing: Joe Ewaskiw, *Senior Director Communications & Public Relations*; Esther Su, *Senior Marketing Manager*; Ryan Garcia, Thomas Talarico, Miranda Villalobos, *Marketing Specialists*

Fodors.com Jeremy Tarr, *Editorial Director*; Rachael Levitt, *Managing Editor*

Technology: Jon Atkinson, *Director of Technology*; Rudresh Teotia, *Lead Developer*; Jacob Ashpis, *Content Operations Manager*

Writers: Claire Deeks van der Lee, Marlise Kast-Meyers, Kai Oliver-Kurtin, Jeff Terich

Editor: Alexis Kelly

Production Editor: Jennifer DePrima

32nd Edition

ISBN 978-1640971-561

ISSN 1053–5950

Library of Congress Control Number 978-0-14-754689-0

All details in this book are based on information supplied to us at press time. Always confirm information when it matters, especially if you're making a detour to visit a specific place. Fodor's expressly disclaims any liability, loss, or risk, personal or otherwise, that is incurred as a consequence of the use of any of the contents of this book.

SPECIAL SALES

This book is available at special discounts for bulk purchases for sales promotions or premiums. For more information, e-mail SpecialMarkets@fodors.com.

PRINTED IN THE UNITED STATES OF AMERICA

10 9 8 7 6 5 4 3 2 1

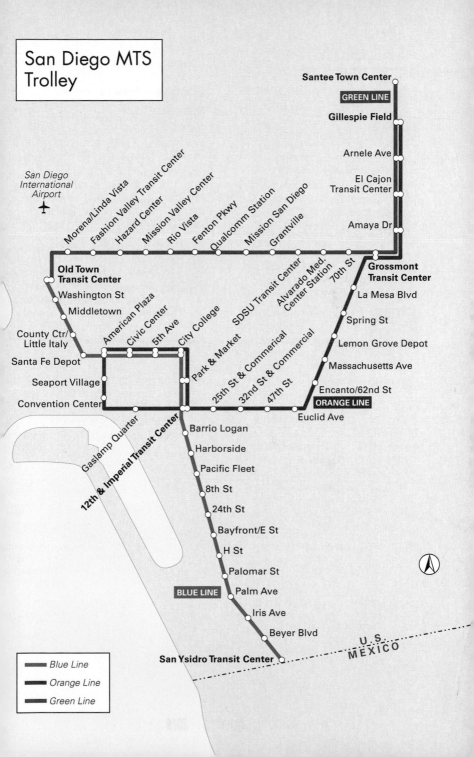

San Diego MTS Trolley

Santee Town Center

GREEN LINE

Gillespie Field

Arnele Ave

El Cajon
Transit Center

Amaya Dr

*San Diego
International
Airport*

Morena/Linda Vista
Fashion Valley Transit Center
Hazard Center
Mission Valley Center
Rio Vista
Fenton Pkwy
Qualcomm Station
Mission San Diego
Grantville

70th St

**Grossmont
Transit Center**

La Mesa Blvd

**Old Town
Transit Center**

Washington St

Middletown

American Plaza
Civic Center
5th Ave
City College
SDSU Transit Center
Alvarado Med.
Center Station

Spring St

Lemon Grove Depot

County Ctr/
Little Italy

Santa Fe Depot

Seaport Village

Convention Center

Park & Market
25th St & Commerical
32nd St & Commercial
47th St

Massachusetts Ave

Encanto/62nd St

ORANGE LINE

Euclid Ave

Gaslamp Quarter

12th & Imperial Transit Center

Barrio Logan

Harborside

Pacific Fleet

8th St

24th St

Bayfront/E St

H St

Palomar St

BLUE LINE

Palm Ave

Iris Ave

Beyer Blvd

San Ysidro Transit Center

U.S.
MEXICO

Blue Line
Orange Line
Green Line

About Our Writers

Veteran traveler **Claire Deeks van der Lee** feels lucky to call San Diego home. An East Coast transplant, she never takes the near-perfect weather for granted. Claire loves playing tourist in her own city, exploring San Diego's cultural attractions as well as its myriad neighborhoods and Balboa Park—so it was a perfect fit for her to work on the Balboa Park and San Diego Zoo, Old Town and Uptown, and the Mission Bay and Beaches chapters of this book. Claire has contributed to *Everywhere* magazine and several Fodor's guides.

Based in North County San Diego, journalist and author **Marlise Kast-Myers** has contributed to more than 50 publications including *Surfer*, *San Diego Magazine,* and the *Union Tribune,* as well as more than 20 Fodor's guides. Her travels have taken her around the world for surfing, snowboarding, and hiking expeditions. Marlise lives at the historic Betty Crocker estate in Valley Center where she and her husband operate an antique business, Brick n Barn. She updated the La Jolla, Point Loma Peninsula, North County and Around, Experience, and Travel Smart chapters.

A freelance writer for the last eight years, **Kai Oliver-Kurtin** loves covering the people, places, culture, and events that embody San Diego's distinct charm and energy. She contributes to various publications including *Condé Nast Traveler, USA Today Travel, San Diego Magazine,* and *Modern Luxury San Diego.* Kai contributed to the Experience chapter.

Jeff Terich is a culture seeker and night owl who is most at home on a barstool, watching live music. He's the web editor at *San Diego Magazine* and a freelance arts and music writer with 19 years of experience writing for publications such as *American Songwriter, Stereogum, Bandcamp,* and *Get Lost.* When he's not breaking in his earplugs at shows in San Diego, he's often traveling with his wife Candice or in search of a good bourbon cocktail. Jeff updated the Downtown and Coronado chapters.